THE CLASH
ON THE CLASH
INTERVIEWS
AND ENCOUNTERS

EDITED BY SEAN EGAN

CHICAGO
REVIEW
PRESS

An A Cappella Book

Copyright © 2018 by Sean Egan
All rights reserved
Published by Chicago Review Press Incorporated
814 North Franklin Street
Chicago, Illinois 60610

ISBN 978-1-61373-745-3

A list of credits and copyright notices for the individual pieces in this collection can be found on pages 365–66.

Library of Congress Cataloging-In-Publication Data
is available from the Library of Congress

Typesetting: Nord Compo

Printed in the United States of America
5 4 3 2 1

CONTENTS

INTRODUCTION

The Clash thought they could change the world. They never did, but in the attempt they created some of the greatest popular music of all time.

The band's eponymous 1977 debut LP was punk rock to its core. Its lyrics were a perfect snapshot of a grey, low-waged, strife-torn Britain, and its music an exquisite blitzkrieg. A maladroit production to which no established rock act would have attached its name actually served to enhance the record's menacing edge.

Following imperishable stand-alone singles "Complete Control" and "(White Man) in Hammersmith Palais," the Clash acquiesced to big-name American producer Sandy Pearlman helming their second album. On 1978's *Give 'em Enough Rope*, their songs of street life were given a glossy treatment which, though sometimes incongruous, made for a worthy follow-up to their already hallowed debut.

Resplendent tunes, wide-screen production, adroit assimilation of multiple genres, and blush-making humanity ensured that with third album *London Calling*, released in their home country in 1979, the Clash created a new punk paradigm that proved dissident music needed to be neither glum nor abrasive. Meanwhile, the band finally came unequivocally good on their incessant men-of-the-people posturing: they successfully insisted on the double set retailing for the price of a single LP.

After that triumph there followed an unexpected dip in the Clash's fortunes, at least on home turf. American fans remember the early eighties as a glorious period in the Clash's career culminating in them closing down Times Square as they performed seventeen consecutive concerts at Bond International Casino. In Britain, in contrast, they were becoming a joke, perceived as neglecting their native fans and having "gone all American"—a particularly grievous offence for the composers of the broadside against cultural imperialism "I'm So Bored with the U.S.A."

Them releasing triple album *Sandinista!* (1980) was deemed another betrayal, smacking of the rock-aristocracy self-indulgence against which they had loudly set out their stall. Stripped down to a single disc, the record would have revealed the Clash to be as excellent and relevant as ever, but consumers and critics were understandably resentful about wading through dross to get to gold.

By the time of a planned British tour to promote fifth album *Combat Rock* (1982), UK interest in the Clash had so declined that rhythm guitarist, chief lyricist, and main singer Joe Strummer had to stage a disappearance to drum up sales. Although it featured the harrowing anthem of the dispossessed "Straight to Hell," the album was uncertain and spotty. Yet a manageable single-disc format, industrious marketing, and the infectious, antifundamentalist single "Rock the Casbah" saw the band finally properly break America.

Internal division resulted in Mick Jones being fired by the group in September 1983. Those who thought preposterous the idea of a Clash bereft of their lead guitarist and Strummer's songwriting foil seemed to be proven right by *Cut the Crap*, a cringe-making self-parody released in 1985. The final Clash studio album, it besmirched a great band's legacy.

Although sorely diminished at the point of their split, the Clash's reputation posthumously soared. They were increasingly celebrated for the excellence of their corpus and the skepticism they had shown toward their own celebrity, while the fact of their early dissolution ensured no tarnishing of their legend by the familiar music-industry pattern of long, slow artistic decline. *The Clash* and *London Calling* regularly featured in critics' polls to determine history's greatest albums. They were popular inductees into the Rock & Roll Hall of Fame.

Clash interviews had always revealed four distinct personalities. Strummer had a habit of snarling through his broken front teeth—often when his supposedly shameful bourgeois hinterland was raised—but behind the belligerent exterior pulsated a huge warmth and a brain buzzing with ideas for social justice. Jones was frequently sweet and sensitive, spurning the hauteur that had become all too common in rock stars; then again he was often a prima donna as petulant and self-absorbed as any of the old guard the Clash were supposedly making redundant. Bassist Paul Simonon was cooperative and pleasant but didn't have much insight to offer; he concentrated on stage design and working on his smoldering looks. Drummer Nicky "Topper" Headon was a complex character. The son of teachers, his respectable background didn't stop him falling prey to a debilitating heroin addiction that eventually saw him thrown out of the band.

Those Clash interviews were multitudinous and mesmerizing. Infused with the messianic punk spirit, the Clash engaged with the press like no rock group before or since, treating the interview almost as an address to the nation. The frequency (weekly) and multiplicity (four) of British music papers meant that they were never out of them, new product or no.

In print, they were at once gratingly naïve and stirringly idealistic. They were forever making promises, among them that there would never be a Clash album costing six pounds or more, that they would never agree to perform on populist BBC-TV chart show *Top of the Pops*, that they would not allow exorbitantly priced concert tickets, that they would not play seated venues, that they would set up a club or live venue for the kids and a radio station for people who liked less mainstream sounds. This is not even to mention all the covenants about refusal to compromise and art-over-commerce made implicit by their confrontational image and defiant songwords.

Their pronouncements were welcomed, but put the Clash in a no-win situation from the beginning. In the hysterically purist climate engendered by punk, scrutiny was pitiless. Desperate that rock never again lose its sociopolitical relevance like it had in the first half of the seventies, the British music papers perpetually used the Clash as a sellout litmus test. When the band's ideals inevitably bumped up against the realities of life and exigencies of career, cries of betrayal dogged their steps. The quality of their music literally became a side issue.

Over in the States, the Clash's rebel anthems and urban-guerrilla chic were perceived by music scribes as a refreshing antidote to corporate rock, and the band's spurning of the standard ingratiating interview tone in favor of finger-wagging over the shortcomings of their host country was deemed masochistically exhilarating.

It all means that the Clash's back pages are voluminous, crackle with controversy, and constitute a snapshot of a uniquely fractious period in modern history, music- and politics-wise.

The Clash on the Clash rounds up the best of the band's many landmark interviews. Whether it be their audiences with the simpatico likes of *Sniffin' Glue* and *Zigzag*, their increasingly testy encounters with the correspondents of pious UK weeklies *New Musical Express* and *Melody Maker*, or their friendlier but no less thought-provoking conversations with US periodicals like *Creem*, *Rolling Stone*, and *Spin*, the contents of this book prove that the Clash consistently created copy that lived up to their sobriquet "The Only Band That Matters."

—SEAN EGAN

JOE STRUMMER: BEFORE

Sean Egan | 2000 | Previously unpublished in this form

This is the first part of a transcript of a 2000 interview with Clash front man Joe Strummer. It focused on his musical activities pre- and post-Clash. Much of it is previously unpublished. Part two—"After"—can be found later in this book.

In part one, Strummer discusses his musical grounding and his time in the 101'ers, a group prominent on the R&B-oriented circuit labeled pub rock that provided one of the few high-energy antidotes to the pedestrian mid-seventies rock scene. The "Bernie" mentioned is Bernard Rhodes, a would-be band manager who convinced Strummer to jump ship from the 101'ers to the ensemble that would become the Clash. The Kosmo Vinyl to whom reference is also made was the band's PR man toward the end of the Clash's career. —Ed.

Apparently you were such a fan of Woody Guthrie as a young man that you were known as "Woody" before you became "Joe Strummer"?

Yeah, but I'd say I got to Woody Guthrie after the Stones. The Stones were our Take That. Stones and the Beatles were kicking off [when] I was about ten or eleven, twelve. The '68 blues boom was good for us 'cause then we got to know about all the good blues players. After the blues I got through to the county/folk guys, Woody Guthrie and what have you. But I'd never say I'm an expert or anything.

It must have been quite difficult to get access to some of these records at boarding school?

We used to write to this place called the Saga Mail Order and, luckily for us, it had a kind of blues list, like Sonny Terry and Brownie McGee.

Probably their crappest-ever recordings licensed by some cheapo artist office in Milwaukee, but we heard "I'm Walking" and really great stuff.

What was it about Woody Guthrie in particular that you liked?

The wildness of it, the rambling-round-lifeness of it. 'Cause when you're young, you don't really fancy the idea of settling down in an insurance office—which I'd say a fair few of my mates did—and reading about Woody Guthrie's life is quite different from that. It's a wannabe thing.

So you didn't just know his records, you knew the myth of him as well?

Yeah. I mean that book, *Bound for Glory*, is probably the only source of information I can think we had, and the records.

Was this a communal record player you had at school?

Oh no, this would be after school, Woody Guthrie, well after. But we had a communal record player at school which would be for Stones and Beatles. I'm a big Beach Boys fan, so I would put Beach Boys on and get booed off. And then Cream came in, Led Zeppelin and Cream, and I was the guy who stood there going, "Yes, but the Beach Boys are better." They all went, "Fuck off to you, pal." I was still hanging with the Beach Boys when everyone else was calling it rubbish.

And do you feel you've been vindicated all these years later?

No. I got vindicated when they kicked in with "Do It Again," which was a surprising last gasp, 'cause it had gone a bit crap with "Darlin'" and stuff like that. Their glory years had gone and it had gone a bit weird with *Smiley Smile* and what have you, and then they kicked back in with a number one with "Do It Again." I felt vindicated then, but not for very long 'cause the other guys were right: in came all the new shit.

When did you first start playing guitar?

Oh god, really late. When I was about twenty, twenty-one. I assumed that it was more difficult, 'cause being brought up in the age of Eric

Clapton and all that wiggly-wiggly-wiggly-woo, and all that improvising and what have you, it was a bit of a put-off. My mate built one in wood-work, who's now the drummer of 999, a bloke called Pablo LaBritain. He built a bass guitar type affair and we started to learn "Spoonful," but they were into all that improvising. We didn't have any chance of following that.

I started to play when I went busking with Tymon Dogg, who has a track on the Clash album *Sandinista!* I began bottling for him, which is collecting money in the Underground, and eventually began to learn chords off of him.

You play guitar right-handed even though you're actually left-handed, is that right?

True. 'Cause I had to start learning to play on other people's guitars, so I picked up the rudimentary chords the wrong way round, and finally when I could afford to get a guitar I found myself too lazy to start learning it all again the right way round. On the other hand, there's so many guitarists in the world, it's so hard to find a unique style. Even if it's a bit grungy or a bit crude, I do have a unique rhythm style because having my bad hand with the plectrum in it means that I don't have any finesse there. Which is something I hadn't realized—that guitarists need to be able to pick the first string and then the third string and then back to the first string and then the fifth string, do that very rapidly. In a way I treat the guitar as if it's one string. I can hit it, but that's kind of it. It's all six strings or none. Which has given me a style of my own, although it's hardly beautiful to hear by itself. It does fit into an engine room of a drum kit and a bass guitar. I can put my style into that and make it really work. Even [on] a nonaudible level. It's like a kind of sticky glue or oil that goes into the rhythm, and my style is probably the best for that.

You're in good company, because Buddy Holly always used to hit all six strings at once.

Did he? Ah, cool.

You've said in the past that you almost left it too late to become a guitarist. Would it be fair to say that that had something to do with your background insofar as rock 'n' roll was always associated with working-class musicians?

Well, not really. I'm afraid I talked it up a bit much. You see my father was in the Diplomatic Service, but he was a self-made orphan. He was sent to an orphanage in India. He was born to a guy who went out there to work on the railways, an Englishman, but when his parents were killed in a crash he became orphaned in India so he had a rough time. But he was a bit smart. I haven't inherited his academic brain at all, but he got himself a scholarship to Lucknow College and joined the Indian army. But he had to fight to get papers to become an English citizen. He only got the papers two years before I was born. When he finally reached England in 1948, he decided to join the Civil Service and he joined at the bottom rung, and so he was a kind of self-made man. When I did my first interview and I said my father was a diplomat, I was over-egging it a bit, but I did it because I was dead proud of what my father had done and I knew that he'd love to be described that way. In fact, the highest rung he ever reached was a thing called Second Secretary Information, which isn't that far up the pecking order.

He also got paid nothing his whole life and all we had as a family was a four-room, pebble-dashed bungalow in Warlingham. The MG 1100 was the height of his car-owning. So we really had nothing, and the reason I went to a public school was because that was a perk of the job. You didn't get to see your parents except for once a year. My father was, say, sent to Tehran, then the government would pay a flight out once a year. The good side was they would pay your school fees. Seeing your parents only once a year from the age of nine, you get very mean, you get very rough, in self-protection.

All I cared about was rock 'n' roll from about that moment on. I didn't have any pressure to do anything 'cause I was so academically useless. I came last in every class and got three O-Levels. I didn't have any expectations.

So were the 101'ers your first proper band?

Not really. I had a group in South Wales called the Vultures, which was three students from Newport Art College and myself.

And that was you on rhythm guitar?

Singing, yeah, doing the usual.

How long did that last?

Must have lasted nearly a year.

At that point, were you seriously thinking about becoming a professional musician?

Ah yeah, definitely. I was working for the council for a while, worked in a graveyard for a while, but that's all I would think about all day long. I was always serious about it.

When did the Vultures end and the 101'ers begin? Was that a fairly smooth transition?

No it wasn't really. We blagged some gig in Bristol and we couldn't really play, so a kind of near riot ensued and we had to leg it, and that's when the Vultures broke up. Then I realized that I had to get back into London, which I'd left two years before, and so I just hitched back there and started sleeping on people's floors again, and then me and Tymon Dogg went on a trip to the continent.

Why were you in Wales?

After school, I went to Central Art School, but I dropped out of there. In art school it's so organized you do one foundation year, then you apply again for a three-year course in your specialized whatever it is. We didn't make any effort. I ended up getting bounced out of there during the first year, so I ended up sleeping on people's floors in London and that's always a precarious existence 'cause you're expecting people to put up with you. I knew that some of the mates I'd made in art school had gone to Newport and Cardiff and my girlfriend was in Cardiff. I hitched down to Cardiff and she told me to piss off, and Newport's the next stop back on the motorway so I got a ride back into Newport. Then I started to sleep on the floor of my mates there. Then I figured well at least here I could probably get some kind of a job and rent a room and here's a group that I could join. They were talking about forming a group.

When did the 101'ers happen?

I'd say '74, '75. I'd spent long enough in Newport and realized it was time to get back to London. Me and Tymon Dogg went on a busking tour of the Continent. We got deported from Holland, and then we were busking in London and it was getting really difficult. I saw this Irish trio through the window of a pub and I thought, "Bloody hell, this looks like a better way to get through the summer than being chased all over the Underground by the British Transport Police." That's when I decided to put the 101'ers together and selected the nearest loafers from the squat-rock scene to try and put it together with.

These days, the history books lump the 101'ers into the mid-seventies pub-rock and R&B scene. Did it feel like a movement at the time?

Well, yeah. We were latecomers to it. Dr. Feelgood were the undisputed kings and there was a group called the Michigan Flyers, some of whom were American, that were really good and I've never heard of since, but they were doing a lot on that scene. Bees Make Honey had already come and gone. Ace had gone, and all that lot. The first wave of pub rock had come and gone, and the Tyla Gang had just about split up when we were making it. We were more like the dirty cousins to that scene, 'cause we were squat rockers and a bit younger and a bit more incapable. We didn't know our chops as well. Eventually we got skilled enough to be probably the second-best rhythm and blues group in West London after Feelgood, but it took a year and a half to get there.

At the time did it feel like what you were doing was a reaction to the rock aristocracy and stadium rock?

Yeah, very much, I've got to say. 'Cause you can imagine living in a squat, scraping together, borrowing money to buy an amp. It was pretty desperate living. I can remember there was some ludicrous documentary on Emerson, Lake & Palmer with aerial shots of three huge articulated lorries with one saying "Emerson" and the next saying "Lake" and the next saying "Palmer." We couldn't help but contrast the difference. I had it in my mind that the real world of rock music as business was that world with Emerson, Lake & Palmer, and that five hundred miles underneath was a sort of scab with insects, which was where we were operating, and it never occurred to me that we would ever cross with that world. The other world was so remote, I didn't even bother thinking about trying to take it on. It just was never discussed.

How high would you say your sights were set?

Oh, I know exactly how high. At the end of Chippenham Road there's a pub called the Windsor Castle on Harrow Road. My sights were set at if we could get a gig at the Windsor Castle on Harrow Road, then we had made it! That to me was the Wembley Stadium of our horizon. When you think what we'd come out of was like an utter shambles and none of us could play really, and we'd borrowed and stuck everything together . . . My speakers I'd made out of a pair of drawers I'd found on a skip. So you can imagine that going to the real pub at the other end of the road was, well, that would be it.

It seemed like R&B was the antidote to the lethargy of rock of the time, but it was a very retro scene . . .

Yes it was, but I didn't really know that at the time. Via the thrill of discovering old blues numbers and then learning them and then playing them to people, making them groove, to us it was new and exciting. It was only when I saw the Sex Pistols that I realized how retro it was. Not only the material but in the concept of it, like playing in pubs the same old blues numbers. That kind of Nowheresville.

**You've always admitted that during the 101'ers you were very inse-
cure about your ability as compared to the musicians in the circles
you mixed in. Does it surprise you looking back that you became the
leader of the 101'ers, despite your insecurities?**

Yeah, but often the beauty of some types of personalities is that they
don't know how good they are. One thing that you can say is true in
my case is that if I had known how good I was, I might have started
swaggering about. It's difficult to say, 'cause one's attitude dictates
the way one's life turns out. It's something I think about occasionally
now, 'cause I knew people who had no ability and thought they were
the answer to Elvis Presley. Even on the squat-rock scene, there were
strange part-formed superstars who acted like they were the answer.
I was more like the other way. I had a lot of ability, but I didn't
really realize it. However, I think that in my case [it was] probably
a good thing 'cause I haven't burnt myself out. I think if your ego
is overcooked, it can short-circuit your mind or somehow use it all
up too quickly. Thankfully I don't sit around really thinking about
how to promote myself every day. I like to think about ideas rather
than ambition.

Was "Keys to Your Heart" the first song you ever wrote?

Absolutely. The worst thing in the world is to play to someone the first
song you've ever written, and I've got to thank Mole Chesterton, the
bass player of the 101'ers, who's now dead, I'm afraid. I played it to
him and he went, "Oh, that's bloody good, that is," and that gave me
the confidence to try and write another one. If Mole had said, "That
stinks," I would have packed it in right there. Not that the world would
have been much different anyway, but for myself I have to thank Mole
a thousand tons for that.

Was it about a particular person?

Yeah, it was about the drummer of the Slits, Palmolive, a girl from Anda-
lusia. The Slits wouldn't form for another two or three years, but at the
time she was my girlfriend. In fact, it was probably watching us morons

load vans and unload them and set up gear that set her mind to eventually make the Slits.

Did you find it difficult to write songs?

No. I think once you've got an idea in your noggin then the hard work's over. Okay, there's a lot of hard work in front of you—you've got to form it in the right way and try and present it in an understandable way to people. But if you didn't have the idea in your noggin to start with, then there's no way you will end up with a result. That's what I've learnt about songwriting, is being able to spot the glimmer of opportunity. To actually get in there and get it out is another whole scenario in itself. That's probably where experience comes in.

The 101'ers actually built up quite a reputation on the circuit. What would you say was so special about them as a live act?

Well, it must have looked pretty funny [laughs]. I'm not joking, because although the terrible things that were happening in Chile at the time don't bear repeating, there is an upside to them in that we got a lot of Chilean rock 'n' roll musicians who had to flee to London to avoid being killed. So I ended up with a fantastic saxophone section from Chile who could actually play, who were in rock 'n' roll bands in Chile, which is more than we had been, 'cause we were kind of starting out. So if you can imagine these guys in their pampas outfits or gaucho outfits, ponchos, hats . . . And then I had a very short guy and a very tall guy—some English guys. We also had a pack of wild dogs snarling around our feet, so we must have looked quite an eyeful.

Then I think we really got into it. Because none of us had done it before, we didn't have that kind of . . . Sometimes you get session musicians, they're quite laid-back about what they're doing or they do the minimum. We really got into it with a heave and a ho.

And finally we only chose really fast rock 'n' roll numbers to play, so there wasn't any introspection going on. We used to play a lot of charity gigs to a bunch of stoned hooligans and because we played at full tilt and everyone in the group was really sweating on it, it kept the room dancing.

How long was the brass section a feature of the 101'ers?

Maybe six or nine months until it sort of stripped itself down. We started to actually get booked gigs in RAF bases in Norfolk and so, as the grueling conditions wore on, people would drop out from that. At one time we had three, but only briefly. For a while we had Alvaro Pena, I think his name was, on tenor and Big John, this was the very tall bloke, whose real name was Simon Cassell, he was on soprano, and then we had a drummer, a refugee from Chile called Antonio. That was a fairly good lineup for a while and then Snakehips Dudanski got in on the drums and really the main lineup was myself, Mole, Snakehips, and the Evil C, which was Clive Timperley, on the lead guitar.

As you built up this reputation, were you making a living?

It was pretty poxy. I can remember the figures. The first time we played at the Elgin, it was a fiver. A fiver [was] worth then a lot more than it is now, but it's still pretty poxy. And then when we started to really pack the place out, he moved us to Thursdays and we got a tenner and I remember it wasn't really enough. I think we could just about hire the van, pay the petrol. And we used to go quite far afield, Nottingham, whatever. On such an occasion, I think we could probably hire the van, pay the petrol, drink beer all night, and that's it. There wouldn't be a penny left over.

Were you signing on the dole?

Er, yeah. Now I don't know if they retrogressively, er—

I think you're safe.

Well anyway, I can remember it was ten pound, sixty-four p, which would keep the wolf from the door, so to speak. Also, if we were really starving I'd just go busking down Portobello Road.

You were still living in a squat?

Exactly. We could run the group, but it was definitely no-money-in-the-pocket time.

Was it a big moment for the band when Chiswick Records offered you the chance to do some recordings?

I thought they were out of their minds, I'm telling you. We'd been grinding out for maybe eighteen months and doing pretty good gigs and one night on the South Bank we were in some university and we just blasted out a gig. Ted Carroll and Roger Armstrong came back and they went, "How would you like to cut a record?" And I remember looking at this bloke, Ted Carroll, and thinking, "Cut a- a- what?" It's funny now with everyone rushing up—and so they should—banging out, "Cut your own record." Somehow we were so unimaginative, that to make a record was like something that you didn't even bother thinking about. Then I realized they were serious and it kind of tickled me. I knew we weren't going to make any dosh off of it, but it was nice to go in a studio.

How did you find your first time in a recording studio?

Well, although I still love [it] and I'm glad the place is still there, it was somewhat sobering to realize that the guitarists couldn't stand up straight. Pathway was a very small room. In fact, tiny. And it had sloping-in walls, like obviously there was staircases in other buildings. In order to set the whole group up in there, all the guitarists had to stand and lean forward slightly. But apart from that, we did it. We probably weren't in there more than two hours.

It was almost too small for baffle boards. There was one in front of the kit. There was a kind of alcove that the kit fitted into with a baffle board across the front of it, and then the amps we just pushed as far as they could be into the recesses of the room. They were turned to face the wall a mite. But we weren't going to try and separate the bass. There's no time for all that.

You got some good recordings out of it: "Keys to Your Heart" and "Sweet Revenge."

Yeah. Not bad at all, are they? I can't remember feeling over the moon. I don't know why. Maybe we were too tired to bloody feel.

You and the other guys must have felt that you were finally getting somewhere, but it wasn't too long after this that you decided to leave the band.

We made big inroads for about a year, and then Eddie and the Hot Rods came along and they were a bit flashier than we were, and a bit younger, maybe. Eddie [Barrie Masters] was like a Jagger-esque bloke. They got signed by Island and they were the only people on the scene that had got signed. That must have made me think, "Well that's it." 'Cause we were like rats down in the gutter and it seemed like suddenly a white hand had come down and scooped Eddie and the Hot Rods out. I think they were signed for two grand, or three grand, and at the time it sounded like ten million pounds to the rest of us.

Ted had put out one single, but after he put out one single I remember him and Roger complaining and they went, "We're only going to put out singles by dead people from now on," 'cause it was such a hassle to deal with us or I don't know what. 'Cause they had a Vince Taylor record. So I knew that wasn't really going anywhere. Then there was a long period, maybe nine months, where I just felt we weren't getting anywhere, perhaps 'cause we weren't doing anything interesting.

Had "Keys to Your Heart" been released?

Yeah.

How long after that before you decided to leave the band?

Oh, quite a long time. I remember we tried to get on the radio and Charlie Gillett had the only show. I think it was on Radio London. Imagine for us sewer rats to get on the radio—it's like, you must be joking. Finally, we got a tape to Charlie Gillett and he said on his program as we gathered round the radio in the squat, "Oh and I've got another tape from the 101'ers, but I'm not going to play it 'cause it's the usual 900 miles a minute rushalong stuff . . ." So I felt we were doomed anyway.

And of course you had this crucial experience seeing the Sex Pistols when they supported the 101'ers.

Yeah, at the Nashville.

And this was the first time you'd ever seen them or heard of them?

Yeah. I knew something was up, so I went out in the crowd, which was fairly sparse. I think it was a Tuesday night. And then I saw the future with a snotty handkerchief right in front of me.

How were they so different and such a breath of fresh air?

Let's just contrast the two styles, between punk and pub rock. Pub rock was, "Hello you bunch of drunks, I'm going to play these boogies and I hope you like them." The Pistols came out that Tuesday evening and they went—they didn't say this but the concept of attitude was—"Here's our tunes and we couldn't give a flying fuck whether you like them or not. In fact, we're going to play them whether you fucking hate them." So suddenly the boot was on the other foot or something had shifted. A cog in the universe had shifted there.

Also—which was something I didn't realize at the time—they quite smartly sent the Pistols out on the same kind of circuit we were treading all around the country, and so by the time they hit the Nashville and places like that, they were a really firing live unit. There's something magical about Steve Jones's guitar ability. He had a Gibson plugged into a Fender Twin. I don't think I've ever seen any guitarist—and I must have seen them all—that can get a sound with just his fingers out of a Fender Twin, the sound of, like, ten guys playing the guitar. Steve Jones is very good at chords and me and him used to walk past each other and go, "B flat 7" and see who could find it on the guitar first. You had Rotten's amazing presence and Matlock is a fantastic bass player—as good as Paul McCartney—and then Steve Jones, and then Paul hammering. When they were all together it was a real live unit, no smoke or mirrors needed.

Is it true that at one point Steve Jones was considered for the Clash?

Not me, but I think that was a wet dream of Bernie's always, 'cause the history of the Clash is really Bernie arguing with Mick, day in, day out, year in, year out, decade in, decade out.

Bernie is the one who headhunted you, is that right?

Yeah.

How did you feel about that? Did you feel a little bit guilty about leaving the guys behind in the 101'ers?

Well, not really. I'd started to fuck the band around after seeing the Pistols, 'cause it took a while for these things to happen. Evil C left or got fired. I can't remember which to be honest, but I gave him his Gibson that the band had paid for anyway. Then I got Martin Stone in. So the whole thing was impacting anyway, and I'd fired Mole when I shouldn't have done sometime earlier. And then punk hit London and suddenly—which side of the line were you on?

When you say punk hit London, wasn't it just the Pistols?

Yeah, the Pistols and the people walking around [with them]. All right, there was only ten of them, but it was starting to mushroom. And we were on the very bottom rung, where ideas come in very quickly. There was a vast number of hippies left over, 'cause it's only '75 end of, early '76, so you were either against punks or with them. You couldn't stand up saying, "Well, we're not sure." So the group really had to fall apart because most of the people in my group were against them and I was with them.

Was the proposition put to you by Bernie, "This is a band that's going to be in the mold of the Pistols"?

Not really. He came along with Keith Levene, who I liked immediately, and he said, "Look, here's one of the geezers in this group I'm putting together. I want you to come along and meet the other two." So I went along and I met Paul and Mick and I decided there and then to throw my lot in, 'cause the 101'ers had really disintegrated anyway.

Were you conscious of the Ramones at the time?

Oh, absolutely. I definitely remember playing along with it while Simmo [Paul Simonon] was learning how to play bass. We were also aware of a group called the Saints from Australia, who were in there very early with a record.

How do you look back now on your time in the 101'ers?

Oh it was brilliant. Absolutely brilliant. In fact, I just toured the States a couple of months back and an amazing number of people were asking about them.

Do you think the 101'ers compilation *Elgin Avenue Breakdown* is a good summary of what the band were about?

Yeah. I mean, it has to be really, 'cause half of that album is cut off a cassette tape. There aren't that many tapes around. I think that's pretty good. There's a great Bo Diddley cover from the Roundhouse. Yeah I think it's pretty good. It has to be really, 'cause that's the only documented evidence left.

MICK JONES: BEFORE

Sean Egan | 2007 | Previously unpublished in this form

The hinterland of Mick Jones, Joe Strummer's songwriting foil in the Clash, involves a band more myth than reality: the London SS. Despite their nebulous nature, however, the London SS were extremely influential on the punk scene.

This 2007 interview—never previously published in this form—sees Jones and his London SS colleague Tony James reminisce about an ensemble without which a musical revolution may never have happened. —Ed.

Mick Jones is famously always late.

A major strand of his well-documented prima-donna behavior is his inability to turn up when supposed to—apart, ironically, from the day that his airs finally got him sacked from the Clash. True to form, he walks in half an hour or so tardy to the small West London rehearsal space of his new musical venture Carbon/Silicon. His partner in Carbon/Silicon, Tony James, holds the fort pending his arrival. (Because James and Jones are such similar surnames, henceforth the two will be referred to by their first names.)

Mick is also apparently not one for small courtesies, at least to journalists. Upon his entrance, he apologizes for his lateness to Tony but not to me, then shares a can of lager with Tony without offering any to your correspondent. After the interview, I send Mick a gratis couple of books for his popular-culture museum and receive no thank-you note.

During the interview, however, he, like his colleague, is warm and friendly. Although Tony's hair is thinning, he is surprisingly youthful for a man in his midfifties, dressed casually and in trainers. Mick looks older in both physique and dress, his almost bald pate a startling contrast to his Keith Richards mane of yore, and his quasi-Edwardian jacket-and-trouser combination a far cry from the old confrontational Clash look. One thing retained from his days in the Clash is his propensity to accentuate a point with, "You know what I mean?"

Both are excited about their new project. When Mick turns up, Tony points at a pile of the freshly arrived Carbon/Silicon release *The News*, saying, "Look—records." "Oh, bloody hell," responds a delighted Mick, as he invokes *This Is Spinal Tap*. "*Sniff the Glove*—it's here!"

Though their joint vision is fixed on future horizons, they are still more than happy to talk about the old days when they first worked together in a group destined to go down as the Big Bang of punk: the London SS. From the ranks of this loose and briefly lived aggregation came a snarling attitude, a back-to-basics musical philosophy, and half a dozen crucial bands. Overseeing this musical activity was the pair of Malcolm McLaren and Bernard Rhodes, businessmen with an eye on becoming rock-music managers—which they eventually did with the Sex Pistols and the Clash respectively.

"Mick and I had met after Mick had been chucked out of his first group and we were trying to form a group," says Tony, estimating the crossing of paths to be in 1974.

Mick was a pupil at Hammersmith School of Art, while Tony was studying for a maths degree at Brunel University. "In those days you went to art school or university," Tony recalls. The motivation to attend either establishment was pretty much the same: "They gave you a grant to buy your guitar with. These days you go to university and you've got to pay *them*! I bought a Rickenbacker with my first grant and my amplifier with my second grant." Mick offers, "Every time I'd get [a grant], I'd buy a piece of equipment or another thing towards it. And then have hardly any money for the rest of the term. I went to art school because I wanted to get in a band. The traditional way: all the people I liked had gone to art school. It wasn't that I wanted to be an artist."

Being a true believer in rock 'n' roll carried its costs. "I liked Johnny Thunders," says Mick of the lead guitarist of the pioneering glam-trash quintet the New York Dolls. "So I used to turn up at art school in high heels, the biggest hair, and a Sex [McLaren's shop] T-shirt or something. And it was a half-building school as well, so it wasn't only artists, and they're all going—in the queue for the canteen—'Aaah!' I didn't care."

Being conspicuous was not an uncommon experience for either. Tony: "At that time in London there were no groups like the group that we wanted to form. So we were running ads every week in the paper looking for people into the Stooges, the MC5, the New York Dolls, and it was like a desert. In those days, you couldn't even go and buy a pair of sunglasses or a leather jacket—it seems ludicrous—let alone find musicians who liked that same kind of music."

Of that specialist taste, Mick says, "One of the things that made me get into it was my mum lived in the States and she used to get me *Roxy* and *Creem* magazines. She'd subscribe to them and then send them back to me, so I knew about a lot of those groups."

Albums-wise, Mick says, "*Nuggets* was a really important record." Tony adds another couple of key albums to that Lenny Kaye compilation of sixties garage rock: *Kick Out the Jams* by the MC5 and *Fun House* by the Stooges. Mick describes the MC5, the Stooges, and the New York Dolls as "an axis of superb brilliantness." He then laughingly appends a comment that might raise eyebrows among those who have a problem with the London SS's name: "That was like the Hirohito, Hitler, and Mussolini, if you like."

In fact, Mick is now remorseful about the London SS handle, even though its Nazi-tinged provocativeness was punk prescience. "I worked at Social Security at the time, so we were trying to pass it off as that," he says, "but we didn't realize the true horribleness of the name. We thought it was like 'New York Dolls.' We were stupid and, when we were confronted with the reality of it, we balked." The name has also come back to haunt them. Now that he has entered into another partnership with Tony, interlocutors always bring up their first joint musical forays. "It's mad innit?" Mick says. "We want to do something new, but obviously people are going to look for a little byline. It's a full circle of penance and remorse. I'm a Jewish kid and so it's particularly wrong."

Tony explains, "London SS existed as a group that auditioned people for about a year, and various members came through that audition process." Mick: "It was like a big fluid situation. All the people who were into that type of music at that time all knew each other 'cause it was only a real small scene. A few pockets." Mick also emphasizes, "The thing was, you never stay together because there was a thing called 'Let's go for a drink.' And that meant: 'You're fired.' You were only with the group for a couple of days or a week or so. Everybody was always trying to get on, in a way."

Mick adds, "If anybody sounded any good—what they were into and stuff—then we'd take them round to our caff in Praed Street where we'd stack the jukebox with all the stuff we liked and then we'd give them a pre-audition audition. Then if they passed that one, we'd take them round the corner to our little rehearsal [studio]."

Tony says, "Ultimately I suppose you could say the core of the group was me, Mick, Brian James, and a drummer called Roland."

At one point however, Chrissie Hynde, a woman of an assertiveness unusual for the era, was considered as a focal point. Mick reveals that Rhodes was pushing for Hynde to be the singer, with the group name changed to Schoolgirl's Undies and Hynde masquerading as male. "Then when the group became successful, she'd go, 'Ha ha, I'm a girl!' and that will be the big trick."

The London SS never played any gigs, although Mick points out, "People came down to the studio [to watch]." Adds Tony of their rehearsal space in the Praed Street café's basement, "It was a room much like this really." This would mean it was no larger than an average-sized living room.

One Praed Street band practice took place in front of two relatively distinguished guests. "We played through what we'd learned in front of Bernie and Malcolm," recalls Tony. Mick: "Malcolm came, but he, like, threw peanuts. He went, 'Is this going to change the world?'"

The performance to which McLaren and Rhodes bore witness was actually captured for posterity and is the only sonic legacy of the band. At one point, Tony intriguingly points to a laptop on a nearby desk and says it can be found on there. However, there is no offer to air it. "There is an album's worth that no one ever gets to hear," he says. "We've never played it to anyone. The weird thing was, it was lost for twenty years. I found it about a year ago."

In 1978, before it went walkabout, Tony boasted of the tape to journalist Pete Frame, "Raw rock 'n' roll . . . it drives like fuck." "He's bigging it up!" scoffs Mick. "It's just us doing a few old Flamin' Groovies and old tracks from *Nuggets* and stuff . . . It was just us forming. Mind you, there's even worse stuff from before. The stuff that we did when we were in Warrington Crescent." The latter is a reference to a basement flat that hosted other Jones pre-Clash musical activity. It was situated around the corner from Mick's childhood home in Wilmcote House, over the Westway, which he and the band would almost fetishize as they cultivated an image of what one journo termed "tower-block rock."

As 1976 dawned, the London SS were coming to the end of their brief and uneventful life. "We started to drift apart," says Mick. "We could never get it together." Tony: "People always [say], 'How did you split up?' but we were just sort of going, 'Oh, we can't find a singer . . .'"

There was one particular voice around town that the band and their manager had their eyes on. "We used to go and see Joe play," says Tony to Mick of a certain Mr. Strummer. "All the time we used to go and see the 101'ers play and Bernie was suggesting maybe you could work with Joe, and Paul Simonon had come down . . ."

Mick: "But he only come down with the drummer. He wasn't actually coming down to audition himself."

This leads into reminiscence about another building central to the band's story. Tony: "Also, you were living in Davis Road then with Sid [Vicious] and Keith Levene in that squat." Mick has few fond memories of the aforesaid Shepherd's Bush house, at which Simonon was also domiciled and which doubled as home and rehearsal space. "The room we practiced in, we put egg boxes on the walls but it was like Paul's room as well and Paul's got no sense of smell whatsoever," he says. "It was only about this size. You can just imagine: we'd crowd in there and we'd start rehearsing."

Tony: "I'd met Billy Idol and we drifted apart. People are always saying, 'Wasn't there some sort of animosity?' because somehow you could say Paul took over my job. But in fact what nobody knows is the first bass guitar Paul Simonon had, I gave him. It was a Perspex guitar that I'd built when I was at school."

As for Strummer, Mick observes, "We'd met him a couple of times really briefly: once in the street [and] we looked at each other in the DHSS [Department of Health and Social Security, where the unemployed would "sign on"]. He was playing already. He needed taking out and putting into the new thing . . . Joe was from pub rock almost. He came, he saw the future, and decided, 'Oh, I want a bit of that. This is over.'"

Both Mick and Tony feel they learned from their time in the London SS. "Masses," says Tony. Singled out for particular praise is Rhodes, whose forensic—and sometimes extremely agitated—dissection of his charges' attitudes has become legendary. "The School of Bernie," says Tony. "The ground rules. What's the idea?" "What we still stick to now," adds Mick. "'What are you about?' That was the big question."

Humble, casual, and even smelly as their modus operandi and milieux may have been, the London SS made a lasting impression. They spun off a host of notable groups. Among the ensembles to feature London SS members were Chelsea and Generation X (Tony James), the Damned (Brian James and Rat Scabies), the Pretenders (Chrissie Hynde), and the Boys (Matt Dangerfield and Casino Steel). They were particularly influential on the Clash: Mick Jones, Paul Simonon, Keith Levene, Terry Chimes, and Topper Headon all at some point became long-term members of the Clash after passing through the ranks of the London SS as either courted auditionee or recruited member.

Such was their central place within the mid-seventies minisociety of people hungering for edgy music that the ripples the London SS created become ever more apparent the closer one looks. For instance, Levene and Sid Vicious wound up in Flowers of Romance with Palmolive and Viv Albertine. From there, Vicious graduated to the kings of the punk pile, the Sex Pistols. Palmolive and Albertine went on to form the premier female punk act, the Slits. Levene ultimately found his way into Public Image Ltd, the band formed by Johnny Rotten/John Lydon following the Pistols' implosion. Journalist Nick Kent was also a sort-of London

SS member, and naturally the fact that he later championed punk bands in print was beneficial to the movement.

Possibly more important than those musical chairs, though, was the push and pull of the friendship/rivalry of Rhodes and McLaren, whose joint enthusiasm, irreverence, and rhetoric set the insurrectionary ground rules for punk. They vied for the status of manager of the top band in said movement and each, at different points, did indeed inhabit that role.

It's an astonishing legacy for such a fleeting operation. "When you look back, it seemed like it was years, but actually it was weeks," says Tony. "Groups formed, made an album, and split up in those days in the time people take to do a remix these days."

"I FOUND IT EMBARRASSING TO BE IN THE CLASH"

Sean Egan | 2003 | Previously unpublished in this form

Keith Levene is the forgotten Clash member.

A guitarist in the group before they had a name or a singer, his only official musical legacy is his one-third songwriting credit on "What's My Name," a track on their first album, released seven months after he left the band.

This Keith Levene interview was conducted for a 2003 magazine feature on the genesis of that first album. Most of it has never previously been published. In an impassioned, profane, discursive, and sometimes contradictory discourse, Levene tells of the Clash's grand visions and petty disputes—as well as how they might conceivably have ended up as the Phones.

Notes: Levene is wrong about the sequence of the Black Swan and Rehearsal Rehearsals gigs: the former took place on July 4, 1976, the latter on August 13.

The Clash did not support Patti Smith at the Roundhouse: Levene seems to be conflating two separate 1976 concerts at the London venue, one by the Patti Smith Group in May at which the two bands socialized, the other a Clash gig the following September.

In UK parlance, a "Tory" is someone politically aligned to the center-right Conservative Party. —Ed.

How did you wind up in the Clash?

I'd learnt how to play guitar and I left school when I was fifteen for my birthday. I ended up working for Yes as a roadie. They were my favorite band. After I came back from that, I said, "Fuck that, I want to be in a band." Most of my best friends were, like, three years older than me and they were quite hip to the West London scene. They ended up getting this squat in Davis Road, which is off the Uxbridge Road in Shepherd's Bush, and by default I could live there.

I was born in 1957. I met Mick Jones at the tail end of 1975, early 1976. He just came round to Davis Road one night. He was called "Rock 'n' Roll Mick." He looked a bit like Tiny Tim. He had long hair and he had these leopard-skin trousers on and this really cool velvet jacket and these blue suede shoes, these winkle-pickers, which he gave to me. We just got on really, really fucking well. We just all loved Mick.

This is the real genesis of punk. We'd all go and see the 101'ers. We'd seen the Pistols at the Nashville. Then Mick said to me, "Look, I know this bloke Bernard Rhodes, right, and there's this bloke, Malcolm McLaren." I said, "The Sex Pistols bloke?" He said, "Yeah. They've had this really bad row over Let It Rock, this shop. He wants to meet you."

[Musician and cofounder of punk club the Roxy] Barry Jones had this little four-track recording studio in Warrington Crescent in West London. I went round there one day and Mick was there. So they're having this makeshift jam. I think it was Chris Miller on drums—Rat Scabies—and Mick's playing guitar and Barry's in there. Mick went away and came back and I was playing guitar. I was just playing something that I was making up at the time and he went, "Oh, fucking 'ell. I've never seen a bass player play guitar like that." And I said, "No, I'm a guitarist, actually—you've never seen a guitarist play bass like that."

He phoned me up and he said, "Come down Portobello Road with us all." What's really happening is, we're going to meet Bernard but I didn't know that. When the market died down about two o'clock, he said, "Look, Bernard's coming over, he's going to pick us up in the car and we're going over to Camden Town." So I met Bernie.

So Bernie was involved from the very outset . . . ?

Absolutely. Without a doubt, Bernie is as responsible for the Clash as fucking anyone.

It's part of rock 'n' roll folklore that the reason Bernie put together the Clash and molded them is because he wanted his own Sex Pistols. Would that be a fair thing to say?

Yeah. So, we meet Bernard. "I want to talk to you, blah, blah, blah, blah. What's the thing you most want to do?" "The only thing I know I definitely want to do is I really want to get a band together." He said, "Mick thinks you're the best find he's ever found," and I said, "Actually I kinda knew that, but that's really flattering." So that afternoon I went down and he's playing us all these reggae records and showing us what we were calling red-label Levis, which he'd saved, and brothel creepers. He had this room just full of fucking treasures.

I just loved Bernard. He was a nervous Jewish guy. I understood his jokes, I understood his wisdoms, I understood what he was talking about, and I also understood what he was saying when he was saying, "Fuck your friends, they're not going to help you. Get rid of your friends, forget all the people you go around with, forget the arseholes you used to play guitar with, forget this, forget that. If you're gonna do this, you're gonna have to *do* this." In that sentence I've encapsulated Bernard's general attitude. After Bernard got that place Rehearsal Rehearsals in Camden, it was great. There was loads of space there. There was enough to just have a nice loft upstairs and a great place to play downstairs and never, ever get a complaint. It was fantastic. It was a fucking dream. He said, "Get all your hippie friends over here and fucking get them to paint it," and stuff like. He was so clever. He was so funny.

He was competing with Malcolm. He was going, "This is the hippest scene you're ever going to be on." I'm quoting him. "This is the hippest scene in London and you are on it. In fact, you *are* it. There're people that's gonna latch onto you, not just because you're in a band, but because of what you are and who you are." And this was before we had a band or we had a name or we had a bass player. We never really had a drummer, until I left. I mean, I left and they put out the record and it was ages until they got Topper.

I always thought that Terry was quite a decent drummer.

Terry was a fantastic drummer. Basically there was nothing wrong with Terry Chimes whatsoever. The only thing that was wrong with Terry Chimes was he was upper middle class and he was very, very straight, but he played fucking great drums. There was nothing wrong with Terry, and yet Mick had to call him "Tory Crimes" on the album. What a cunt. It was definitely Mick's doing. No doubt about it. Take it from the horse's mouth.

I didn't even know they were going to credit me for a third of a song. I wrote all those songs with them. I made them sound the way they sounded. Where I drew the line was with "White Riot" and "1977."

You said this was the beginning of punk, but you were traditionalists: your favorite band was Yes and Mick himself was a true believer in rock 'n' roll.

Mick was more into these what I call annoying bands like the Dictators. Now, I like the Dictators, but the Dictators weren't serious. I was very much into the whole Trojan reggae thing and porkpie hats and all that kind of thing, which very luckily Paul Simonon was very, very tuned into and Bernard was totally, totally tuned into. And I was very into the dub thing.

Bernard didn't put me and Mick together. Mick put me and Bernard together. It's very important you understand that, because if Bernard put me and Mick together, I probably would have stayed in the Clash. Bernard was really interesting. Bernard said, "You know, I've heard things about you," and I said, "Like what?" He said, "I've heard you've taken drugs. Well, I think if you know about drugs, you know about other things, other things the other guys don't know about." And I said, "I think I know what you're talking about." And he said, "The element that you add to the band is the element I love."

I'm jumping forward a bit, but in a later conversation I was saying to Bernard, "I can't take it anymore. They've all got the right haircut and I've got the wrong haircut, but I feel like actually I've got the right haircut and they've all got the wrong fucking haircuts. I'm leaving because it's either Mick's band or my band. This band can't work in that democratic way where it's just a band. It seems to have to be led." We'd do a version of a song. I'd work it out with Joe, Paul, and Terry and then I'd come in and they'd play this tune and I'd go, "What's that? It went that way the other day, why's it go this way now?" "Well, Mick wants it to have a verse and a chorus and this and that." I said, "Well that can be another tune." The only tune they'd accept from me was "What's My Name," where I did a verse and the frigging chorus.

It's easier to talk in hindsight because you can tell by what I did with PiL [Public Image Ltd] and everything what I was into more. That I was trying to break ground in music. It was about not being scared to play something that was—in inverted commas—wrong, and repeat it. I was trying to bring a big dub influence. I was trying to bring a big subtractive influence. Dub is about subtraction.

Mick is a big Mott the Hoople fan and that sort of stuff.

Like myself. We had a lot of things in common. We loved Mott the Hoople, we loved that scene, we loved the glam-rock thing. He wasn't as into Bowie as I was, but maybe I wasn't as into the New York Dolls as he was.

So those very early rehearsals at the squat, what kind of music were you knocking up then? Were there any original songs? Was Mick writing stuff?

I'll tell you how it worked. Mick said, "Do you want to be in a band with me?" "Yes, absolutely yes." So, it's me and Mick. I go round to his granny's flat in that tower block off Harrow Road [over] the Westway. We're playing fucking electric guitars not even plugged in. He's going, "I've got this song, it goes 'de diddle de . . .'" He's playing me "Protex Blue" and I'm going, "Yeah, but that's um, that Rolling Stones tune, innit?" He'd play me another tune. I'd go, "Yeah, but that's fucking *Goat's Head Soup*, isn't it?" And he's going, "Oh, shut up." I'm sort of half taking the piss and I'm half respecting him because he's writing songs. Where I wanted to go was you don't have to play a verse and a chorus, you can just play a repetitive theme and sing different vocal lines over the top of it and that will change it, or come in at a different time and that will completely change it. He couldn't get his head around that at all.

Mick had about five songs at that time and he was going, "We've got to get a bass player. I've got an idea for this guy. He comes across a bit thick, but he's really good. He's really good-looking and he's an artist." That was Paul Simonon. So I met Paul one day and I really liked him, he was great. Then Paul moves in at the squat at Davis Road, so I really get to know him. He's just like this big, big, big kid. But he's really hard, too. He's the real thing and he loves all the things I love. He loves reggae, really old Bowie like the Laughing Gnome, new Bowie, Lou Reed stuff, and Patti Smith. He liked Yes! Anyway, he couldn't play bass and Mick had this thing of saying, "Go, like, 'de de de dum de,'" and I was like, "Mick, instead of showing him how to play like that, why don't you just tell him where you're playing and show him that you're doing the barre chord and the tonic note, and let him make up his bass lines, because then he might come up with something." I just thought I could see what's going to happen here: Mick's just gonna robot this guy into these songs and he's going to learn how to play bass in a very, very one-dimensional, traditional way.

Wasn't Paul really brought in for his good looks and for his front-man potential?

No. Paul was brought in because we needed someone that was good. We needed people that were good personalities. I'm not saying we knew we were going to make it, because I don't think we were trying to make it. We were just trying to make a great band. I hadn't really blossomed into anything that great-looking, but I had personality. I knew exactly what I wanted to do with music and everything. The thing about Paul was he did look good. He was designed to be in a band.

We've all been through our shit now, we've all been through being ripped off by the record companies, no longer being in the really popular band, walking round the streets miserable, all that shit. I remember seeing Paul—he turned up at a gig—and he was the only person that actually went, "Keith, Keith, oh, fucking hell, I haven't seen you for ages." I saw Joe Strummer in L.A. in 1989, somewhere around there, and he's rehearsing and all the guys he's rehearsing with, I'd just made a record with the day before. I just happened to walk into the rehearsal studio because I needed to pick up my little amp and I saw Joe and I went "Joe! Joe!" and I ran over and I grabbed him. And he was almost acting like "Erh, erh, who are you, erh, erh, erh, I don't know you." He totally fucking knew who I was and he really upset me. I felt like a total prick and I was totally embarrassed and I totally hated him for responding like that.

I've turned up at a few Clash gigs after I left. I turned up at three of the gigs at Bond's [Casino, New York] when they played at Bond's for about a year. I felt like a Clash gig was always an hour and a half too long. It used to just drain me inside watching them and I used to think, "I'm so glad I left that band." By that time I was in PiL and I was like, "If we do a gig, it's an event." And I learned all that off Bernard! What's the point of doing a gig every night, 'cause then people can see you every fucking night and they think, "Well, we can see those guys any time, so fuck them. Let's go and see someone else." That's another Bernard Rhodes quote.

But Bernie changed, because he was the manager of the Clash again at the Bond's gigs.

Yeah, he was. You see, Bernard would never call himself the manager of the band. He didn't want to be the manager. It was, like, he wanted to work *with* us and I really liked that. A lot of my manifesto, I inherited from Bernard.

I'll tell you a few more things about the Clash, anyway. Me and Mick and Bernard went down to High Wycombe, got this guy, forgotten his name, I'm sorry. So we had a singer and I think we were using Terry Chimes. So we had Paul, me, Mick, this singer, and Terry Chimes. This singer, I mean, you couldn't have a guy more like Mick Jagger. It wasn't like he was doing anything wrong. He just wasn't for that band.

I've always wondered how that five-man Clash worked with three guitarists.

Well, it didn't. That's why I left.

The 101'ers, they were like a misdirected rock band that was sort of fifties. Joe would come on in a big Zoot suit. You couldn't understand a word he was fucking saying, he had terrible teeth, but he'd fucking *move*, and he'd be like this big pile of sweat. He was such a mover and a shaker. But he didn't do it in this Elvis way, he did it in this really unique way. Anytime you went and saw the 101'ers, it didn't fucking matter that you knew all the fucking numbers or whether you liked them or not 'cause Joe was just gonna fucking blow you away. The reason they were called the 101'ers [was] 'cause they lived at 101 Chippenham Road. They had a squat there.

We've now come to know and love Joe's idiosyncratic enunciation.

You might, but I don't. What I saw in Joe was amazing potential. So me and Bernard go to this 101'ers gig and he goes, "I've seen you around." I said, "Listen, I want you to come over to my place in Davis Road, meet my mate Paul and have a little jam with me." He went "Why?" Bernard said, "Have you heard of the Sex Pistols?" and Joe went, "Yeah" and he went, "Well, we've got this band that is the only band that can rival the Sex Pistols. But we're not trying to be the Sex Pistols, we're gonna be the *other* band. You know like the Beatles/the Stones." I think I'm making that quote up a bit, but that's what we were putting across.

The Pistols had supported the 101'ers, hadn't they?

I don't know, but I think that was really funny if they did. Only because the 101'ers were so fucking good. I was really into the 101'ers. There was a few tunes I really loved, one being "Keys to Your Heart."

They were a good band but even back then it was very, very retro.

That's the thing. I was saying, "Listen mate, you're wasted in this band. What the fuck are you doing here with your fucking Zoot suits? You've got all this energy. When you come on there and you can know what your direction is and you can come on there with your fucking comrades, your fucking gang, the people you feel confident walking down the street with, the people you know will take a bullet for you. You want to walk on stage with a band like that, not a band that's thinking like, 'Fucking 'ell, that singer's so good, he might fire us at any time.'" And he went, "Ah ha ha ha!"

Anyway, I don't know how we did it, but I made it that he come over one Saturday, the squat. I have him singing with me. I wasn't thinking my main objective is to get him in the band. I was just like, "Joe's coming over, let's play, man." We just play, we just have fun together. Actually, it was really funny, 'cause he was covered in sweat and he made this comment. He said to me, "You never sweat, do you, man? You're so cool." That was his first observation. And then he went, "God, I love the way you play guitar, you just play anything. I love the way you make things up." I said, "You can *have* that." I couldn't help doing that: it just came out. I went, "You can be part of that." We did "Keys to Your Heart" and I'm singing it with him and he's going, "Oh, I fucking love you" and he just grabbed me and he said, "I'll do it, I'll do it, I'm gonna do it, I'm gonna do it. Okay. What's the band called?" I said, "I don't know, but I know one thing now: we've got a fucking killer singer."

Then we had to tell Mick that we'd asked him to come over, but I think by the time Mick got that news, I'd already snagged him into the band. And there was no way Mick was gonna say, "No fucking way."

Wouldn't Joe have agonized about leaving the 101'ers?

He was well agonized about it. I totally respected that and understood that was gonna hurt to him. It's almost like me going to one of the members of the Hives and saying, "Join the Strokes."

After years of struggling, the 101'ers had just done these recordings for Chiswick. They were getting there, even if really slowly.

Well, you see we weren't so career-oriented. We didn't give a fuck. What Joe was singing about in the 101'ers, was "A little less conversation, a little more action," and in the Clash, Bernard's giving him all these fucking books on like Trotsky and socialism and Nietzsche, I don't fucking know what. I'm going, "Joe, Joe, you're taking this a bit too seriously, you're almost quoting these fucking books, man."

All right, so Mick's accepted it, so now it's Keith, Mick, Joe, Paul, and the drummer, who was never respected. Terry was like the drummer that was lucky to be drumming with the other hippest band in London. Then we had this little discussion. We're sitting upstairs at Rehearsal Rehearsals. We've done a few rehearsals, the songs are sounding good.

Very quickly after we got Joe we did this thing in the loft—sorry, I keep calling it the loft—in Rehearsal Rehearsals.

That was after the first gig, wasn't it?

That *was* the first gig.

Didn't you play the Black Swan first?

No, no, no, other way round. You see, what we did was, we played our own rehearsal studio and we had Caroline Coon there and a bunch of other people who were the people at the time. Maybe Vivienne Goldman was there.

Have you ever seen Rehearsal Rehearsals? It had something to do with the Underground. If you went in there, it was like a club. There was a stage, there was a place to stand up on, and then there was a lower bit.

We did this gig and it was really, really successful. It really went down fucking great. Then afterwards we went back to Caroline Coon's boat and we're sitting around and sort of doing our first schmoozing, socializing thing and we got written up in *NME* and *Melody Maker* for it, because Bernard made sure all the right people were there.

Was that first gig recorded at all?

Not to my knowledge.

And how many people would have been in the room?

I would assess fifty.

So the songs played at that first gig, would we recognize any of them?

Yeah, first album. All those tunes. Not "What's My Name," 'cause we hadn't written it yet. I wrote that at the Black Swan gig. I wrote it at the soundcheck. What was going on was we were doing tester gigs and we supported the Pistols at the Black Swan.

Now, by this time, I'd been a bit moody with the band. It had been a bit argumentative. I was just trying things out. I was still very influenced by Steve Howe [of Yes]. The Ramones was one of the most influential things on me. The Ramones was what straightened me out. We're in Davis Road. [Mick] comes in with the Ramones album and I look at it and I say, "The Ram Ons," and he goes, "The fucking Ramones, you fucking idiot." Then we put it on and it's just everything we wanted it to be and more. It was just like this wall of guitar. No fucking lead. And it was just like a fucking revelation, man.

Also, it made me realize that that's what is really getting me down about the fucking Clash. That every time I really do unleash myself, it's not allowed. "We'll let Keith do it, but when he does the gigs, he'd better do it the way I want," which is Mick.

When you say, unleash yourself, what do you mean by that—guitar solos?

No, the exact opposite.

So, this is interesting, because you're saying you were more "punky" than the rest of the Clash?

I didn't put it in those words. I'm just telling you how it came about. The Ramones was just like the big stiff drink I needed to just say, "Relax, just do what the fuck you like, man."

So we do the gig at the Black Swan, and by then I'd been well moody at rehearsals, to the point that I knew they were talking about me. They were also talking about this song called "White Riot," which I was going, like, "No. Fucking. Way. What the fuck have we got to riot about? Forget it. You know: when we've got something to riot about, okay, let's just fucking do the riot and then just write about the riot after we've done it. I ain't gonna fucking sing 'White Riot.' I'm not gonna do it." "You're just being awkward, Keith." "Fuck you." "Don't say fuck you . . ." And then it got to this thing: "I don't think you wanna be in the band anymore and you're always so miserable."

So we're doing the Black Swan. Mick's going, "What are you fucking wearing?" I'd just got this green shirt that I liked. He's going, "You're wearing a fucking bowling shirt, Reebok training shoes . . ." I don't know what else I was wearing. No one else had a problem with it. And by then, Mick was being really critical of everything I did.

It was about two things. One was Viviane Albertine. He was crazy about her and she was crazy about me and she knew me before she knew Mick. The next thing was, the day I was eighteen we were waiting at this bus stop, me, Viv, and Mick. Viv went, "It's Keith's birthday today," and he went, "Oh, how old are you? Twenty?" I went, "No, eighteen." He went, "You're never eighteen." I said, "Yeah, yeah, eighteen today. I'm fucking really getting old now." And I said, "Well, how old are you, Mick?" And he went [embarrassed voice], "Oh, twenty-one." So I thought maybe he was twenty-two then. After that, he never treated me the same. After that, he was so horrible to me.

So, anyway, we were at the Black Swan. I noticed that John Lydon was sitting at one corner of the gig on his own. I was sitting on my own at the sort of perpendicular corner and having nothing to do with my band, and John was having nothing to do with his band. At some point or another, I strolled over. I said, "John, I hate my band, I fucking hate it and I'm gonna leave it." And he went, "Well I tell you what, if I can ever get out of this, we'll get a band together." And I said, "Well, I can't see that happening, but if there's anyone I'd want to be in a band with, it's you." He went, "Listen man, I've been trying to get you in the Pistols. I can't get that thicko out. I'll never get him out. I can't be in the Pistols."

And we did the Mucky Duck, as Joe Strummer called it—the Black Swan—and it was a good gig. Went back to London, did the Round-house. We supported Patti Smith. And Patti Smith's talking to Bernard, and I run up to Bernard and I go, "It was fucking awful, it was the most fucking embarrassing fucking set I've ever been involved in and I fucking hate this fucking band." And Bernard pulled me aside and said, "Don't ever say anything like that about the fucking group in front of anyone." I said, "It doesn't fucking matter 'cause I'm not going to be in the fucking group anymore." He said, "Don't pull that fucking drama with me," and I said, "Bernard, I never fucking pull drama. I've made a decision tonight, and you've seen it coming, because you've seen me and you arguing for the last fucking six months while Paul, Mick, Joe, and whoever the fucking drummer was at the time were just leaning against the wall and it would be me and you arguing, wouldn't it? And what would we be arguing about? We'd be arguing about how fucking uncool the fucking Clash is and how stupid the fucking name is and what a load of fucking wankers they are. Because we weren't arguing about what a wanker I was, were we?" And Bernard went, "Suppose not," and he went, "Please, I understand, I understand what you're doing—go." And he gave me this blue Les Paul Junior and I left.

I thought that this had been presented to Bernie as a fait accompli, that you'd been sacked . . .

Absolute bollocks. I'm telling you the truth.

So, just backtracking a little bit, with regard to three guitars in the lineup, did that make a problem?

What three guitars? Well, Joe didn't count. He may have counted more when I left [laughs]. But because I was there, Joe didn't have to play. In fact, I used to turn his amp down. Because it was awful.

We're in situations like sitting in the Speakeasy and he'd be sitting there drunk and going, "Oh come on, Keith, come on, you don't want to leave the band," and all this kind of stuff. They didn't believe me. They didn't believe I wanted to leave.

There was a vote. I said, "Well, look, I don't *wanna* leave the band but the way the band is, I *do* wanna leave it, so unless you're gonna let me have a hell of a lot more input, you guys can decide. Is the band better with Keith or does the band make more sense without Keith? I think it's either my band or Mick's band, because that's the way this band works. Now if it was my band, I wouldn't be telling Joe to read books and how to sing and I wouldn't be showing Paul what notes to play."

But Mick could always turn around to you and say, "Well, these are my songs."

It wasn't a question of that. Mick had already written the foundation of the bulk of the songs, but until I came along and added my bit to it, and added my sound to it, they sounded like shit. Put it this way, "Protex

Blue." He's playing the chords and I'm going, "De, de, de, de, de." After I did that Mick went, "That's my favourite lick, that's my favorite lick." It just worked so great, and then he's singing the song and I'm going, "Ooh-ooh." He'd got the music that he wanted that he couldn't do himself. He got everything. He got his songs and then he got them sort of finished off and produced. So it wasn't like an upper-hand thing. Mick was very miffed about the fact that I could fucking just wipe the floor with him on guitar, but that wasn't my thing. I didn't care about that.

So, Mick was coming up with the tunes and the lyrics and you were filling in with licks and guitar parts?

Well, this was the sequence of events, right? He runs into a seventeen-year-old. We become fast friends. Four months is pretty quick to become friends and say we're going to be in the same band and have a guy leave the London SS, which was his big main project and he's twenty already, or something, and feeling very old already.

Was the London SS a real band?

Yes, it was. It was Tony James, Mick Jones, and I don't know the names of the other guys. One of them ended up in Sigue Sigue Sputnik. I can't remember who. I only know Tony [James] was in Sigue Sigue Sputnik.

So the sequence of events was they had this vote because you had indicated you were unhappy with things?

This is the deal. They didn't want me to leave the band. I said, "Well, you guys decide then." So what happened was, Mick says—

But was this after the thing with Bernie at the Patti Smith gig?

Oh no, that was just like that night at the gig. He was right. You don't walk up to your manager when they're talking to an influential person like Patti Smith or somebody in the business and say you think your band's shit. He taught me something there. I don't even think the other guys even fucking knew about it. It had blown over by the time Patti

Smith had come on stage. I was almost holding hands with Bernard going, "She's so great, she's so fucking great, man."

But it was after this that there was this vote. Presumably you weren't in the room?

No, I was in the room. That's the whole point. I was sitting upstairs on my own and they came up and they said, "Why are you always so moody and miserable?" I said, "I work out a tune with Joe and it goes one way and then when I come back, it goes another way. I don't get it. I don't get any say in it. I like rock 'n' roll, but I think it's been done. The Rolling Stones sort of dealt with that. So, I want that to change a bit, and I want more freedom to do what I do. I'm not being allowed to do what I do by psychic inference." And I said, "Well, fuck it, you decide." And so Mick said, "Out." And Joe said, "Um." And Terry said, "Definitely not—in." And then I looked at Paul and I knew Paul was going to go with the majority. Paul wasn't going to make any waves. Because Paul says, "No," Joe said, "No." And I said, "Well, I'm really glad that happened because I just saw the way you did that and it sort of answers other questions. It tells me I'm right not to do this band and this is the right time to get out." And I said to them, "Look, if you change your mind, let me know. I'm only talking about in the next couple of weeks. I'm not leaving this band to be nasty. I'm leaving this band because I think it's better for the band."

Yeah, there was a vote, but I could have said after that vote, "Look actually, I really want to be in, I've changed my mind" and stayed in the band. And by the way, Bernie says, "This is crazy, this is so insane," and Bernard met me separately and asked me to stay in the band. Joe met me separately in a drunken state twice and asked me to stay in the band.

So just going back a bit, the reason you didn't like "White Riot," was it because you didn't want any politics at all in the music?

No. I mean, it's one thing saying, "It's difficult to get jobs, no future," and all that kind of bollocks, right? They were just trying to be militant and they were doing a really poor job of it.

Presumably something like "Career Opportunities," that would be more up your street?

Well, "Career Opportunities" made more sense. That was post-me, but it was definitely being toyed around with.

Would "London's Burning" have been in the set?

Yeah, I remember doing that.

Was that more the kind of thing that you preferred?

No. You know the one I liked? And we totally ripped off "Pretty Vacant." That was "Janie Jones." That was the first song Mick showed me. That's what made me like him so much.

I don't know how that was done when you were in the band, but on the album it's got continuous Ramonesy blurred rhythm guitar all the way through.

Yeah, funny that, innit?

Was that the way that was done when you were in the band?

That's the way I did it. You see when Mick showed me it, I'm going, "One note is so much more powerful."

So you were talking about having written "What's My Name" at the Black Swan . . .

I thought of [Sex Pistols bassist] Glen Matlock, and I thought, *What's the sort of thing Glen Matlock would do?* I thought of a riff that Glen Matlock would do, that was a typical kind of run up, and I did that. They went, "What's that?" and I went, "It's a song I'm writing." And they said, "What's the rest of it?"

It's got a really spooky ambience to it. It sounds kind of menacing as well.

I was taking the piss out of the Clash.

What about "48 Hours"—was that knocking around?

Yes. I never had the album. Even though I had a credited tune on it. I just didn't like it enough.

Have you heard the album?

Oh, yeah, certainly, I've heard it. But when you're naming these specific songs, it's a bit difficult because I probably know how they go, but I just don't know what ones they are.

There's a lot of people around who talk about it as one of the greatest rock 'n' roll records ever made. Some even go a bit further than that and say it's the best. How do you relate to that?

Are you saying people are saying the first Clash album is the best album they made?

No, there's a lot of people who say it's one of the best albums ever made by anyone.

Oh, I think that's insane. It just doesn't make any sense to me. How can it be remotely close to the best album ever made? There's so many better records out. *Graceland* pisses all over the first Clash album. The first Clash album was a great—in inverted commas—punk-rock album. I'm looking at an album in front of me here called *Physical Graffiti*. There's one track on there called "Kashmir" that's better than that whole album. I mean, how the fuck can the first Clash album be the best album when you've got an album like *Hunky Dory*? *Revolver. Here Come the Warm Jets*. It's insane. Nirvana—*Nevermind*.

Do you actually remember this incident when Paul is supposed to have given the Clash their name?

Yeah, I do. We were all sitting around thinking of names. I don't particularly remember suggesting any good ones and Paul said, "You know, I think 'the Clash' is good." And it sort of went round the room a couple of times. Then a couple of other names came up. They were coming up with names like the Mirrors.

Was the Phones one of the names?

Yeah. I remember liking the Phones. I remember thinking, *I like the Phones a load more than the Clash.*

I think there was also the Heartdrops.

That's right, yeah.

And the Psycho Negatives.

Don't know about that. I remember the Negatives and I said, "Yeah, we should be a load of black guys with dyed blond hair!" The point was, it had been done. But I do remember Paul thought the Clash was quite a good idea, that it sort of represented what had happened amongst us and what we were doing within the scene [but I thought] that's for other people to decide, sort of thing. I just didn't think the name was cool enough.

What about this idea that Paul had read the *Evening Standard* one day and he kept seeing in it there was a clash of this and there was . . .

That was true. That was another reason they liked it, 'cause it came up a lot: there was a clash in this situation, or the clash over benefits, or the clash over pensions.

I'm just wondering whether the band have pushed this story of Paul reading the *Standard* and seeing "the clash" because it sounds a bit better than—

Is that the story? Because the story was that Paul did come up with the name the Clash and he thought it sort of represented where we were at and I said, "I can't disagree with where you're coming from, but I just think the name's a bit corny and I think that we've got enough dork factors going through at the moment . . ."

Paul wasn't one of them. That's what was so weird. Because Joe was cool, Mick was cool, I was cool, Paul was cool, Terry was cool, even though they just wouldn't acknowledge it. It's one thing to listen to Bernard or let Bernard give you books and everything, but it's another thing to make up your own mind about what you think of something. You don't read something and get a load of new information and just spout it out. You have to give yourself time to assimilate something. I think if Joe had assimilated this new information that Bernard was piling on him, he could have come up with something a lot more confident. He might have been smart enough to get Mick to sing on a lot more things with him.

But that wouldn't have left much for Joe to do, because his guitar skills weren't that great, were they?

No, but he was a great front man and he could have had a situation where we could have backed him up a lot more singing. But he looked good with a guitar hung round his neck, and the fact that he could play it enough that he knew the songs, and if we wrote a new one he could learn it and always know where to be in it, if he did want to play the fucking thing. He was Joe Strummer. It's true. He got his name right—he is Joe Strummer.

What were relations like after you left the Clash?

The Clash were doing fine, so they were a little bit like, "Oh, Keith lost out, Keith blew it by leaving." I never felt like that, personally, and when I did the PiL thing, they were really intimidated by it. They were treating it like the tables were turned.

THE VERY ANGRY CLASH

Steve Walsh and Mark Perry | October 1976 | *Sniffin' Glue* (UK)

It's appropriate that this first proper Clash interview feature appeared in *Sniffin' Glue*. Though a low-circulation, photocopied amateur magazine, it was the bible for the musical and social movement just beginning to be tagged "punk."

The interview took place in the last week of September 1976 at Rehearsal Rehearsals, the North London building rented by Bernard Rhodes that served as practice room and sometimes home for his charges. Although the article was originally formally credited to Steve Walsh, *Sniffin' Glue*'s founder Mark Perry belatedly arrived to throw in some questions of his own.

A footnote explained that drummer Terry Chimes hadn't been present. This invisibility on Chimes's part was standard: his lack of interest in their political slant ensured he wasn't invited when the Clash held court to the media.

The article's title is accurate: Strummer, Jones, and Simonon virtually froth at the mouth about the shortcomings of both UK society and contemporary music. Although Jones primly disavows the "lawlessness" he considers to go with "arnachy" (original spelling has been retained throughout as a reflection of the ground-level nature of punk fanzines) the article contains an example of the irresponsibility about violence on the part of Strummer that littered early Clash interviews. This is despite taking place a few days after an incident at the 100 Club punk "festival" in which a girl lost an eye to a thrown glass.

As with much of the coverage of the band in the early days, the definite article in the band's name is treated as optional and Paul Simonon's surname is rendered as "Simenon." Also standard for early Clash coverage is the wholesale quoting of their lyrics: journalists were clearly impressed that these people's songs had something to say.

The feature gave rise to one of the most memorable of all Clash quotes: "Like trousers, like brain!"

Notes: For "Paul Simenon" read "Paul Simonon"

For "Bryan James" read "Brian James" —Ed.

"All the power is in the hands,
Of people rich enough to buy it,
While we walk the streets,
To chicken to even try it,
And everybody does what they're told to,
And everybody eats supermarket soul-food,
White riot!"

('White Riot' by the Clash).

The CLASH rehearsal studios are situated somewhere between Dingwalls and the Roundhouse. Inside it has been decorated—pink and black colour scheme—by the band. The downstairs studio, where the band rehearse, is equipped with a juke-box, pink drapes hang from the cieling—very tasteful. I talked to three of the band (Micky Jones—guitar, Paul Simenon—bass and Joe Strummer—guitar) in the upstairs office.

Mick tells me, he and Paul have been together for about 6-months and with Joe since the 101'ers broke up. They told me boredom inspires their songs—"It's just that I can't stand not doing anything", Joe explained.

SW-What's the name about, why call yourselves Clash?

Paul-Well, it's a clash against things that are going on . . . the music scene, and all that we're hoping to change quite a lot.

SW-Does this mean you're political?

Mick-Yes, we're definitely political!

Joe-We wanna be the apathy party of Great Britain, so that all the people who don't vote go out and don't vote for us!

Mick-We're really into encouraging creativity . . . we ain't a bunch of raving facists!

SW-Are you a bunch of raving arnachists?

Joe-I don't believe in all that arnachy bollocks!

Mick-Yeah, arnachists believe in lawlessness . . . look, the important thing is to encourage people to do things for themselves, think for themselves and stand up for what their rights are.

SW-You hate apathy?

Mick-Oh, I fuckin hate apathy but I hate ignorance more than anything.

SW-Do you try to put this over in your songs?

Mick-All our songs are about being honest, right? The situation as we see it, right?

SW-Right! So the songs relate directely to you and your enviroment?

Mick-Right, otherwise we'd be writing bullshit!

SW-So, what do you want to happen today?

Joe-What I'm most aware of at the moment, is that most people in London are going out every night to see groups or something and they're making do with rubbish and because everything else around is rubbish, it's not immediately apparant that it's rubbish. People are prepard to except rubbish, anything that's going. I mean, every single LP anybody plays me in any flat I go to and they say, "this is good" . . . it's rubbish and they have got nuthin' else to play . . . the thing is they've got to think it's good, otherwise they go insane . . .

Mick- . . . and it's all shit!

SW-What's shit?

Mick-All them records, right . . . you know, you can't go out and buy a record 'cause you know it's just, like, fuckin' bollocks . . . just a load of shit!

Joe-The only good one is that Ramones one.

Mick-Yer, the Ramones record is good.

(Doorbell rings—in strolls Mark P. to spoil my fun).

HERITAGE.

Joe-It's our heritage . . . "What are we livin' for, two-room apartment on the second floor". That's English, not what's goin' on now.

Mick-They're the most important English band. Like Mott the Hoople's Ian Hunter always spoke to the kids straight and even when they went to the States and they were getting a bit flash and a bit dopey he still used to sing about the dole and he had to translate for the Americans and say, "look, this is really the welfare". They don't know what the fuckin' dole is, where as we're all down the dole anyway, coppin' our money off Rod Stewart's taxes!

> In 1977, I hope I go to heaven,
> Cos I been too long on the dole,
> And I can't work at all.
> Danger, stranger! you better paint your face,
> No Elvis, Beatles or Rolling Stones, in 1977!"
> ('1977' by the Clash).

SW-What do you think is wrong with people today?

Mick-They're apathetic . . . boring . . . boring music bores me! Boring 'cause it's not new, boring 'cause it's not . . .

Joe-It's a lie . . .

Mick- . . . they ain't pushin' themselves nowhere they ain't being creative.

Joe-Where's that picture of the George Hatcher Band?

Paul-Oh yeah, that's a real joke, that is . . .

Joe-We found this to be . . .

Mick-Hilarious, have you seen it?

(They hold up a advertisment for the George Hatcher Band showing to members in typical stage pose).

Joe-I mean, the whole thing is a lie, it means nothing.

Mick-Except that they're on tour with Dr. Feelgood.

Joe-All this crap like, oh yeah, they've got long hair and his got his arm up here and look at his cowboy shirt and the trousers.

SW-What have clothes got to do with it?

Mick-Well, this is what rock'n'roll's supposed to look like . . .

Joe-It's a state of mind.

Mick-What's the difference between this ad. and the cover of last weeks NME, it's the same pose ain't it? I think that's the same pair of trousers, from 'Jean Machine'.

(Mick was referring to the previous weeks' cover-pic of the Rod's Dave Higgs).

MP-But they're a pair of trousers!

Joe-No, you can't say that's clothes and this is music, it's a state of mind, a complete thing. If anything was going on in that blokes head he would do something about it.

Mick-To show he was a person, he would've done something to himself. Now, he's just showing that he's one of the many—a consumer, i.e: I eat shit all the time!

SW-Everyone's a consumer, I mean, if you go down to 'Sex' and buy a pair of leather trousers your still a consumer. That's the odd thing about the '70's, in order to change society you must first consume it. (You can tell he's been to art-school -Ed).

Mick-Yeah, but if it comes out of creativity. Some people change and some people stay as they are, bozos, and they don't try to change themselves in any way.

Joe-We deal in junk, you know, I just realised that the other day. We deal in junk. We deal in like, the rubbish bin. What we've got is what other people have put in the rubbish bin. Like Mick's shirt was gonna be put in the bin until he paid 10p for it. I mean, you ain't gonna go down to 'Sex' with yer ten quid stuffed in yer pocket and buy some stupid . . . er . . . I dunno, I've never even been down there.

Mick-I think it's a bit easy to go down there and look great, I mean, there stuff's pretty good. Looks good to me, but I think the way we do it is much more accessible to kids cos' anyone, at very little price and it encourages 'em to do something for themselves. It's to do with personal freedom . . . I don't think it's just the trousers though, I mean, the trousers reflect the mind.

Joe-Like trousers, like brain!

"WHITE RIOT, I WANNA RIOT!
WHITE RIOT, A RIOT OF ME OWN!"

SW-Would you say your image is violent or suggestive of violence?

Mick-It reflects our 'no nonsense' attitude, an attitude of not takin' too much shit. I don't like violence tough.

SW-What do you think of the aura of violence that surrounds the Pistols, I mean, it can easily get out of hand.

Joe-I think it's a healthy sign that people arn't going to sleep in the back-row.

Mick-I think people have got to find out where their direction lies and channel their violence, into music or something creative.

SW-Thing is, you talk about being creative but say the thing got so popular that we had all those fuckin' footballs and discos and all that lot coming down to see Pistols gigs. They'd take the violence at face value and go fuckin' crazy!

Mick-So you think it can get out of hand?

SW-You bet it can . . .

Mick-It got out of hand on Tuesday (100 Club fest-glass throwing incident).

SW-I reckon it could get worse.

Mick-I definitely think it could escalate but the alternative is for people to vent their frustrations through music, or be a painter or a poet or whatever you wanna be. Vent your frustrations, otherwise it's just like clocking in and clocking out . . . clock in at the 100 Club, every one comes in, everyone clocks out, it ain't no different.

SW-How much change do you want, d'you want a revolution?

Joe-Well . . . yeah!

SW-A bloodless one or do you want just total chaos?

Joe-No, I'm just not into chaos, and I don't believe it when people say they are 'cause you've got to be a special type . . .

SW-Of maniac?

Joe-Well, a Frenchman, about 100 years ago could be into chaos 'cause it was possible then, but nowdays, this is like sleepytown. So, when someone tells me they're into chaos I don't believe it.

Joe-What I would like to see happen is, very much . . . I realise a lot of people are quite happy, you know, at that market down the road from here. All them people, they're as 'appy as sandboys and I'd just like to make loads of people realise what's goin' on. Like, all those secrets in the government and all that money changing hands and every now and then it comes to light and someone gets sacked and someone else comes in the back-door, know what I mean? I'd like to get all that out in the open and just see what's goin' on. I just feel like no one's telling me anything, even if I read every paper, watch TV and listen to the radio!

RADIO.

SW-What was that with the radio at the 100 Club gig?

Joe-Well, all that was . . . I'd been lucky and bought a cheap transister in a junk-shop for ten-bob and it worked quite well. I'd been goin' around with it on my ear for a few days just to see what it was like. When someone broke a string I got it out and it just happened to be something about Northern Ireland.

Mick-A state of emergency . . .

SW-Yeah, bombs . . . I thought it was interesting I thought maybe it was part of the way you approach your audience.

Mick-That was part of it, but we've tried other things since then, like at the Roundhouse . . . er . . . we 'talked' to the audience . . .

Joe-But they were half asleep . . .

Mick-The ones who were awake were pretty clever.

Joe-I didn't think so, I mean, *you* could hear them, I couldn't. How can I answer smartass jibes when I can't hear 'em? All I could hear was some girl sayin', "nyah, nyah, nyah!" and then every-one goes,"aha,ha,ha (Bursts out laughing)". If you can't hear what they're saying, then you can't really get out your great wit!

Mick-Well, I'm sure they were funny 'cause everyone was laughing at 'em but when Joe said something like, you know, "Fuck off, fatso!", there was just complete silence!

(More laughter).

SW-So, what do you wanna do to your audience?

Joe-Well, there's two ways, there's that confronting thing right! No . . . three ways. Make 'em feel a bit . . . threaten 'em, startle 'em and second—I know it's hard when you see rock'n'roll bands, to hear the lyrics are but we're workin' on getting the words out and makin 'em mean something and the third thing is rythmn. Rythmn is the thing 'cause if it ain't got rythmn then you can just sling it in the dustbin!

"He's in love with rock'n'roll, wooaghhh!
He's in love with getting stoned, woooagh!
He's in love with Janie Jones, wooagggh!
But he don't like his boring job, no-oo!"
('Janie Jones' by the Clash).

ANY INFLUENCES?

Joe-That's a tricky question . . . Paul's are the Ethiopians and what's that other band?

Paul-The Rulers.

Joe-I've never heard of 'em!

Mick-Up until now, I thought everything was the cat's knackers and every group was great. I used to go to all the concerts all the time and that's all I did. Until, somehow, I stopped believing in it all, I just couldn't face it. I s'pose the main influences are Mott the Hoople, the Kinks, the Stones but I just stopped believing. Now, what's out there (points out the window) that's my influence!

SW-What changed your way of looking at things?

Mick-I just found out it wern't true, I stopped reading all the music papers 'cause I used to believe every word. If they told me to go out and buy this record and that, then, I'd just go out and do it. You know, save up me paper round and go out and buy shit and now I'm in a position where I'm selling the records 'cause I don't have much money and they're showing me how much my shits' worth! 'Cause I paid 2 quid for them albums and they give me 10 pence down the record shop, that's how much they think you're worth!

MICK.

Mick-I've played with so many arse'oles and my whole career has been one long audition. Like, I was the last kid on my block to pick up a guitar 'cause all the others were repressing me and saying—no, you don't want to do that, you're too ugly, too spotty, you stink!" . . . and I believed 'em. I was probably very gullible and then I realised that they wern't doing too well and I said, ah fuck, I can do just as well!

"LONDON'S BURNING WITH BOREDOM,
LONDON'S BURNING, DIAL 999!"

SW-What do you think of the scene so far?

Mick-Well, it's coming from us, the Pistols, Subway Sect and maybe the Buzzcocks, that's it, there are <u>no</u> other bands!

MP-What do you think of bands that just go out and enjoy themselves?

Mick-You know what I think, I think they're a bunch of ostriches, they're sticking their heads in the fuckin' sand! They're enjoying themselves at the audience's expense. They're takin' their audience for a ride, feeding the audience shit!

MP-What if the audience say they're enjoying themselves?

Joe-Look, the situation is far too serious for enjoyment, man. Maybe when we're 55 we can play tubas in the sun, that's alright then to enjoy yourselves, but now!

Nick-I think if you wanna fuckin' enjoy yourselves you sit in an armchair and watch TV but if you wanna get actively involved, 'cause rock'n'roll's about rebellion. Look, I had this out with Bryan James of the Damned and we we're screamin' at each other for about 3 hour 'cause he stands for enjoying himself and I stand for change and creativity.

Joe-I'd rather play to an audience and them not enjoy it, if we we're doin' what we thought was honest. Rather than us go up and sing—"Get outta Denver, baby" and do what we didn't think was honest.

Mick-If they enjoy us then they come with us. If you ask me what I think of groups like the Hot Rods, I think they're a load of bozos and they're not telling the audience to do anything other than stay as they are. They're playing old stuff and I don't think much of their orginals. The situation is where the Hot Rod's audience are bozos and it's easy to identify with a bozo. I mean, obviously they're goin' down . . . like, people queing outside the Marquee, they've got a great thing goin' for themselves, but it's not to do with change, it's just keeping people as they are!

SW-What do you think the scene needs now?

Mick-Ten more honest bands!

Joe-More venues . . .

Mick-More events!

Joe- . . . just more people who care, if we could get out hands on the money and get something together . . . immediately. None of the promoters running any of the venues in London, care. Ron Watts, the 100 Club bloke, has done something but no one else really cares. They don't give a shit about the music, not one shit!

CLASH: DOWN AND OUT AND PROUD

Caroline Coon | November 13, 1976 | *Melody Maker* (UK)

Journalist and drug reform campaigner Caroline Coon was a famous figure on the "scene" during 1967's Summer of Love. A decade later, she remained sufficiently hip to realize that a new musical and social revolution was taking place. It was she who—in cahoots with Malcolm McLaren and fellow journalist John "Jonh" Ingham—formally gave the name "punk" to the music and fashions of the bands she was witnessing and enthusing about in print during the summer of 1976.

This article by Coon was the first Clash interview feature to appear in a mainstream print outlet. It's suffused with poverty chic and mythmaking: Strummer was at this point twenty-four, not the twenty-two Coon seems to have been told, and by all accounts his father was not the uptight figure he paints but a Marxist who was proud of Strummer's work in the Clash. There is also much posturing: the band members pledge to never sell out and to give any riches they earn back to their community.

Coon's predictions for the Clash in her final sentence show astonishing prescience about a band not yet even signed to a record label.

Notes: For "Denigh" read "Deny"

For "Protex Blues" read "Protex Blue"

For "Portabello" read "Portobello"

For "Paul Simenon" read "Paul Simonon" —Ed.

THREE weeks ago at London's ICA, Jane and Shane, regulars on the new-wave punk rock scene, were sprawled at the edge of the stage. Blood covered Shane's face. Jane, very drunk, had kissed, bitten and, with broken glass, cut him in a calm, but no less macabre, love rite.

The Clash were not pleased. "All of you who think violence is tough—why don't you go home and collect stamps? That's much tougher," roared Joe Strummer. Then he slammed into the band's anthem "White Riot."

> *"All the power is in the hands*
> *Of people rich enough to buy it,*
> *While we walk the streets*
> *Too chicken to even try it*
> *And everybody does what they're told to,*
> *And everybody eats supermarket soul-food.*
> *White Riot, I wanna riot*
> *White riot—a riot of my own!"*

The song, played with the force of an acetylene torch, is no less politically uncompromising than the other numbers in the band's repertoire—numbers like "Denigh," " Protex Blues," "Career Opportunities" and "1977." To hammer home their impact, the Clash play with enough committed force to bring down the walls of Babylon, Jericho, Heaven and Hell if necessary. And their audiences go wild.

But, far from wanting people to hurt each other, Joe Strummer (vocals, guitar), Mick Jones (guitar), Paul Simenon (bass) and Terry Chimes (drums) insist that their aim is to shake audiences into channelling their frustrations into creative outlets. It's difficult, however, trying to maintain a balance between positive reaction and violence.

How easy it is though, when you examine the Clash's background (one only too similar to that experienced by the thousands of young people who identify with the new-wave rock bands), to explain their emotional intensity.

Aware that, like the rest of the band, he'd rather not talk about his childhood, I asked Joe (22) where he came from. "That's the trouble, see." He speaks fast, using words economically.

"The only place I considered home was the boarding school, in Yorkshire, my parents sent me to. It's easier, isn't it? I mean it gets kids out the way, doesn't it?" Then he adds defiantly: "It was great! You have to stand up for yourself. You get beaten up the first day you get there.

"And I'm really glad that I went because I shudder to think what would have happened if I hadn't gone to boarding school. I only saw my father twice a year. If I'd seen him all the time I'd probably have murdered him by now. He was very strict."

While Joe is talking, Paul (20) is sitting next to him pointing and shooting a realistic, replica pistol—bang—at the posters on the walls—bang—at Mick across the room—bang—at Gertie the roadie's dog—bang, bang—anywhere at all.

"I get on all right with my parents," he says. "But I don't see them very much. They split up when I was eight. I stayed with my mum but I felt it was a bit soft with her. I could do whatever I liked and I wasn't getting nowhere so I went to stay with my Dad.

"It was good training because I had to do all the laundrette and that. In a way I worked for him—getting money together and that—down Portabello market and doing the paper rounds after school. It got me sort of prepared for when things get harder."

Paul liked school. "I never learned anything. All you done is play about . . . there were forty-five in our class and we had a Pakistani teacher who didn't even speak English."

Mick, (21) like Paul, comes from Brixton. His father is a taxi driver and his mother is in America. "They kind of left home one at a time," he says. "I was much more interested in them than they were in me. They decided I weren't happening, I suppose. I stayed with my gran for a long time. And I read a lot.

"Psychologically it really did me in. I wish I knew then what I know now. Now I know it isn't that big a deal. But then, at school, I'd sit there with this word 'divorce, divorce' in my head all the time. But there was no social stigma attached to it because all the other kids seemed to be going through the same thing. Very few of the kids I knew were living a sheltered family life."

When he was sixteen, Mick believes he had two choices—football or Rock 'n' Roll. He chose Rock. Why? "Because he couldn't afford toilet rolls," quips Joe. Much laughter. Mick explains: "I thought it was much less limiting. And it was more exciting and, I got into music at a very early age.

"I went to my first rock concert when I was twelve. It was free, in Hyde Park and Nice, Traffic, Junior's Eyes and the Pretty Things were playing.

"The first guitar I had was a second-hand Hofner. I paid sixteen quid for it and I think I was ripped off. But, I tell you something—I sold it for thirty to a Sex Pistol." Everyone laughs again, gleefully.

Laughter is a cheap luxury when, like Clash, you never have the money for a square meal and when, like Joe, you live in a squat—or like Paul, you 'crash' in your manager's vast unheated, rehearsal room (where this interview took place) with no hot water or cooking facilities.

After Paul and Mick left school, they both eventually ended up as casual art students. Mick was already in a group when a friend of his dragged Paul down to a rehearsal. "The first live rock 'n' roll I can remember seeing was the Sex Pistols, less than a year ago. All I listened to before then was ska and bluebeat down at the Streatham Locarno.

"But when I went to this rehearsal, as soon as I got there Mick said 'you can sing, can't you?' And they got me singing. But I couldn't get into it. They were into the New York Dolls and they all had very long hair so it only lasted a couple of days."

Ten days later however, Paul had "acquired" a bass guitar, Mick had cut his hair, they had formed a group called the Heartdrops (although the Phones, the Mirrors, the Outsiders and the Psychotic Negatives were also names for a day). Then walking down Golbourn Road with Glen Matlock of the Sex Pistols, they bumped into Joe.

The meeting was auspicious. "I don't like your group (the 101ers)" said Mick. "But we think you're great."

"As soon as I saw these guys" says Joe "I knew that that was what a group, in my eyes, was supposed to look like. So I didn't really hesitate when they asked me to join."

How did Joe first get into a rock 'n' roll band? "Because I owned a drum kit. Someone gave me a camera and then I met this guy who had a drum kit in his garage and I had a go on it one day. And I thought 'this guy's going to swap me this little camera for all that kit.' And I said 'here you are.'

"Then I went down to Wales and I ran into a band who had a drummer but no drum kit. But I didn't want to play drums because I wanted to be the star of the show, right? So I said 'if you use my drum kit you're going to have me as your singer.' And they had no option but to accept."

Before Joe joined the band they were called Flaming Youth. He changed their name to the Vultures. They did six gigs before Joe decided to come back to London to form the 101ers.

Joe broke up the 101ers directly as a result of seeing the Sex Pistols. A few months ago he told me: "Yesterday I thought I was crud. Then I saw the Sex Pistols and I became a King and decided to move into the future."

Today he says: "As soon as I saw them I knew that rhythm and blues was dead, that the future was here somehow. Every other group was riffing their way through the Black Sabbath catalogue. But hearing the Pistols I knew. I just knew. It was something you just knew without bothering to think about."

What is it about punk-rock which is so important to Joe? "It's the music of now. And it's in English. We sing in English, not mimicking some American rock singer's accent. That's just pretending to be something you ain't."

Continues Mick: "It's the only music which is about young white kids. Black kids have got it all sewn up. They have their own cultural music. Basically young white kids are relying on a different time to provide for their kids."

But what's so different about youth today then? Silence. Joe stands up and, relishing the drama, he turns to reveal the stark, hand-painted graffiti on the back of his boiler suit. HATE AND WAR glare letters in red and white across his shoulders. It's the hippy motto reversed.

"The hippy Movement was a failure" is Joe's explanation. "All hippies around now just represent complete apathy. There's a million good reasons why the thing failed, O.K. But the only thing we've got to live with is that it failed.

"At least you tried. But I'm not interested in why it failed. I'll jeer at hippies because that's helpful. They'll realise they're stuck in a rut and maybe they'll get out of it."

The pervading, resentful feeling on the New Youth Front is that the older generation, squandering the opportunities of the rich Sixties, has left them with the shell of a disintegrating society. One of the reasons drummer Terry Chimes is notable for his absence is that he is having a serious argument with Joe. Terry wants to 'get out' of the country while there's still time. Joe thinks he should stick around to see IT—the political chaos they see as inevitable—through.

What do they feel about society today? "It's alienating the individual," says Mick. "No one gives a s—about you."

Says Joe: "There's nowhere to go. Nothing to do. The radio's for housewives. Nothing caters for us.

"All the laws are against you. Whoever's got the money's got the power, The Rent Act's a complete mockery. It's a big joke. I just have to f—off into the night for somewhere to sleep."

Adds Paul, with feeling: "At the moment what the Government should do is put licences on clubs so that kids can have somewhere to go. But they're clamping down on all that. But it's great because there's going to be kids on the streets. And they're going to want something to do. And when there ain't nothing to do you wreck up cars and that.

"The situation that is beginning to happen now is their fault. If we end up wrecking the place it's the Government's fault. They'll bring back National Service and we'll all be sent down to South Africa or Rhodesia to protect white capital interest. And then we'll all be slaughtered . . ."

They may knock society, but they're all on the dole aren't they? "Yeah. We get a little freedom from social security. Otherwise I'd have to spend 40 hours a week lifting cardboard boxes or washing dishes, or whatever I done in the past. But because we're on the dole—which is £9.70 a week—I can get a Rock 'n' Roll band together.

"If I got up at 4.00 a.m. and went to Soho and joined a queue I could get a job as a casual washer-upper. That's the other opportunity I've got. Or the opportunity to work in a factory!"

But someone's got to work in a factory? "Why have they?" demands Mick. "Don't you think technology is advanced enough to give all those jobs over to a few people and machines.

"There's a social stigma attached to being unemployed. Like 'Social Security Scroungers' every day in the Sun. I don't want to hear that. I cheer them. You go up North and the kids are ASHAMED that they can't get a job."

Aren't they being rather pious when all they are doing is playing in a Rock 'n' Roll band? "No," says Paul. "It's the most immediate way we can handle it. We can inspire people. There's no one else to inspire you. Rock 'n' Roll is a really good medium. It has impact, and, if we do our job properly then we're making people aware of a situation they'd otherwise tend to ignore. We can have a vast effect!"

Oh yer, I jibe, rock stars have usually started out saying they're going to change everything. Joe reacts first. "But you learn by mistakes. The Rolling Stones made mistakes. But I want to do something useful. I'm not going to spend all my money on drugs.

"I'm going to start a radio station with my money. I want to be active. I don't want to end up in a villa on the South of France watching colour TV."

Do they want money then? "Yes." says Paul. "Money's good because you can do things with it. Bands like the Stones and Led Zeppelin took everything without putting anything back. But we can put money back into the situation we were in before and get something going for the kids our own age."

Not that there are any profits at all at the moment—which completely belies the resentment in some quarters that these new-wave bands are 'having it easy and don't deserve all the exposure they're getting.' Apart from playing such—as Mick Jones himself so aptly puts it—"wonderfully vital" music, which deserves all the encouragement it can get, these bands are struggling harder than ever to stay on the road.

"We make a loss at every gig," says Joe. "It's the promoters who we want to attack. I bet you can only name one or two who really care about music and I'm amazed that there isn't one that really cares about what's happening at the moment. We're really having to get down on our knees and grovel for venues."

No doubt life will be easier when the Clash sign the contract dangling under their manager's nose. They are more politically motivated than the Damned, perhaps more musically accessible than the Pistols. Their lovingly painted clothes (the same on and off stage, of course), which are acrylic spattered with the ferocity of a Jackson Pollack action painting, have started one of the most creative fashion crazes of the year.

And their acute awareness, and ability to articulate the essence of the era which inspires their music will ensure that their contribution to the history of rock is of lasting significance.

KONKRETE KLOCKWORK

Kris Needs | April 1977 | *Zigzag* **(UK)**

By the spring of 1977, the new wave was unstoppable: the Clash's crude, rude, and cheaply recorded debut LP was just about to crash into the upper reaches of the UK album chart despite minimum publicity. *Zigzag* felt obliged to cover the scene with a special issue, although, such was the disdain for it among the magazine's hippie staff, they insisted on the new music being referred to only as "p*nk."

This article finds the Clash moving on. They were between drummers. Not only were they now recording artists, but they had replaced their homemade paint-splattered outfits with clothes with multiple and oddly positioned zips, designed for them by Alex Michon, who would collaborate with them on all their future outfits. Early the following year, Mark Perry of *Sniffin' Glue* would tell a television interviewer that punk died the day the Clash signed a £100,000 contract with CBS records, but some were already talking about the commodification of punk. The Clash—who were themselves lamenting the commercialism of the scene in their new song "Garageland"—assert herein their retention of punk integrity by repeatedly boasting they have "complete control." This, though, would come back to haunt them.

The "Julian" mentioned is in fact Julien Temple, who would go on to be a big-time motion-picture director.

Notes: For "Paul Simenon" read "Paul Simonon"

For "Keith Levine" read "Keith Levene"

For "the 101ers" read "the 101'ers"

For "Garage Land" read "Garageland" —Ed.

At the moment there isn't a group in the New Wave that comes within spitting distance of The Clash, live or on record. Within a year they have become the most exciting live band in the country, and shortly they will release an album which is the most stunning debut for years . . . I believe it'll be as important as the first Rolling Stones album in shaping a new direction for rock'n'roll.

The New Wave groups who have so far made albums - The Hot Rods and The Damned - have been OK for party music, but The Clash are something far more important and vital. Not only is their music original and lethally energised, but it encompasses a whole new attitude of positive creativity which, if it rubs off on their audience, can only be a good thing. They are trying to wake people up to reality as well as plumbing the fine essence of ultimate rock'n'roll.

First time I saw The Clash was at their first out-of-London gig at Leighton Buzzard's Tiddenfoot Leisure Centre, about an hour's drive out of London. The hall was like a large hotel lounge, which encouraged the crowd to drape itself over the seating.

The Clash taking the stage was like an injection of electricity into the smoky air. They charged headlong into 'White Riot' with shattering energy, strutting and leaping like clockwork robots out of control. They never let up for half an hour. Despite sound problems they were astounding, almost overpowering in their attack and conviction.

The Clash are: Mick Jones (lead guitar, vocals); Joe Strummer (vocals, guitar); Paul Simenon (bass, vocals). They haven't got a permanent drummer, although Terry Chimes has done most gigs with them and plays on the album.

They are managed by one Bernard Rhodes and rehearse/hang out in this huge ex-warehouse he found in Camden Town between Dingwalls and The Roundhouse. They converted it to a rehearsal room downstairs, with pink drapes and old barber's chairs for added home comforts; and upstairs is where the group create their outfits, revamping jumble sale purchases with acrylic paint spatterings and slogans . . . cheap and striking.

Mick: "We encourage the kids to paint their clothes. That way they get involved, feel part of it. Now they come along and show us ideas we like".

Back to the music. They write all their own songs, no Clash number is longer than three minutes, and not many exceed two. Each is fast, razor-sharp and rocking, with insanely catchy choruses. The songs are viciously topical and directly inspired by the group's London environment.

'White Riot', for example, was written after Joe and Mick got caught in the Notting Hill riots last year.

'Janie Jones' concerns the bloke with a boring job who gets off by being in love with Janie Jones (the imprisoned vice queen). 'London's Burning' ("with boredom") is "A celebration of the Westway under a yellow light" - Joe Strummer. '1977' is a cold look at the future/present: "No Elvis, Beatles or The Rolling Stones in 1977", and "Ain't so lucky to be rich; sten guns in Knightsbridge". There's loads . . . all vital, power-packed SONGS.

The Clash are very much a London band. They couldn't live anywhere else or their music would suffer.

"We love the place - blocks of flats, concrete", says Joe. "I hate the country. The minute I see cows I feel sick", says Mick, who says he has never lived at ground level.

The Clash formed a year ago this month. Originally Mick, who like Paul comes from Brixton, was a member of the London S.S., arguably the first New Wave group. The line-up also included Brian James (now with The Damned) and Tony James (bassist with Generation X). They were rehearsing in 1975, and Paul came down to a rehearsal one day and met Mick, who got him singing, "I'd never sung or played bass before in my life".

The S.S. "didn't work out" and split before they'd done a gig. Mick got together with Paul and formed The Heartdrops, which later became The Clash. Paul learned bass by sticking white dots on the fret board of the machine he'd acquired.

There was another guitarist too . . . Keith Levine, who left mysteri-ously last autumn and is getting his own band together.

They needed a singer, and one day when Mick and Paul were walking down a street in Shepherds Bush they bumped into Joe, who was still with the 101ers. Mick told him that he was great but his band stunk, and asked him to join The Clash. Joe was bored with singing pub rock standards, and despite that fact that the 101ers were rising fast, he broke them up and joined The Clash (on April 1st, to be precise).

By the time the 101ers single 'Keys To Your Heart' came out, Joe was firmly involved with The Clash. Goodbye rhythm & blues, hello 1976! When they were ready The Clash unveiled themselves to a rehearsal room full of press and friends. The date was Friday 13th. Reaction was immediate and they got rave reviews.

There followed a select series of London dates at places like the 100 Club (they did the p*nk rock festival last summer), the Sex Pistols all-nighter at the Screen On The Green, and two at the Institute Of Contemporary Arts (the last one being the time when Patti Smith leapt on stage during 'I'm So Bored With The U.S.A.').

The Clash have always taken gigs seriously, never being content to just trundle round the circuits night after night. They've only done The Roxy once (January) and they often organise their own gigs . . . that way everything's right and it becomes a complete event. They might lose money, but it's made for some great gigs. There've been the ICA gigs, one at the Royal College of Art, where hippy art students threw glasses at the stage, and the last one, which was on March 11th at Harlesden Colosseum (more later).

The Clash were also part of the Sex Pistols ill-fated "Anarchy" tour last December, along with The Damned and The Heartbreakers. As you must know, most of the gigs were blown out by timid moral guardians after the Pistols said naughty things to the baiting Bill Grundy.

Mick: "That was soul-destroying. We thought we were the greatest rock'n'roll bands, conquering the world. Everyone was really excited . . . but the day before it started, the Grundy thing went down and gigs started being cancelled".

Paul: "It was really bad it was cancelled. The tour turned into a cause, in a way . . . us kids just wanted to play. We were stuck in hotel rooms for a couple of days waiting to play, then we'd be told the gig was cancelled, and we'd wait for another three days in the hotel room. It was good fun to read about it in the papers, though".

Mick again: "The Pistols suffered quite terribly. It was really tragic, but we learnt so much from it. You knew the time had to come".

The bureaucratic petty opposition The Clash encountered on that tour solidified one of the things they are against - oppression.

"There's a lot of oppression around today", says Mick. "We're making people aware of it and opposing it".

One of the best gigs I've been to recently was The Clash's self-organised one at Harlesden Colosseum. It was a lesson in organisation (only a ten minute gap between bands!).

It was an important gig for each group on the bill, The Slits, the first all-girl p*nk band, were making their world debut; The Subway Sect hadn't played since November; The Buzzcocks were making their first appearance since reorganising the line-up after singer Howard Devoto's departure; and The Clash were playing their first gig in three months since signing with CBS.

Harlesden Colosseum usually serves as a Pakistani porn pit, attracting vast crowds of up to three a night. The Clash noticed the place when they were rehearsing for the "Anarchy" tour at the Roxy theatre up the road. They liked the look of it and thought it would be a great place for rock gigs. Bernard decided to have a go and see how it worked out.

Inside, the Colosseum is the classic definition of a flea pit, all peeling paint and stained seats. The owners seemed rather bemused by the sudden invasion of p*nks.

When I got to the Colosseum at about 2.30, all the bands were there apart from The Clash, although Mick has come down early 'cos he's so excited about the gig.

While the roadies build the stage and groups wheel in their gear, Mick and I adjourn to the balcony and look down on the bustle of activity going on below.

"It's great isn't it", enthuses Mick, "our own gig . . . I'm really excited. This is more than a gig, it's an important event!"

Mick is also bubbling over about the forthcoming album. It only took two weeks to do and CBS, who signed The Clash for a six figure sum, gave them complete control.

As soon as the group made their marks on the CBS contract they knew they'd be accused of selling out - "I've been numbered wherever I go", says Mick.

But the deal hasn't turned them into big-spending superstars. They got some new equipment, Joe got a place to live, Mick got a stereo, but they're the same group, except with a means and outlet for their music. CBS is one of the biggest record companies in the world, so it follows that more people will get to know and hear about The Clash album than if they'd signed to a small label, or done a private pressing job.

Mick: 'I think it's important that we don't change. What is happening right now is that at last we've got a chance to make records. It all comes down to records . . . that's why we had to do one. You've got to make records.

"You can do your own label and not many people will hear it. This way more people will hear our record . . . I don't care if they don't like it or don't buy it, as long as they hear it.

"We've got complete control. Everything is our own ideas. We knew what we wanted to do, so we went in the studio and learnt as we went along".

The Clash did some recording at Polydor studios, and at one time there was a running battle for their signatures between that label and CBS. Guy Stevens, the infamous loony who produced Mott's early albums, did those sessions.

"It was great recording with Guy Stevens . . . fantastic when we were doing it. He was really inciting us, but when it came down to the mixing, it was a bit untogether".

So the next sessions saw The Clash's sound mixer, Micky Foote, in the producer's chair. 'White Riot' and '1977' were recorded. Compared to the album, 'White Riot' has a very raw, chaotic sound and slightly buried vocals, but it's still a real scorcher.

Mick: "It's not as brave as the album production, but it's still a great rock'n'roll song".

And the album?

"Well, we're really excited about it . . . I mean, AN ALBUM! It's destined to be a classic!"

Paul added later: "It sounds really good . . . so much better than the single. I think we've definitely captured the live sound".

Mick agrees, but says that the album has also succeeded in being a real studio product, rather than just a reproduction of the stage act. "We used the studio to make it sound good".

It's got 14 tracks, including stage faves like '48 Thrills', 'London's Burning', 'I'm So Bored With The USA", 'Protex Blue', 'Hate And War', and another "more wild" version of 'White Riot'. There's also a big surprise in the form of a six minute rock version of Junior Murvin's huge-selling reggae hit of last year, 'Police & Thieves', which is going to surprise a few people.

I can't mince words here. I've only heard it once, but I know this is the most exciting album I've heard in years. I can't think about it for more than a minute without feeling like I'm going to explode (let alone write about it!). You can hear all the words, there's the hardest guitar/drum sound ever, various studio tricks enhance the production and make some songs even more effective . . . but most important, it's captured the essence of The Clash. Their intense conviction is here in all its blazing glory. The whole thing's magnificent! If it don't sell, I'm Hughie Green. Even if you don't buy it, at least HEAR it . . . it's one of the most important records ever made.

I asked Mick about the daring inclusion of 'Police And Thieves'. He replied: "It's a logical progression. There's obviously a lot of links between us and what's happening with the Rastas. It just seemed right to do it. We had lots of our own material, but we wanted to do one song by someone else. What would we do? Not a 60s rehash . . . let's do something which is '76, right? Let's try and turn people on. This is a rock'n'roll track in 4/4, but it's experimental. We've incorporated dub reggae techniques. We'll probably get slagged to bits for it, but we don't care. They can't understand that what we're trying to do is redefine the scene and like make it clear to people the way to move . . . You've got to take risks all the time. That's why we did it . . . as a risk". (And it works - you wait and hear it, you'll be amazed!)

Mick says his favourite track is a new song called 'Garage Land' - the last track - "Where we're moving on next. The chorus is "We're a garage band and we come from garage land". . . That's just what we are.

It's also commenting on the current situation with all the groups being signed up".

How will The Clash move on?

"Well, it'll always be rock'n'roll, but we're hoping to improve the aura of the sound".

The Clash would like to do something about an alternative radio station as well. There are plans, but they need money.

Harking back to Mick's point about all the bands being signed up, I asked what he thought of this situation.

"It's a snowball. You form a group and the next week you've got a recording contract. That's great if they make great records, but so far they haven't made great records. No really good groups have come up just recently . . . just average groups. They don't move me to the point where it's rock'n'roll. The general quality of the music is a bit rough. They're like TV films . . . but I'd rather hear them than a shopping list. It's certainly growing".

Mick's really happy to see people making the effort to form groups. So's Paul: "What's great about this scene is the way kids are starting up bands. The only thing is, they have to do something original, and that's really hard. If you try and be like another band that can really slow you down".

What about the New Wavers who've got records out at the moment and enjoyed some success with 'em? (Rods, Stranglers and Damned in particular.)

Mick: "They're obviously going to clean up, but they've got nothing to do with us. That's all there is to it. I don't consider them important groups. They're cleaning up at the moment because there isn't any great alternative, recording especially".

We turn off the tape to check out what's happening down below. Mick takes the stage and plugs in his new plexiglass guitar. Paul, who is sporting newly-bleached yellow hair, and I have a chat in the ladies loo . . . well, it was the only quiet place (apart from when ladies came in!).

It was soon time for The Clash's soundcheck. They ironed out the sound problems with 'London's Burning' (twice), 'Garage Land' (which on first hearing sounded like a corker), and . . . I recognise those chords! . . . Jonathan Richman's 'Roadrunner', with the chorus changed to "Radio One"! Sounds fantastic Clashified. Mick says they may do it as an encore, but it doesn't happen. "We couldn't get it together". Paul says he hates the song anyway.

As The Clash retire to their dressing room - the place where they do the projecting from! - the people start to come in. Considering the place is in deepest Harlesden and it's raining there is a good turnout. The atmosphere builds up all evening . . . it's electric by Clash time!

First on were The Slits, who were great, making up for their sound problems with pure energy. 14 year old singer Arianna, who was alluringly decked out in black leather mini-skirt and fishnet tights, stamped and screamed like a little girl throwing a tantrum at a party . . . she reckoned we couldn't hear her, but we could! It was great when she came on in a big mac and flashed her legs like an old tosser before throwing it off.

The Slits careered through half an hour of their songs, propelled with astounding force by a drummer called Palmolive, who kept flattening her floor tom-tom. I'm looking forward to seeing The Slits again.

Next were Subway Sect, who are now managed by The Clash's Bernard. They'd changed from the rambling, two-chord outfit I'd seen in November. They've been rehearsing a lot at The Clash's studio and have a whole stock of unusual new numbers, which are complicated and a bit weird. The singer, Vic, ended the set by stumbling backwards and falling over - he'd been motionless for the whole set.

The reorganised Buzzcocks went down well. Pete Shelley, the bloke with only half a guitar, is centre stage front man now. He wore black, while the rest of the group sported hand-painted Mondrian shirts (i.e. they had squares on them, if you're not arty). With Pete loosening up (he played some weird guitar solos) the 'Cocks have got a lot of potential.

It was The Clash's night, though, and they played a blinder - despite little obstacles like one of the hired hippy sound men accidentally pulling out a lead.

It was great seeing them back on stage, in new zip-festooned outfits to boot. The crowd in front of the stage went potty, pogoing right up into the air, screaming the words, shaking themselves to death and falling into twitching heaps. They couldn't have been able to see what was going on though, which is a show in itself!

There were some great announcements from Joe. Someone yelled something about the CBS contract. "Yeah, I've been to the South of France to buy heroin", he said. Another time: "I'm Bruce Lee's son", he declared, before slamming the band into another devastating two minute burn-up. It was a great set.

Next day I saw a video recording of the gig. A bloke called Julian is making a video film of The Clash. He's a student at the London Film School, and, using their equipment, has been filming gigs and interviews since the "Anarchy" tour. It's not certain that the film will be shown, but I hope we get to see it somehow, 'cos it's dynamite!

Watching the recording of Friday's gig showed just how impressive The Clash are onstage. In the excitement you're bound to miss some things, like Mick's guitar strap breaking, and him holding up the guitar like a machine gun to finish the number; Joe jerking across the stage like an electrocuted piranha fish; or Paul ripping a giant chord from his bass with a violence so intense that his arm is nearly torn from its socket.

That's The Clash . . . pushing themselves to the limits. The least you can do is give them a listen . . . you'll never be the same again!

STEN-GUNS IN KNIGHTSBRIDGE??
THE CLASH NAPALM CHELTENHAM

Tony Parsons | April 2, 1977 | *New Musical Express* (UK)

This interview was conducted on the London Underground's Circle Line. Its audio version would shortly be released on the "Capital Radio E.P.," a *New Musical Express* giveaway that became a collector's item. Said audio version shows the band to be much more profane than they are depicted herein, which shows either that even a punk-friendly paper like the *NME* had its limits or that Tony Parsons didn't want to unnecessarily use up his wordage.

Despite her perceptiveness about the Clash's potential, Caroline Coon was from an older generation and ver-ah posh. The *NME*'s Tony Parsons was from younger and coarser stock, something which led to him disdaining Coon's occasional skepticism for wholehearted collusion in Clash mythmaking. He refuses to challenge the morality of their boasts of violence—or indeed its authenticity (Strummer's altercation with a Ted sounds like a shaggy-dog story, while the gentle Jones was the most unlikely participant in fisticuffs).

While it's easy to mock the apocalyptical tone of Parsons's rhetoric, it did reflect the feelings of many UK residents at a time when the country was riven by endless labor strikes and ever-escalating inflation.

Notes: The Hughie Green to whom repeated mention is made was the unctuous host of *Opportunity Knocks*, a TV talent show to which the refrain of Clash song "Career Opportunities" happens to be an allusion.

Knightsbridge is an upscale area of London.

"GBH" means the criminal offence Grievous Bodily Harm.

For "Paul Simenon" read "Paul Simonon"

For "Glenn Matlock" read "Glen Matlock" —Ed.

"IT AIN'T PUNK, IT AIN'T NEW WAVE, it's the next step and the logical progression for groups to move in. Call it what you want—all the terms stink. Just call it rock 'n' roll . . ."

You don't know what total commitment *is* until you've met Mick Jones of The Clash.

He's intense, emotional, manic-depressive and plays lead guitar with the kind of suicidal energy that some musicians lose and most musicians never have. His relationship with Joe Strummer and Paul Simenon is the love/hate intensity that you only get with family.

"My parents never . . . the people involved with The Clash *are my family* . . ."

THE CLASH and me are sitting around a British Rail table in one of those railway station cafes where the puce-coloured paint on the wall is peeling and lethargic non-white slave labour serves you tea that tastes like cat urine.

Joe Strummer is an ex-101er and the mutant offspring of Bruce Lee's legacy—a no-bullshit sense of tough that means he can talk about a thrashing he took a while back from some giant, psychotic Teddy Boy without the slightest pretension, self-pity or sense of martyrdom.

"I was too pissed to deal with it and he got me in the toilets for a while," Joe says.

"I had a knife with me and I shoulda stuck it in him, right? But when it came to it I remember vaguely thinking that it wasn't really worth it coz although he was battering me about the floor I was too drunk for it to hurt that much and if I stuck my knife in him I'd probably have to do a few years . . ."

When The Clash put paint-slashed slogans on their family-created urban battle fatigues such as "Hate And War" it's *not* a cute turnaround of a flowery spiel from ten years ago—it's a brutally honest comment on the environment they're living in.

They've had aggravation with everyone from Teds to students to Anglo-rednecks, all of them frightened pigs attacking what they can't understand. But this ain't the summer of love and The Clash would rather be kicked into hospital than flash a peace sign and turn the other cheek.

"We ain't ashamed to fight," Mick says.

"We should carry spray cans about with us," Paul Simenon suggests.

He's the spike-haired bass-player with considerable pulling power. Even my kid sister fancies him. He's from a South London ex-skinhead background; white stay-press Levi strides, highly polished DM boots, button-down Ben Sherman shirt, thin braces, eighth-of-an-inch cropped hair and over the football on a Saturday running with The Shed because for the first time in your life the society that produced you was terrified of you.

And it made you feel good . . .

Paul came out of that, getting into rock 'n' roll at the start of last year and one of the first bands he ever saw was The Sex Pistols. Pure late-Seventies rock, Paul Simenon. In Patti Smith's estimation he rates alongside Keef and Rimbaud. He knew exactly what he was doing when he named the band The Clash . . .

"THE HOSTILITIES," Mick Jones calls the violent reactions they often provoke.

"Or maybe those Lemon Squeezers," Paul says, seeking the perfect weapon for protection when trouble starts and you're outnumbered ten to one.

The rodent-like features of their shaven-headed ex-jailbird roadie known, among other things, as Rodent break into a cynical smirk.

"Don't get it on their drapes otherwise they get *really* mad," he quips.

He went along to see The Clash soon after his release from prison. At the time he was carrying a copy of "Mein Kampf" around with him. Prison can mess up your head.

Strummer, in his usual manner of abusive honesty, straightened him out. Rodent's been with them ever since and sleeps on the floor of their studio.

The Clash demand total dedication from everyone involved with the band, a sense of responsibility that must never be betrayed no matter what internal feuds, ego-clashes or personality crisis may go down. Anyone who doesn't have that attitude will not remain with The Clash for very long and that's the reason for the band's biggest problem—they ain't got a drummer.

The emotive Mick explodes at the mention of this yawning gap in the line-up and launches into a stream-of-consciousness expletive-deleted soliloquy with talk of drummers who bottled out of broken glass confrontations, drummers whose egos outweighed their creative talent, drummers who are going to get their legs broken.

"Forget it, it's in the past now," Joe tells him quietly, with just a few words cooling out Mick's anger and replacing it with something positive. "If any drummer thinks he can make it then we wanna know."

"We're going to the Pistols' gig tonight to find a new drummer!" Mick says excitedly. "But they gotta prove themselves," he adds passionately. "They gotta believe in what's happening. *And they gotta tell the truth . . .*"

THE BAND and Rodent have their passport photos taken in a booth on the station. Four black and white shots for twenty pence.

They pool their change and after one of them has had the necessary two pictures taken the next one dives in quickly to replace him before the white flash explodes.

When you're on twenty-five quid a week the stories of one quarter of a million dollars for the cocaine bill of a tax exile Rock Establishment band seem like a sick joke . . .

The Human Freight of the London Underground rush hour regard The Clash with a culture-shock synthesis hate, fear, and suspicion.

The Human Freight have escaped the offices and are pouring out to the suburbs until tomorrow. Stacked haunch to paunch in an atmosphere of stale sweat, bad breath and city air the only thing that jolts them out of their usual mood of apathetic surrender is the presence of The Clash.

Because something's happening here but The Human Freight don't know what it is . . .

"*Everybody's doing just what they're told to / Nobody wants to go to jail / White Riot / I wanna Riot / White Riot / A Riot of me own! / Are you taking over or are you taking orders? / Are you going backwards or are you going forwards?*"

"White Riot" and The Sound Of The Westway, the giant inner city flyover and the futuristic backdrop for this country's first major race riot since 1959.

Played with the speed of The Westway, a GBH treble that is as impossible to ignore as the police siren that opens the single or the alarm bell that closes it.

Rock'n'roll for the late Nineteen Seventies updating their various influences (Jones—the New York Dolls, MC5, Stooges, vintage Stones; Simenon—Pistols, Ramones, Heartbreakers; and Strummer, *totally* eclectic) and then adding something their very own. The sense of flash beach-fighting Mods speeding through three weekend nights non-stop coupled with an ability to write songs of contemporary urban imagery that are a perfect reflection of the life of any kid who came of age in the Seventies.

The former makes The Clash live raw-nerve electric, a level of excitement generated that can only be equalled by one other band—Johnny Thunders' Heartbreakers.

The latter makes The Clash, or maybe specifically Jones and Strummer (as Simenon has only recently started writing), the fulfilment of the original aim of the New Wave, Punk Rock, whatever; that is, to write songs about late Seventies British youth culture with the accuracy, honesty, perception and genuine anger that Elvis, Beatles or The Rolling Stones or any others in the Rock Establishment could never do now that they're closer to members of the Royal Family or face-lift lard-arse movie stars than they are to you or me . . .

BUT SO MANY bands coming through now are churning out cliched platitudes and political nursery rhymes. The Blank Generation is the antithesis of what The Clash are about . . .

Strummer and Jones disagree on the best environment for a new band to develop and keep growing.

Joe thinks it's all too easy right now and having to fight every inch of the way when the band was formed a year ago is the healthiest situation—whereas Mick believes in giving every help and encouragement possible while being totally honest with bands who are just not delivering the goods.

"I'm as honest as I can be," he shouts over the roar of the tube train. "All the new groups sound like drones and I ain't seen a good new group for six months. Their sound just ain't exciting, they need two years . . ."

The sound of The Clash has evolved, with their experience this year in the recording studio first with Polydor when they were dangling a contract, and more recently recording their first album after CBS snapped them up at the eleventh hour.

The change in the sound first struck me as a regulation of energy, exerting razor-sharp adrenalin control over their primal amphetamined rush. It created a new air of tension added to the ever-present manic drive that has always existed in their music, The Sound Of The Westway . . .

And, of course, the subtle-yet-indefinite shift in emphasis is perfect for the feeling that's in the air in the United Kingdom, one quarter of 1977 already gone:

"In 1977 you're on the never-never / You think it can't go on forever / But the papers say it's better / I don't care / Coz I'm not all there / No Elvis, Beatles or the Rolling Stones / In 1977."

"1977", the other side of the single, ends with the three-pronged attack shouting in harmonies derived from football terraces: "1984!"

THE PRESSURE. That's what they call the heavy atmosphere in Jamaica, the feeling in the air that very soon, something has got to change . . .

The Jamaican culture is highly-revered by The Clash. They hang out in black clubs, pick up reggae import singles in shops where it ain't really wise for them to tread and express their disgust at the undeniable fact that in the poor working-class areas of London where they grew up and still live the blacks are treated even worse than the whites.

But, ultimately, they know that White Youth needs its *own* sense of identity, culture and heritage if they're going to fight for change.

A riot of their own . . .

But can the masses take to the incisive reality of what The Clash are about the way they lap up the straight-ahead rock bands who push nothing more than having a good time?

"Maybe the reason those bands are so big is because they *don't* say anything," Mick says. "But we ain't gonna preach and sound like some evangelist."

I mention to Joe what happened when he walked on stage at Leeds Poly for the first gig that actually happened on the Pistols' Anarchy tour.

He said a few words before the band went into the set that they'd been burning to play for weeks about how the gutter press hysteria, local council butchery and Mary Whitehouse mentality of The Great British people was preventing certain young rock bands getting on stage and playing for the people who wanted to see them.

I remember him saying that 1984 seemed to have arrived early as the Leeds Poly students bawled abuse at him.

With the minds and manners of barnyard pigs the over-grown schoolchildren conveyed the message that they didn't give a shit.

"I think they will take to us, but it'll take time," Joe says. "But I don't want to go *towards* them at all, I don't wanna start getting soft around the edges.

"I don't want to compromise . . . I think they'll come round in time but if they *don't* it's too bad."

"We ain't *never* gonna get commercial respectability," Mick says, both anger and despair in his voice.

Paul Simenon takes it all in and then ponders the nearest station that has a bar on the platform.

THAT'S THE DIFFERENCE between their attitudes to, how you say, Making It.

Strummer is confident, determined, arrogant and sometimes violent in the face of ignorant opposition (a couple of months back in a club car park he faced an American redneck-rock band with just his blade for support).

Mick Jones is a rock equivalent to a Kamikaze pilot. All or nothing.

The Clash gives him both the chance to pour out his emotional turmoil and offer an escape route from the life the assembly-line education the country gave him had primed him for.

When a careers officer at school spends five minutes with you and tells you what you're gonna do with your life for the next fifty years. More fodder for the big corporations and the dole.

Mick is beating them at their own game by ignoring all the rules.

"*Someone locked me out so I kicked me way back in,*" he declares in "Hate And War".

His uncanny resemblance to a young Keef Richard allowed him to relieve an early identity problem by adopting the lookalike con-trick which fools no-one but yourself. Then he met Strummer who told him he was wearing a Keith Richard identikit as though he had bought it in a shop.

"I got my self-respect in this group," Mick says. "I don't believe in guitar heros. If I walk out to the front of the stage it's because I wanna reach the audience, I want to *communicate* with them. I don't want them to suck my guitar off . . ."

And Paul Simenon: total hedonist.

His fondest memories of the Anarchy tour are hotel room parties and broken chairs, things trod into the carpet and girls who got you worried because you thought they were gonna die like Jimi Hendrix if they didn't wake up. He's a member of The Clash because they're the best band in the country and it gets him laid a lot.

So what did they learn from the Anarchy tour, so effectively butchered by the self-righteous Tin Gods who pull the strings?

"I learned that there's no romance in being on the road," Mick says.

"I learned that there's lots," Joe smiles.

"I learned that if they don't want you to play they can stop you," Joe says seriously. "And no-one's gonna raise any fuss . . ."

"For the first four days we were confined to our rooms because the *News Of The World* was next door," Mick continues.

"We thought—shall we go out there with syringes stuck in our arms just to get 'em going? Yeah, and furniture seemed to have labels saying, 'Please smash me' or 'Out The Window, Please'."

And when they finally got to play, the minds in the Institutes Of Further Education were as narrow as those in Fleet Street. So Strummer gave them something—even though they were too blind to see it . . .

"This one's for all you *students*," he sneered before The Clash tore into the song that they wrote about Joe being on the dole for so long that The Department Of Employment (sic) wanted to send him to rehabilitation to give him back the confidence that they assumed the dole must have destroyed, together with Mick's experience working *for* the Social Security office in West London, and, as the most junior employee, being told to open all the mail during the time of the IRA letter-bombs.

The song is called "Career Opportunities": *"Career Opportunities / The ones that never knock / Every job they offer you / Is to keep ya out the dock / Career Opportunities. / They offered me the office / They offered me the shop/ They said I'd better take ANYTHING THEY GOT. / "Do you wanna make tea for the BBC? / Do you wanna be, you wanna be a cop?" / I hate the army and I hate the RAF/ You won't get me fighting in the tropical heat / I hate the Civil Service rules /And I ain't gonna open letter bombs for you!"*

"MOST BANDS and writers who talk about the dole DUNNO WHAT THE DOLE IS!" Mick shouts.

"They've never been on the dole in their life. But the dole is only hard if you've been conditioned to think you've gotta have a job . . . then it's sheer degradation.

"The Social Security made me open the letters during the letter bomb time because I looked subversive. Most of the letters the Social Security get are from the people who live next door saying their neighbours don't need the money. The whole thing works on spite.

"One day an Irish guy that they had treated like shit and kept waiting for three hours picked up a wooden bench and put it through the window into Praed Street."

Mick shakes his head in disgust at the memory of the way our great Welfare State treats its subjects.

"Every time I didn't have a job I was down there—waiting. And they degrade the black youth even more. They have to wait even longer. No-one can tell me there ain't any prejudice . . ."

WE MAKE FOR "Rehearsal Rehearsals", the North London studio of The Clash. An enormous building once used by the British Rail for a warehouse. Only part of it is in use at the moment, a large expanse of property ruled by no lighting, rats and water.

Upstairs Joe, Mick and Paul look glad to have guitars in their hands again. The walls are covered with posters of Bruce Lee, Patti Smith, the Pistols and The Clash themselves.

A large map of the United Kingdom faces the old TV set where Hughie Green is being sincere with the speech turned down. Biro graffiti stains the screen. The television is not treated like the Holy Grail in *this* place . . .

I watch Joe playing a battered old guitar with all but two of its strings missing and think about his comments when I wanted to know how he would cope with financial success when/if it came . . .

"I ain't gonna fuck myself up like I seen all those other guys fuck themselves up," he said. "Keeping all their money for themselves and getting into their head and thinking they're the greatest.

"I've planned what I'm gonna do with my money *if* it happens. Secret plans . . ."

I could be wrong, but at guess the development of Rehearsal Rehearsals into anything from a recording studio to a rock venue to a radio or TV station seem like possible Strummer visions for when The Clash get the mass acceptance they deserve.

As we talk about how The Clash have reacted to putting their music down on vinyl I tell them that the major criticism people not cognisant with their songs have expressed is that the unique Strummer vocal makes understanding their brilliant lyrics almost impossible for the uninitiated.

"The first time we went into a studio with a famous producer he said, 'You better pronounce the words, right?'" Joe remembers with his amused sneer.

"So I did it and it sounded like Matt Monroe. So I thought I'm never doing that again . . . to me our music is like Jamaican stuff—if they can't hear it, they're not supposed to hear it. It's not for them if they can't understand it."

THE CLASH SAY that being signed with CBS has had no interference with the preservation of their integrity and, even with the band's attitude of No Compromise, a termination of contract in the manner of the Pistols seems most unlikely.

They believe the sound on the album to be infinitely superior to that of the single because the latter was cut during one of their first sessions in the studio after the decision to let their sound man Micky Foote produce the band even though he had no previous experience in production.

"We tried the famous ones," Joe grins. "They were all too pissed to work."

"Outside, there ain't no young producers in tune with what's going on," Mick says. "The only way to do it is to learn how to do it yourself."

"You do it yourself because nobody else *cares* that much," Micky Foote, Boy Wonder Producer tells me, his sentiments totally in keeping with the clan spirit in The Clash camp.

The band talk of their respect for their manager Bernard Rhodes, who has been a major influence on all of them, and who has made enemies because of his obsessive commitment to The Clash. But Joe, Mick and Paul are free spirits, unlike a lot of bands with heavy personality management.

"He really pushes us," Paul says.

"We do respect him," Mick adds. "He was always helping and giving constructive criticism long before he was our manager." Mick then points at the other members of the band and himself. "But the heart is there."

I ask them about their political leanings. Do they believe in left and right or is there just up and down?

They reply by telling me about a leftist workshop they used to frequent because they enjoyed the atmosphere—and also because it gave them an opportunity to nick the paints they needed for their artwork.

"It was really exhilarating there," Mick says. "They used to play Chinese revolutionary records and then one day the National Front threw bricks through the window.

"The place didn't shut, though. So one day they burned the whole joint down and they *had* to close down . . ."

"In 1977 there's knives in West Eleven / Ain't so lucky to be rich / Sten guns in Knightsbridge / Danger stranger / You better paint your face / No Elvis, Beatles or the Rolling Stones / In 1977 / Sod the Jubilee!"

"I always thought in terms of survival," Mick says.

"And these people are the opposition of free speech and personal liberty. And they're trying to manipulate the rock medium."

Then he repeats something he said earlier, reiterating the importance of The Clash: "And I ain't ashamed to fight . . ."

IT HAS BEEN over a year since Mick Jones, Paul Simenon and their friend Glenn Matlock first met Joe Strummer down the Portobello Road and told him that he was great but his band was shit.

Later Joe talked to Bernard Rhodes and twenty-four hours after he showed up on the doorstep of the squat where Mick and Paul were living and told them he wanted in on the band that would be known as The Clash.

And from the top of the monolith tower block where they wrote their celebration of the Westway you can gaze down through the window of—as Mick Jones puts it—one of the cages and see that London is still burning . . .

"*All across the town / All across the night / Everybody's driving with four headlights / Black or white, turn it on, face the new religion / Everybody's drowning in a sea of television. / Up and down the Westway / In and out the lights / What a great traffic system / It's so bright / I can't think of a better way to spend the night / Than speeding around underneath the yellow lights. / But now I'm in the subway looking for the flat / This one leads to this block and this one leads to that / The wind howls through the empty blocks looking for a home / But I run through the empty stone because I'm all alone / London's burning, baby . . .*"

"Each of these high-rise estates has got those places where kids wear soldiers' uniforms and get army drill," Mick says quietly.

"Indoctrination to keep them off the streets . . . and they got an *artist* to paint pictures of happy workers on the side of the Westway. Labour liberates and don't forget your place."

He looks down at the fire hundreds of feet below.

"Can you understand how much I hate this place?" he asks me.

1977 is the year of The Clash.

SIX DAYS ON THE ROAD
TO THE PROMISED LAND

Lester Bangs | December 10, 17, and 24, 1977 | *New Musical Express* **(UK)**

When CBS International decided to spread the word on the Clash beyond Britain, they put them together with veteran US music journalist Lester Bangs. It turned out to be a perfect match.

Bangs's gonzo style was appropriate for a band into streetwise vignettes and colloquialism, while his leftism and disillusion with the non-punk music scene made him highly susceptible to the virtues of an ensemble in possession of—to use his term—"righteousness." However, his infatuation with the group and their world didn't prevent him taking them to task for an ugly incident inconsistent with their values.

The *NME* allowed Bangs to spread his impressions of his week with the Clash across a three-part feature (part one of which was actually called "Six Days on the Road with The Foremost Garage Band in the Land"; the common title of the second and third parts has been used here as an overall title). The result was a classic piece of rock journalism.

Although only fleetingly mentioned, the Clash had a new drummer, Nick Headon, soon to be known as "Topper."

Note: For "White Boy In Hammersmith Palais" read "(White Man) In Hammersmith Palais" —Ed.

Part One: Six Days on the Road with The Foremost Garage Band in the Land

THE EMPIRE may be terminally stagnant, but every time I come to England it feels like massive changes are underway.

First time was 1972 for Slade, who had the punters hooting, but your music scene in general was in such miserable shape that most of the hits on the radio were resurrected oldies. Second time was for David Essex (haw haw haw) and Mott (sigh) almost exactly two years ago: I didn't even bother listening to the radio, and though I had a good time the closest thing to a musical highlight of my trip was attending an Edgar Froese (entropy incarnate) press party. I never gave much of a damn about pub rock, which was about the only thing you guys had going at the time, and I had just about written you off for dead when punk rock came along.

So here I am back again through the corporate graces of CBS International to see The Clash, to hear new wave hands on the radio (a treat for American ears) and find the empire jumping again at last.

About time, too. I don't know about you, but as far as I was concerned things started going downhill for rock around 1968; I'd date it from the ascendance of Cream, who were the first fake superstar band, the first sign of strain in what had crested in 1967. Ever since then things have just gotten worse, through Grand Funk and James Taylor and wonderful years like 1974, when the only thing interesting going on was Roxy Music, finally culminating last year in the ascendance of things like disco and jazz-rock, which are dead enough to suggest the end of popular music as anything more than room spray.

I was thinking of giving up writing about music altogether last year when all of a sudden I started getting phone calls from all these slick magazine journalists who wanted to know about this new phenomenon called "punk rock." I was a little bit confused at first, because as far as I was concerned punk rock was something which had first raised its grimy snout around 1966 in groups like The Seeds and Count Five, and was dead and buried after The Stooges broke up and The Dictators' first LP bombed.

I mean, it's easy to forget that just a little over a year ago there was *only one thing*: the first Ramones album.

But who could have predicted that that record would have such an impact—all it took was that and the ferocious *edge* of The Sex Pistols' "Anarchy In The UK," and suddenly it was as if someone had unleashed the floodgates as ten million little groups all over the world came storming in, mashing up the residents with their guitars and yammering discontented *non sequiturs* about how bored and fed up they were with everything.

I was too, and so were you—that's why we went out and bought all those shitty singles last spring and summer by the likes of The Users and Cortinas and Slaughter and the Dogs, because better Slaughter and the Dogs at what price wretchedness than *one more* mewly-mouthed simper-whimper from Linda Ronstadt. Buying records became fun again, and one reason it did was that all these groups embodied the who-gives-a-damn-let's-just-slam-it- at-'em spirit of great rock 'n' roll. Unfortunately many of these wonderful slices of vinyl didn't possess any of the other components of same, with the result that (for me, round about *Live at the Roxy*) many people simply got FED UP. Meaning that it's just too goddam easy to slap on a dog collar and black leather jacket and start puking all over the room about how you're gonna sniff some glue and stab some backs.

Punk had reaped the very attitudes it copped (BOREDOM and INDIFFERENCE), and we were all waiting for a group to come along who at least went through the motions of GIVING A DAMN about SOMETHING.

Ergo, The Clash.

YOU SEE, dear reader, so much of what's (doled) out as punk merely amounts to saying I suck, you suck, the world sucks, and who gives a damn—which is, er, ah, somehow *insufficient.*

Don't ask *me* why, I'm just an observer, really, But any observer could tell that, to put it in terms of Us vs. Them, saying the above is exactly what They want you to do, because it amounts to capitulation. It *is* unutterably boring and disheartening to try to find some fun or meaning while shoveling through all the shit we've been handed the last few years, but merely puking on yourself is not gonna change anything. (I know, 'cause I tried it.) I guess what it all boils down to is:

(a) You can't like people who don't like themselves; and

(b) You gotta like somebody who stands up for what they believe in, as long as what they believe in is

(c) Righteous.

A precious and elusive quantity, this righteousness. Needless to say, most punk rock is not exactly OD-ing on it. In fact, most punk rockers probably think it's the purview of hippies, unless you happen to be black and Rastafarian, in which case righteousness shall cover the land, presumably when punks have attained No Future.

It's kinda hard to put into mere mortal words, but I guess I should say that being righteous means you're more or less on the side of the angels, waging Armageddon for the ultimate victory of the forces of Good over the Kingdoms of Death (see how perilously we skirt hippie-dom here?), working to enlighten others as to their own possibilities rather than merely sprawling in the muck yodelling about what a drag everything is.

The righteous minstrel may be rife with lamentations and criticisms of the existing order, but even if he doesn't have a coherent program for social change he is informed of hope. The MC5 were righteous where The Stooges were not. The third and fourth Velvet Underground albums were righteous, the first and second weren't. (Needless to say, Lou Reed is not righteous.) Patti Smith has been righteous. The Stones have flirted with righteousness (e.g., "Salt Of The Earth"), but when they were good The Beatles were all-righteous. The Sex Pistols are not righteous, but, perhaps more than any other new wave band, The Clash are.

The reason they are is that beneath their wired harsh soundscape lurks a persistent humanism. It's hard to put your finger on in the actual lyrics, which are mostly pretty despairing, but it's in the kind of thing that could make somebody like Mark P. write that their debut album was his life. To appreciate it in The Clash's music you might have to be the sort of person who could see Joe Strummer crying out for a riot of his own as someone making a positive statement. You perceive that as much as this music seethes with rage and pain, it also champs at the bit of the present system of things, lunging after some glimpse of a new and better world.

I know it's easy to be cynical about all this; in fact, one of the most uncool things you can do these days is to be committed about anything. The Clash are so committed they're downright militant. Because of that, they speak to dole-queue British youth today of their immediate concerns with an authority that nobody else has quite mustered. Because they do, I doubt if they will make much sense to most American listeners.

But more about that later. Right now, while we're on the subject of politics. I would like to make a couple of things perfectly clear:

1. I do not know shit about the English class system.

2. I don't [*sic*] not care shit about the English class system.

I've *heard* about it, understand. I've heard it has something to do with why Rod Stewart now makes music for housewives, and why Townshend is so screwed up. I guess it also has something to do with another *NME* writer sneering to me "Joe Strummer had a fucking middle class education, man!" I surmise further that this is supposed to indicate that he isn't worth a shit, and that his songs are all fake street-graffiti. Which is fine by me: Joe Strummer is a fake. That only puts him in there with Dylan and Jagger and Townshend and most of the other great rock song writers, because almost all of them in one way or another were fakes. Townshend had a middle-class education. Lou Reed went to Syracuse University before matriculating to the sidewalks of New York. Dylan faked his whole career; the only difference was that he used to be good at it and now he sucks.

The point is that, like Richard Hell says, rock 'n' roll is an arena in which you recreate yourself, and all this blathering about authenticity is just a bunch of crap. The Clash are authentic because their music carries such brutal conviction, not because they're Noble Savages.

HERE'S a note to CBS International: you can relax because I liked The Clash as people better than any other band I have ever met with the possible exception of Talking Heads, and their music it goes without saying is great (I mean *you* think so, don't you? Good, then release their album in the U.S. So what if it gets zero radio play; *Clive* knew how to subsidize the arts.)

Here's a superlative for ads: "Best band in the UK!"—Lester Bangs. Here's another one: "Thanks for the wonderful vacation!"—Lester Bangs. (You know I love you, Ellie.) Okay, now that all that's out of the way, here we go ...

I WAS sitting in the British Airways terminal in New York City on the eve of my departure, reading *The War Against The Jews 1933-1945* when I looked up just in time to see a crippled woman in a wheelchair a few feet away from me. My eyes snapped back down to my book in that shameful nervous reflex we know so well, but a moment later she had wheeled over to a couple of feet from where I was sitting, and when I could fight off the awareness of my embarrassment at her presence no longer I looked up again and we said hello to each other.

She was a very small person about 30 years old with a pretty face, blonde hair and blazing blue eyes. She said that she had been on vacation in the States for three months and was now, ever so reluctantly, returning to England.

"I like the people in America so much better," she said. "Christ, it's so nice to be someplace where people recognize that you *exist*. In England, if you're handicapped no one will look at or speak to you except old people. And they just pat you on the head."

IT IS four days later, and I've driven from London to Derby with Ellie Smith from CBS and Clash manager Bernard Rhodes for the first of my projected three nights and two days with the band. I am not in the best of shape since I've still got jet-lag, have been averaging two to three hours sleep a night since I got here, and the previous night was stranded in Aylesbury by the Stiff's Greatest Hits tour, hitching a ride back to London with a roadie in the course of which we were stopped by provincial police in search of dope and forced to empty all our pockets, something which had not happened to me since the hippie heydaze of 1967.

This morning when I went by Mick Farren's flat to pick up my bags he had told me "You look like 'Night Of The Living Dead.'"

Nevertheless, I make sure after checking into the Derby Post House to hit the first night's gig, whatever my condition, in my most thoughtful camouflage. You see, the kind of reports we get over in the States about your punk rock scene had led me to expect seething audiences of rabid little miscreants out for blood at all costs, and naturally I figured the chances of getting a great story were better if I happened to get cannibalized. So I took off my black leather jacket and dressed as straight as I possibly could, the *coup de grace* (I thought) being a blue promotional sweater that said "Capitol Records" on the chest, by which I fantasized picking up some residual EMI-hostility from battle-feral Pistols fans. I should mention that I also decided not to get a haircut which I desperately needed before leaving the States, on the not-so-off chance of being mistaken for a hippie. When I came out of my room and Ellie and photographer Pennie Smith saw me, they laughed.

When I got to the gig I pushed my way down through the pogoing masses, right into the belly of the beast, and stood there through openers The Lous and Richard Hell and the Voidoids' sets, waiting for the dog soldiers of anarch-apocalypse to slam my skull into my ankles under a new wave riptide.

Need I mention that nothing of the kind transpired?

Listen: if I were you I would take up arms and march on the media centers of Merrie Old, *NME* included, and trash them beyond recognition. Because what I experienced, this first night and all subsequent on this tour, was so far from what we Americans've read in the papers and seen on TV that it amounts to a mass defamation of character, if not cultural genocide. Nobody gave a damn about my long hair, or could have cared less about some stupid sweater. Sure there was gob and beercups flung at the bands, and the mob was pushing sideways first right and then left, but I hate to disappoint anybody who hasn't been there but this scene is neither *Clockwork Orange* nor *Lord Of The Flies*. When I got tired of the back-and-forth group shove I simply stuck my elbows out and a space formed around me.

What I am saying is that I have been at outdoor rock festivals in the hippie era in America where the vibes and violence were ten times worse than at any of the gigs I saw on this Clash tour, and the bands said later that this Derby engagement was the worst they had seen. What I am saying is that contrary to almost all reports published everywhere, I found British punks everywhere I went to be basically if not manifestly *gentle* people. *They are a bunch of nice boys and girls and don't let anybody (them included) tell you different.*

Yeah, they like to pogo. On the subject of this odd tribal rug-cut, of course the first thing I saw when I entered the hall was a couple of hundred little heads near the lip of the stage all bobbing up and down like anthropomorphized pistons in some Max Fleischer cartoon on the Industrial Revolution.

When I'd heard about pogoing before I thought it was the stupidest thing anybody'd ever told me about, but as soon as I saw it in living *sproing* it made perfect sense. I mean, it's obviously no more stupid than the seconal idiot-dance popularized five years ago by Grand Funk audiences. In fact, it's sheer logic (if not poetry) in motion: when you're packed into a standing sweatshop with ten thousand other little bodies all mashed together, it stands to reason you can't dance in the traditional manner (ie sideways sway).

No, obviously if you wanna do the boogaloo to what the new breed say you gotta by dint of sheer population explosion shake your booty and your body in a *vertical* trajectory. Which won't be strictly rigid anyway since because this necessarily involves losing your footing every two seconds the next step is falling earthward slightly sideways and becoming entangled with your neighbours, which is as good a way as any of making new friends if not copping a graze of tit.

There is, however, one other aspect of audience appreciation which ain't nearly so cute: gobbing. For some reason this qualifies as news to everybody, so I'm gonna serve notice right here and now: LISTEN YA LITTLE PINHEADS, IT'S NAUSEATING AND MORONIC, AND I DON'T MEAN GOOD MORONIC, I MEAN JERKED OFF. THE BANDS ALL HATE IT (the ones I talked to, anyway) AND WOULD ALL PLAY BETTER AND BE MUCH HAPPIER IF YOU FIGURED OUT SOME MORE ORIGINAL WAY OF SHOWING YOUR APPRECIATION.

(After the second night I asked Mick Jones about it and he looked like he was going to puke.

"But doesn't it add to the general atmosphere of chaos and anarchy?" I wondered

"No," he said. "It's fucking disgusting.")

END OF moral lecture. The Clash were a bit of a disappointment the first night. They played well, everything was the right place, but the show seemed to lack energy somehow. A colleague who saw them a year ago had come back to the States telling me that they were the only group he'd ever seen on stage who were truly *wired*. It was this I was looking for and what I got in its place was mere professionalism, and hell, I could go let The Rolling Stones put me to sleep again if that was all I cared about.

Back up in the dressing room I cracked "Duff gig, eh fellas?" and they laughed, but you could tell they didn't think it was funny. Later I found out that Joe Strummer had an abcessed tooth which had turned into glandular fever, and since the rest of the band draw their energy off him they were all suffering. By rights he should have taken a week off and headed straight for the nearest hospital, but he refused to cancel any gigs, no mere gesture of integrity.

A process of escalating admiration for this band had begun for me which was to continue until it broached something like awe. See, because it's easy to *sing* about your righteous politics, but as we all know actions speak louder than words, and The Clash are one of the very few examples I've seen where they would rather set an example by their personal conduct than *talk* about it all day.

Case in point. When we got back their hotel I had a couple of interesting lessons to learn. First thing was they went up to their rooms while Ellie, Pennie, a bunch of fans and me sat in the lobby. I began to make with the grouch squawks because if there's one thing I have learned to detest over the years it's sitting around some goddam hotel lobby like a soggy douchebag parasite waiting for some lousy high and mighty rock'n'roll band to *maybe deign* to put in an imperial appearance.

But then a few minutes later The Clash came down and joined us and I realized that unlike most of the bands I'd ever met they weren't stuck up, weren't on a star trip, were in fact genuinely interested in meeting and getting acquainted with their fans on a one-to-one, non-condescending level.

Mick Jones was especially sociable, so I moved in on him and commenced my second mis-informed balls-up of the evening. A day or two earlier I'd asked Mick Farren what sort of questions he thought might he appropriate for The Clash, and he'd said, "Oh, you might do what you did with Richard Hell and ask 'em just exactly what their political *program* is, what they intend to *do* once they get past all the bullshit rhetoric. Mind you, it's liable to get you thrown off the tour."

So, vainglorious as ever, I zeroed in on Mick and started drunkenly needling him with what I thought were devastating barbs. He just laughed at me and parried every one with a joke, while the fans chortled at the spectacle of this oafish American with all his dumbass sallies. Finally he looked me right in the eye and said, "Hey Lester: why are you asking *me* all these fucking questions?"

In a flash I realized that he was right. Here was I, a grown man, travelling all the way across the Atlantic ocean and motoring up into the provinces of England, just to ask a goddam rock 'n' roll band for the meaning of life! Some people never learn. I certainly didn't, because I immediately started in on him with my standard cultural-genocide rap: "Blah blah blah depersonalization blab blab blab solipsism blah blab yip yap etc . . ."

"What in the fuck are you talking about?"

"Blah blab no one wants to have any emotions any more blab blip human heart an endangered species blah blare cultural fascism blab blurb etc. etc. etc. . . ."

"Well," says Mick, "don't look at *me*. If it bothers you so much why don't *you* do something about it?"

"Yeah," says one of the fans, a young black punk girl sweet as could be, "you're depressing us *all!*"

Seventeen punk fan spike heads nod in agreement. Mick just keeps laughing at me.

SO, HAVING bummed out almost the entire population of one room, I took my show into another: the bar, where I sat down at a table with Ellie and Paul Simonon and started in on them. Paul gets up and walks out. Ellie says, "Lester, you look a little tired. Are you sure you want another lager . . . ?"

Later I am out in the lobby with the rest of them again, in a state not far from walking coma, when Mick gestured at a teenage fan sitting there and said "Lester, my room is full tonight; can Adrian stay with you?"

I finally freaked. Here I was, stuck in the middle of a dying nation with all these funny looking *children* who didn't even realize the world was coming to an end, and now on top of everything else they expected me to turn my room into a hippie crash pad! I surmised through all my confusion that some monstrous joke was being played on me, so I got testy about it, Mick repeated the request and finally I said that Adrian could *maybe* stay but he would have to go to the house phone, call my hotel and see if there was room. So the poor humiliated kid did just that while an embarrassed if not downright creepy silence fell over the room and Mick stared at me in shock, as if he had never seen this particular species of so-called human before.

Poor Adrian came back saying there was indeed room, so I grudgingly assented, and back to the hotel we went. The next morning, when I was in a more sober if still jetlagged frame of mind, he showed me a copy of his Clash fanzine *48 Thrills* which I bought for 20p, and in the course of breakfast conversation learned that The Clash make a regular practice of inviting their fans back from the gigs with them, and then go so far as to let them sleep on the floors of their rooms.

Now, dear reader, I don't know how much time you may have actually spent around bigtime rock 'n' roll bands—you may not think so, but the less the luckier you are in most cases—but let me assure you that the way The Clash treat their fans falls so far outside the normal run of these things as to be outright revolutionary. I'm going to say it and I'm going to say it slow: most rockstars are goddamn pigs who have the usual burly corps of hired thugs to keep the fans away from them at all costs, excepting the usual select contingent of lucky (?) nubiles who they'll maybe deign to allow up to their rooms for the privilege of sucking on their coveted wangers, after which often as not they get pitched out into the streets to find their way home without even cabfare. The whole thing is sick to the marrow, and I simply could not believe that any band, especially one as *musically* brutal as The Clash, could depart so far from this fetid norm.

I mentioned it to Mick in the van that day en route to Cardiff, also by way of making some kind of amends for my own behaviour: "Listen, man, I've just got to say that I really *respect* you . . . I mean, I had no idea that any group could be as good to its fans as this . . ."

He just laughed. "Oh, so is that gonna be the hook for your story, then?"

AND THAT for me is the essence of The Clash's greatness, over and beyond their music, why I fell in love with them, why it wasn't necessary to do any boring interviews with them about politics or the class system or any of that: because here at last is a band which not only preaches something good but practices it as well, that instead of talking about changes in social behaviour puts the model of a truly egalitarian society into practice in their own conduct.

The fact that Mick would make a joke out of it only shows how far they're going towards the realization of all the hopes we ever had about rock 'n' roll as utopian dream—because if rock 'n' roll *is* truly the democratic artform, then the democracy has got to begin at home, that is the everlasting and totally disgusting walls between artists and audience must come down, elitism must perish, the "stars" have got to be humanized, demythologized, and the audience has got to be treated with more respect. Otherwise it's all a shuck, a ripoff, and the music is as dead as the Stones' and Led Zep's has become.

It's no news by now that the reason most of rock's establishment have dried up creatively is that they've cut themselves off from the real world of everyday experience as exemplified by their fans. The ultimate question is how long a group like The Clash can continue to practice total egalitarianism in the face of mushrooming popularity. *Must* the walls go up inevitably, eventually, and if so when? Groups like The Grateful Dead have practiced this free-access principle at least in the past, but the Dead never had glamour which, whether they like it or not (and I'd bet money they do) The Clash are saddled with—I mean, not for nothing does Mick Jones resemble a young and already slightly dissipated Keith Richard— besides which the Dead aren't really a rock 'n' roll band and The Clash are nothing else but. And just like Mick said to me the first night, don't ask me why I obsessively look to rock 'n' roll bands for some kind of model for a better society . . . I guess it's just that I glimpsed something beautiful in a flashbulb moment once, and perhaps mistaking it for a prophecy have been seeking its fulfillment ever since. And perhaps that nothing else in the world ever seemed to hold even this much promise.

It may look like I make too much of all this. We could leave all significance at the picture of Mick Jones just a hot guitarist in a white jumpsuit and a rock 'n' roll kid on the road obviously having the time of his life and all political pretensions be damned, but still there is a mood around The Clash, call it "vibes" or whatever you want, that is positive in a way I've never sensed around almost any other band, and I've been around most of them. Something unpretentiously moral, and something both self-affirming and life-affirming—as opposed, say, to the simple ruthless hedonism and avarice of so many superstars, or the grim tautlipped monomaniacal ambition of most of the pretenders to their thrones.

BUT ENOUGH of all that. The highlight of the first day's bus ride occurred when I casually mentioned that I had a tape of the new Ramones album. The whole band practically leaped at my throat: "Why didn't you say so before? Shit, put it on *right now!*" So I did and in a moment they were bouncing all over the van to the strains of "Cretin Hop". "Rocket To Russia" (Nick Kent = *fool)* thereafter became the soundtrack to the rest of my leg of the tour.

I am also glad to be able to tell everybody that The Clash are solid Muppets fans. (They even asked me I had connections to get them on the show.) Their fave rave is Kermit, a pretty conventional choice if y'ask me—I'm a Fozzie Bear man myself. That night as we were walking into the hall for the gig in Cardiff, Paul said, "Hey Lester, I just figured out why you like Fozzie Bear—the two of you do look a lot alike!" And then he slaps me on the back.

All right, at this point I would like to say a few words about this Simonon fellow. Namely that HE LOOKS LIKE A MUPPET. I'm not sure which one, some kinda composite, but don't let that brooding visage in the photos fool you—this guy is a real clown. (Takes one to know one, after all.) He smokes a lot right, and when he gets really out there on it makes with cartoon non sequiturs that nobody else can fathom (often having to do with manager Bernie), but stoned or not when he's talking to you and you're looking in that face you're staring right into a red-spiked bigeyed beaming cartoon, of whom it would probably not be amiss to say he lives for pranks. Onstage he's different, bouncing in and out of crouch, rarely smiling but in fact brooding over his fretboard ever in ominous motion, he takes on a distinctly simian aspect; the missing link, cro-magnon, Piltdown man, Cardiff giant.

It is undoubtedly this combination of mischievous boychild and paleolithic primate which has sent swoonblips quavering through feminine hearts as disparate as Patti Smith and Caroline Coon—no doubt about it, Paul is the ladies' man of the group without half trying, and I doubt if there are very many gigs where he doesn't end up pogoing his pronger in some sweet honey's hive. Watch out, though, Paul—remember, clap doth not a Muppet befit.

The gig in Cardiff presents quite a contrast to Derby. It's at a college, and anybody who has ever served time in one of these dreary institutions of lower pedantry will know what manner of douse that portends. Once again the band delivers maybe 60% of what I know they're capable of, but with an audience like this there's no blaming them. I'm not saying that all college students are subhuman—I'm just saying that if you aim to spend a few years mastering the art of pomposity, these are places where you can be taught by undisputed experts.

Like here at Cardiff about five people are pogoing, all male, while the rest of the student bodies stand around looking at them with practiced expressions of aloof amusement plastered on their mugs. After it's all over some cat goes back to interview Mick, and the most intelligent question he can think of is "What do you think of David Bowie?"

Meanwhile I got acquainted with the lead singer of The Lous, a good all-woman band from Paris. She says that she resents being thought of as a "woman musician," instead of a musician pure and simple, echoing a sentiment previously voiced to me by Talking Heads' Tina Weymouth. "It's a lot of bullshit," she says. I agree; what I don't say is that I am developing a definite carnal interest which I will be too shy to broach. I invite her back to our hotel; she says yes, then disappears.

When we get there it's the usual scene in the lobby, except that this time the management has thoughtfully set out sandwiches and beer. The beer goes down our gullets, and I'm just about to start putting the sandwiches to the same purpose when I discover somebody has other ideas: a clot of bread and egg salad goes whizzing to *splat* right in the hack of my head! I look around and confront solid wall of innocent faces. So I take a bite and *wham!* another one.

In a minute sandwiches are flying everywhere, everybody's getting pelted, I'm wearing a slice of cabbage on my head and have just about accepted this level of chaos when I smell something burning.

"Hey Lester," somebody says, "you shouldn't smoke so much!" I reach around to pat the back of my head and—some joker has set my hair on fire! I pivot in my seat and Paul is looking at me giggling. "Simonon you fuckhead—" I begin only to smell more smoke, look under my chair where there's a piece of 8 × 10 paper curling up in flames. Cursing at the top of my lungs, I leap up and get a chair on the other side of the table where my back's to no one and I can keep an eye on the red-domed Muppet. Only trouble is that I'll find out a day or so hence that it wasn't him set the fires at all: it was Bernie, the group's manager. Eventually the beer runs out, and Mick says he's hungry. Bernie refuses to let him take the van out hunting for open eateries, which we probably wouldn't be able to find at 4 a.m. in Cardiff anyway, and we all go to bed wearing egg salad.

NEXT MORNING sees us driving to Bristol, a large industrial city where we put up in a Holiday Inn, much to everyone's delight. By this time the mood around this band has combined with my tenacious jet-lag and liberal amounts of alcohol to put me into a kind of ecstasy state the like of which I have never known on the road before.

Past all the glory and the gigs themselves, touring in any form is a pretty drab and tiresome business, but with The Clash I feel that I have re-apprehended that aforementioned glimpse of some Better World of infinite possibilities, and so, inspired and a little delirious, I forego my usual nap between vantrip and showtime by which I'd hoped to eventually whip the jet-lag, spending the afternoon drinking cognac and writing.

By now I'm ready to go with the flow, with anything, as it has begun to seem to me delusory or not that there is some state of grace overlaying this whole project, something right in the soul that makes all the headache-inducing day to day pain in the ass practical logistics run as smoothly as the tempers of the people involved, the whole enterprise sailing along in perfect harmony and such dazzling contrast to the brutal logistics of Led Zep type tours albeit on a much smaller level . . . somehow, whether it really is so or a simple basic healthiness on the part of all involved heightened by my mental state, I have begun to see this trip as somehow symbolic pilgrimage to that Promised Land that rock 'n' roll has cynically sneered at since the collapse of the Sixties.

At this point, in my hotel room in Bristol, if six white horses and a chariot of gold had materialized in the hallway, I would have been no more surprised than at room service, would've just climbed right in and settled back for that long-promised ascent to endless astral weeks in the heavenly land.

What I got instead around 6 p.m. was a call from Joe Strummer saying meet him in the lobby in five minutes if I wanted to go to the sound check. So I floated down the elevators and when I got there I saw a sheepish group of little not-quite punks all huddled around one couch. They were dressed in half-committal punk regalia, a safety pin here and there, a couple of little slogans chalked on their school blazers, their hair greased and twisted up into a cosmetic weekend approximation of spikes.

"Hey," I said, "You guys Clash fans?"

"Well," they mumbled, "sorta . . ."

"Well, whattaya mean? You're punks, aren't ya?"

"Well, we'd like to be . . . but we're *scared* . . ."

When Joe came down I took him aside and, indicating the poor little things, told him what they'd said, also asking if he wanted to get them into the gig with us and thus offer a little encouragement for them to take that next, last, crucial step out into full-fledged punk pariahdom and thus sorely-needed self-respect.

"Forget it," he said. "If they haven't got the courage to do it on their own, I'm bloody well not gonna lead 'em on by the hand."

On the way to the sound check I mentioned that I thought the band hadn't been as good as I knew they could be the previous two nights, adding that I hadn't wanted to say anything about it.

"Why not?" he said.

I realised that I didn't have an answer. I tell this story to point out something about The Clash, and Joe Strummer in particular, that both impressed and showed me up for the sometimes hypocritical "diplomat" I can be. I mean their simple, straightforward honesty, their undogmatic insistence on the truth and why worry about stepping on people's toes because if we're not straight with each other we're never going to get anything accomplished anyway.

It seems like such a simple thing, and I suppose it is, but it runs contrary to almost everything the music business runs on: the hype, the grease, the glad-handing. And it goes a long way towards creating that aforementioned mood of positive clarity and unpeachy morality. Strummer himself, at once the "leader" of the group (though he'd deny it) and the least voluble (though his sickness might have had a lot to do with it), conveys an immediate physical and personal impact of ground-level directness and honesty, a no-bullshit concern with cutting straight to the heart of the matter in a way that is not brusque or impatient but concise and distinctly nonfrivolous.

Serious without being solemn, quiet without being remote or haughty, Strummer offers a distinct contrast to Mick's voluble wit and twinkle of eye, and Paul's looney toon playfulness. He is almost certainly the group's soul, and I wish I could say I had gotten to know him better.

From the instant we hit the hall for the sound-check we all sense that tonight's gig is going to be a hot one. The place itself looks like an abandoned meatpacking room—large and empty with cold stone floors and stark white walls. It's plain dire, and in one of the most common of rock 'n' roll ironies the atmosphere is perfect and the acoustics great.

MEANWHILE BACK in the slaughterhouse, another thing occurs to me while The Clash are warming up at their soundcheck. They play something very funky which I later discover is a Booker T number, thus implanting an idea in my mind which later grows into a conviction: that in spite of the brilliance manifested in things like "White Riot", they actually play better and certainly more interestingly when they *slow down* and get, well, funky. You can hear it in the live if not studio version of "Police and Thieves", as well as "White Boy In Hammersmith Palais," probably the best thing they've written yet.

Somewhere in their assimilation of reggae is the closest thing yet to the lost chord, the missing link between black music and white noise rock capable of making a bow to black forms without smearing on the blackface, get me! It's there in Mick's intro to "Police And Thieves" and unstatedly in the band's whole onstage attitude. I understand why all these groups thought they had to play 120 miles per hour these last couple of years—to get us out of the bog created by everything that preceded them this decade—but the point has been made, and I for one could use a little funk, especially from somebody as good at it as The Clash. Why should any great rock 'n' roll band do what's *expected* of 'em, anyhow? The Clash are a certain idea in many people's minds, which is only all the more reason why they should *break* that idea and broach something else. Just one critic's opinion y'understand but that's what god put us here for.

In any case, tonight is the payload. The band is taut terror from the instant they hit the stage, pure energy, everything they're supposed to be and more. I reflect for the first time that I have never seen a hand that *moved* like this: most of 'em you can see the rockinroll steps choreographed five minutes in advance, but The Clash hop around each other in all configurations totally non-selfconsciously, galvanised by their music alone, Jones and Simonon changing places at the whims of the whams coming out of their guitars, springs in the soles of their tennies.

Strummer, obviously driven to make up to this audience the loss of energy suffered by the last two nights' crowds, is an angry live wire whipping around the middle of the front stage, divesting himself of guitar to fall on one knee in no Elvis parody but pure outside-of-self frenzy, snarling through his shattered dental bombsite with face screwed up in all the rage you'd ever need to convince you of The Clash's authenticity, a desperation uncontrived, unstaged, a fury unleashed on the stage and writhing in upon itself in real pain that connects with the nerves of the audience like summer lightning, and at this time pogoing reveals itself as such a pitifully insufficient response to a man by all appearances trapped and screaming, and it's not your class system, it's not Britain-on-the-wane, it's not even glandular fever, it's the cage of life itself and all the anguish to break through which sometimes translates as flash or something equally petty but in any case is rock 'n' roll's burning marrow.

It was one of those performances for which all the serviceable critical terms like "electrifying" are so pathetically inadequate, and after it was over I realized the futility of hitting Strummer for that interview I kept putting off on the "politics" of the situation. The politics of rock 'n' roll, in England or America or anywhere else, is that a whole lot of kids want to be fried out of their skins by the most scalding propulsion they can find, for a night they can pretend is the rest of their lives, and whether the next day they go back to work in shops or boredom on the dole or American TV doldrums in Mom 'n' Daddy's living room nothing can cancel the reality of that night in the revivifying flames when for once if only then in your life you were blasted outside of yourself and the monotony which defines most life anywhere at any time, when you felt supra-alive, when you supped on lightning and nothing else in the realms of the living or dead mattered at all.

Part Two: I Do Want a Baby Like That

(IN LAST week's episode, our fearless though slightly misapprehensive Ishmael shipped out only to find the dreaded newpube Leviathan a massive—though not Trojan—lamb, which did not so much allay his quave as charm his pacifist heart. This week he continues on the White Star Liner to Coventry, a voyage fraught with anecdote and ruminations both utopian and pragmatic. So keep a close eye on him and a ratchet handy 'cause he could slip back into this penny-dreadful prose at a moment's notice . . .)

BACK AT the hotel everybody decides to reconvene in the Holiday Inn's bar to celebrate this back-in-form gig. I stop off by my room and while sitting on the john start reading an article in *Newsweek* called "Is America Turning

Right?" (Ans: yes.) It's so strange to be out here in the middle of a foreign land, reading about your own country and realising how at home you feel where you have come, how much your homeland is the foreign, alien realm.

This feeling weighed on me more and more heavily the longer I stayed in England—on previous visits I'd always been anxious to get back to the States, and New York homesickness has become a congenital disease whenever I travel. But I have felt for so long that there is something dead, rotten and cold in American culture, not just in the music but in the society at every level down to formularised stasis and entropy, and the supreme irony is that all I ever read in *NME* is how fucked up it is for you guys, when to me your desperation seems like health and my country's pabulum complacency seems like death.

I mean, at least you got some stakes to play for. *Our* National Front has already won, insidiously invisible as a wall socket. The difference is that for you No Future means being thrown on the slagheap of economic refuse, for me it means an infinity of television mirrors that tell the most hideous lies lapped up by this nation of technocratic Trilbys. A little taste of death in every mass inoculation against the bacteria of doubt.

But then I peeked behind the shower curtain: Marisa Berenson was there. "I've got films of you shitting," I said.

"So what?" she said. "I just sold the negatives to WPLJ for their next TV ad. They're gonna have it in neon laserium. I'll be *immortal*."

I mean, would you wanna be a ball bearing? That's how all the television families out here feel and that's how I feel when I go to discos, places where people *cultivate* their ballbearingness. In America, that is. So what did I go down into now but the Bristol (remember Bristol?) Holiday Inn's idea of a real swinging disco where vacationing Americanskis could feel right at home. I felt like climbing right up the walls, but there were girls there, and the band seemed amused and unafeared of venturing within the witches' cauldron of disco ionisation which is genocide in my book buddy, but then us Americans do have a tendency to take things a bit far.

THIS CLUB reminded me of everything I was hosannah-glad to escape when I left New York: flashing dancefloors, ball bearing music at ballpeen volumes, lights aflash that it's all whole bulb orgone bolloxed FUN FUN FUN blinker city kids till daddy takes the console away. I begin to evince overt hostility: grinding of teeth, hissing of breath, balling and banging of fists off fake naugahyde. Fat lot of good it'll do ya, kid. Discotheques are concentration camps, like Pleasure Island in Walt Disney's *Pinocchio*. You play that goddam Baccara record one more time, Dad, your nose is gonna grow and we're gonna saw it off into toothpicks.

I'm seething in barely suppressed rage when Glen Matlock, a puckish pup with more than a hint of wry in his eye, leans across the lucite teen-tall flashlight pina colada table and says, "Hey, wanna hear an advance tape of the Rich Kids album?"

"Sure!" You can see immediately why Glen got kicked out of the Pistols: I wouldn't trust one of these cleanpop whiz kids with a hot lead pole. But I would tell 'em to say hello. I don't give shit for The Raspberries and Glen looks an awful lot like Eric Carmen—except I can't help gotta say it not such a *sissy*—and it's all Paul McCartney's fault anyway, and I mean McCartney ca. Beatles wonderwaxings we all waned and wuvved so well, but in spite of all gurgling bloody messes we're just gonna have to keep on dealing with these emissaries from the land of Bide-a-Wee and His Imperial Pop the Magic Dragon, besides which I'd just danced to James Brown and needed some Coppertone oil and band-aids.

Let's see, how else can I insult this guy, shamepug rippin' off the galvanic force of our PUNZ flotilla with his courtly gestures in the lateral of melody, harmonies, Hollies, all those lies? So he puts it on his tape deck and it's the old Neil Diamond penned Monkees toon, "I'm a Believer".

"Hey!" I said. "That's fuckin' *good!* That's *great! You* gotta helluva band there! Better than the original!"

Ol' Puck he just keeps sitting back sipping his drink laughing at me through lighthouse teeth. Has this tad heard "Muskrat Love?"

"Whattaya *laughin'* at?" I quack. "I'm *serious.* Glen, anybody that can cut the Monkees at their own riffs is okay in my book!"

Then the next song comes on. It's also a Monkees toon. "Hey, what is this—you gonna make your first album 'The Monkees' Greatest Hits'?"

Well, I know I'm not the world's fastest human . . . from the time it was released until about six months ago I thought Brian Wilson was singing "She's giving me *citations*" (instead of the factual "excitations") in "Good Vibrations", I thought the song was about a policewoman he fell in love with or something. So as far as I'm concerned The Rich Kids SHOULD make their first album (call it this too, beats "Never Mind The Bollocks" by miles) "The Monkees Greatest Hits". *I'd* buy it. *Everybody'd* buy it. Not only that, you could count on all the rock critics in *NME* to write lengthy analyses of the conceptual quagmire behind this whole helpful heaping scamful—I mean, let's see Malcolm top that one. Come to think of it, the coolest thing the Pistols could have done when they finally got around to releasing their album would be to've called it "Eric Clapton". Who cares how much it helps sales, think of the *important* part: the *insult.* Plus a nice surprise for subscribers to *Guitar Player* magazine, would-be closet hearthside Holmstrummed Djangoes, etc. *They* don't want a baby that looks like that, even if it's last name is Gibson. Les Paul, where are you? Gone skateboarding, I guess.

With Dick Dale.

OH YEAH, The Clash. Well, closing time came along as it always has a habit of doing at obscenely punescent hours in England—I mean, what is this eleven o'clock shit anyway? Anarchy for me means the bars stay open 24 hours a day. Hmmm, guess that makes Vegas the model of Anarchic Society. Okay, Malcolm, Bernie, whoever else manages all those like snorkers and droners all over the place, it's upROOTS lock stock and barrel time, drop the whole mess right in the middle of Caesar's Palace, and since Johnny Rotten is obviously a hell of a lot smarter than Hunter S. Thompson we got ourselves a whole new American Dream here. No, guess it wouldn't work, bands on the dole can't afford past the slot machines, cancel that one. We go up to Mick's room for beer and talk instead.

He's elated and funny though somewhat subdued. I remark that I haven't seen any groupies on this tour, and ask him if he ever hies any of the little local honeys up to bed and if so why not tonite?

Mick looks tireder, more wasted than he actually is (contrary to his git-pikkin hero, he eschews most all forms of drugs most all of the time) (whole damn healthy bunch, this—not a bent-spoon man or parlous freaksche in the lot). "We don't get into all of that much. You saw those girls out there—most of 'em are too young." (Quite true, more later.) "But groupies ... I dunno, just never see that many I guess. I've got a girlfriend I get to see about once a month, but other than that ..." he shrugs, "when you're playin' this much, you don't need it so much. Sometimes I feel like I'm losin' interest in sex entirely.

"Don't get me wrong. We're a band of regular blokes. It's just that a lot of that stuff you're talking about doesn't seem to ... apply."

See, didn't I tell you it was the Heavenly Land? The Clash are not only not sexist, they are so healthy they don't even have to *tell* you how unsexist they are; no sanctimony, no phonies, just ponies and miles and miles of green Welsh grass with balls bouncing ...

Now I will repeat myself from Part One that THIS is exactly and precisely what I mean by Clash = model for New Society: a society of *normal* people, by which I mean that we are surrounded by queers, and I am not talking about gay people. I'm talking about ... well, when lambs draw breath in Albion with Sesame Street crayolas, we won't see no lovers runnin' each others' bodies down, get me. I mean fuck this and fuck that, but make love when the tides are right and I *do* want a baby that looks like that. And so, secretly smiling across the rain, does William Blake.

NEXT DAY was a long drive South-West. Actually this being Sunday and my three days *assignment* up I'm sposed to go back to London, but previous eventide when I'd told Mick this he'd asked me to stick around and damned if I didn't—a first for me. Usually you just wanna get home, get the story out and head beerward.

But as y'all can see my feelings about The Clash had long ago gotten way beyond all the professional malarkey, we liked hanging out together. Besides which I still kept a spyglass out for that Promised Land's colours seemed so sure to come a-blowin' around every fresh hillock curve, hey there moocow say hello to James Joyce for me, gnarly carcasses of trees the day before had set to mind the voices "Under Milk Wood"... land rife with ghosts who don't come croonin' around no Post Houses way past midnite with Automatic Slim and Razor Totin' Jim, no, the reality is you could be touring Atlantis and it'd still look like motorway :: car park :: gasstop :: pissbreak :: souvenir shop :: at deadening cetera.

Joe kills the dull van hours with Nazitrocity thrillers by Sven Hassel, Mick is just about to start reading Kerouac's *The Subterraneans* but borrows my copy of Charles Bukowski's new book *Love Is a Dog From Hell* instead which flips him out so next two days he keeps passing it around the van trying to get the other guys to read certain poems like the one about the poet who came onstage to read and vomited in the grand piano instead (and woulda done it again too) but they seem unimpressed, Joe wrapped up in his stormtroopers and Paul spliffing in bigeyed space monkey glee playing the new Ramones over and over and everytime Joey shouts "LOBOTOMAAY!!" at the top of side two he pops a top out of somebody's head, the pogo beginning to make like spirogyra, sprintillatin' all over the place, tho it's true there's no stoppin' the cretins from hoppin' once they start they're like *germs* that jump. Meanwhile poor little Nicky Headon the drummer who I won't get to know really well this trip is bundling jacket tighter in the front seat and swigging cough mixture in unsuccessful attempt to ward off miserable bronchold. At one point Mickey, the driver, a big thicknecked lug with a skinhead haircut, lets Nicky take the wheel and we go skittering all over the road.

Golly gee, you must get bored reading such stuff. Did you know that this toot is costing IPC (who, for all I know also put out a you're-still-alive monthly newsletter for retired rear Admirals of the Guianean Fleet) seven and a half cents a word? An equitable deal, you might assert, until you consider than in this scheme of things, such diverse organisms as "salicylaceous" and "uh" receive equal recompense, talk about your class systems or lack of same. NOW you know why 99% of all publicly printed writers are hacks, because cliches pay good as pearls, although there is a certain unalloyed ineluctable Ramoneslike logic to the way these endless reams of copy just plow on thru and thru all these crappy music papers like one thickplug pencil's line piledriving from here on out to Heaven.

I mean look, face it, both reader and writer know that 99% of what's gonna pass from the latter to the former is justa buncha jizjaz anyway, so why not just give up the ghost of pretence to form and subject and just make these rags ramble fit to the trolley you prob'ly read 'em on . . . you may say that I take liberties, and you are right, but I will have done my good deed for the day if I can make you see that the whole point is YOU SHOULD BE TAKING LIBERTIES TOO. Nothing is inscribed so deep in the earth a little eyewash won't uproot it, that's the whole point of the so-called "new wave"—to REINVENT YOURSELF AND EVERYTHING AROUND YOU CONSTANTLY, especially since all of it is already the other thing anyway, The Clash a broadside a pamphlet an urgent hand-bill in a taut and moving fist, *NME* staff having advertised themselves a rock 'n' roll band for so many years nobody can deny 'em now, as you are writing history that I read, as you are he as I am we as weasels all together, Jesus am I turning into Steve Hillage or Daevid Allen, over the falls in any case but at least we melted the walls leaving home plate clear for baseball in the snow.

ARE YOU an imbecile? If so, apply today for free gardening stamp books at the tubestop of your choice. Think of the promising career that may be passing you by *at this very moment* as a Greyhound. Nobody loves a poorhouse Nazi. Dogs are more alert than most clerks.

Plan 9: in America there is such a crying need for computer opera-tors they actually put ads on commercial TV begging people to sign up. British youth are massively unemployed. Relocate the entire under-25 population of Britain to training centres in New Jersey and Massachu-setts. Teach them all to tap out codes. Give them lots of speed and let them play with their computers night and day. Then put them on TV smiling with pinball eyes: "Hi! I used to be a lazy sod! But then I dis-covered COMPUTROCIDE DYNAMICS INC., and it's changed my life completely! I'm happy! I'm useful! I walk, talk, dress and act normal! I'm an up and coming go getter in a happening industry! Good Christ, Mabel, I've got a *job*." He begins to bawl maudlinly, drooling and drib-bling sentimental mucous out his nose. "And to think . . . that only two months ago I was stuck back in *England* . . . unemployed, unemployable, no prospects, no respect, a worthless hunk of human shit! Thank you, Uncle Same!"

So don't go tellin' me you're bored with the U.S.A., buddy. I've heard all that shit one too many pinko punko times. We'll just drink us these two more beers and then go find a bar where you know everybody is drinkin' beer they bought with money they owned by the sweat of their brow, from *workin'*, get me, buddy? 'Cause I got a right to work. Niggers got a right to work, too. Same as white men. When your nose is pushin' up grindstone you got no time to worry about the size of the other guy's snout. Because you know, like I know, like we know, like both the Vienna Boys' Choir and the guy who sells hot watches at Sixth Avenue and 14th St. know, that we were born for one purpose and one purpose only: TO WORK. *Haul* that slag! Hog that slod! Whelp that mute and look at us: at our uncontestible NOBILITY: at our national biological PRIDE: at our stolid steroid HOPE.

Who says it's a big old complicated world? I'll tell ya what it comes down to, buddy: one word: JOB. You got one, you're okay, scot-free, a prince in fact in your own hard-won domain! You don't got one, you're a miserable slug and a drag on this great nation's economically rusting drainpipes. You might just as well go drown yourself in mud. We need the water to conserve for honest upright workin' folks! Folks with the godsod sense to treat that job like GOLD. Cause that's just what it stands for and WHY ELSE DO YOU THINK I KEEP TELLING YOU IT'S THE MOST IMPORTANT THING IN THE UNIVERSE? Your ticket to human citizenship.

One man, one job. One dog, one stool.

THE HOTEL has a lobby and coffeeshop which look out upon a body of water which no-one can figure out whether it's the English Channel or not. Even the waitresses don't know. I'm feeling good, having slept in the afternoon, and there's a sense in the air that everybody's up for the gig. Last night consolidated energies; tonight should be the payload.

We wind through narrow streets to a small club that reminds me much of the slightly sleazy little clubs where bands like the Iron Butterfly and Strawberry Alarm Clock, uh, got their *chops* together, or, uh, paid whatever *dues* were expected of them when they were coming up and I was in school. This type of place you can write the script before you get off the bus; manager a fat middle-aged brute who glowers over waitresses and rockbands equally, hates the music, hates the kids but figures there's money to be made. The decor inside is ersatz-tropicana, suggesting that this place has not so long ago been put to uses far removed from punk rock. Enrico Cadillac vibes.

I walk in the dressing room which actually is not a dressing room but a miniscule space partitioned off where three bands are supposed to set up, almost literally on top of one another. The Voidoids' Bob Quine walks in, takes a look and lays his guitar case on the floor; "Guess this is it".

Neither of the opening acts have been getting the audience response they deserved on this tour. These are Clash audiences, people who know all their songs by heart, have never heard of The Lous and maybe are vaguely familiar with Richard Hell. Richard is totally depressed because his band isn't getting the support he hoped for from their record company on this trek. The "Blank Generation" album hasn't been released yet—The Voidoids think it's because Sire wants to flog a few more import copies, although I hear later in the week that strikes have shut down all the record pressing plants in Britain. The result is that the kids in the audience don't know most of the songs, the lyrics, nothing but that Ork/ Stiff EP to go on, so they settle for gobbing on the band, screaming for The Clash.

I tell Hell and Quine that I have never heard the band so tight, which is true—there's just no way that night-after-night playing, in no matter how degraded circumstances, can't put more gristle and fire in your playing. Interestingly enough, Ivan Julian and Marc Bell, Hell's second guitarist and drummer, are both in good spirits—they've toured before, know what to expect—while Hell and Quine are both totally down.

Someday Quine will be recognised for the pivotal figure that he is on his instrument—he is the first guitarist to take the breakthroughs of early Lou Reed and James Williamson and work through them to a whole new, individual vocabulary, driven into odd places by obsessive attention to "On the Corner" era Miles Davis. Of course I'm prejudiced, because he played on my record as well, but he is one of the few guitarists I know who can handle the supertechnology that is threatening to swallow players and instrument whole—"You gotta hear this new box I got," is how he'll usually preface his latest discovery, "it creates the most *offensive noise* . . ."—without losing contact with his musical emotions in the process. Onstage he projects the cool remote stance learned from his jazz mentors—shades, beard, expressionless face, bald head, old sport-coat—but his solos always burn, the more so because there is always something constricted in them, pent-up, waiting to be let out.

Tonight's crowd is good—they respond instinctively to The Voidoids though they're unfamiliar with them, and it doesn't seem at all odd to see kids pogoing to Quine's Miles Davis riffs. (He steals from *Agharta*! And makes it *work*!) Hell and the Voidoids get the only encore on my leg of the tour, and they make good use of it, bringing Glen Matlock out to play bass. The Clash's set is brisk, hot, clean—consensus among us fellow travellers is that it's solid but lacks the cutting vengeance of last night.

Even on a small stage—and this one is tiny—the group are in constant motion, snapping in and out of one anothers' territory with electrified sprints and lunges that have their own grace, nobody knocking knees or bumping shoulders, even as The Voidoids in certain states which they hate and I think among their best reel and spin in hair's-breadth near-collisions with each other that are totally graceless but supremely driven. You can really see why Tom Verlaine wanted Hell out of Television—he flings himself all over the stage as if battering furiously at the gates of some bolted haven, and if Ivan and Bob know when to dodge you can also see plainly why Hell would have been in a group called The Heartbreak-ers—because that sumbitch is hard as oak, and he's just looking for the proper axe because something inside seethes poisonously to be let out.

I would also like to say that Richard Hell is one of the very few rockers I've ever known who I could slag off in print and still be friends with. After my feature on him in this magazine I was half-wondering if I was gonna have another Patti Smith (cracked and bitter "I am the Oracle!") on my hands, but he was totally cool if contentious about it—a *sane* person, in other words.

BACK IN the dressing room I met some fans. There was Martin, who was 14 and had a band of his own called Crissus. I thought Martin was a girl until I heard his name (no offence, Martin) but look at it this way: here, on some remote southern shore of the old Isle, this kid who is just entering puberty, this *child* has been so inspired by the New Wave that he is already starting to make his move. I asked him whether Crissus had recorded yet, and he laughed: "Are you kidding?"

"Why not? Everybody else is". (Not said cynically either.)

I asked Martin what he liked about The Clash in particular as opposed to other New Wave bands. His reply: "Their total physical and psychic resistance to the fascist imperialist enemies of the people at all levels, and their understanding of the distinction between art and propaganda. They know that the propaganda has to be palatable to the People if they're going to be able to a) be able to listen to it b) understand it, and c) react to it, rising in Peoples' War. They recognise that the form must be as revolutionary as the content—in Cuba they did it with radio and ice cream and baseball and boxing, with the understanding that sports and music are the most effective vectors for communist ideology. Rock 'n' roll as a form is anarchistic, but if we could just figure out some way to make the *content* as compelling as the form *then* we'd be getting somewhere!

"For the present, we must recognise that there is only so much revolutionary information that can be transmitted in so circumscribed a space and time, after all, and so we must be content in the knowledge that the potency of form ensures the efficacy of content, that is that the driving primitive African beat and boarlike guitars will keep bringing the audience back for repeated hypnotised listenings until the revolutionary message laid out plainly in the lyrics cannot help but sink in!"

Martin was bright for his age. Not quite as bright as all that, though. Or maybe brighter. Because of course he didn't say that. I made that up. What Martin said was, "I like The Clash because of their clothes!"

And so it went with all the other fans I interviewed over the six nights I saw them. *Nobody* mentioned politics, not even the dole, and I certainly wasn't going to start giving them cues. This night, I got such typical responses as: "Their sound—I dunno, it just makes you jump!" "The music, which is exciting, and the lyrics, which are heavy, and the way they look onstage!" (which is stripped down to zippers and denims for instant combat, or perhaps stage flexibility).

As we were all wandering out, Mick in the middle of a cluster of fans as usual, not soaking up adoration but genuinely interested in getting to know them, about halfway between bandstand and door, the owner of the club began making noises about "Bleedin' punk rockers—try to have a decent club, they come in here and mess it up—"

Mick looked at him indifferently. "Bollocks."

"Look, you lot, clear out, now, we don't want your kind hanging round here," and of course he has his little oaf-militia to hustle them toward the exits. Finally I said to him, "If you dislike them so much, why don't you open a different kind of club?"

Instantly he was up against me, belly and breath and menace: "Wot're you lookin' for some trouble, then?"

"No, I just asked you a question."

You know, it's like all the other similar scenes you've ever seen all your life—YOU REALLY DON'T WANT TO GET INTO SOME KIND OF STUPID VIOLENCE WITH THESE PEOPLE, but you finally just get tired of being herded like swine.

WHEN WE got out front a few Teds showed up—first I'd seen in England, really, and I had the impulse to go gladhanding up to them every inch the Yankee tourist gawker dodo: "Hey, you're *Teds,* aren't you? I've heard about you guys! You don't like anything after Gene Vincent! Man, you guys are one bunch of stubborn motherfuckers!"

I didn't do that, though—I looked at Mick and the fans, and they looked wary, staring at indistinct spots like you do when you scent violence in the air and don't want it. They were treading lightly. But then, outside of certain scenes with each other, almost all the punks I've *ever* seen tread lightly! They're worse than hippies! More like beatniks.

But what was really funny was that the Teds were treading lightly too—they just sort of shuffled up with their dates, in their ruffled shirts and velour jackets and ducktail haircuts, shoved their hands in their pockets and started muttering generalities: "Bleedin' punks . . . shit . . . buncha bloody freaks . . ." Really, you had to strain to hear them. They seemed almost embarrassed. It was like they had to do it.

I had never seen anything quite like it in the U.S., because aside from certain ethnic urban gangs, there is nothing in the U.S. quite like the Teds-Punks thing. We've got bikers, but even bikers claim contemporaneity. The Teds seemed as sad as the punks seemed touching and oddly inspiring—these people know that time has passed them by, and they are not entirely wrong when they assert that it's time's defect and not their own. They remember one fine moment in their lives when everything—music, sex, dreams—seemed to coalesce, when they could tell everybody trying to strap them to the ironing board to get fucked and know in their bones that they were right. But that moment passed, and they got immensely scared, just like kids in the U.S. are mostly scared of New Wave, just like people I know who freak out when I put on Miles Davis records and beg me to take them off because there is something in them so emotionally huge and threatening that it's plain "depressing."

The Teds were poignant for me, even more so because their style of dress made them as absurd to us as we were to them (but in a different way—they look "quaint," a very final dismissal). They looked like people who had had one glimpse in their lives and were supping at the dry bone of that memory forever, but man, that glimpse, just *try* to take it away from me, punk motherfucker . . . not that the punks are trying to infringe on the Teds—just that unlike the punks, who pay socially for their stance but at least have the arrogance of their freshness, the Teds looked like people backed into a final corner by a society which simply can't accept anybody getting loose.

In America you can ease into middle age with the accoutrements of adolescence still prominent and suffer relatively minor embarrassment: okey, so the guy's still got his sideburns and rod and beer and beergut and wife and three kids and a duplex and never grew up. So what? You're not supposed to grow up in America anyway. You're supposed to consume. But in Britain it seems there is some ideal, no, some dry river one is expected to ford, so you can enter that sedate bubble where you raise a family, contribute in your small way to your society and keep your mouth shut. Until you get old, that is, when you can become an "eccentric"—do and say outrageous things, naughty things, because it's expected of you, you've crossed to the other mirror downslide of the telescope of childhood.

In between, it looks like quiet desperation all the way to an outsider. All that stiff-upper-lip, carry-on shit. If Freud was right when he said that all societies are based on repression, then England must be the apex of Western Civilisation. There was a recently published conversation between Tennessee Williams and William Burroughs, in which Burroughs said he didn't like the English because their social graces had evolved to a point where they could be entertaining all evening for the rest of their lives but nobody ever told you anything personal, anything *real* about themselves. I think he's right. We've got the opposite problem in America right now—in New York City today there's a TV talk show host who's so narcissistic that every Wednesday he lays down on a couch and pours out his insecurities to his analyst . . . *on the air!*

You guys strike me as a whole lot of people who laugh at the wrong time, who constantly study the art of concealment. Then again, it occurs to me that it could actually be that there is something irritating me that you don't suffer from—which is certainly not meant as self-aggrandizement on my part—but that you've been around a while, have come to wry terms with your indigenous diseases, whereas we Americans got bugs under our skin that make us all twitch in Nervous Norvusisms that must amuse you highly. But even here there is a difference—at our best we recognise our sickness, and stuggle constantly to deal with it. You're real big on sweeping the dirt under the carpet. So it's no wonder that, like Johnny Rotten says, you've got "problems"—more like boils bursting, I'd say.

AND NOW, as I get ready to close off, I feel uncomfortably pompous and smug—I'll be back with the payoff next week, the sum of what I see in this whole "punk" movement, for anybody who want to hear it—but here I sit on what feels like a sweeping and enormously presumptuous generalisation on not just the punks but your whole country.

Well, then, let the fool make a fool out of himself, but I'll tell you one thing: the Teds are a hell of a symptom of the rot in your society, much more telling in their way than the punks, because the punks, much as they go on about boredom and no future, at least offer possibilities, whereas the Teds are landlocked. You cocksuckers have effectively enclosed these people, who are only trying to not give up some of their original passions in the interests of total homogenization, in an invisible concentration camp. Your contempt stymies them, so they strike out at the only people who are more vulnerable and passive than they are: the punks.

The almost saintly thing about the punks is that for the most part they don't seem to find it necessary to strike out with that sort of viciousness against anybody—except themselves.

So to anyone who is reading this who is in a position of "status," "responsibility," "power," unlike the average *NME* reader, I say congratulations—you've created a society of cannibals and suicides.

Part Three: A Little Poetry, Some Violence, and Ten Thousand Trembling Lambs

"RECENT HISTORY is the record of the vast conspiracy to impose one level of mechanical consciousness on mankind and exterminate all manifestations of that unique part of human sentience . . . which the individual shares with his Creator. The suppression of contemplative individuality is near complete.

"The only immediate historical data that we can know and act on are those fed to our senses through systems of mass communication.

"These media are exactly the places where the deepest and most personal sensitivities and confessions of reality are most prohibited, mocked, suppressed . . .

"A few individuals, poets, have had the luck and courage and fate to glimpse something new through the crack in mass consciousness . . . the police and newspapers have moved in, mad movie manufacturers from Hollywood are at this moment preparing bestial stereotypes of the scene . . .

"How many hypocrites are there in America? How many trembling lambs, fearful of discovery? What authority have we set up over ourselves, that we are not as we Are?—*Allen Ginsberg, "Poetry, Violence, and the Trembling Lambs."*

WE'RE STILL standing around in front of the club, and Mick (Jones) and I have been talking to three fans who've hitchhiked from Dover for the gig. They're invited back to the hotel in the more or less loose way these things happen, and Mick looks at me: "Lester, can you put them up in your room tonight?"

It's two girls and a guy and my room is small but they're nice and the conversation's been good so far so I say sure if they don't mind sleeping on the floor. We all climb in the van and immediately Mickey, the driver, begins to bitch about having to carry extra people.

He's a big thicknecked plug with a skinhead haircut, not the most sanguine vibes in the world but it's been a long drive from Bristol today and cats like him got no stage to let it out on. So I try to mollify him a bit, telling him he's like Neal Cassady (because on those long stretches of motorway he is).

"Yeah," he snaps. "I'm a drivin' *star!*"

When we get back to the hotel the surliness escalates. I'm wandering around the lobby trying to locate some beer, so I miss the first part of the trouble. The fans, Mickey the driver, Mick's friend and travelling companion Robin, Paul Simonon and Nicky Headon sitting there, and the sandwiches are flying as usual, so at first I don't notice what's going on. But when I sit down in my chair I realise that most of the sandwiches are being thrown by Mickey and Robin at the male fan.

I look around at the fan, who seems to be wearing bits of tomato, egg, lettuce, mayonnaise and bread all over his body, is shrinking back in his chair in the most abject humiliation. Confused, I hand him a beer and tell him it's all right.

Mickey: "It is *not* all right!" He leaps up and runs across to us, pummelling the fan with his fists. The kid tries to roll up into a ball. A moment later Robin is over; first he grinds the remainder of the sandwich glop all in the kid's hair and clothes, then he's grabbed a cushion off one the chairs and is smothering his face in it. Finally everybody sits down, and ugly silence falls.

I don't want to get my face punched in, but finally I've got to say something. I look at Mickey, speaking calmly. "Why are you acting like such an asshole?"

"What's an asshole?" he demands.

"There are all kinds," I say. "You just know one when you see one."

"That little fucker fucked up my jacket!"

He indicates a small stain on his windbreaker.

"So what?" I say. "If you're gonna start throwing sandwiches you've gotta expect stuff like that."

"We didn't start it—*he* did," says Mickey.

"Oh," I say, knowing full well it's lie.

Another even nastier silence. Finally I say, "Well, I'm sorry about your jacket. You must value it a lot."

"Fucking right I do."

"Would you have punched one of them if they'd stained it?" I ask, indicating Paul and Nicky, who are still sitting there in silence.

"Yeah." Then he starts in on me, verbally, trying to incite whatever he can. I won't bore you with the details. After a few minutes, Robin stands up and asks me if I want to go up to Mick's room. After everything that has just happened, I can sit there and say, "Yeah, that sounds pretty good." I look at Liz, one of the girl fans.

"Wanna go up and see Mick?"

"No," she says.

So the three fans and I head for the elevator to my room. Somehow, only when we get there does the full sense of the scene just past hit me. "I guess they're hypocrites, aren't they?" says the kid with food smeared all over him. The girls are incensed. It won't be until tomorrow that it occurs to me that I've been reading *The War Against the Jews 1933-1945*, trying to figure out how a whole nation could stand by and let atrocities happen, yet I sit there somehow *refusing to perceive* for several minutes that someone sitting right next to me was being verbally abused and physically brutalised for no reason at all.

By the time we get up to my room the kid is already making excuses for The Clash. "I'm not mad at anybody," he's saying. "It's not the band's fault."

By this time I'm seething. "What do you mean? They sat right there and let it happen! "I sat there and let it happen! What gives anybody the right to do shit like that to you?"

I curse myself again and again for not having acted. Because now I'm sitting in my room, heart pounding, nerves which I've pushed to the breaking point by not pacing myself on this tour twitching, uptight and itching to smash somebody in the face. I realise that that *goon* down there has only infected me with his own poison, but there is nothing I can do about it except try vainly to cool out.

The girls are enraged at The Clash, the kid is slowly admitting to his own anger past utter mortification, and we keep hashing it over and over until we realise that's not going to do us any good. So the conversation turns to other things. The kid works in a hotel in Torquay, a really swanky place, and regales us with stories of some of the foibles and antics of famous guests such as Henry Kissinger and Frank Sinatra. He tells us what pigs most of the big-name rock groups that have stayed there are. The only guests who are worse then the rock stars, he says, are the Arabs. When the rock stars leave, the rooms arc decimated; when the Arabs leave, they're decimated and full of bullet holes. Which of course brings us right back to tonight's incident.

"What they don't realise," he says, "is that when they throw food all around like that, it's somebody like me who's got to get down on his hands and knees and clean it up."

WHICH MEANS somebody like The Clash themselves. I suppose I'm going to seem very moralistic about this, and I don't mean for this incident to dominate this story, but if I close my eyes it will not go away.

I recall the first time I read about The Clash, the cover story *NME* ran last spring, being a little surprised when it is said that on their first tour they were (already?) tearing up hotel rooms. I mean even then it struck you a bit odd, coming atop all their righteous rhetoric. If somebody screws around with you, fine, smash 'em back if you want. But random destruction is so . . . *asinine.* And so redolent of self-hate.

I suppose there's no basic difference between The Clash thrashing hotels and their fans leaving beermug shards all over concert hall floors, that it's all just the product of frustration and no big deal. But some things you just gotta see as a package deal. Meaning that the nature of any enterprise at all levels is defined by what's coming down from the top. What's at the top with most of the big rock groups is just totally diseased, so their whole operation reflects the sickness, down to the employment of brutal thugs to keep the fans away from them in the name of "security" (whose?). What's at the top in The Clash organisation seems so basically good, moral, principalled, all that, that it's no wonder that except for this incident everything has seemed to run smoothly on this tour, everybody has seemed so happy.

When Led Zeppelin or the Stones tour everybody's got to suffer to compensate for indulgence of the big babies at the top, so all kinds of minor functionaries and innocent bystanders can get around into shit. But even Led Zeppelin don't invite their fans back to the hotel *and then* beat them up.

At about four a.m. one of the girls said to the boy fan, "Looks like you've got a shiner." You could begin to see the discolouration in his right eye. By the time they left, it would have turned into a purple lump half an inch thick and the width of a shilling.

I sat up all night with them, getting to know each other in that transient, pleasant intimacy common to travellers. We exchanged addresses and warm goodbyes and they left to hitchhike back to Dover in a mild drizzle around 7:30 a.m. The scene with Mickey had left me too wound up to sleep, and we were all supposed to show in the lobby at 9 for the drive to Birmingham. So I showered, dressed, packed and went down for breakfast, where I met and talked with a guy named John who was replacing Mickey for today's drive. Which was fortunate, because I would have hopped the first train to London rather than spend another few hours in a van with that shithead.

In fact I didn't say anything on the drive to Birmingham. I figured there was no point in getting into what could be a prolonged argument with anybody in a small enclosed space. But as soon as we checked into the hotel that afternoon, I called Mick's room and asked if I could come over. It had been eating at me since it happened, and I had to get it out of my system. Mick, Robin, and Paul were there, and I repeated what had happened. They didn't seem particularly concerned. When I asked Paul why he hadn't done anything, he said, "Mickey's just that kind of bloke; you don't want to get in his way. Besides, it seemed like it was all in fun—I 'ave a tussle with me mates every once in awhile."

Yeah, I said, but there's nothing vicious in you. (It was the difference between a cub and a beast.) Robin didn't remember what had happened— "I was pissed"—and Mick said that Mickey was a good mate of theirs from back home. So I pushed the issue, and when I was done Mick said, "Well, I feel as if I've just had a severe reprimand."

"Yeah," said Robin. "You sound like my father."

I told them I didn't mean to set myself up as judge and jury. But you could see that Mick was upset; more than anybody else in The Clash, he love's the group's fans. After a short depressed silence, he said he was going out for a walk, got up and left the room. After talking for a while to Robin, who turned out to be a decent guy sober, I went back to my room, where I was finally able to fall asleep in the bath.

THE MOOD at the Birmingham concert hall was ominous. Clash road manager Corky was handing out "I WANT COMPLETE CONTROL" buttons to the kids going in the door, and police were confiscating them as soon as they got inside. The mood of the crowd was ugly—they gobbed all over Richard Hell even more than usual, and he started gobbing back, which was a mistake.

When I walked into the dressing room Joe Strummer immediately confronted me: "Lester, what's all this shit you're raisin' then?"

"You mean about last night?"

"Yeah. That guy was a bleedin' little ligger . . ."

Rather than tell him he was wrong and get into a hassle just before showtime, I left the dressing room. Out in the hall Mick came up to me, obviously still concerned. "I've heard four different stories about what happened last night," he said, "but the main thing is that it better not happen again."

Later there was a party in a disco above the hall, and I spoke briefly to Bernie Rhodes, The Clash manager. I told him I loved the group, and liked Mick the best. He sighed, "Yeah, but Mick's my biggest problem . . ."

The real problem, of course, is how to reconcile Mick's attitude towards the fans with the group's escalating popularity in some realistic manner. Meaning that just like with that recent Joe-Strummer-turned-his-back-on-me letter in *NME*, eventually you have to draw the line, and who's going to decide when and where it's to be drawn? Without this one-on-one contact with their audience, The Clash would seem likely to fall into the same elitist alienation as most bands preceding them, but if it gets to the point that several thousand people want into your hotel room you've got to find some way of dealing with it. I certainly don't have the answer—all I know is that the total access is as unreasonable as Zep/Stones style security can be fascistly offensive.

Anyway, in spite of tension between police and audience, the band had played a great set, channelling all the frustration in the room through the music into a liberating mass seizure. I couldn't help comparing this, especially in the light of most of the publicity accorded punks in the dailies, to the last time I was in Birmingham, for Slade in 1972. At that show I'd been warned not to take my tape recorder into the audience because they'd surely break it; they didn't, but they did smash every seat in the house, fights broke out everywhere, and Dave Hill was injured by flying shrapnel.

Of course, that *was* your standard football audience, and what's a little authentic violence in the face of a generation five years on who would seem to prefer rebellion by clothes and hairstyles?

Speaking of which I experienced a revelation of sorts at the after-gig party. I am loath to confess it, but I must say that try as I might I have never been able to find punk girls sexy. Somehow that chopped hair will just douse you every time, never mind the thought of trying to kiss somebody with a safety pin through their mouth (by the way, I didn't see a single safety pin through the flesh the entire time I was in England)—but now, in the disco upstairs, with Don Letts manning the turntable alternating punk and reggae at mindmelting volumes, a whole pack of punkettes got out on that dance floor and started pogoing away and . . . well . . . suddenly it all began to make real tight *sense* . . .

In fact, it was one of the highlights of my trip. I tried dancing a little bit, but mostly I just had to stand there and stare and stare, as one girl in black leather did James Brown steps, while Ari Up of The Slits, in all sorts of rags and a fishnet shawl, hopped highfooting around the dancefloor like some incredible mix of spider and strutting ostrich, and the drummer from The Lous first walked around the floor on her knees, then got down on all fours and walked the dog for real as my eyeballs and than brains fell out a little at a time.

I suppose all you English tots are used to this sort of thing and blase, but for this American it was Tod Browning's *Freaks* doing the Cretin Hop in the hypnotantalizing pulsating flesh. Like, if anybody starts asking me about the *sociological significance* of all this punk stuff I'm just gonna flash back to that Lous drummer down on all fours marching in circles, recalling most vividly her face as she did so: the fact that it was serene, *blank,* unconcerned, *totally unselfconscious.*

MUCH THE same sort of thing strikes me next night, when for my last night on the tour, I attend a gig in Coventry with fellow rock critic Simon Frith. Simon, his wife Jill and I are surrounded by these strange children, the age difference somehow even more accentuated when there are three of us instead of just me blending with the geeks.

We note things like nonfunctional zippers sewn into the middle of shirts, and I'm almost passing out on my feet after six days of three hours sleep a night on the road when suddenly something very strange and totally unprecedented in my experience runs over me. It's a kid moving through the crowd in a jagged mechanical pivoting career, like a robot with crossed circuits and staring fixedly at nothing I can see, certainly not seeing me as we collide and he spazzmos on. When I ask Simon what in the hell that was he says they do it all the time—"Curious, isn't it?"— and when I ask if such a gait might be the byproduct of amphetamine abuse he laughs: "This is no pill scene. Most of these kids have never had anything stronger than stout." (The Clash, contrary to reputation, are not into speed either, at least not on the road.) Then we stare for a moment at the pogoing army, and Simon says, "Very tribal, isn't it?" *(Bleedin' ol' voyeur sociologist bore—Ed)*

That it is. Between The Voidoids' and The Clash's sets, the PA broadcasts "Anarchy In The UK," and the whole audience, pogoing wildly, sings the entire song. I reflect how such a sight must strike terror, or something, into the heart of a middle-aged policeman looking on; but then I recall Slade getting their audience to sing along to "You'll Never Walk Alone" in '72, and the symmetry is inescapable. I *know* about the dole, I recognise the differences, but I wonder just exactly what, in the end, we can all understand this thing to be about.

When The Clash come in on Coventry, Joe repeats a little speech he first tried out in Birmingham: "Listen—before we play anything, we'd like to ask you one favour: please don't spit on us. We're just trying to do something good up here, and it throws us off our stride." It worked in both places, although I heard people complaining about it. But what gobbing really represents to me, besides nausea, is *people doing what they think is expected of them rather than whatever it is they might really want to do.*

Which of course *should* be what the New Wave is against.

Or rather, the converse should be what it's all about. At its best New Wave/punk represents a fundamental and age-old Utopian dream: that if you give people the license to be as outrageous as they want in absolutely any fashion they can dream up, *they'll be creative about it*, and do something good besides. Realise their own potentials and finally start doing what they really want to do. Which also presupposes that people don't want somebody else telling them what to do. That most people are capable of a certain spontaneity, given the option. That, like Richard Hell says, anybody can reinvent him or herself and should.

As it is, the punks constitute a form of passive resistance to a slick social order, but the question remains of just what alternatives they are going to come up with. Singing along to "Anarchy" and "White Riot" constitutes no more than a show of solidarity, and there are plenty of people who think this is all no more than a bunch of stupid kids on a faddist's binge. They're wrong, because at the very least all of this amounts to a gesture of faith in mass and individual unrealised potentials, which counts for a lot in an era when there are plenty of voices who would tell you that all human behaviour especially including music can be reduced to a formula.

But if anything more than fashions and what usually amounts to poses is going to finally come of all this, then everybody listening is going to have to pick up the possibilities with both hands and fulfill 'em themselves. Either that or end up with a new set of surrogate mommies and daddies, just like hippies did, because in spite of whatever they set in motion that's exactly what, say, Charles Manson and John Sinclair were.

Like Joe Strummer said when I asked him to sit down for a tape recorded interview as the "leader" of the group: "*I'm* not the leader. We don't have no fuckin leader."

The paradox for me is that the punks, in their very gentleness behind all the sneers and attitudes copped, are lambs—and believe me, I'm with the lambs over the bullies and manipulators of this world all the way—but what are lambs without a shepherd? Rastas aside, I don't want no Jesuses in *my* Promised Land, and if I didn't find it at the end of my road with The Clash I did catch a glimpse of it, on that road, in the way they acted towards their fans, towards me, towards people who worked for them, towards women, and ultimately towards themselves, every day. Meaning that even if we don't need any more leaders, we could do with a lot more models. If that's what the punks really amount to, then perhaps we actually do have the germ of a new society, or at least a new sensibility, that cuts through things like class and race and sex.

If not, well . . . I started talking to a girl who knew Simon and Jill, who I figured was a student in one of Simon's classes. She was very fresh, very wholesome, very young in a jacket covered with buttons bearing groups' names, and very miffed that The Clash had asked the audience not to spit on them. "After all," she said, "*they* started it!"

"But look," I said, "They play better when you don't."

"I don't care! I just want to jump up and down! That's all my students want, too!"

I blinked. "Your *students*? Wait a second, how old are you?"

"Twenty-four. I'm a schoolteacher."

Honestly, I couldn't help myself.

"Then . . . but . . . what are you doing here? I mean, why do you like The Clash?"

"*Because they make me jump up and down!*" And she pogoed away.

THE END

CLASH ON TOUR:
FORCES OF LIGHT AND SHADOW

Chris Salewicz | July 15, 1978 | *New Musical Express* (UK)

In mid-1978, the Clash were suffering second-album blues. In the extended gap since their long-playing debut, their fans had had to make do with a series of powerful stand-alone singles, including the incendiary "Complete Control," in which the band lambasted their own record company for undermining their previous interview boasts of autonomy. Pending that long-awaited LP follow-up, the Clash made sure to keep in touch with their public by regularly taking to the road.

This evocative and harrowing dispatch from a British Clash tour is the real-life version of the type of milieu addressed in more stylized terms in "I Fought the Law," the Bobby Fuller Four rebel anthem later covered by the Clash. It certainly puts into context assumptions about the violence of punks: the brutality herein is meted out by bouncers and police officers. The incidents Salewicz describes were later dramatized in the Clash motion picture *Rude Boy*.

The article also sees Strummer talking movingly about his brother, who committed suicide when Strummer was seventeen. Jones meanwhile asserts the continuing integrity of Keith Richards (or "Richard" as he was then more commonly known, as demonstrated by previous *s*-less references). The pictures accompanying the article showed the now long-haired Jones to be bearing an uncanny resemblance to his Rolling Stones guitar hero.

Notes: For "Joseph Mellors" read "John Mellor"

For "*The London Weekend Programme*" read "*The London Weekend Show*" —Ed.

IT'S AS IF THE Clash's "Police And Thieves" stage backdrop has suddenly transmogrified into moving 3-D.

The scene: the cobbled street down the side of the Glasgow Apollo. Round about midnight.

The dramatis personae: The Clash, fifty to sixty Clash fans, Clash drivers and security guys, an indeterminate number of members of the Glasgow constabulary.

The sound:

CR-U-N-C-H!!!

There it goes again: Paul Simonon impeccably street-cool despite the Johnsons royal-blue shot-silk suit and Scotch House scarlet cashmere sweater, sinking down on his DMs onto the damp cobbles in a perfect staccato frozen-frame sequence as the back of his neck becomes the object of a manic, self-brutalising, truncheon-waving charge by an anorak-clad plainclothes Glasgow cop.

It's a disgusting incident. Highly emotive, riddled with flashes and waves of fear and terror and shock.

There's a whole pattern of ironies binding this little scenario together: the Apollo bouncers, the police, even some of the kids outside the back of the theatre, all hating The Clash because The Clash threaten the basic status quo on which their hatred has been erected. As the plainclothes cops suddenly emerge, chain-weighted truncheons in hand, from the shadows, they stir up eerie images of battles between the forces of good and evil.

BACKSTAGE BEFORE the Apollo gig, a Glaswegian punk is haranguing Simonon. "You still doin' all that politics stuff? That's not music."

"It's not politics," Simonon replies, taking a hit from a bottle of Smirnoff vodka. "It's just the difference between right and wrong."

"Yeah. But a lot of punks don't understand the politics. They're just here for the music."

"Well," Simonon shakes his head, "I don't understand it either. I just know what's right and wrong. Like closing this place—that's wrong."

There's something horribly appropriate in The Clash being the last rock band ever to play the Glasgow Apollo—always (in)famous for having some of the best rock audiences and the most psychotic bouncers in the UK—before it's turned into a bingo hall.

More than any other band, The Clash really do *care*—no, not care, *love*—their audiences. And, by extension, their fellow-men, though maybe that's another matter.

Anyway, the bouncers, apparently, have long been standing by for this night.

Tonight's the night, Jimmy, when they get their own back on the kids. "Here!" One of them proudly pulls up his vest to show the band's 'personal', Steve English. "This scar's from the David Bowie show. And this one's from The Faces. And this" (he shows a thick welt across his belly) "is from the last time The Clash played here."

The instant the band hit the stage it's like the Apocalypse is upon us and performing live in the stalls. Pogoing kids being dragged to the back of the hall and having the shit kicked out of them . . . Pogoing kids having the shit kicked out of them in front of the stage . . . "I'M SICK OF BLOOD. I'M SICK OF FUCKIN' BLOOD." Joe Strummer backs off from the mike and shakes his head to himself after pleading with the bouncers and kids to stop attempting to dismember each other.

They do stop. A little bit. But there are still obscene sights like a bouncer with shoulder-length hair diving head-first off the front of the orchestra pit onto the heads of the audience . . . .

As he's coming off the stage, one of the bouncers is waiting in the wings for Joe. Whisky-breathed, he leers six inches away from Strummer's face: "Ah'm gonna have y-e-e-ew."

The word is that the bouncers are intending to come up to the dressing-room to tear the band apart limb from limb. They are detained, however, by a young lady whom the theatre management have thoughtfully hired to stand on the stage and remove her clothes and do clever tricks with bottles.

Meanwhile, the band, Strummer with a bottle of lemonade in his right hand, head for the car that's parked just a few yards away from the stage-door.

As soon as they're out the door Joe is screamed at by kids who'd been kicked out of the theatre by bouncers. "Why'd you no' do anything to help us?" berates a guy who was beaten on and kicked out for pogoing during the first number. "Ye're jes' big egoed pop stars," snarls another.

Strummer, who'd been in tears after the gig over the way the fans had been treated, swears back and exasperatedly flings his bottle of lemonade onto the road. Instantly his arms are grabbed by two uniformed cops who've appeared from nowhere. As he's dragged out into the road, both uniformed and plainclothes cops appear to emerge from every crack in the pavement.

Simonon moves in to attempt to drag Strummer free . . . which is where you came in.

Topper Headon is chased up the road and manages to slip away and get back up into the dressing-room where Bernie Rhodes, the band's manager, is entertaining an American promoter who maintains he's never seen *anything* like the scenes he's just witnessed inside the theatre.

Mick Jones is dragged away in a state of total shock by some fans, who smuggle him through the prowl-car filled streets and back to the band's hotel . . .

STRUMMER, ONE of his brothel creeper laces replaced with a guitar string, and Simonon spend the night in the cells. "The people inside," says Strummer later, "the people up for drinking and nicking, they really treated us great. Giving us dog-ends and stuff."

A certain new wave spirit is maintained by the arrested punk fans spending much of the night singing chorus after chorus of "The Prisoner", the B-side of "(White Man) In Hammersmith Palais".

Contrary to the fears of those waiting for the pair back at the hotel, neither Joe nor the bassist have too rough a time of it down the police station—although as Joe points out, "Just as we were leaving for the last time one of the cops on the door said to the one in charge of us, 'How come you didn't beat them up? Are you reformed or something?'

"So I suppose they could've done that. But it never really seemed on the cards."

The magistrates court where the pair appear the next morning—both are on breach of the peace charges, with Simonon also charged with something like "attempting to free a prisoner"—reeks of austere, tiled Scottish Calvinism.

After a whole troop of casualties—crippled eighty-year-old drunks, 18-year-old hookers—have been led before the magistrate for him to sharpen his wit on, Strummer, appearing under his real name of Joseph Mellors, is called.

So authentic is Strummer's quite classic Brando slouch—head to one side, left lower lip hanging open, hands thrust deep in the pockets of his semi-drape jacket—that the real Gorbals heavies on the front bench of the visitors gallery turn round and nudge each other respectfully.

"Do you understand the charge against you?" demands the clerk of the court.

"Yeah," snarls Joe.

"Yeah what?" interrupts the magistrates.

"Yeah, sir," Joe snaps back sullenly.

"What is the name of your group?" enquiries the magistrate.

"Vuh Clash," Joe enunciates proudly.

"How appropriate," titters the magistrate, just like he's seen them do it in court-room scenes at the movies, too.

Both Strummer and Simonon whose appearance is something of a replay of Joe's, plead guilty. (Hey Joe, how come Paul pleaded guilty when he was quite obviously innocent? "Cos I told him to. So we could get on to Aberdeen".)

Joe is fined £25, whilst Paul, who must be especially punished for going to the assistance of a friend, has to cough up £45.

As each leaves the court to pay their fines, the hard man poses are dropped and first Joe, then Paul, beams the kind of broad smirk that the bad kids in class always used to have on tap for walking back to their desks after they'd just been slippered in front of the whole form.

In the street outside the court Strummer turns to Simonon and grins: "Maybe it was a mistake calling this tour 'Clash On Parole'."

ALTHOUGH HE BELIEVES himself to have "trouble with words" and had equal difficulty adding up, Clash bassist Paul Simonon is actually far more articulate than the average rock musician.

Like guitarist and group founder Mick Jones, Simonon spent the early years of his childhood in Brixton, South London. Also like Jones, the bassist is the product of a broken marriage—although both would appear to present strong arguments for the single parent family.

In fact, Simonon tells me, it was because his father was always looking for some place to dump him for a few days that Paul became interested in art.

Sent out to stay with a painter friend of his dad's in East Acton when he was about seven, Paul waited until the artist had gone out one day and then sat down with a book of paintings by Matisse and copied them all out in pencil. "After a while," he tells me, "you find you can like draw a woman with just one flowing line."

Sitting in his Earls Court flat following a secret pre-tour warm-up gig in Fulham, Simonon recalls how he first came to join the band.

Mick Jones and Generation X bassist Tony James were attempting to get the London SS out of the rehearsal studio and onto some kind of stage, when Simonon turned up one day from the exclusive Byam Shaw art school in Holland Park, to which he had a scholarship, and, as a perfect David Bowie lookalike, auditioned for the role of lead singer by singing the words "I'm a roadrunner, I'm a roadrunner" over and over for ten minutes until he was requested to stop.

Later, Jones looked him up again and told him that if he wanted to be the bass player in a new group he was forming then he (Jones) would teach him.

Since taking up the bass and joining The Clash, Simonon feels his drawing and painting have suffered. "But then," he says, pouring me out a cup tea, "I'm getting better on the bass all the time. I just want to transfer that simplicity from drawing and painting to bass-playing; to say an incredible amount with just one flowing line of notes just like Leonardo used to paint."

Leonardo Da Vinci, in fact, is one of Paul Simonon's major influences. All he wanted to do when he went to the Byam Shaw was to learn how to draw cars and tower-blocks "in the style of Leonardo". Going into the bed-room of his flat to get me a Clash tour poster, he shows me one of his paintings, a stark, sinister car dump with (almost a Clash cliche) the Westway as background.

Simonon learnt his bass technique by playing along with The Ramones, the Pistols and reggae records. Although a skinhead in his early teens, he claims he never actually got into their field sport of Pakki-bashing, though he didn't blanch at going thieving down Pakistani supermarkets.

West Indians, though, were viewed very differently. "When I was at school in South London I used to always want to be mates with the hardest kids in school. So I could get to figure 'em out. And most of those guys tended to be black.

"Anyway, I used to hate all that Deep Purple and Hawkwind stuff and just listen to reggae 'cos I was a skinhead. Those reggae records really used to say a lot to me. Some of them really meant quite a lot."

As an English bassist who doesn't stick himself away back by the amps but chooses instead to move and dance about by the mike, Simonon is something of an iconoclast. And that's just for starters: "I want to able to stick the bass behind my neck and play it like Jimi Hendrix played the guitar. Really elevate its status. Show people all the possibilities that it has in its simplicity."

He puts a Rothmans between his lips, flicks his Zippo lighter but holds it, flaming, in front of him without lighting the cigarette. "The last couple of years," he muses, "have been like being born again.

"Although I did always believe in doing the best in everything that I did . . . Even if it was only carrying carpets."

AH YES, THAT CLASH Pursuit Of Excellence that is the prime reason for my being at Simonon's . . .

Simonon, in fact, is about to play me the rough tapes of some of the new material The Clash have recorded for their next LP, the record for which the group have been in the studios laying down tracks since last summer.

After the slightly abortive alliance with Lee Perry—apparently whilst they wanted Scratch to give them a reggae production, the Upsetter himself was anxious to learn how to get a 'punk' sound—the band spent some months working on their own, though mainly only in the rehearsal studio, until the sudden appearance at the beginning of this year of one Sandy Pearlman, Witchfinder General for Blue Oyster Cult.

The introduction of the American Pearlman into the Clash camp can be seen as just one pointer to the fact that The Clash have now indubitably transcended 'punk'—in its musical rather than social definition—and become A Rock Band.

Not just any rock band, mind you. Indeed, it is probable that right now The Clash are the finest rock band in the world. The hassles of the past year—finding the right record producer, the constant frictions between the band and record company and, it appears, with their management too, plus Joe Strummer's hepatitis bout in the early months of this year and the band's regular run-ins with the law—all these troubles appear to have enriched the band with new inner strength and righteous power.

Whatever, it's fitting that the band should have cut a track entitled "Last Gang In Town"—because that really does seem to be how The Clash see themselves. "We're the only one left," Mick Jones tells me, though he'll later qualify that by offering a fairly substantial list of other outfits who are trying to remain true to what he sees as the essential spirit of rock'n'roll.

Being on tour with The Clash, though, you do gradually begin to see the band as they seem to see themselves—or certainly as Jones and Strummer view it: like Peckinpah's vision of the Western outlaw in *The Wild Bunch*, the loners whose high moral sense is one of the last relics of another time.

Except that in The Clash's case they are not anachronisms but the forerunners of better times. The advance guards, the emissaries of the New Age when Babylon's flaky hold on rock music (and on life) will finally fall . . .

THE CLASH now appear to be approaching the future from firm foundations.

Although none of them has been as big a hit as it should have been, The Clash have put out a trio of classic singles in the subversive "Complete Control", their very own group anthem in "Clash City Rockers" and now the near-epic 'ballad' "(White Man) In Hammersmith Palais", probably the best single of 1978 so far.

Of course, had "Capital Radio" had an official release you could have chalked that up as *four* classic singles . . . but the band decided to give it away free instead. Still, Jah was probably quite happy about that.

Besides, "Capital Radio", along with "Complete Control", is being included on the U.S. release of the band's first LP. American CBS are finally beginning to wise up and, though it seems unlikely that anyone there fully understands what they're dealing with, they do at least see that The Clash are capable of earning them a large amount of money.

Listen, there is a lot of magic going on in the rough tapes Simonon plays me. All the indications are that when The Clash do finally release their second album it will be a rock music landmark.

Particularly notable are:—

• "Safe European Home". Written after Strummer and Jones returned to England from their trip to Jamaica shortly before Christmas of last year. Originally the lyrics were some fifty lines long, now shortened to twenty. (Much of the material the band have recorded was written, incidentally, whilst the pair were tucked away in their room at the Pegasus Hotel, Kingston, a matter to which we will return later. Topper Headon, incidentally, claims that they didn't just do a *bit* of writing whilst out in JA, but that the band's songwriting duo actually turned out some two and a half albums' worth of tunes.)

• "Guns On The Roof". The first Clash number to be co-authored by all the band. Details the Simonon/Headon pigeon-shooting incident, of which both Mick Jones and I heartily disapprove.

• "Stay Free". A Mott The Hoople-like anthem written and sung entirely by Jones, about the gang he was in at school. A great, stirring number that could be a Top Five single hit were it not for the number of four-letter words.

• "Tommy Gun". An uptempo rocker, as they were once described, that is fast becoming an onstage fave. None of the lyrics seem decipherable.

Other titles? "Julie's In The Drug Squad", "Groovy Times Are Here Again", "Scrawl On The Bathroom", "One Emotion" and the very excellent "Cheapskates".

It should not necessarily be assumed that any of these songs will be on the album, however.

JOURNEYING UP TO Glasgow from the Manchester gigs—in addition to the scheduled Sunday theatre date, The Clash also played a 'secret' gig at Rafters Club the following day—Mick Jones and I have the choice of either a very cramped car or the wonder of British Rail InterCity.

As Jah has specially delayed the Royal Scot by nearly two hours, we pick it up at Preston three minutes after disembarking from the commuter train that brought us from Manchester.

This ensures that we arrive at the hotel in Glasgow at *exactly* the same minute as the rest of the band, thereby dismissing manager Bernie Rhodes' taunt that Jones was only travelling this way to be 'flash', and that he would inevitably cause that evening's show to be delayed.

The group founder, Jones, like Simonon and Strummer, is a product of the English art school system.

While the rhythm section, and particularly the bassist, provide the truly primal punk aspects of The Clash, the central core of the group's being appears to emanate from Jones, with Strummer operating as an external expression of that soul. (It is interesting to note that although Strummer and Simonon are both fire signs—Leo and Sagittarius respectively—both Jones and Headon are Cancers, a water sign. Though logically one might expect the water to cancel out the fire, it seems reasonable to surmise that that indefinable warm tension within The Clash is a direct result of this astrological chemistry.)

Settling back in the empty dining-car which we've found, Jones crushes an empty Coke can in his right hand and soliloquises on his craft. "Rock'n'roll really is an art form—the most immediate there is, the most vital in terms of reaching out to the masses.

"But maybe one day if this all becomes dissatisfying I might go back to painting. Though it's one of the most introverted existences there is.

"Every morning when you get up and go and look at what you've done the previous day, in those moments you almost have to examine every aspect of your life. And if you're a painter—or an artist of any sort, come to that—then it's a full-time existence.

"I've no patience with people who claim to be artists and then just talk about it. Just get on with it: whatever you're doing."

Sandy Pearlman, Jones tells me, just appeared to "arrive" one day. "There's definitely some inner magic circle—whether conscious or otherwise—within rock'n'roll. We've encountered it enough times already to be certain of that. People seem to have been *sent* to see us, to tell us we're on the right path, to tell us to keep it up.

"I think Pearlman definitely saw in us all the possibilities of that *black* side of rock'n'roll. He immediately seemed to see in us another possibility for what he really wanted to do with the Blue Oyster Cult. He knows the Cult don't really do it. And he knows we know it, too."

Working with Pearlman began to appear something like the Grand Quest. Which it was/is as far as the U.S. division of CBS is concerned: The Quest For A Hit Album.

As the producer has laboured in Island's Basing Street studio until six every morning, making the band go through as many as twenty takes of each track, executives from CBS in New York have flown in to check out the progress. As the tapes have been played back to these upwardly mobile young men, it has sometimes been necessary for all four members of The Clash to be present in order to have enough people coughing and dropping books on the floor when particularly subversive or obscene lyrics came through the speakers.

Towards the end of the sessions, Pearlman became increasingly anxious over leaving what it seems he had begun to regard as Sandy's Perfect Studio Album in the hands of the band for the final mixing—particularly as they'd already been bitching about the cleanliness of the sound and expressing a desire to murk it up somewhat.

Matters reached something of a head shortly before Pearlman flew back to the States just prior to the tour. At a Blue Oyster Cult party thrown by CBS, Topper Headon placed a large cake on the head of the wife of Blue Oyster Cult's "gnome guitarist" Buck Dharma. Unfortunately the cake somehow slipped and splattered all over the good lady's head, with the result that several Cult roadies were on the brink of tearing Topper to pieces.

Not so Pearlman, however. *He* knew who was the *real* culprit. "He turned to me and said, 'You put the eye on him, didn't you? You made him do that, didn't you?'" grins a somewhat bemused Mick Jones.

THE ROCK AGAINST Racism festival in Hackney once again appeared to put The Clash in a position of conflict with other bands.

"We said we didn't *want* to top that bill." Jones shakes his head. "We just wanted to be part of it.

"And then backstage there were all these numbers going down with Tom Robinson's management—and someone turned the power down on us and made sure the PA wasn't working properly.

"But," he nods with a smile, "when we went onstage the sun started shining, so obviously the forces must have been with us.

"However, there are so many groups who do treat their fans as if they're complete rubbish. I can't think of many groups at all who really still care.

"Who is there? Well, we haven't given up. Neither have The Slits either. Nor Generation X. I certainly don't think John Rotten's given up . . . Nor Jimmy Pursey . . . Actually, I don't think Keith Richard ever gave up really. Mick Jagger certainly did, though."

We talk for a few minutes about the new material. Joe had told me that the anthem-like new number, "Stay Free", was about a friend of Jones' whom I'd met on several occasions in his role as dilettante journalist.

"It's not just about him," the guitarist says. "It's about all my gang in Brixton. That guy's the lucky one—he's escaped.

"Two of the others both work in butchers' shops and are in the National Front. Twenty-three and they're in the Front.

"I don't not talk to them because of that, though. I go and see them. Show them what *I've* done. Show them the possibilities.

"You know," he free-associates, "it seems to me there are only three types of possible relationships: master-pupil, or pupil-master, or—and this is the really rare one that I've had about twice—a one-to-one relationship where you both help each other. That's the one to quest for, isn't it?

"Actually, I've been reading a lot about orgone energy lately. I've suddenly started realising that all of these bands who are into pulling loads of girls backstage obviously can't be fulfilling their full potential when they're performing.

"Mind you," he admits, "all of this band are a right bunch of studs. I was the only one who slept on his own last night.

"But we *do* try and treat them with respect. In some ways we're probably the first group to ever do that. And it's quite difficult: making them realise that you really *are* a human being is something of a necessary strain in the job. It's quite understandable, though. When I first met musicians I never saw them as just people.

"But I think a lot of people are keeping their eyes on us. Waiting for it to crack. So it can't, of course.

"Listen, somewhere we played the other day there was some girl showing us the bruises this other band had given her.

"I mean, where's that at?"

ALMOST EXACTLY twelve hours later Mick and I are sitting in his room at the Albany Hotel in Glasgow, drinking whisky and smoking and recovering from the police aggro that's ensured neither Joe nor Paul will be using their rooms tonight.

Mick, who has been unfairly criticised for being a poseur by people who don't seem to understand that a certain dedication to looking sharp and stylish has always been an integral aspect of rock 'n' rolling, demonstrates a vision all too rare among rock 'n' rollers.

"You know when Joe was going over the top a bit in the dressing room tonight?" he asks through tight lips. "Well, the first reason that he could offer for those kids getting hurt in the Apollo was that it was all because of his giant ego, all because of his obsessive need to appear onstage.

"Except that it's not that at all. Totally the reverse, in fact.

"I sometimes really do wonder if someone hasn't set out to get us.

"But then, everytime you start thinking that maybe the answer is not to play at all, I start noticing all these strange things which we can't put down to just coincidence. Like the train today, or talking about that guy from *Melody Maker* and then he walks through the door.

"Coincidence, maybe. But there's too many of them. It really does seem sometimes like there's someone out there caring for us.

"Joe understands all that, too. That's why it really is something of a strain sometimes. Like living out your destiny everyday."

IN EIGHT DAYS I see The Clash play six gigs—two of them, in Fulham and at Rafters in Manchester, totally unscheduled and slotted in the day before the gig because the band found they had the time and the facilities to play.

The Rafters gig is notable not only for not being sold out ("Not only is it a return to playing club dates, but a return to playing club dates that aren't even sold out—makes sure you keep your perspective," says Jones), but also for a certain drama involving Topper Headon and a girl—a situation that puts him in a position where he is forced to decide between his emotions and his loyalties to the group.

"He's beginning to understand the full extent of his responsibilities," says Mick Jones as, fortified by half a bottle of vodka, the drummer tapes the hideous blisters on his hands that drumming on the tour has already caused him and drags himself out onto the stage.

Replacing Terry Chimes after the first LP had been completed, Headon joined The Clash just in time for the White Riot tour in the spring of last year. A karate freak—in Manchester Strummer spends his last sixteen quid in the HMV shop on a Bruce Lee import that he knows Topper ought to have—his musical pedigree includes having played with Pat Travers.

He now seems a totally integrated member of the band.

The vibe at the Clash theatre dates is akin to what it once seemed only The Faces were capable of attaining—a warm, positive empathy between performer and audience in which no one person's contribution is any more or any less vital than anyone else's. Except that The Faces only attained that level on about one in every ten gigs—and beneath that superficial empathy there always seemed to exist a subtly disguised contempt for their audience.

The Clash get up there every night. Moreover, their sound, which in the past has frequently been *erratic* to say the very least, has now been sorted out to an extent where you know this is a big league rock band you're witnessing and not some mere experiment in anarchic creative situations.

The set is about 50/50 old and new material—which, considering the paradoxically reactionary nature already evident in certain of the hardcore punk fans, is brave indeed.

And almost always it works.

After the first number—which I *think* is generally "Complete Control", although that might be complete mental aberration—you get (not necessarily in this order) "Tommy Gun", "Bang Bang" (featuring Mick Jones' Ron Wood-like runs across the stage), "Capital Radio", the splendid "Stay Free", a "Police And Thieves" that frequently segues into a verse of "Blitzkrieg Bop", plus the one that really seems to confuse them, "When Johnny Comes Marching Home". The Clash also play "Cheapskates" and "London's Burning" and "White Riot" (generally as the encore) and "Janie Jones" and "Clash City Rockers" and, of course, the superb "(White Man) In Hammersmith Palais". Plus several others that I've temporarily forgotten.

It's no wonder really that the kids at the front always seem into trashing the hall. The chemical fusion onstage is producing near-nuclear possibilities. After all, all influences duly considered, The Clash really do produce the best, the warmest, the most involving, the most enjoyable rock'n'roll shows I've ever seen.

Indeed, there were even rash moments during the quite magnificent Aberdeen gig when I start hallucinating that The Clash really were the '70s Beatles.

ON THE WAY BACK to the Piccadilly Hotel in Manchester after Jones and Strummer had been out scoring some sounds—Jones had bought cassettes of Peter Tosh's "Legalise It", Al Green's "Let's Stay Together", Neil Young's "On The Beach" and Randy Newman's "Little Criminals"— we pass a piece of Manchester United graffiti which, via an intelligent usage of paint, has transmuted into MU . . . NF.

"About the best piece of art-work they'll ever manage," snarls Strummer sibilantly through the gap in his front teeth.

A couple of hours later Mick Jones, Mary (the fan-club secretary, who's distraught at having only been given £15 by the Clash's management to form the band's appreciation society), and I are sitting up in Joe's room watching a highly emotive *World In Action* expose on the puerile macho fantasies of the Front, when a slightly tense version of the Strummer hip rockabilly gunslinger strolls in.

He stands scowling at the programme for maybe two or three minutes.

"Did you talk to Bernie about all these problems with the fan-club?" enquires Jones, as Mary disappears into the bathroom.

In a sudden spasm of rage, Joe takes a penalty kick at the wastepaper basket, a cassette just misses my head, and the band's onstage frontman storms out, followed shortly after by Jones who cools him down and discovers that the reason Joe's uptight is because he's been told he's going to have problems getting kids in to the Rafters gig for nothing.

As a matter of fact, this Strummer incident is somewhat atypical—although, in typical Leonine manner, he goes over the top a couple of times more in the next few days. In the Glasgow Apollo dressing-room he grabs by the throat a fan who is berating him for not having done more to stop the bouncers (this is perhaps a salutary lesson for the fan: later it is he who leads Mick Jones through the streets away from the police). But the days when those close to the band would tell you that "the real problem in The Clash is Joe Strummer", the days when Joe would be found lying drunk in the gutter outside Dingwalls with rainwater washing into his mouth, now seem to be over.

The occasional losses of control on the road are purely due to The Pressure, mon.

In the past, though, as Joe himself admits, they were down to "the demon drink"—a problem which was solved when his bout of hepatitis earlier in the year obliged him to lay off the booze altogether for the next six months if he didn't want a permanently weakened liver.

"It doesn't half make you lose your friends, though, not going down the pub," he laughs. He also vigorously denies that the hepatitis was due to any ingestion of impure stimulating powders. Cocaine he considers to be "complete muck. If you snort coke you're in on your own. You don't *want* anybody and you don't *need* anybody. Which is a *horrible* place to be."

Joe has a very powerful aura about him.

Onstage, he *never* smiles. This hard man stage persona, like the pre-hepatitis love of booze, may well be an extension of the belligerent Scotsman within him. His mother is Scottish and he claims that the sound of bagpipes renders him most emotional. (Jones, incidentally, is also a half-Celt—his mother is Welsh whilst his father is Jewish.)

He is also, as are all The Clash, a very sensitive and perceptive bloke, though not necessarily a near-intellectual in the same way that Jones certainly is.

When he was about 18 (he's 25 now) and just getting set to leave the minor public school in Epsom to which his parents had sent him (and where they told him he wasn't "university material", which is how he ended up going to Central Art School in London for a year before deciding it was a waste of time), Joe's brother committed suicide.

Although he comments no further than that "it happened at a pretty crucial time in my life," it seems certain that this event had a significant bearing in creating Joe Strummer, ally of the powers of positivism and light.

His brother, 18 months older than Joe, was a member of the National Front and was obsessed with the occult. In every way he seems to have been Joe's opposite. "He was such a nervous guy that he couldn't bring himself to talk at all. Couldn't speak to anyone.

"In fact, I think him committing suicide was a really brave thing to do. For him, certainly. Even though it was a total cop-out."

HE LEANS BACK on the bed-head in his Aberdeen hotel room. It's two in the morning and we're both pretty done in. All the time, he tells me, underlining what Mick had said earlier in the day, he keeps getting signs—whether in the form of actual emissaries or less tangible incidents—that he, and this band, are on the right path.

"I go in for that mumbo-jumbo a lot myself," he smiles. "Like, when me and Mick went to Jamaica I was quite convinced we were going to die. At Heathrow someone dropped this ketchup all over the floor in front of us—and then we get there and we're driving through Trenchtown and I glance up at this wall and just see this one word: BLOOD.

"Mind you, nothing happened at all like that, and when I got back I thought, 'What a lot of time I wasted worrying.'"

Jamaica, mind you, was not a particularly pleasant experience for the pair, who went over to JA kitted out as hard-line punks. Instead of welcoming them, black Jamaicans were calling them "white pigs" in the street. Unable to find *anyone* connected with the music scene—they spent their last Jamaican dollars on an abortive cab ride looking for Lee Perry's place—they stuck themselves away in their hotel rooms with a load of ganja and got down to writing songs.

Didn't they think they might look somewhat provocative?

"Sure," Strummer smirks. "We fuckin' went out on the streets dressed to the nines. We thought we'd show 'em where it was at." He laughs. "Cos they all like looking sharp, too.

"Boy, we got some funny looks. Sometimes when it got a bit heavy we'd pass ourselves off as merchant seamen."

Of course, one of the contradictions within The Clash is that all the warmth and positivism are hemmed in by overtly aggressive imagery— and here I'm thinking of the "White Man" gun logo, the militaristic stage backdrops, even the song titles: "Tommy Gun", "Guns On The Roof" . . .

"It keeps coming up, doesn't it?" Strummer nods. "I think it's just a reflection of what's out there. I really do think we *are* a good force, but we're dealing with the world and those images are just a reflection of what it is."

Strummer first recalls singing "When Johnny Comes Marching Home" as a kid in singing lessons at school. Rather than being about the American Civil War, as is the original, The Clash's version is subtitled "The English Civil War".

"It's already started," says Joe matter-of-factly. "Sure it has. There's people attacking Bengalis with clubs and firing shotguns in Wolverhampton . . .

"What really gets me is it's *so-o-o* respectable to be right-wing. All those big geezers in the Monday Club will probably switch over to the Front if they start making any headway. That's what happened in Germany—they turned round and said, 'Oh yeah, I've been a Nazi all along, mate.'

"It's a pity when the skins go out on the rampage, that they don't go down the House of Commons and smash *that* place up.

"Any time there's any urban disturbances they always occur on the poor areas of town. Why don't they happen in the rich areas? More things would get smashed up if they did.

"If it's in London it's always in either the East End or in Notting Hill. Or it's in Belfast or in Londonderry—they're like bomb-sites, the slums out there.

"You know, I was in Notting Hill the other day and I was walking along and I saw that all of Tavistock Crescent is gone. And they used to seem to really know how to build houses fit for human beings to live in in those days.

"I mean, round by Westbourne Park Road these real egg-boxes have suddenly sprung up from behind the corrugated iron. Which is just brutal. I'd like to blow the head off the guy who designed those—or, better still, force him to live in it."

DESPITE HIS serious intent, Strummer agrees that many Clash listeners seem to miss out on the humour in their lyrics. I tell him that there are certain tracks on the first album that make me burst out laughing everytime I hear them.

"Yeah," he smiles. "I think some of it's really hysterical stuff. We *all* used to burst out laughing too, when we first started playing them . . ."

Mick Jones has told me that he finds it a strain when people try to look on the band as evangelists . . .

"Yeah, that's a bore. Just a load of old crap. I think you've always just got to be grateful for what you've achieved and then just try and achieve some more."

But why do you think you've got to that position where people think The Clash have The Answer?

"We give 'em good stuff. That's all. There aren't that many other groups around doing it. Sham's doin' it. So's The Slits and Siouxsie."

So look: it's nearly two years on from when the band first started. How does it feel now?

"I could've told you the answer without hearing the question. *We're a good group.* That's the only answer.

"And when you're in a good group you feel good."

CLASH: WHAT, THEM AGAIN? FRAID SO. NO APOLOGIES . . . ON THE ROAD FAX

Nick Kent | December 2, 1978 | *New Musical Express* (UK)

This *NME* on-the-road report is a happier affair than the Chris Salewicz article of five months previously. After a period in which the Clash had thought, Jones admits herein, that they were commercially finished, their new album *Give 'em Enough Rope* had taken them to number two in the UK chart. Although its lyrics attracted allegations of self-aggrandizement and glamorization of violence, and although history hasn't adjudged it as worthy as the albums that preceded and succeeded it, at the time . . . *Rope* made a point by proving that the band's working-class tableaux could be given plush settings without losing grit and authenticity.

Early champion Caroline Coon was now holding the Clash management reins following a bust-up with Bernard Rhodes.

Notes: Ian Penman was an *NME* journalist with a notoriously impenetrable prose style.

For "The 101ers" read "The 101'ers" —Ed.

JUST WHAT the world needs—another *NME* piece capturing The Clash On The Road Part 128, you say?

Well yes and no, the writer demurs. Nothing lengthy in the Bangsian style of extended narrative, nor is there any grim detailing of spiralling trauma like Chris Salewicz depicted in his article penned during The Clash's last tour of Britain.

The tee-shirts printed for this current fling read in simple white lettering on a black background—*"The Clash—The Sort It Out Tour"* and although the person actually wearing the garment, a newly drafted Welsh roadie, will claim otherwise, that particular statement of intent is, it seems, being adhered to both practically and ideologically with a fair degree of success.

The gig I caught at Manchester's Apollo Theatre apparently fell into a linear focus for, as far as the opening stretch of a tour can gauge, The Clash's particular working policy is successfully being implemented.

Certainly as a musical entity, the band are in ripe old form, the current set kicking off with Safe European Home" and seguing through a strong rendition of The Bobby Fuller Four's "I Fought The Law" and "Jail Guitar Doors". It manages to take in most of the "Rope" album with its sturdy detours like "Police And Thieves" denoting a more varied tempo allocation until the set's climax with a brace of the first album's little classics; basically "Janie Jones", "Bored With The USA" and "White Riot".

"It's that 'White Riot' that gets 'em up every time," growls one of the roadies after the set's conclusion, which tonight, like every other time, draws the front row of kids onto the stage itself on instinct—as though they were being physically impelled there by some perverse form of suction.

It's the band's expressed desire that the kids who've amassed on stage for the closing minutes of the set are allowed to remain there that appears to be causing dissension amongst The Clash road crew. And Caroline Coon, the band's new manager, will state this dilemma diplomatically to a surprised Joe Strummer at the hotel bar later; "They don't feel as though they're doing their job properly."

Mick Jones, however, baulks at this latest problem and remarks jaundicedly about the roadies' apparent suppressed functions.

And so it goes. They still spit at bands up North, by the way—something I hadn't witnessed for a while and thus considered obsolete—and Strummer gets a good drenching for his troubles while Jones gamely sports a large white globule of phlegm on his current lacquered-back haircut.

"What can you do? Tell 'em to stop? Of course, it's repellent. We've always said that," says Jones philosophically.

But after all, it's better than that very real cut-throat violence that the band were having to face up to at virtually every gig on the last tour.

WHEN our own Chris Salewicz ran into the band on that particular trek (in Glasgow) earlier this year the report he filed was a vivid, frightening documentary of a band totally out of control of its audience and becoming prey to all manner of random violence.

It turns out that Salewicz wasn't over-estimating anything either, as both Jones and Strummer reminisce over the daily trials and tribulations of that last escapade.

Jones, for example, recalls "breaking down in tears all the time" at what was going on around him—events which included a near-fatality (a personal roadie almost "offed" by Strummer in a car accident) and a cocaine bust for the guitarist himself.

"Two years ago we did the band's first interview," recalls Jones re the latter charge. "On Janet Street-Porter's *London Weekend Programme,* it was, and me being all young and naive, I blamed bands taking too many drugs for the great mid-70s drought in rock. I recall saying it really well. And a year or so later, I found myself doing just as many drugs as them!

"Y'know, taking drugs as a way of life, to feel good in the morning, to get through the day. And it's still something I'm getting over right now."

Now, however, instead of cocaine, or more pertinent to this band, amphetamines ("I was so into speed," states Jones, "I mean I don't even recall making the first album"), The Clash appear to be adhering strictly to a steady dosage of vitamins for maintaining energy.

Jones himself pinpoints the making of the second album as an important point of departure here. "It was really a question of me saying to myself, 'Well, do you really want to make a great album or what?' In which case, I knew that I had to be straight at least part of the time. Which I was."

The making of "Give 'Em Enough Rope" appears, from the outside anyway, to have been a period of much turmoil. Jones himself concurs by denoting just one of the pressures on the project from the internal hierarchy of CBS.

"It was at a point right in the middle of the mixing and Sandy Pearlman was getting this incredible rush of insecurity and sheer panic because CBS were calling him up and saying that the first mixes were of absolutely no substance. And me 'an Joe were having to do this whole number on our side, telling him that this effort represented absolutely his last shot at any kind of aesthetic success.

"Meanwhile, unbeknown to us, two geezers from CBS—Muff Winwood and Jeremy Ensall—were taking the tracks, doing their own fuckin' mixes and going back to CBS saying, Well look what we've done—it's much better than Pearlman's efforts'."

Finally, in order to placate the opposition, and keep their creation from being wrecked by extensive tampering, the band conceded to a deadline which they narrowly held together. The immediate result is a satisfied Mick Jones, who laughingly claims that he wouldn't even mind seeing Pearlman on a social level again.

"His big thing is that he invented the word 'Heavy Metal'," Jones comments on Pearlman, again with tones of hilarity not entirely absent, before describing a fairly noxious aspect of the Blue Oyster Cult's one-time theorist which manifested itself through a desire to employ a somewhat ghoulish dwarf as a gofer.

"Joe and me had to really keep checkin' him over that. Like, keep on at him about this fuckin' guy being around and all."

TALK OF gofers moves perhaps a touch too coincidentally onto one of the primary Clash 'pressing issues' of the present moment, which equates itself into the little matter of former manager Bernie Rhodes becoming 'persona non grata' amongst the band members whom Rhodes himself claims he "took off the street".

The 'official' Clash line on this little chapter has the group democratically muttering "No hard feelings" as a display of good diplomacy in the face of the purportedly aggrieved Rhodes.

Indeed, the last 'official' interview I read with Messrs Strummer and Simonon—in *Melody Maker*, just before the onslaught of this latest tour—had the latter at least agreeing with Rhodes's "I-took-them-from-nothing" side of the story whilst also filling in details of the split by claiming that Rhodes's ideals had become redundant in the light of the band's progress and consequent need for better technology.

Mick Jones, however, allowed for some of the 'unofficial' essence to be sucked into print here.

The 'unofficial' side, mostly manifested through rumour-mongering, has several barbed pointers in the recounting of the latter days of the Clash-Rhodes pairing.

It was certainly a well-recounted story of the time that Malcolm McLaren, just before his interests were all-consumed by the latest Sid Vicious drama, had gotten in touch with Rhodes again and was buttering up his former partner-of-sorts by slyly informing him that The Clash had 'betrayed' Rhodes.

The McLaren Sex Pistols and Rhodes Clash aspect of the situation has always, apparently, been crucial. There was this terrible feeling—manifested implicitly in the very origin of McLaren and Rhodes's quarry would be immediately second-best to brother Malcolm's treasure.

Mick Jones was very aware of his feeling of being second-best at one time. He admits that The Clash were made to feel that, in the shade of the Pistols' all-pervading lustre, they were very much immediate runners-up.

He also admits that at the time—up until somewhere betwixt the creation of their two albums, Jones reckons—the seeds of dissention were force-fed by this awareness.

"There was this time when that feeling of being second-best was really getting to us. And, of course, Malcolm would help it along by throwing in some story like, oh Christ, there was this time when we heard that the Pistols had come over and nicked some of our gear. As a gesture of contempt, so to speak.

"So we'd immediately be up in arms . . . like, y'know, 'let's get 'em, let's go over to their rehearsal place and rip off their microphones', always something petty. Like there was this time—the first time—the Pistols actually slagged us off in print, in a *Melody Maker* interview, I think it was—so, right, we got off together and confronted John (Rotten) in a pub (laughs), and John was pretty shocked, probably because he saw how petty we were all becoming, fighting among ourselves, just stupid squabbling when there was a very real enemy out there probably laughing its head off." *(Ian Penman?—Ed.)*

Jones recalls that when the feeling of being 'second-best' to the Pistols suddenly lifted, "it didn't even matter anymore"—which he goes on to prove by expressing a kind of dolorous awe at the Pistols' greatness, and great pity at the way they came to career-termination.

However, it's dubious whether McLaren has ever gotten over this in-built feeling of superiority. It's a moot point, for example, that he thought of The Clash as an 'easy pickings' second division to the still intact Pistols.

Thus, last Christmas, when matters came to a head, it was 'assumed' that Paul Simonon would be available for transfer to Pistols-prominence, although the bassist was doubtless never asked about it.

The Clash, however, were later to make this position clear, when 'powers-that-be' (you only need to guess who) quite recently attempted to move Steve Jones into Mick Jones' Clash position.

"Yeah, that's all true," mutters Jones now, adding slyly: "Course I wasn't going to have any of that! And, more to the point, neither were the rest of the group. But yeah, there were all sorts of little undercover swaps being arranged."

Jones, though, had an advantage in securing a kind of advance knowledge relating to these dodgy activities, partly because he's no fool and partly because of all Clash members he was the first to encounter Rhodes & McLaren—when the latter was making tentative plans for the importing into England of one Richard Hell.

"Yeah, like just before The Clash there was this thing where Richard Hell was writing to Malcolm saying, 'Honest, I'm not a junkie, I really wanna come over to London.' So I was in line for that. Meanwhile, Malcolm or Bernie would be planning some new group or other and I'd be sent over to some rehearsal (laughs) . . . Like, there was a pool of us musicians that they'd have 'on tap', expecting us to form bands ultimately.

"At one point, me and Chrissie Hynde would be half-heartedly rehearsing away and Bernie would rush in and say, 'I've got a new idea. We'll call the band 'Big Girl's Underwear' or something like that."

Jones's involvement with The Clash project was more his own doing, however. After all, it was he who taught Simonon the rudiments of bass-playing—"for all of three days (laughs) . . . Which means Paul got pissed off after those three days and would go away and then return some days later to try again."

More pointedly, Jones—and Simonon—went after the services of Joe Strummer, then of The 101ers, a self-confessed pub rock band.

More pointedly, Jones—and Simonon—[*This sentence was repeated and text omitted in article as originally published —Ed.*] y'know, amongst the McLaren bunch, of thinking 'yeah, well' *they're* pub-rock—they're below us'. Whereas with Joe I could see he was a great performer saddled with a duff band."

THE WHOLE Bernie Rhodes subject is according to at least one source, currently a 'sub-judice' matter, which may account for the official 'no hard feelings' front. In his place are a posse of lawyers and former Release prime-mover and freelance journalist Caroline Coon who, as Paul Simonon's girlfriend appeared a fairly obvious choice as personal manager.

For her part, after just a handful of dates, it's hard to tell whether this move has been for the best, although brief chats with the roadcrew denote that Ms. Coon is quickly learning the practical day-to-day facts necessary for a manager's vocation.

In her favour, though, is the feeling of great togetherness noticeable on this current tour. Coming off at a time when the "Rope" album has literally bulleted in at a staggering "No 2" in the official album charts, this latter show of faith has had a noticeably confidence-building effect on a band who'd had to watch virtually single after single nose-dive into the bottom reaches of the Top 30 before disappearing from sight.

"We honestly thought it was virtually finished for us in terms of commercial force", Jones now admits, pinpointing the four previous singles' lack of success as chief demonstration to this feeling.

That added to the constant barrage of letters that seemed to hit paydirt in the columns of the various music papers, almost every week berating the latest petty Clash let-down until a little under a month ago, and one begins to get only the outline of the problems that have been pelted down from what appeared like some monstrous frowning deity on the band themselves, as though their name itself warranted such treatment.

Jones points to the sequence of events that simply naming a tour, say, seems to have sparked off. The last one, for example, boasting that "On Parole" sign, appeared to virtually supernaturally guarantee at least one bust.

So this time it's down to simply "sorting it out". And this The Clash may actually achieve at least a semblance of this time around. The halls still get packed out, and visually the band may look a little the worse for wear—particularly Strummer, whose teeth seem in terrible shape after being chipped and battered by a fan manhandling of the singer's mikestand.

Yet The Clash's philosophy, not to mention the broad design of a deep interlinking set of friendships that hold this band together against often brutal odds is succinctly hinted at by Mick Jones when he talks about the latest slag-off and its perpetrators, namely our own Messrs. Parsons and Burchill and their book *The Boy Looked At Johnny*, which attempts a brittle dissection of the band—based, The Clash maintain, mostly on half-truths and warped malice.

"It's like, ultimately, who cares? So, two more people think rock'n'roll's dead? So what? Should we all drop our guitars down and fall apart? It's like too many people are letting the negative aspects get to them, get them into some terminal form of depression.

"Fuck it, I get depressed just as much, but what can you do? 'Cos if you start shouting about the death of something, you're just copping out really. To me, it's like rock'n'roll is dead? Oh alright then. See you at the next gig."

CLASH: ANGER ON THE LEFT

Mikal Gilmore | March 8, 1979 | *Rolling Stone* **(US)**

Give 'em Enough Rope was not only a domestic revitalization, but constituted a product sufficiently glossy for the Clash's US label Epic—who had denied their lo-fi debut an American release—to put its weight behind it. (The debut would appear Stateside the following July—albeit with a tweaked tracklisting—after reputedly becoming the biggest-selling import in history.) Accordingly, in February 1979, the Clash took their proletarian, English-accented rock across the Atlantic.

Rolling Stone prepared for their arrival by dispatching a reporter to take in a London show and meet up with them. Mikal Gilmore found a band whose weariness with the UK's relentless discourse about whether they were living up to their ideals made them ready and willing to explore new markets.

The assumption that the Clash were political artists is somewhat brought into question by the disdain Strummer expresses herein for the Tom Robinson Band, a quartet doing well in the UK with a brand of Clash-inspired hard rock whose lyrics had a current-affairs specificity that the Clash's records, for all their posturing and street-level perspectives, almost always avoided.

Notes: For "the 101ers" read "the 101'ers"

For "Keith Levine" read "Keith Levene" —Ed.

"NEVER MIND that shit," says Joe Strummer, the thuggish-looking lead singer of the Clash, addressing some exultant kids yelling "Happy New Year" at him from the teeming floor of the Lyceum. "You've got your *future* at stake. Face front! Take it!"

In sleepy London town, during a murky Christmas week, rock & roll is being presented as a war of class and aesthetics. At the crux of that battle is a volcanic series of four Clash concerts—including a benefit for Sid Vicious—coming swift on the heels of the group's second album, *Give 'Em Enough Rope,* which entered the British charts at Number Two. Together with the Sex Pistols, the Clash helped spearhead the punk movement in Britain, along the way earning a designation as the most intellectual and political New Wave band. When the Pistols disbanded early last year, the rock press and punks alike looked to the Clash as the movement's central symbol and hope.

Yet, beyond the hyperbole and wrangle that helped create their radical myth, the Clash brandish hearty reputation as a rock & roll band that, like the Rolling Stones or Bruce Springsteen, must be seen to be believed. Certainly no other band communicates kinetic, imperative anger as potently as the Clash. When Nicky "Topper" Headon's single-shot snare report opens "Safe European Home" (a song about Strummer and lead guitarist Mick Jones' ill-fated attempt to rub elbows with Rastafarians in the Jamaicans' backyard), all hell breaks loose, both on the Lyceum stage and floor.

Like the Sex Pistols, the Clash's live sound hinges on a massive, orchestral drum framework that buttresses the blustery guitar work of Jones, who with his tireless two-step knee kicks looks just like a Rockettes' version of Keith Richards. Shards of Mott the Hoople and the Who cut through the tumult, while Strummer's rhythm guitar and Paul Simonon's bass gnash at the beat underneath. And Strummer's vocals sound as dangerous as he looks. Screwing his face up into a broken-tooth yowl, he gleefully bludgeons words, then caresses them with a touching, R&B-inflected passion.

Maybe it's the gestalt of the event, or maybe it's just the sweaty leather-bound mass throbbing around me, but I think it's the most persuasive rock & roll show I've seen since I watched Graham Parker rip the roof off a San Francisco nightclub almost two and a half years ago.

I try to say as much to a reticent Joe Strummer after the show as we stand in a dingy backstage dressing room, which is brimming with a sweltering mix of fans, press and roadies. Strummer, wearing smoky sunglasses and a nut-brown porkpie hat, resembles a roughhewn version of Michael Corleone. Measuring me with his wary, testy eyes, he mumbles an inaudible reply.

Across the room, Mick Jones and Paul Simonon have taken refuge in a corner, sharing a spliff. "You a Yank?" Jones asks me in a surprisingly delicate, lilting voice. "From 'ollywood? Evil place, innit? All laid back." According to the myth encasing this band, Jones, who writes nearly all of the Clash's music, is the band's real focal nerve, even though the austere Strummer writes the bulk of the lyrics. In the best Keith Richards tradition, the fans see Mick as a sensitive and vulnerable street waif, prone to dissipation as much as to idealism. Indeed, he looks as bemusedly wasted as anyone. I've ever met. He's also among the gentler, more considerate people I've ever spent time with.

But the next evening, sitting in the same spot, Mick declines to be interviewed. "Lately, interviews make me feel 'orrible. It seems all I do is spend my time answering everyone's charges—charges that shouldn't have to be answered."

The Clash *have* been hit recently with a wide volley of charges, ranging from an English rock-press backlash aimed at what the critics see as reckless politics, to very real criminal charges against Headon and Simonon (for shooting valuable racing pigeons) and Jones (for alleged cocaine possession). But probably the most damaging salvo has come from their former manager, Bernard Rhodes, who, after he was fired, accused the band of betraying its punk ideals and slapped them with a potentially crippling lawsuit. Jones, in a recent interview, railed back. "We're still the only ones true to the original aims of punk," he said. "Those other bands should be destroyed."

THE CLASH FORMED as a result of Joe Strummer's frustrations and Mick Jones' rock ideals. Both had been abandoned at early ages by their parents, and while Strummer (the son of a British diplomat) took to singing Woody Guthrie and Chuck Berry songs in London's subways for spare change during his late teens, Jones retreated into reading and playing Mott the Hoople, Dylan, Kinks and Who records. In 1975, he left the art school he was attending and formed London SS, a band that, in its attempt to meld a raving blend of the New York Dolls, the Stooges and Mott, became a legendary forerunner of the English punk scene.

Then, in early 1976, shortly after the Sex Pistols assailed London, Mick Jones ran into Strummer, who had been singing in a pub-circuit R&B band called the 101ers. "I don't like your band," Jones said, "but I like the way you sing." Strummer, anxious to join the punk brigade, cut his hair, quit the 101ers and joined Jones, Simonon (also a member of London SS), guitarist Keith Levine now a member of Public Image Ltd) and drummer Terry Chimes to form the Clash in June of 1976. Eight months later, under the tutelage of Bernard Rhodes, the Clash signed with CBS Records for a reported $200,000.

Their first album, *The Clash* (unreleased in America; Epic, the group's label stateside, deems it "too crude"), was archetypal, resplendent punk. While the Sex Pistols proffered a nihilistic image, the Clash took a militant stance that, in an eloquent, gutteral way, vindicated punk's negativism. Harrowed rhythms and coarse vocals propelled a foray of songs aimed at the bleak political realities and social ennui of English life, making social realism—and unbridled disgust—key elements in punk aesthetics.

But even before the first album was released, the punk scene had dealt the Clash some unforeseen blows. The punks, egged on by hysterical English press, began turning on each other, and drummer Chimes, weary of ducking bottles, spit and the band's politics, quit. Months passed before the group settled on Nicky Headon (also a member of Mick Jones' London SS) as a replacement and returned to performing. By that time, their reputation had swelled to near-messianic proportions.

When it was time for a new album, CBS asked Blue Oyster Cult producer Sandy Pearlman to check out the Clash's shows. "By a miracle of God," says Pearlman, "they looked like they believed in what they were doing. They were playing for the thrill of affecting their audience's consciousness, both musically and politically. Rock & roll shouldn't be cute and adorable; it should be violent and anarchic. Based on that, I think they're the greatest rock & roll group around." Mick Jones balked at first at the idea of Pearlman as their producer, but Strummer's interest prevailed. It took six months to complete *Give 'Em Enough Rope*, and it was a stormy period for all concerned. ("We knew we had to watch Pearlman," says Nicky Headon. "He gets too good a sound.")

But nowhere near as stormy as the album. *Give 'Em Enough Rope* is rock & roll's *State of Siege*—with a dash of *Duck Soup* for comic relief. Instead of reworking the tried themes of bored youth and repressive society, Strummer and Jones tapped some of the deadliest currents around, from creeping fascism at home to Palestinian terrorism. The album surges with visions of civil strife, gunplay, backbiting and lyrics that might've been spirited from the streets of Italy and Iran: "A system built by the sweat of the many/Creates assassins to kill off the few/Take any place and call it a courthouse/This is a place where no judge can stand." And the music—a whirl of typhonic guitars and drums—frames those conflicts grandly.

THE DAY AFTER THE Clash's last Lyceum show, I meet Joe Strummer and Paul Simonon at the Tate Gallery, an art museum. Simonon leads us on a knowledgeable tour of the gallery's treasures until we settle in a dim corner of the downstairs cafe for an interview.

We start by talking about the band's apparent position as de facto leaders of punk. Strummer stares into his muddy tea, uninterested in the idea of conversation, and lets Simonon take the questions. Probably the roughest-looking member of the group, with his skeletal face and disheveled hair, Simonon is disarmingly guileless and amiable. "Just because I'm up onstage," he says in rubbery English, "doesn't mean that I'm entitled to a different lifestyle than anyone else. I used to think so. I'd stay up all night, get pissed, party all the time. But you get cut off from the workaday people that way. I like to get up early, paint me flat, practice me bass. I see these geezers going off to work and I feel more like one of them."

But, I note, most of those same people wouldn't accept him. They're incensed and frightened by bands like the Clash.

Strummer stops stirring his tea and glowers around. "Good," he grunts. "I'm pleased."

This seems a fair time to raise the question of the band's recent bout with the British rock press. After *Give 'Em Enough Rope*, some of the band's staunchest defenders shifted gears, saying that the Clash's militancy is little more than a fashionable stance, and that their attitude toward terrorist violence is dangerously ambiguous. "One is never entirely sure just which side [the Clash] is supposed to be taking," wrote Nick Kent in *New Musical Express*. "The Clash use incidents . . . as fodder for songs without caring."

Strummer squints at me for a moment, his thoughtful mouth hemming his craggy teeth. "We're against fascism and racism," he says. "I figure that goes without saying. I'd like to think that we're subtle; that's what greatness is, innit? I can't stand all these people preaching, like Tom Robinson. He's just too direct."

But that ambiguity can be construed as encouraging violence.

"Our *music*'s violent," says Strummer. "We're not. If anything, songs like 'Guns on the Roof' and 'Last Gang in Town' are supposed to take the piss out of violence. It's just that sometimes you have to put yourself in the place of the guy with the machine gun. I couldn't go to his extreme, but at the same time it's no good ignoring what he's doing. We sing about the world that affects us. We're not just another wank rock group like Boston or Aerosmith. What fucking shit."

Yet, I ask, is having a record contract with one of the world's biggest companies compatible with radicalism?

"We've got loads of contradictions for you," says Strummer, shaking off his doldrums with a smirk. "We're trying to do something new; we're trying to be the greatest group in the world, and that also means the biggest. At the same time, we're trying to be radical—I mean, we never want to be *really* respectable—and maybe the two can't coexist, but we'll try. You know what helps us? We're totally suspicious of anyone who comes in contact with us. *Totally.* We aim to keep punk alive."

The conversation turns to the Clash's impending tour of America. "England's becoming claustrophobic for us," says Strummer. "Everything we do is scrutinized. I think touring America could be a new lease on life."

But the American rock scene—and especially radio—seems far removed from the world in flames that the Clash sing about. (While the Clash may top the English charts, they have yet to dent *Billboard*'s Top 200. "We admit we aren't likely to get a hit single this time around," says Bruce Harris of Epic's A&R department. "But *Give 'Em Enough Rope* has sold 40,000 copies and that's better than sixty percent of most new acts.") I ask if a failure to win Yankee hearts would set them back.

"Nah," says Strummer. "We've always got here. We haven't been to Europe much, and we haven't been to Japan or Australia, and we want to go behind the iron curtain." He pauses and shrugs his face in a taut grin. "There are a lot of other places where we could lose our lives."

Those may seem like boastful words, but I doubt that's how Strummer means them. Few bands have fought more battles on more fronts than the Clash, and maybe none with better instincts. Of course, it's doubtful that the American and British underclass—or the teenage middle class for that matter—are any more willing than the music industry to be shaken up as much as the Clash would like.

As producer Sandy Pearlman says: "No one's really very scared of punk, especially the record companies. They've sublimated all the revolutionary tendencies this is based on. The Clash see the merit in reaching a wider audience, but they also like the idea of grand suicidal gestures. We need more bands like *this* as models for tomorrow's parasites."

YES, IT'S STRUMMER IN THE CITY (BOILIN' RED HOT)

Charles Shaar Murray | June 30, 1979 | *New Musical Express* (UK)

They may not have been as political as the Tom Robinson Band, but that the Clash always saw themselves as more than just a rock band is evidenced by this feature, in which Joe Strummer talks about virtually everything but music.

The singer enthuses about playing benefit gigs, setting up alternative means by which to purvey music, and changing the finances of the recording industry.

Notes: The GLC was the Greater London Council.

Rudi Can't Fail was ultimately released as *Rude Boy*.

For "Ray Gant" read "Ray Gange" —Ed.

HOT TOWN! Strummer in the city: walks into the Kings Road pub that serves as his temporary local while he's staying in Fulham dead on time. Nine o'clock on nose: Dave Allen has time for precisely one and a half jokes before Joe arrives, one degree haggard but punkabilly sharp. A few things to clear up, a few ideas to kick around. A Guinness changes hands.

"I've got a few things to tell you but first I'll just get this out of the way," he begins. On his mind is the allegation made by Jah Wobble in Danny Baker's PiL outing a fortnight back to the effect that The Clash blew out their American tour because Public Image Ltd. refused to support them.

"Like Johnny says, there's two sides to every story. What really happened was that me and Mick were trying to cook up a good bill and we began noticin' that there was a similarity between PiL's set-up and our set-up.

"We'd both broken away from mentors and we were both manager-less groups who wanted to direct their own futures. So we just went down their house to see if they'd do the States with us. We said, 'We don't mind goin' on before if you wanna follow us.'

"We didn't mean for them to support us; we were thinkin' about an alternating headline. They said no because they were already planning their own Stateside tour. We didn't in the end, and neither did they.

"There's this bloke called Wayne who we work with in New York and who does our booking. I phoned him and said that we were gonna try and get PiL and he said, 'Yeah, that's a good idea'. When I called him back to say that they didn't wanna come he just said 'oh well' because we were working on a load of other ideas at the time.

"I don't know who's telling PiL things or from where they get their information, but I think someone's geein' 'em up a little.

"What do you think of that Buzzcocks-in-the-park thing? Did you hear what the GLC said? Imagine if you were a Buzzcock and you were told 'It's okay, you're safe enough to play in the park.'

"I was trying to see if we could stop all the bitching going on and I was working with John Dennis from Rock Against Racism and I fed him the idea of all the big names in punk or New Wave or whatever having a big jammin' show in the park and recording it for an LP to sell for RAR to help the cause. Something positive, something for the summer.

"I thought it'd be interesting if all the groups shattered each in different combinations or something. But people are too arrogant: they'd say, 'I'm not goin' on stage with him' or 'They stink' . . . everyone's a bit too fussy.

"And with the GLC we haven't got a hope in *hell!* The Buzzcocks are just safe enough, but they ain't gonna stand for Clash, Pistols, Sham and Banshees and Undertones and stuff, are they?"

Well, they let the Stones do it at a time when *they* were still considered subversive . . .

"Tell ya, the '60s are really in, aren't they? We got *Juke Box Jury,* mods and everything. It's a piss-off. Who needs the past? I'm so sick of all this delving into the past. It's on a really short cycle now as well. It's stupid. Everyone's looking for yesterday because tomorrow's so shitty. There's 10,000 days of oil left. It's finite."

Ten thousand days in which to break our independence on oil?

"10,000 days to play the guitar, mate. Everyone's got to spend that time in their own way, but I think I'll play the guitar. Everything else gets boring . . ."

The Clash are in a deep hole at the moment. The separation from Bernie Rhodes—their manager from the early days before the interim period when Caroline Coon did their business—has necessitated legals, and that's why the American tour is off (okay, Wobble?). It doesn't look to be rancorous, but it still takes time and money, and The Clash are severely in debt.

Strummer gestures towards a rubbish skip a few yards down from where we're sitting. "You'd have to fill that with five pound notes to get anywhere near paying off our debts."

Despite all of that—and The Clash have the responsibility of trying to run their business as well as their music—Strummer is also jacking his energy into trying to set up a network of musicians in order to create a musician-owned venue in London and into trying to get in touch with London Weekend TV chiefs to create a *real* rock and roll TV show.

"It's time for a new pop show, and we want to get right in there. We've hung back from all that other stuff, because we didn't want to put whatever energy we've got into what's on at the moment. It's tough shit for us now, because all we get is 22 or 23 in the chart, but in the long run it's gonna be for the best."

We discuss *Quadrophenia* and I tell him it's maybe the best film about kids in Britain that I've ever seen.

"Don't say that too soon, mate. Wait'll you see our film. It's called *Rudi Can't Fail.* Ray Gant is the boy from nowhere." (The next day, Joe phones up to ask me to make that the slob from nowhere".)

"The Who . . . you remember Misty getting smashed up in Southall? Well, us and The Who are working on doing a couple of shows for them, and it's going to happen in the middle of next month. The Who have been really good about it. They're lending a lot of gear and they're really keen to play. Roger Daltrey's particularly keen to play. It's a really bad thing when a group gets beaten up and all their stuff gets smashed . . ."

And Clarence, Misty's manager, who was put in hospital that evil night, is walking and talking again, no complications. Positive.

"You know what John (Lydon) said about us being desperate? I think that being desperate is one of the best things you can be. That's what it was all about, being desperate. If you get desperate on one side, what's the opposite? Arrogant complacency?

"They're a good group, PiL: no doubt about it. You know Wobble was saying that he was a natural? I think he is. But you know something? If I was just walkin' around and I didn't know anything about Clash and I didn't know anything about PiL, I'd be saying, 'What the fuck are Clash and PiL actually *doing*?' That's what I'd be saying and I think it's a very good question.

"If we get this musicians' venue going, we're going to call it Buckingham Palais. The average music fan is really great, because they fund this whole thing. If they didn't come, nothing would happen. I don't care what it's like as long as it's good. It's got to be good, that's all. I like singing. I don't like talking."

Between The Clash and the plans are the obstacles, which are . . .

"We got a debt so big we'd have to fill that skip with five pound notes. We're involved in court actions which we don't want, and we're having to deal with the whole thing ourselves. We're working on crazy plans.

"See: everything in the world is cost-related except for records. I shouldn't say this, but I'm a man whose knees are dusty from begging on record company floors—I got no pride—but I wanna survive and I want The Clash to survive. The only thing that we got is The Clash.

"I shouldn't be saying this, but we've been mucking around with some sound gear and we've got some crazy ideas like . . . some LPs, like a Bee Gees LP, will cost hundreds of thousands of pounds to make, so it's gonna cost—what is it now?—six quid soon.

"Suppose a group came along and decided to make a 16-track LP on two Teacs, which dramatically diminishes the cost factor called 'studio costs'.

"Suppose you presented that tape to the record company and told 'em that it cost just these few quid to make. So even when they've added their mark-ups and a cut for him and a cut for *him,* you can still get a fucking LP for two or three quid. So why can't *that* be cost-related?"

Well, with independent labels it can, but the majors don't like doing that sort of thing because it sets unhealthy precedents and because they just *love* making money.

"It's a serious thing about managers. You know the people who've approached us?"

I've heard everyone from Peter Grant to Brian Lane.

"Bet you ain't heard Kerry Packer. Bet you ain't heard Harry Hyams. Bet you haven't heard Freddie Laker. . . . I'll tell you one thing about managers: the whole reason they exist is that groups are supposed to think about the songs while the manager thinks about the affairs.

"But times change, we're moving into the future and we're in the position of doing both things. It's pretty schizophrenic: you're either playing the guitar or you're on the phone and you could say that us and PiL are working in a Jamaican kind of way: we do what we feel like, *soon come,* but there's still that burning question. *What the fuck are they doing?* It's got to be answered, and that's why we're gonna get hold of some guy in America to do the American end and we'll handle things here ourselves, or maybe we'll work with someone we know.

"We're working on quite a wide front. We got all these things cookin' and we're trying to bring 'em to the boil. We've had our fill of various sorts of bullshit, and now we're back to the drawing board. We're really fucked, but I don't think we're fucked enough to quit. We're way beyond *that.*"

CLASH: ONE STEP BEYOND

Chris Bohn | December 29, 1979 | *Melody Maker* (UK)

By the end of 1979, the Clash had some reasons for optimism.

They may have recently been beset by legal, financial, and musical worries—some of which were still ongoing—but their new album, *London Calling*, was superb. Moreover, its release enabled what Strummer terms in this article "our first real victory over CBS." Relations had been prickly between the band and their record label ever since CBS had provoked their infuriated writing of "Complete Control" by putting out unauthorized single "Remote Control." The Clash had finally exacted suitable revenge by tricking the label into making *London Calling* a double set priced as though it were a single album.

For reasons of kindness or sentimentality, Strummer propagates something of a lie about the album: that credited producer Guy Stevens—mentor of Jones's heroes Mott the Hoople—was a major force behind it. Although the Clash have stuck to this line ever since, other album participants have asserted that, with the exception of "Brand New Cadillac," Stevens was obstructive or absent and that the record's real producers were Mick Jones and engineer Bill Price.

The feature also finds Strummer musing on his mortality—at the grand old age of twenty-seven. —Ed.

INSIDE the Clash's new rehearsal studio, under a railway bridge somewhere in South London, Joe Strummer is singing a slow country blues about rolling boxcars, twisting his head way down under to reach a low mike, perched next to an electric piano.

To his right, Mick Jones, dressed in black shirt, vest and trousers, looking like a maverick from a Western B-movie, messes around with a bottleneck; while to his left Simonon slouches on a barstool, as if posing for the silhouette logo on "Top Of The Pops". Behind them, Topper Headon drops an occasional beat to throw drumsticks for his dog.

This is the new Clash, relaxed and unfettered by the chains—or "bullshit," as Joe would have it—with which some would bind them to their past. They will later worry about the lack of work they're getting done, but undoubtedly the music will be as tough and as tight as it ever was by the time they reach the stage in January.

By then, their attack will be strengthened by an influx of new songs from their third album, "London Calling", which showcases an ardent, much younger-sounding band, for the first time allowing itself the expression of a full range of emotions, rather than just those sentiments we all wanted to hear. The sound is exhilarating, jumping from the loping, lightweight "Jimmy Jazz" to the swinging political punch of "Clampdown", to the "white trash" reggae of "Lover's Rock" and the upstart, rocking "I'm Not Down" or "Hateful".

The songs' source-material is rock 'n' roll, old movies, Raymond Chandler, anything—not just personal experiences or responses, which limited the scope of "The Clash" and "Give 'Em Enough Rope".

Those albums were necessarily narrow, pushing forward the punk message. But life goes on, things change, people grow, and in doing so the Clash have broken out gloriously from their own confines. They've learnt from their mistakes, which were many, and today they're far more cautious in what they say off the record, friendly and helpful, without volunteering the "good copy" they used to deliver, and which they've been forced to live down ever since.

"THE trouble is the newspaper men have forgotten why humans like music," says Strummer. "It's like the fairy-tale, when people forget the basic thing because they're too involved with the bullshit. And that's the moral of this fairy-tale—they can't see the wood for the trees any more.

"We're just a group and we release records, and that's the face of the situation, I'd say, but people think they've got to swallow all the bullshit with it. That's why I thought Blind Date, which you used to have in your paper" (MM used to carry single reviews by a guest musician who wasn't allowed to see the label or the artist's name before passing comment) "was so good, because the reviewer had to judge it on the tune and the beat—what it should be judged on, you know, not what kind of trousers he's got on. Aw, I dunno."

Easy to say that now, but the Clash—with or without Bernie Rhodes, whom they've previously acknowledged as being important in establishing the political character of the band at the beginning—formed the blueprint for the whole movement of socio-political punk bands, and thrived on confrontation at all levels: with authority, with their record company (CBS), and with their public—the last category perhaps still to come.

The Clash coming clean will shock those harbouring illusions about them being front-line troops, though the band began the whole mobile-guerrilla-unit thing themselves. Even on the new album, on "Spanish Bombs", Strummer glamourises the "artists at war" image.

"I got that from reading—Orwell and people like that," he says. "It's been pretty well covered. But me, I've gone through my Starsky and Hutch stage. If there was another one, I don't think I'd rush out there and get in the front line. Who lives by the gun dies by the gun—never was a truer word said."

THE emphasis has shifted. The Clash still shoulder responsibilities, like making sure the songs are right and the band are fit to play them and to give their all onstage.

"It ain't like sitting on a stool, it's about 300 times more physical than that. I'm now 27 and it's something you gotta learn by the time that you're 25, that before then your body doesn't keep a record of what you do to it. After that you get real sick, sort of burning the candle at both ends—especially doing the stuff that we do. All this junkie he's-so-out-of-it rock 'n' roll stuff doesn't appeal to me at all. That's the easy way out, you know?"

He adds: "I wrote 'Rudie Can't Fail' about some mates who were drinking brew for breakfast. They think nothing of it. Me, I'm past the stage where I can. I can drink brew for breakfast, but not every day, and that's what made me notice them. I thought it was a hell of a way to start a day."

Their commitment comes in the positive exuberance of the songs, concentration on getting the basics right and helping people in the most direct way they know—cutting the price of the album to the minimum. Eighteen tracks for £5, as the ad goes. Most of them worth having, too.

Ironically, bearing in mind the music's healthy vitality, the Clash were at their lowest when they began planning "London Calling". Reeling from expensive court hearings, extricating themselves from former manager Bernie Rhodes, then leaving his successor, Caroline Coon, the Clash were going through a radical reappraisal of their whole approach.

First, they took control of their management, only recently relinquishing it to Blackhill Enterprises when they had the album in the can, because "we didn't wanna spend all day on the 'phone".

But they were at rock-bottom, and desperately needed to find a way out. Says Strummer: "Economically, we were really tight at the time. This album woulda been our last shot, never mind if we didn't have the spirit for it, which we did. I don't know why, but the problem seemed to relax us, the feeling that nothing really mattered anymore, that it was make or break time.

"Desperation. I'd recommend it."

He continues: "We thought of this idea to create the £2 wall of sound, by recording it on two Teac recorders to keep the costs low, so we could release it cheap. Then the music would have to be fucking good to cover this fucking insanity. We just said to ourselves that we'd never put out a Clash album for six quid.

"But to do that, we knew we'd have to pay for the recording costs ourselves, otherwise CBS woulda told us to fuck off and sent us another list of debts when we asked them to put it out cheap."

They got CBS to agree to the lowest price category, which would also cover a free 12-inch single; they played a festival in Finland—"it was good dough and would pay for the recording costs at Wessex studios," says Strummer—and recorded between May and August.

"We gave CBS 20 tracks and told them to put eight on the 12-inch single. They freaked out, so we said, 'Look, make it a fiver', and against my expectations they agreed to put it out as a double-album.

"I'd say it was our first real victory over CBS."

MORE important, the double-album format allowed them to keep lighter, nonsensical tracks, like the free-ranging "Jimmy Jazz" or the misunderstood "Lovers Rock", alongside more conventional Clash songs like "Clampdown", "Hateful" and "Death Or Glory".

"Jimmy Jazz" is the Clash at their most relaxed, working out on a bluesy tune, with Strummer scatting along, taking more care with his voice than the words:

"What started me thinking, is that it's not only the message, but the way it's said. So a piece of nonsense can have a powerful meaning to me. Like, you know, 'Well, they all call me Speedo / But my real name is Mr Earl.' But in this post-Dylan age, if you unleashed that on the political critics, they'd go 'tedious nonsense', whereas in fact it's the greatest thing that ever walked the earth along with all the other things."

Mick Jones begins miming Gene Vincent doing "Be bop a lula" and Strummer continues:

"Like, I saw that TV programme when they were taking the piss on a panel show, by reading out the lyrics of 'Be bop a lula, she's my baby / Be bop a lula, I don't mean maybe.' They didn't understand that it's Gene Vincent and that's it—the meaning of life is revealed immediately (laughs).

"But," he says, "I put a lot of thought into the whole process of writing lyrics. Some days, I just can't see the point, and then I get worried because it's the only thing I've been solely preoccupied with for I-don't-know-how-many years."

Strummer's at his most passionate these days talking about method rather than content, except in a rather extraordinary defence of "Lovers Rock". It's a song I'd considered lightweight before he volunteered, out of the blue, his reasons for writing it, opening up a whole new area previously left uncovered by the Clash.

He says that the song's based on "The Tao Of Love And Sex", which is about "The Chinese way of fucking. A lot of people in the Western Hemisphere have problems. No-one really wants to talk about this kind of thing, but it's very common, especially with boys turning into men—you get some great bird and fuck it up, right?

"This song mainly tries to tell you how to do it properly. It goes: 'You Western man, you're free with your seed / When you make lovers rock / But whoops there goes the strength you need—to make real cool lovers rock.'

"Another thing," he adds, "it's about how you can have a good time without her either having to take the pill or have a baby. The pill leads to dreadful depressions with some girls. Taking the pill every day, sometimes getting fat and they don't know why, and that makes them feel worse.

"I mean, I was a dwarf when I was younger, grew to my normal size later on, but before then I had to fight my way through school.

"Anyway, that's why I wrote the song, even though it's a bit of a touchy subject. I don't agree with the pill at all. Then you got the Pope saying Catholics can't take it . . ."

Strange: the Clash, musically closer than ever to the rock 'n' roll mainstream, moving further away in their concerns. Strummer does deflate his explanation somewhat, though, saying: "The song is, kind of, having a laugh, too."

IN retrospect, "Give 'Em Enough Rope" was more of a mistake of execution, Sandy Pearlman succeeding only in diminishing the Clash's passion, without playing up their force. It just doesn't compare with Guy Stevens' more sympathetic, less obtrusive job on "London's Calling".

Strummer remarks on the difference: "Guy is that private thing called an X-factor. He comes in and grabs me by the throat and says, 'I deal with emotions', and that's it. He doesn't deal with knobs or whatever else producers deal with.

"He's very off the wall, and he understands the spontaneity of the moment—priceless. If you can get that moment when you play a song just so in front of a tape machine, you got a million dollars. He understands that.

"Sandy's just a knob-twiddler. Well, not even that—he oversees others twiddling knobs. But Guy Stevens no longer knows what a machine is, only that it's a means to an end, while Pearlman half-knows that, but he's not sure. He's too obsessed with the machinery of it. He's kinda forgotten that it's only there to give us some soul."

THE myth-making of "Guns On The Roof", "All The Young Punks" and "Last Gang In Town" indicated that the band were taking themselves and their history a bit too seriously in those days. Strummer counters:

"Yeah, that was another stream of bat-piss, you know? But I think sometimes you need to do that. We like to gee ourselves up a bit, but it's not strictly serious, like 'Last Gang' wasn't anything to do with us at all. I never for one minute imagined that we were the last gang in town, but the fact it was one of our song-titles became a handy headline for newspaper editors.

"In fact, I was taking the piss out of violence by inventing a mythical gang. Every day I was hearing about a new gang, first the teds, then the punks—then they were fighting—then the rockabilly teds and the zydeco kids, who were rumoured to wear straw cowboy hats and Doc Martens covered in cement.

"All this was at the height of the violence, an' I came across it lots of times. I just wanted to take the piss, you know? So we invented this mythical gang, like 'Boy, you better come running, because here's the last gang in town.'"

Less interesting were the continually publicised clashes with CBS, the remote-control / complete-control games that still go on, but now they don't talk about them so much.

"Hmm. I must agree it's not the point at all, fighting record companies. It's a waste of time, but with 'Complete Control' I thought strongly about it, and the phrase kept cropping up everywhere after we seized on it, so I think, looking back, it was worth latching on to."

STRUMMER today is more pragmatic, less prone to lash out at easy targets. Mick Jones is the same. In casual conversation, he's friendly and open. When he drifts in on the interview, he contents himself with a few quips or corrections. He'd rather continue the rehearsal that the meeting has interrupted.

With both, some subjects are taboo. The Clash film for instance, which they're adamant won't be released. No further comment. On the band's past political involvement, Strummer tends to sidestep questions by talking about the medium rather than the message.

He says: "I personally like a pokey lyric, because unless there's something really good about it, it bores me to hear about jealousy and straight heterosexual complaining songs. Unless, say, Chrissie Hynde—I wouldn't care what she's singing. Her voice is the sweetening to the pill. But unless it's someone like that, I prefer a pokey lyric—by which I mean a lyric covered in barbed wire.

"Look, we're just trying to do the best we know how. Our ability has widened slightly. Ya gotta learn, ain't ya? You wake up the next day and know there's more to be done, and carry on hoping that you won't make the same mistakes. You gotta keep your eyes open."

"ANOTHER thing I'm fed up with," Strummer adds, getting more animated, "if you don't mind me saying so, and that's calling the kettle black—(singing low, deadpan): 'It's a shitty situation/A lot of mess today / It's a shitty situation.' What I'm trying to say is one step beyond. I hope we've gone through that stage.

"Listening to all this cold, grey brave-new-world music—with a K— you know, I wouldn't play it to a cage of hamsters. It wouldn't do them any good. It doesn't do me any good. What we're trying to do is make some music. It's just, you know, the sound of finger-clicking. You know what I mean? This is out of place in the modern world.

"It's bullshit, the new kind of bullshit, and it's just as well to spot it when you can, otherwise you follow it like sheep.

"Like, there we were in '71 following Emerson, Lake & Palmer to the brink of disaster, but luckily everybody snapped out of it. I don't like this neu pop musik, because it just ain't got swing, or soul.

"Dogma?" he continues. "We kind of need that stuff, but we ain't gonna set it to lifeless, cold, grey music, because we realise there's no point in trying to get a message across unless it's somehow sweet—so that your unconscious will reach out to it.

"Anyway, we always tried to play just as good as we could. What we play now is what we can do. It wouldn't be fair to do ranting music, because we've mastered a time-change. We can play in another rhythm. So there's just no point. We do a bit of ranting, just to keep it up, but we don't do it all the time. We do something now which we couldn't do before."

THE CLASH CLAMP DOWN ON DETROIT—OR: GIVE 'EM ENOUGH WISNIOWKA

Susan Whitall | June 1980 | *Creem* (US)

London Calling could be termed sugarcoated punk: an album that—deliberately or not—wrapped up the genre's social conscience and studied Britishness in enough fine tunes, wide-screen production, and emotional warmth as to give it universal appeal.

It was therefore unsurprising that it was the album that saw the Clash make headway in the United States, not least because the single it bequeathed—Jones's soul lope "Train in Vain (Stand By Me)"—was the group's first bona fide love song.

This is a dispatch from the Clash's early 1979 Pearl Harbour tour to promote their first US top thirty long-player. It found Strummer talking about the differences between the American and British music press, the importance to the group of reggae, and the division of songwriting duties within the Clash. Plus a subject that, for all their social conscience, was rarely essayed by the band: feminism. Susan Whitall secured some interesting comments from Strummer on a subject only ever addressed in song by the Clash—and even then nominally or elusively—in "Lover's Rock," "Death Is a Star," and "Sex Mad War."

Notes: For "Kozmo Vinyl" read "Kosmo Vinyl"

For "Working For The Clampdown" read "Clampdown"

For "Don Etts" read "Don Letts"

For "the punk rock movie" read *The Punk Rock Movie* —Ed.

London Calling/Now don't look to us
Phony Beatlemania has bitten the dust
                    —"London Calling"

DETROIT—On a cloudy, cold March night tall skinny radical activist of amorphous persuasion M-50 stood outside the Motor City Roller Rink shivering and passing out leaflets that read: "THE CA$H SOLD OUT!"

M-50 feels he was let down, after the pain and fury of the first two Clash albums. His feelings are not likely to be soothed by the fact that the Clash's music is finally palatable to the dons at *Rolling Stone*, or by their album marching resolutely up the charts to sit, fat and smug, at #27. There's gotta be something wrong, and M-50 figures bucks must be involved. The Clash had to sell out to sell records, right?

Most of the people filing into the roller rink for the Clash's March 10th benefit for Jackie Wilson tossed the fliers away, but the rumbling's coming from both sides of the rock 'n' roll fence: FM programmers are "happy the Clash has made an album acceptable to AOR." They finally stopped shouting and made a nonthreatening album.

M-50 and pals would agree: *they sold out.*

The truth is that the Clash, arrogant as ever, have made exactly the album they wanted to make and piss on *you.*

They had no reason to do otherwise; at the time of recording *London Calling* the band was at bottom emotionally and financially. Lengthy managerial hassles had depleted their money and devastated them personally. *London Calling* could very well have been their last shot. Recorded cheaply and released at an economic $9.98, it is a stirring emotional comeback. They had nothing to lose, as Joe Strummer pointed out later:

"It was like, let's *rock out* before they bug us out of the studio."

I told him about a misinterpretation of the album in the magazine *Us*, where it was slagged off as negative in spirit and punkily perverse.

"I don't think that we *could* have made a negative record," he replied, shaking his head sadly. "It would have been too depressing."

More than any other band to come out of punk, the Clash are burdened with their fans' emotional expectations. Not the new fans of *London Calling* (like Bootsy Collins, who plays "Train In Vain" every day), but the fans who cherished their import copies of the first two albums of passionate, political music. The people from Kansas who drove in for the Jackie Wilson benefit because it was the closest the Clash would come to them (700 miles is *close*? 700 MILES IS CLOSE?).

This burden does not sit lightly on Joe Strummer's shoulders. While the band seems to genuinely enjoy giving their fans treats (like the impromptu concert they played instead of just a soundcheck for the early arrivals at the Detroit gig), the more intense feelings of their congregation seem to worry them.

As my *CREEM* cohort Mark Norton and I sat around behind the stage of the roller rink, soaking up the fan ambience, the band finished their soundcheck/preview and disappeared up the stairs to the dressing room. Strummer had barely made it to the third step, though, when cries of "Joe! Joe!" brought him doubling back down, guitar still strapped on. "Joe!" a leather-jacketed teenager yelled. "I just wanta touch ya." Strummer's face broke into a gaptoothed grin, and he pumped the kid's hand. This gave a kid just behind the first one his chance to grab the hapless singer and bearhug him. Joe's attention to them both seemed to gently imply, "See, I'm just a flesh-and-blood schmoe like you," especially confronted with their adulation. It probably had the opposite effect—it probably thrilled them to the bone.

While talking later at the hotel, my comrade-in-pens Norton had gone into a Brando/*Apocalypse Now* impression, in the course of an impassioned discussion on flicks: "'Strummer!" he choked in a strangled Brando mumble, "What do you call it . . . when the assassin . . . accuses the assassin . . . (See, Brando's still got the cotton in his mouth from *The Godfather*)."

Joe laughed. "That's how I feel, every day, when I try to talk to people . . . like [does English Brando mumbling] . . . sometimes I think I'm their Godfather, just grunting away."

Picture Joe, in his pale broad brimmed hat, spliff firmly in mouth, mumbling "You shall have your justice" to a desperate soul. He mumbles well.

"Like, in Boston," he related. "We'd just got out of the coach, and there were all these people shouting 'Ban Don Law,' 'ban Don Law,' just like that, and handing out pamphlets. The guy turns out to be the promoter, and I'm thinking, here we go for the classic punch-out gig, you know. And we get in there, and they're taking all the seats out, and that's made their demonstration irrelevant. They were complaining about being harassed, and told to stay *in* their seats, but they'd actually taken out the seats, like everywhere should. *Like everywhere should.*

"They were complaining that this guy, Don Law, uses guerillas . . . But I went to those people—I went to the biggest guy I could see. And I said, 'There's no chairs here, right?' And he said, 'No.' And I said 'Well, what are you gonna do when there's people standing there?' And he says 'I'm not gonna do nothing to them.' 'Well, what if they start jumping around?' 'Well, we got the chairs here to protect us, so I don't give a fuck.' That kind of eased the tension a bit, I reckon. But we're *always* walking into that, 'cause it's hard to be a group from somewhere else, and come steaming three thousand miles in, and you have to go with the guy in town, say Bill Graham in Frisco. If you don't go with Bill Graham in Frisco, he's gonna bar cars from the street the gig's on and turn it into a car park before you get out of the airport."

Against all odds, Mark and I finally made contact with Kozmo Vinyl, vital for any Clash press business. (After numerous calls to Kozmo at the hotel, an exasperated desk clerk asked, "Did his *mother* give him that name?") Kozmo was everything we'd heard he was and more. A record company friend who'd been put through the mill by Ian Dury nonetheless spoke warmly of Kozmo; it was universal. Now I know why: Kozmo strives to please *everybody*. He may end up scattered, running to and fro while confusion reigns, but nobody gets mad because *he tries*. He talks to you. He makes you laugh. Said Joe Strummer: "He's more than a PR man, he . . . keeps the spirit up. You know what I mean? You need someone, when you're flagging, to keep your spirit up so you can get back up there. Kozmo's one of those sorts of human beings, he's all razzle-dazzle and no downs, which is quite special, doing a tour and stuff."

Kozmo transported us upstairs to meet the Clash before the show; we'd talk afterwards.

The moment of truth had arrived: would we be eaten up by the Clash machine and spewed out like so much journalistic excrement? Would we be verbally trashed? Would Joe get mad and hit our tape recorder? Would they laugh at our clothes?

This was a terrible dilemma; as with any Clash fan, their personal morality was abnormally important to me, and I knew a few journalists who were devout Clash fans but had emerged from their interview encounters . . . shaken. How could they hate such devoted nice guys as Simon Frith (who their then-manager Bernie Rhodes had advised to check for his wallet after he left the band), and Dave DiMartino? Simon probably appeared, in late 1977, dangerously mature and too intellectual to be a Clash fan. But he was. Dave did what pisses *me* off: gross indecencies with a cigarette (albeit in all innocence). Still, were the Clash righteous assholes peddling moralistic Sunday School lessons to their fans, only to trample on kindly human souls in real life?

Topper and I made contact sartorially—we were wearing identical green Air Force jackets (mine so unspeakable my mother won't sit in the same room with me wearing it). We laughed, and then he went back to his brooding. (Understandable as he was nursing a cracked pelvis *and* a torn ligament in his hand, so anything above a snarl was probably a superhuman effort.) Freddie, a muscular guy in the band's employ, demanded "So is this a *cover* story?" menacingly, but Mick was effervescent and entertaining, and Joe smiled genuinely and answered all questions with care. Kozmo gave us Dutch beer: was there any limits to this British hospitality? Our fragile American illusions remained intact.

And so, the gig: As soon as DJ Birry Myers spun "Higher & Higher" we knew the Clash were imminent; they came bursting out with "Clash City Rockers" and a long, frenzied gig was underway. The Clash seemed to look at the audience as curiously as they themselves were scanned from the teeming masses on the roller rink floor. Joe decided to break the ice with a little grooming foreplay, asking the audience for a comb (just like our monkey ancestors licking each others' fur?). Presented with a brush, he protested but made do. He's just lucky it wasn't Ted Nugent's—the guitar-playing deer hunter had driven in two hours from his farm near Jackson to experience the Clash in Detroit. And indeed, he experienced a *cultural* clash when the band gleefully sent out a roadie with a pair of scissors and the message that Ted could come back and meet them if he cut off his frizzy mane. All in fun, but Ted didn't get the joke, and huffed out. An apologetic letter from the Clash's manager was sent out the next day. "After all," said an Epic person, "what if someone said they wouldn't talk to Joe Strummer unless he fixed his teeth? *How rude.*" The Clash didn't insult anybody else in Detroit, though; in fact they played a long set, covering each album generously, re-emerging manfully for encores, and surprising the crowd with one last turn onstage when everybody'd given up on them, already having had several hour's worth of music. Whether by playing long, or by playing well, the Clash were determined to give Jackie Wilson's benefactors their ticket's worth.

The Detroit FM stations were playing the two "radio" cuts from *London Calling*—"Train In Vain" and "London Calling"—only, so a good deal of the audience were politely attentive but had never heard a lot of the Clash's earlier numbers, as they hadn't been played on the radio. Another portion were the hippie "show me" types. One such fellow stunned me by never moving so much as a hair in the long mane floating down to his waist. It was incredible—not *one* muscle moved in even a spasm of rhythm. But it struck me, listening to Mick Jones thrashing out precise, thundering power chords that maybe someone like Nugent was getting off on this . . . or even Mr. 1969.

Hippies like the Clash. So do black people—I watched two black girls dancing, to see whether they favored the reggae-flavored numbers or not. They didn't. They're American girls, after all.

This ever-broadening audience of the Clash's, being American, is so large and uncouth and . . . unhip that maybe it's a natural conclusion on the part of the avant-gardists that the Clash are unhip, too. These people in their audience don't even know how to dress; this goddamn hippie may have bought every one of their albums, but what does he know? Right? He might as well be at a Molly Hatchet show, if looks are anything. Next my mother will want an album, and M-50 will be furious: How dare they appeal to such people?

I told Joe Strummer during our interview that I found *London Calling* full of American rhythms, and thus its appeal to Americans wasn't very hard to fathom. I do believe that touring the length and breadth of the New World listening to their rockabilly and 50's rock 'n' roll tapes was responsible for deepening the texture of their sound, resulting in the versatile combo showcased on *London Calling*. It's embarrassing when the Clash are slavishly acclaimed by critics as *the* rock 'n' roll band of the decade—and yet, what other band has so successfully absorbed the music of so many cultures, digested it, and emerged with a startling, evocative language of their own?

———

After the show, Mark and I awaited Kozmo and our journalistic destiny at the foot of the dressing room stairs, mingling with the kids, country punks, Detroit media superstars, etc. A chap next to us, Carl Nordstrom of "Free Radio Now," announced authoritatively: "We can't see the Clash because they're upstairs giving an interview to *CREEM*." The price of fame, blah, blah. Mark and I nod understandingly.

———

Fashion note: all of the Clash still favor their late 50's/early 60's greaseball hair styles, which of course necessitates frequent, Kookie-like combing sessions. (Ask your older brother who Kookie is . . .) In the dressing room after the show, as we explained to Kozmo how punch press operators in the auto factories have their hands clamped to their machines, Paul, Mick and Joe lined up in front of a trunk mirror and made some impressive comb moves, maneuvering their heads so each could see himself.

———

> The men at the factory are old and cunning,
> You don't owe nothing so boy get runnin'
> It's the best years of your life they want to steal.
> —"Working For The Clampdown"

It being decided that the Clash required a bar to satisfy their post-gig cravings (and our interview wishes), we were called on to choose the place, and fixed upon our old haunt Lili's, in Hamtramck. Coordinating a large bus crammed with people with our Mustang took some doing, but we arrived with half an hour left before closing. Despite the entourage who'd followed us down the freeway (as we entered the club one fellow snorted to his pals: "Don't you EVER try to talk me out of following anybody!" as he took his place at the bar next to the Clash), the bar wasn't too raucous—Mick settled down to drinking tequila with a tableful of friends, and I could see Joe's hat planted at the bar, where Lili, the Polish Zsa Zsa Gabor, poured rounds of wisniowka. Joe was instructed on the proper pronunciation of the Slavic toast "Nazdrowie," which magically brought more and more of the red liquid to his glass. It's a tribute to the alcoholic capacity of the average Englishman that our interview was ever conducted at all once Lili got through with Joe.

Packed snugly by a crowd of Detroit "pals," Joe called me over to explain that he needed to relax in the bar, as it was "normal," and, after a gig, he needed desperately to feel normal. We agreed to do a formal interview later, at the hotel. As I passed by Mick's table, I also heard the word "normal" issued from the Jones mouth to describe the place. Strange, when we're used to suspicious English visitors like Elvis Costello or reclusive megastar groups like the Stones, to encounter a group so eager to mingle with the natives and observe the local scene. If they wanted equal, low-key treatment this was the place; Lili didn't know exactly *who* they were, but any friends of friends of hers are given the wisniowka treatment and a hearty welcome.

Since Detroit was the last date of this truncated tour, the mood back at the hotel was distinctly non-business. My compadre and I walked despondently to Lee Dorsey's room, where a soul hootenanny was taking place. Photographer Pennie Smith offered helpfully, "Well . . . you can always do an atmosphere piece."

And we have the perfect atmosphere tape; a roomful of assorted Clash well-wishers, Kozmo Vinyl, visiting friend Pearl E. Gates, fans from Kansas (*not* the band), Clash employees, and, of course, Lee Dorsey, and ourselves, singing every old soul/gospel/R&B song we could think of. But no C.C. Rockers in sight; subject Simonon was long in bed, resting his moody profile as he was off to Vancouver the next day to begin shooting on a movie; subject Jones was off, intent on chatting with a pretty blonde; subject Headon was nowhere to be found; subject Strummer had been seen ducking into his room.

But, as we laughed in the face of interview disaster, drank beer and sang, Joe kept the faith by returning to Lee's room, where he lounged back on the bed, still behatted, listening to our wailing with no small amusement. Since Topper came in and broke the caterwauling up by slapping on a Taj Mahal tape (boooo), we agreed with Joe to adjourn to his room, where Joe fielded questions cheerfully, offering us Clash t-shirts and buttons in return for the R. Crumb *CREEM* t-shirts we gave him. It was 5:30 or 6:00 in the morning, and the distinctive Strummer voice was reduced to a hoarse whisper, but we sipped beer and slogged on.

First he questioned us: "What would it take," he asked in that distinctive monotone, "for a reggae record to go to number one in America?"

Probably it would have to be a novelty record like "My Boy Lollipop" or "The Israelites," I offered. "Novelty" to American ears, anyway . . . What about the anti-reggae backlash in the English papers?

"That's the devil talking, if you ask me," Joe replied. "A couple of years ago I thought the same thing; I thought, well maybe it's going to go into a slump now, you know? But then, it's just cooking away, and it's even going to break through—bigger than what I even thought before. And so I've changed my opinion on that. I read that too, I think . . . some guy going "Blah blah." I think he's a fool."

What about the 2-Tone sound?

"Bluebeat? The trouble is . . . this one summer I'd gone to live with this bloke, called Don Etts who'd made the punk rock movie, kind of a home movie—he's done a lot of filming for us—well, I'd moved into his house, I rented a room he had spare, and he gave me this Trojan album, 'cause he was digging the "now sound of roots rock reggae," right? And he didn't want—they're not interested in the old stuff. They think it's boring if it ain't new, you know? Which is quite a good attitude. But anyway—he said he didn't want it . . . so I got hold of it, I put it on . . . and I was just *wiped away* for six months, 'cause it's just like the cream, in a triple album set, the cream of all the bluebeat stuff.

"And then all that new stuff came up—I felt that there was a danger sign 'cause they were just rippin' off the licks, you know? Like even if they had their own song, they just put in a famous bluebeat lick, you know? [Joe hummed the intro to "Gangsters"] . . . and that's all off old records. I felt like ringing them up and telling them, 'Hey, put yourself in there, get some input in, 'cause otherwise it becomes too dangerously . . . *retreading*, you know what I mean?

"I see in London the papers are full of that kind of—1001 ska bands, all doing all the old ska hits, and probably ruining them all forever! I don't know . . ."

What about the possibility that the Specials-type ska will—being popish—influence Americans to go back and listen to the real thing?

"That's a thought, yeah," Joe replied. "I think it probably will. 'Cause I like those bands, that said. That's my reservation. Apart from that, I like those bands, I think they're fucking great." He took the offensive again. "Is it true you can tour the Motown studios? Are they far from here?"

We confirmed that there was a tour, and offered to take him over the next morning.

"Ahhh, you won't remember. Could you be here at 11:00? Nah, you won't make it. I'll bet you five dollars you won't."

We accepted the challenge. What about songwriting; the songs are credited Strummer/Jones—did Joe compose mostly lyrics, and Mick mostly music? That was probably the image most people have.

"You could say that was a rough definition, but I wouldn't even ever say *that*, because it's just not true. Mick wrote all the lyrics to 'Complete Control.' *And* all the music.

"We collaborate on everything . . . there ain't any method to it at all. It's a big jumble up, really. You'd probably be surprised if you knew who contributed what—they think just because I sing it, I wrote it, or because he sings it, he wrote it, but it ain't like that at all."

I offered him a cough drop, but Joe lit up another Camel Light.

"I just believe that . . . it's difficult but good to have a meeting of minds . . . it's difficult because everyone's got an ego, and you obviously think that what *you* think up is better than what anybody else thinks up. Or you do if you're like me, anyway," he laughed. "So it's good to collaborate . . ."

What about the American press?

"Well, I read what I can find, but I haven't been able to find very much." He laughed silently, his hoarseness growing worse. "A little review in the *New York Bollocks* or whatever that said we was like . . . volume merchants or something. Ira something. Ira Schnub.

"But I *like* to be given the duff review," he rasped happily. "You know? Especially by a square. Like on newspapers, they send back some guy who's got an attitude before he walks in the door, and he reviews the concert from that point of view, and they come up with some *beautiful* sentences . . . like one I read tonight, it's fantastic! It was really an over-the-top sentence, and I'm kind of rooting for them, going *yeah!*" he chortled hoarsely, beside himself. "Say something worse! 'Cause the worse they say, I know the better it is, you know what I mean? Because if *they* don't get it, that means it *really* must be there.

"Lee Dorsey was *really hurt*," he continued. "He read in *Billboard* [March 15th, *Talent In Action*]: 'Lee Dorsey came on and played a 45-minute, tight, unexciting set.' End of sentence, right? And you know, that's probably his first review in . . . *whew*. And you know, he really takes it bad, the way I used to take it when we first started, when we were on tour. I could see he was really taking it bad, so I told him about the Elvis reviews that I read the other day from 1956—in the *New York Times*, like 'Elvis Presley cannot sing, cannot dance, he has no talent whatsoever and he is going nowhere.' BAM! There goes Elvis! There it is, down in cold print. I told him that, to make him feel better," Joe mused. "But I don't think it had any effect."

And the English press?

"It's good to have a lot of information passing around the four papers every week—there's a lot of information going round, and I think *ideas* can go round," he said. "But the negative side is all this *bitching* over the fine points of anything—you know? Anything, there's a crowd of vultures bitching about it . . . sometimes I read them, and I feel depressed, so down, that I don't read 'em for a month."

Were they sometimes too hard on the Clash, did he think?

"Naaaah," Joe laughed. "There's no point—if you're gonna pick up a guitar or open your mouth, you've gotta make sure you've got a six-foot thick skin before you start—know what I mean?

We passed Joe his t-shirts, which prompted him to ponder R. Crumb's fate.

"Guy's a genius! He's probably drinking wine tonight or something." Joe paced up and down the room. "There's a few slick cartoonists in England, right, and they do stuff that looks just like this," he pointed to the girl's arm on the Mr. Dreem Whip shirt. "That crosshatching on that bird's arm—those strokes. If they're drawing someone's leg they do that Robert Crumb crosshatching on the side."

Inspired, Joe continued to walk about, chanting, "Bring back Robert Crumb . . . bring back Robert Crumb . . . *only he can save us.*"

We discovered Joe's taste in films to be right up (or *down*, possibly) our alley—he'd make a lively luncheon companion for our own Edouard Dauphin (*Drive-In Saturday*) on the subject of movies, as both favor the trash aesthetic in films. Joe revealed himself to be "a *Dark Star* fanatic," having seen the embryonic Carpenter film three times in England.

"Oh, *God*, they filmed that *so cheap*," Mark cried out, in acute pain. "American cinema is actually a lot better than that."

Joe was firm. "I know, but that's a *fucking great film.*"

It is, it is . . .

"I don't care about the budget, I care about the *idea*," he emphasized, getting up to pace around.

"Joe! Sit down!"

"When they're trying to talk to the Commander," he laughed.

"The Commander was on ice, and he's talking: 'I am dead, but I will talk to you . . .'"

"Did you see *The Fog*?" Joe queried, eager for the news.

I responded that it'd been . . . disappointing.

"Boo, boo, boo, boo!" he exclaimed. "By the way, do you get the films that nutter make down in Cleveland—the guy—the *Pink Flamingoes* guy?"

John Waters, from Baltimore—affirmative.

"They just got that one in England made back in '74—*Desperate Living*," Joe enthused.

"'Hey schtoopid, you got your clothes on backwards!'"

We questioned how Joe had come to see so many weird American flicks.

"In London there's quite a lot of people who get into those films, actually," he said. "They're classics! They should be shown on TV, American prime time TV! I'll ring up my friends at CBS and tell them to stick it on their TV."

In describing the Polish/Ukrainian neighborhood Lili's bar was located in to Joe, we got into the subject of the depressed local economy (Chrysler, etc.), the similarities over in England, and Joe introduced a topic dear to his heart: guitars and their manufacture. He spoke fondly of his '61 Esquire and his '63 Telecaster (although whether the '61 was an Esquire or not was the subject of heated debate).

"What the fuck are we going to do in ten years?" he said. (With older guitars.)

Take care of them . . .

"Yeah, but is it still gonna be working?" Joe queried.

You change the pods and pickups . . .

"But what about the nut?"

Stradivariuses last 300 years . . .

"Yeah," he countered, "but did the guy play the Stradivarius every night at the show? He didn't bang it on the back of fucking amps because he couldn't stand to hear it go *twanging* . . ." Joe looked heartbroken. "My brand new '61 Esquire, right? My *little baby* . . ."

How could you . . . break a beautiful instrument?

"Ah, some nights are like that, you know."

The daylight was getting more and more insistent, so I trotted out my awkward question . . . what about the Clash's feminist consciousness?

They'd been known for insisting on female opening acts; the lyrics of "Lovers Rock" on *London Calling* actually proposed that men take some responsibility for birth control, and their partner's pleasure. While heavy metal musicians of whatever nationality are the worst offenders, casual observation of English male musicians generally reveals a pretty primitive attitude towards women. (And not just the stereotyped super-star/groupie scene.) Along with European charm comes a certain subtle chauvinism . . . which makes the Clash's view of women all the more intriguing—and admirable.

"Well, I think it's something you have to watch, because it's inbred," Joe proffered.

Sexism?

"Yeah. It's inbred, you don't even notice it. Sometimes I catch myself saying that are just . . . *stupid*, you know?"

Did he think rock 'n' roll was particularly sexist?

"Well, all the early passion was derived from . . . a sort of *lust*."

But *lust* isn't sexist.

"Yeah, but it tended to bend that way," he replied. "When taken to an extreme . . . 'I'm a hog for ya baby/Can't get enough of your love'—you could say that's a love song . . . and this guy comes along, and it ends up in England, going like . . . I don't even want to say it. I don't even want to say it . . . it's really dumb."

Heavy metal seemed to twist a lot of honest sex around . . .

"That's what it turned into," Joe said. "I mean, those early sort of passion numbers turned into . . . just *macho*. What do they call it? Cock-strutting routines. And I can't stomach that.

"You just say one word, *chicks*," Joe snapped his fingers. "Says it all, right? We used to find—we'd be standing in the warehouse in Camden Town [their practice room] and these kind of surveyors were coming in off the pavement, and they'd go 'Oh blah blah blah, these *chicks*, man!' . . . And I remember we'd kind of get up and say: 'You can call them *girls* . . . or *birds* . . . or *women* . . . but you can't call them *chicks*.' Know what I mean? *Chickens*. I remember sometimes, they really could get my goat. And then, the other day, I found myself saying it."

Joe leaned against the window of the hotel room, looking over-whelmed by it all, the worried Godfather of his own description.

Did he have any new impressions of America this time around?

"Well," he sighed. "I think America's really *too big* . . . to fit into. Playing at one time. If you put New York in . . . Boston, Philadelphia, Georgia, South Carolina, and Louisiana—and these places stick out in the back of your head—by the time you get round to Oregon, and Utah . . ." he sighed again.

Now that the Clash had broken through successfully in Detroit, was he going to continue the Clash crusade in America?

Finally surrendering to fatigue—mental and physical, Joe drooped on the radiator. "Well, noooo."

We prepared to leave. It was 7:00. "So," he perked up. "Are you going to meet here at 11:00 to go to Motown? Bet you five dollars you don't make it. I'll be in that coffee shop across the street."

(Note to Strummer: do you take checks?)

JOE STRUMMER ANSWERS THE CALL-UP

Paolo Hewitt | December 13, 1980 | *Melody Maker* **(UK)**

Although now viewed as a classic, on its release *London Calling* actually attracted not inconsiderable criticism: some thought its slick grooves and occasionally internationalist lyrics constituted a sellout of punk values.

Such sentiments only increased over the following year, albeit with somewhat greater justification. For instance, the band that had once professed themselves so bored with the U.S.A. seemed to be spending a lot of time there, either touring or, in the case of Mick Jones, as resident. This itself caused a creative problem: the songs the Clash continued to write about poverty in their home country assumed a phony aura. Meanwhile, songs they wrote about other countries such as "The Call Up" and "Washington Bullets" had an air of irrelevance: the draft and Latin American nationalism were not exactly burning issues for UK council-estate youth. The triple-album format of new album *Sandinista!* was for many the height of hubris, as was its cold, substandard self-production. To cap it all, the band were looking increasingly comical, swathed—as on the cover of *Sandinista!*—in an arbitrary jumble of military and outlaw chic. Not even the album's low price could mollify ex-fans.

Perhaps because of this recent wave of criticism, Strummer had gone back on his assertion to Susan Whitall only six months previously that he had "a six-foot thick skin." In this interview, he complains that journalists don't understand how "sensitive" musicians can be.

Strummer is in alternately defiant and defeated mood, admitting the naivete of past stances and acknowledging that the Clash have lost ground in their home country. It's particularly noteworthy how catty he is about the Jam. Enmity between the Clash and the

Jam was long-standing. Enraged by the then politically conservative leanings of Jam front man Paul Weller, Strummer had gone so far as to ridicule the Jam on record in "(White Man) in Hammersmith Palais." It can't have amused him, then, to have seen the group that were once the runts of punk's litter lately overtaking the Clash and all the rest of their peers to become what the Clash had always dreamed of being: a group who scored chart-toppers with social protest.

Notes: Lord Denning compiled a report on a notorious sixties sexual scandal involving a government minister.

For "*Sandinista*" read "*Sandinista!*"

For "Wells End Estate" read "World's End Estate"

For "FSLM (Frante Sandinista Liberation Nicaragua Nationale)" read "FSLN (Frente Sandinista de Liberación Nacional)"

For "Black Parenza" read "La Prensa"

For "Jose Chemaro" read "Joaquín Chamorro"

For "Paul Moreley" read "Paul Morley" —Ed.

WORKING on the theory that if you give him enough rope he'll either hang or save himself, the following pages are left basically for the words of Joe Strummer.

The reason for this is simple. Since that violent eruption of upturn, promises and rebellion in 1977, no band has received more flak and criticism for the directions their career has taken than the Clash.

The Pistols blew themselves up; the Damned became an even bigger joke; and the Jam grew from strength to strength. The Clash, meanwhile, came under constant fire for their determined pursuit of success in America, superficial politics, chic guerrilla poses, and worst of all, their forsaking of furious music, for safe, formulated rock 'n' roll.

From the band who once sneered so viciously with boredom at the U.S.A., whose leader used to wear "Rock 'N' Roll Is Dead" T-shirts, we had cover versions of oldies like "Brand New Cadillac", time spent in American studios, and worse still, promises, however rash and heady, ignored and rarely fulfilled.

After all the fuss, may be that's all they were and ever could be . . . the new Rolling Stones.

Now, the Clash have recorded a new triple album, "Sandinista" (whose main highlights are explained and discussed overleaf), became a lot bigger in the U.S.A., and became frustrated by the sycophancy with which they have often been treated by well-meaning, but misguided, critics.

This interview offered a chance for Joe Strummer to answer criticisms.

It took place at CBS's London headquarters and a nearby pub, and is the result of a five-hour talk re-arranged accordingly to allow Joe to fill in all sides of the story.

Make of it what you will, but I must say Joe Strummer couldn't have been nicer, or more honest.

How are relations between the Clash and CBS right now?

We're tied here for a ten-album deal. Did you know that?"

I thought it was five.

That's what we thought. But we were had and I don't mind admitting it. Sick of pussyfooting around. We've been trying to get out of that for ages, and there's no way we can do it. The only way is to sue Bernie (Rhodes, the group's original manager who signed them to CBS) and his lawyer, but I don't want to sue Bernie . . . I think Bernie's great.

Like "London Calling" it counted as one album not as two. This counts as one (pointing to "Sandinista" cover) not three, because we say, 'We want it cheap' and they say, 'Well if you want it cheap, we're not going to accept it as more than one'.

We can't have our cake and eat it. So we choose, but we have to because we want to get the record out now we've made it. If we went to court it would be a three-year case and we'd lose. We haven't got the money to pay. The legal situation is really appalling and there's nothing else we can do. *This* is what we can do (grabbing the "Sandinista" cover). You can get this for £4.29 in Virgin in a couple of weeks. This is our answer to the jam we're in, but I *will* say we're in a jam just maybe to prevent over people following us. Obviously we went through every alternative, but I've come to accept it, especially now we've got a record out.

Profits

Why not break up and come back together again under a different name?

I don't like negative solutions to anything and breaking up is negative. Also we're individually signed.

They're keeping their profits intact, it's not as if they're taking a cut in it.

We're taking a cut. In order to keep the price down we had to make concessions and those included not paying us any royalties until certain vast amounts have been sold. But that's just for Britain. I've heard they want to pay us half royalties round the rest of the world, to put it out at the price we've demanded. That's what we're having to accept and as I said before there's not a lot we can do except give value for money.

It's seemed recently that you've become preoccupied with America.

Yeah, but that's what I call the Woking philosophy ... (laughs). Yeah the Woking philosophy because that's one of Paul Weller's things. Like on our last album I wrote a song about Montgomery Clift which went (sings), 'New York, New York, 42nd Street ...' and he says 'you're not allowed to do that right?'

Well I thought what's Paul going to do when he goes to Yankee land or Australia or Japan? What's he going to do? Is he going to look at a picture of Woking and concentrate on that in the bus or train? Or is he going to look at what's going on outside the window? I'm English and I live here, but I'm still aware there's the rest of the world out there.

Can English kids relate to that though?

Yeah, but what about the Americans listening to it? We don't sell records here. The situation has kind of changed very subtly, but we don't sell records here. We can get an album near the top of the charts but it goes (indicates with his hands a quick descent) and if you compare it with other albums that stay in the top of the charts, it really means a lot. I know it's the usual view to say America is the land of the fat slobs with small brains, but that's just not true. There are young people in America who are destroyed by what their government's been doing since the beginning of the century.

The imperialistic attitudes, the supporting of Right Wing juntas around the world and there are people who are well pissed off with it. And they're human beings too. I mean if you're an English band and they're not going to buy your records, then you've got to face up to it.

Perhaps it's because you've lost credibility.

Well I'm not going to sway to them. I haven't got any kind of wish to dance to another person's tune, because the one I hear is too strong. I hear what they're saying, I read everything they say and I shut myself off from them all.

Alive

A lot of people have accused you of failing to live up to the group's original radical image.

I see what you're saying, but I would say to them they must think what they want. It certainly looks like that, but on the inside it's a different story. We're still alive, the Clash, a real ongoing situation, a real bunch of people that are still talking to each other, and we don't intend to stop. We intend to go on and on and we'll see in the end what we do with it. Our thing is that we were too childish to know just what we were walking into. Yet we've matured enough to not let the full impact of that . . . it hasn't broken us up. Like a lot of people don't know how the thing is set up. I didn't know until I was tricked all over the place. I'm talking about the actual business of making records and selling them . . . I had no idea!

So you've been manipulated?

Only by our own stupidity in a way. I'm talking about getting a big advance. A lot of groups are smart enough those days not to, but certainly in those days we had no idea what an advance was. It was just like a big laugh, a *big* laugh, and once we'd blown the advance on a few tours and making a record, we realised. Like people were saying to us, "Now you going to be rich and famous, what are you going to do with it?" and we had loads of ideas. Like radio stations, like put a co-operative venue together owned by musicians because they know what's wanted, and a decent bar with no hassle and all ideas like this.

We came flooding out with these ideas and everybody wrote them down and said, "Well, this is all really good stuff, right on." Then we walked into the door and we realised we weren't getting any money, that they'd been geeing us up going now you're going to be rich and famous . . .

It's a myth! I mean they all expect you believe that, that pop stars are rich and famous. It says it in the papers, so it must be true. *I* certainly thought it was true, but when we walked into that and realised what a massive debt we were into, it meant that any incoming money was sucked in by these people here (sweeps arm around him to indicate CBS), to pay them back for what they'd given us.

Attention

We took a hundred grand and that brought the Clash to the attention of the people, we invested it in that.

Yet it wasn't our hundred grand, we had to pay them back and that meant we were fucked and we're only just getting out of it now. I mean splitting up with our manager didn't help it because he wanted a lot of dough and he, I'm not knocking Bernie because I think he's the best, but that was his idea that we lost that money in order to flog these tours and records. And so he didn't mind that we were thousands and thousands of quid in debt because he anticipated that in the first place.

But not us, in our stupidity, with all these people telling us how rich and famous we were going to be next week! – really thought that was going to happen.

It began to sink in after a couple of years of slogging round the Top Ranks and being gobbed on, it finally began to sink in we weren't getting anywhere.

I mean every time we went to see the accountant it was like, I mean I couldn't get a member of the Clash into that office if I offered them a lift down in a mini cab.

They just wouldn't get in the mini cab.

Angry

It was that kind of depressing story, it took a couple of years for that to sink in, whilst in the meantime all these other people were saying (adopts angry tone), 'Where's all these radio stations? Where's all these wonderful things?' And of course when that begun to sink in . . . phew dear!

And it's taken us the following two years, after we began to feel that effect to dig our way out, and try and get on an even keel.

But I haven't dropped *any* project at all.

In fact I spend my time dreaming more up and we're starting small. We've a four track cassette machine, right, on its own without a room to put it in and that's where we're starting from.

We're trying to keep it together and not let our egos get out of hand, and we're going to slog on from here.

But I don't think people are interested in this. They don't want to hear about this because this is the reality of life and they don't want to hear about all this, what I'm saying, but it's still reality to me and the rest of the Clash and they've got to deal with that.

How do you feel when people cynically describe the Clash as the new Rolling Stones.

To be just like the Rolling Stones? I mean, a thousand groups would give their right arms to be called that, although I don't particularly find it wonderful.

But if we were, wouldn't we have a 24-track studio? For a start we haven't got our own houses. I'm talking about the rock 'n' roll thing.

You get a big house, you build your own 24-track in the basement and when it's all done you can't think of a damn thing to record on it, right?

I mean, all those groups scrabbling round for studio time and there's all these jerks sitting in there and they can't think of anything to tape.

I mean those people would condemn us because they read it somewhere, but I'm not saying I don't have no fuck-up in my life.

I know where every penny is going, I know exactly how much we owe to who, how fast we're paying them off and how we're going to pay the rent to get an office of some kind, or basement to put this tape recorder in, and I know we're starting from the ground like that and I'm not interested in what people think, I'm only interested in the realities of my life. Which are very far removed from what anybody would think. You know, if you're a pop star you're rich and famous and that's all they want to know. They want to hear about Adam Ant's trousers or whether Malcolm McLaren likes geese or something like that. They're not interested in all I've been talking about, like the grim realities of life. Being conned by giant corporations when you're too stupid to know what's been pulled.

I don't regret it because you're not supposed to regret anything, so I don't regret it because I think that's a good attitude. But I'm only interested in . . . we're digging our way out and we're going to do it and people can go fuck themselves.

What did you think of Pennie Smith's book, Before And After: A Book Of Clash Poses? Did you think it had any validity? Any real point other than to glamorise you?

It's a book of photos and at least the chapter is called "Posing". But what are photographs for? Photographs are for other photographers. I'm talking about books like that for people who are into it. I think your argument would have some grounds if we forced every Clash fan into buying a copy. If we could think of some way to do that then your argument would have some grounds, but it's freedom of choice and for £4.99 you can either get that or Paula Yates's book of knickers, right?

Scene

Paul Weller used his position and influence to finance a book of poems written by kids – not just his own fans.

Yeah, but Pennie wanted to put that book out. There's not a lot we had to do with it. Eel Pie published it. Townshend's company, and it was

Pennie's scene you know. Pennie wanted to put that book out, Eel Pie asked her and they came to us to see if we'd say okay.

Doesn't it perpetuate a rock star mythology though?

Well maybe, but that's all part of it. That's part of the lure of hoisting yourself out of some duff environment. You can't take the glamour out of this scene, not matter how hard you try.

Would you like to?

No. I don't see a necessity for it. In fact, it's impossible even if you wanted to. I mean we're real people and they're real places in that book and each of those moments was sweated to, through and beyond, right, and that's just a record of what happened, That's *her* record.

She's an artist, herself, and that's one of her testaments.

She might bring out a book on flora and fauna of the British Isles next. It's her business.

We were pleased that they wanted to bring out a book on us. Who wouldn't be flattered by that? I can see your point, but otherwise it's 'Let's all go down and lay in a black hole somewhere and die'. Hell.

Do you feel self-conscious when you're described as a rock star? Surely you don't want to end up like Mick Jagger – a caricature?

When I say a rock star shouldn't be a rock star, I'm not apologising for existing, you realise that. I'm very serious about it, I'm not apologising for existing. I'm just saying that the arrogance and unfeeling and inhumanity that these people have, they didn't grow up like that, they became like that because of the treatment that was handed out to them, people licking their arseholes from morning to night and they become like that. Arrogant and insincere . . . like Mick Jagger. But when we started out, say they were the big heroes of the day or whatever, we didn't see that you had to end up like that. We knew we were good, we knew that we could write songs that could thrash everybody else's just as well, but that doesn't mean to say we were going to crawl off in a corner and die. Yet there was no need to end up as an arrogant jerk, and that's what I mean by a rock star as defined . . . an arrogant jerk.

Yobbo

Does criticism from the press cut very deep?

I'm not sure if you people realise how sensitive these so-called tough-skinned, yobbo groups can be. I know I get very sensitive in the wrong frame of mind. In a certain frame of mind, a good slagging can just about be the last straw on the camel's back.

But no-one would ever admit that, not really, not in a group, to a journalist like I'm admitting to you. But it is true.

How has your relationship with your fans developed - has there been any deterioration? You always used to pride yourself on how close the group was to its audience.

Well I'm always willing to talk, but I'm not so good at writing back, I must admit that. But I do read and again they never have anything constructive to say. It's facile, easy, the usual stuff, 'Oh you've sold out'. But take them beyond that and they're lost. People are desperate to be trendy, the only thing they've got is to be trendy, so they must follow that. But I'll argue with somebody if they've got a real argument and they really want to know. But mostly I find when I'm in that situation, I take them past their obvious declaration and they don't know what they're talking about. They end up (adopts monotone voice), 'He says so' or 'I read it' or 'It's true', they say.

And there's nothing really beyond it, they're not interested in what's real or not.

Radical

What about the people who continually dismiss the Clash's political songs as 'radical chic'?

I just don't think a song needs a licence or a passport and these people do. It's just too bad. I know people would like to censor my dreams, but they can't.

There's too many rules because rule one is, there is no rule and that was the first rule of punk and the last. That kind of attitude, we can do what we want to do.

How would you define your own political stance?

I'm Socialist, but by persuasion, from my own experiences.

I believe you can't give orders. People have got to want to do it, and to want to do it you've got to be educated enough to think about it. I'm talking about any kind of socialist society.

Paul Simonon went to Moscow a couple of years ago and he said there were shops where tourists and party members could go, but not your average Russian. People walked round with their heads down and he said the whole thing seemed as unequal as anywhere else.

It's obviously not the solution and the Khmer Rouge, they forced that down the throats of a nation and butchered a whole nation. But you've got to realise you can't do it like that. It's the will of the people that must be followed.

Do you have any religious beliefs at all?

I'm one of those people that believes in an after life or a soul lives eternally. I don't believe that surrendering yourself to Jesus is a solution to anything at all, but I believe He existed, but not in the form that, you know, the Bible is as much a political document as it is a spiritual one. I'm sure it's been well censored by the Romans. We've got it today, but it must have passed through many hands . . .

Have you been involved much with drugs?

I've been a little acid freak in my time, though it never caused me to freak out. But there's a part of your brain where you leap in there when you take acid, where not only is there a good energy there, but something that's a malevolent one as well, and that's where a bad trip comes out of. Though I never tripped one myself, I was with plenty of people who did and that's why I gave it up.

I took it about 35 times over a period of a couple of years ('70 and '71).

What do you feel about your contemporaries: Let's start with Rotten?

I like to think that I'm celebrating being alive. We can only open our mouths and sing a tune and when he says he wants to destroy rock 'n' roll, well I've heard that often enough. I'd like him to stop there, go back a bit and define what he's saying so I can understand it. What does he mean by rock 'n' roll? And what does he see to take its place? They never say that. They just go (adopts Rotten voice), 'It must be killed'. It's like dogmatic, but I'm quite interested to know what they mean. If they mean the rock 'n' roll attitude, well I agree, destroy it.

Message

But if he thinks the mode of the music must change, I kind of agree with that as well, but I think if a message of soul is to be delivered, it can only be delivered if the listener is with you.

The way they subscribe to, is to make it sound horrible so that the listener will know how horrible they feel, which I find a bit strange. It's something a bit alien to me. I mean I'm just an r'n'b fanatic.

What's your opinion of the Jam?

The Jam are really opposite to the Clash in that I see them as an organisation. We call it Tory Rock, like tightly organised shit and I don't think you can knock that at all. Paul Weller furthermore is 22, and I got to give him respect, a hell of a lot of respect. But personally, and I'm no expert, it's too organised and dull for me.

And the Damned?

Mature

The Damned I think are great fun but I don't listen to their music. Musically they mean nothing.

Anything to say about 2-Tone?

I'm just glad 2-Tone is more mature than punk ever was.

Any last words on the Pistols?

The Pistols were locked up by McLaren, they weren't allowed to play and they took that out on the Clash. It was that kind of heady daze, it was very aggressive.

They gave it to us and we gave it right back and like we were all giving it to the Damned, so it was just like a load of petty backstabbing from childish, petulant arseholes, but the Pistols I hated them because they slagged us off without intelligence. They took a word like conscription out of a song like 'Career Opportunities' which is worth more now than any of their songs are, except maybe 'Anarchy' and that one about 'eat your heart out on a plastic tray', they took a word like that and in the MM, to an adoring, gushing Allan Jones, who had been slagging them off a couple of weeks before, and gave him what he wanted to hear. 'Conscription' they said and they tore it apart right out of context . . .

Present

Let's talk about the Blockhead connection.

I've just fucked it up. You know that interview you done with the Block-heads, well there I am sitting waiting to be interviewed on Radio One, with a microphone right next to me, and the guy goes, 'I've just read what Mickey Gallagher says here, that you've got one good album, and two thrown in as a Christmas present. What do you say about that?' And I kind of went, on the air, 'Well the guy's jealous. Just because he's taken a year to put together one measly record, of course he's going to slag us for having the audacity to come out with three.' And like Mickey Gallagher's my best mate.

What's going to happen now, though?

But I'm glad you pointed that out because that scene's been great and it is unusual for us to be mates with a group. I hope it continues although it gets sour. Like what we just said, God knows what Mickey is going to say now.

Violence

You seem more mellow than I expected. Do you think violence is ever justified – in any kind of circumstance?

I'm in Gandhi's army and Luther King's army. I tried fighting violence with violence. I tried it in Hamburg and I nearly murdered some guy, because *I* was out of order. They were out of order, but that's no excuse for me to get out of order, and I only just got out of jail alive. So from that day on, life was teaching me something and Luther King and Gandhi were right, you can't fight violence with violence. I don't know, that's my new way of thinking, maybe I'll change my mind if Thatcher books herself in for a 20-year slot . . .

Do you think you were fairly portrayed by "Rude Boy"?

We were most unhappy about what they were doing with the blacks you know. They'd be the first to admit it, Dave Mingay and Jack Hazan who made it, they're middle class twats.

Pockets

I mean I'm a middle class twat, but so are they and we didn't like what they were doing with the black people, because they were showing them dipping into pockets and then they were shown being done for something and that was their only role in the film. And that's a one way view. I think the contribution the black people made to this scene, that's one of the negative contributions . . . the music, the . . . (angry) who wants to propagate that. That's what the right wing use, all blacks are muggers which is a load of rubbish. After that rough showing I've never seen it since and nor have any of the Clash. We've never spoken to them, never seen any dough . . .

Can you briefly sum up the past, present and future of the Clash?

We were too naive and we said too many things, although I will say we meant them and we still do. But we said too many things and that means that the people aren't prepared to give the music a fair hearing obviously. They listen to it with a sneer and I do myself with other artists I hate. I won't give their music a fair hearing and sometimes I have to grudgingly accept that the people I've been slagging off for years have genuine talent. Like Elvis Costello. So I can well understand people listening to it with sneers, but I've learnt to cool down on what I expect.

A final word, then . . .

I'm sure there are answers. The answer is organisation and education.

SANDINISTA! The Strummer Overview of the New Clash Album

WE didn't mean to do it right? We ended up in New York after the tour in February and we booked a couple of days here and there just to sample the recording in that city. Then we were offered a three week block in Electric Ladyland, someone had cancelled or something.

Well I wanted to do it straight off because I knew that was Jimi Hendrix's studio and that was the only thing he'd invested his money in. So I wanted to see that anyway.

We didn't particularly have anything to record actually, I can't quite figure out what we were doing, but we went in there and we really enjoyed it, experimenting stuff, banging things down . . . like this track, (points to "Junkie Slip" on the cover) we made up on the spur of the moment.

We just went straight into that number. It wasn't even written or rehearsed and that's it, exactly it.

It wasn't kind of 'oh my God, let's do another tape', or 'what are we going to do now???' It just seemed to flow in there.

"THE MAGNIFICENT SEVEN"

I'M A person who's always hated not being in touch with funkier disco. A lot of this is written and recorded in New York and we went down to

Brooklyn and Mick picked up some rapping, clapping LPs and played them to me.

That was the first time I really could see what was going on, because it was taking a bit from Jamaican toasting and I really could say I enjoyed this funk immensely. So I couldn't wait to have a go at it.

This is a Karl Marx rapping clapping song.

Get up, go to work, (sings): "AM, the FM, the PM too" making sure you get there . . . it's from my experiences of working I wrote this from.

This is the employer shouting, "You lot!" And the workers going, "What?" then the employer, "Don't stop, give it all you got," and the stuff they pump out for you to buy! I saw an ad last night for a £900 mink coat on ITV. I mean, Jesus! The kind of trap that's set up.

This is more working stuff, "Wave goodbye to the boss, it's for our profit and his loss".

That's Karl Marx and what he's saying.

"Cheeseboiger," this is junk food to fuel you up, and this bit is like a busking lyric. I'm trying to entertain people and earn a few pennies, and yet as soon as I see a cop I've got to pick up the guitar and really move it. "Cops kicking gypsies off the pavement," this is what we've got for entertainment.

And this is like all the drivel that pumps into your senses, "lunar landing of the dentists convention/Italian mobster shoots a lobster . . ." It's like a blast of advertising, news and information that's diverting your attention from this, (points to line about "wave goodbye to the boss . . .") which is the crucial thing we should be thinking about.

But this is what we've got to think about because it's pumping at us in stereo and full colour.

This is what I did when I was working, ("hits the town, he drinks his wages"). I drank all my money. I felt so lousy earning it I had to drink it all before I felt better, and by that time it was Monday again. I've been reading Marx a lot.

The whole set-up about the guy who owns the factory, takes all the profits and pays you as little as he can. I think that an equal share of everything is called for because you're both putting in.

Why shouldn't there be equal profit sharing?

This is a bit of fun here, "Karlo Marx and Fred Engels came to the checkout at the 7-11!"

I know I shouldn't use that stuff, but that's like a grocery store in America, "the 7-11", it felt like a good rhythm.

That was when Marx was living in London, he didn't have no money, but he had the sense to be friends with Fred Engels, because Engels was paying all his bills while his kids were sick and dying, so he could carry on writing, and concentrate on what he should have.

Then this is a couple of more heroes, "Luther King and Mahatma Ghandi, went to park to check on the ball, but they were murdered 50-nil."

That's the kind of Right Wing. Men of peace and they both got shot for their troubles.

Then this is what happened to Socrates. Socrates was told to drink poison because they couldn't handle what he was saying which was the truth, yet Nixon was fiddling everybody, and they both got the same treatment. So how the hell can we set up anything if this is all we've got to go on?

"Plato the Greek or Rin Tin Tin," I'm more interested in reading about Plato than watching some garbage and this is something I read in the News Of The World, "Vacuum cleaner sucks up budgie," written in great big letters. It just seemed to be in the right rhythm of the song, so I threw it in at the end.

"THE LEADER"

THE LYRICS to that come out of reading Lord Denning's report. At the back of the report he collected all the rumours that were going around and obviously had to whitewash them.

The one that tickled me was the one about the Cabinet minister who was said to have presided at the orgies with a velvet mask on. I thought I could see the image of it.

But the hypocrisy of it all is what I'm trying to get at. The way that people are jailed for this and that, and yet up on the Top Floor they're setting no example at all. So how the hell can they dish it out to us?

"HITSVILLE UK"

IT'S about the independents. I wanted to celebrate it, because of my own experiences with the 101'ers. How many doors were shut to us, and now the independents have opened them up.

It goes here, "Mike 'n' boom in your living room,". And the fact that people can make records like that, and are making records like that, to me it's the healthiest thing ever.

It gives you confidence and encouragement to put out a record, because I was flabbergasted when Chiswick asked us, the 101'ers, to do a single.

I'd accepted that attitude that they didn't care about British bands. But now it's as if though Tamla Motown were here, but in a hundred different places and I think that's worth celebrating.

It's a Tamla/soul number and I knew we'd get flak with everyone saying CBS, blah blah and all that, but no-one else has done it. They're probably not objective enough to understand how great it is.

"REBEL WALTZ"

THIS is a song about a dream I had and I just wanted to write it down like I saw it in the dream. The idea for the waltz feel was mine.

The beat that Jamaicans discovered is, as you know, totally opposite to rock 'n' roll, and I thought a waltz was the whitest kind of music you could possibly imagine, the whitest beat. It was just a suggestion, but I wanted to see if we could put down a waltzing track using a reggae, not using a reggae beat at all, but a reggae bass, and a bit of hi hat, snare . . .

It was just an attempt to do something white, but with a really black angle. I didn't really expect it to work. It was one of those crazy ideas, but I think it does because of the way Mick mixed it.

Like he took a lot of care over it and we wanted to do adventurous mixes to go with adventurous songs and I think the way he's done it is really good.

"LOOK HERE"

THIS is a Mose Allison song. Mostly the attraction there was the lyric, what he's saying, like "what do you think you're going to be doing next year?" and "you could use a button on your lip." Good things, some good advice here. A kind of nice potted style.

"SOMEBODY GOT MURDERED"

THAT'S something that happened to this car park attendant on the Wells End Estate. He was stabbed for a fiver and that kind of set me thinking.

I was living there at the time and I saw his blood on the pavement . . ."

"SOUND OF THE SINNERS"

YEAH, well this is taking the piss out of gospel music, really but eh, they got a point somehow these people.

I like the whiplash lyrics that go with these songs, planetary earth shaking lyrics.

But if you think what one of these people is, say the ones who are 'Born Again', Jesus, people like Dylan, they've taken their thought energy inside their mind and they've really given it to a belief. And I was just thinking that a spiritual solution is just as important as a social solution.

A spiritual solution is needed to complement that I reckon. Just solely talking about economics like, say, Marx did, I don't think it's enough.

There's something deeper that should be brought into account.

"WASHINGTON BULLETS"

WELL in 1919 the United States set up this family called Somoza as a dictatorship in Nicaragua, who went the way of all dictatorships, and by 1927 there was an open war in the country.

One of the Generals who was in the Nicaraguan army was called Augusto Cesar Sandino and he's the mainman in this story.

The U.S. Marines were keeping close control on the country at this time, and he took to the mountains with whatever men would follow him. From 1927 to 1934 they harassed and attacked in a kind of Che Guevara action from the mountains, and finally in '34 there was a negotiation and the Somozas agreed to kick the U.S. Marines out.

And that was Sandino's number one rule.

He said he wouldn't put his gun down till the Americans had left. So they kicked them out, and he was invited to the Palace in Nicaragua for negotiations.

So he went to the Palace where there was a big dinner, and after the dinner Somoza had him dragged out and shot in the courtyard.

Since then Somoza's son took over, the one who was murdered the other month, and carried on in the same way.

Eventually it got so bad, like they had this thing called the National Guard, set up and trained by American Marine commandos and Somoza was using this guard. Usual thing. Hundreds of people disappearing each week, and the whole thing was becoming a shit-out.

In 1961 three men met and formed the FSLM (Frante Sandinista Liberation Nicaragua Nationale) in Honduras, because they were exiles and they tried fighting various actions along the Costa Rican border.

They really didn't get anywhere, they were wiped out whenever they struck. So they decided to change their tactics, and work from inside Nicaragua, from inside the people.

They started doing that in 1963 and since then they've split up into three factions.

One that believed in a certain kind of warfare, like guerrilla warfare, another which believed in working and educating the people and another faction which believed in something else.

That hampered their development, but all through the Sixties and the early Seventies they increased, until open warfare finally broke out around 1977.

Whole cities would rise up against the National Guard, and Somoza would aerial bombard these packed slums.

Like he owned 80 per cent of almost everything. He had banks, farms, he was just taking all the money in the country for himself and his toadies.

Meanwhile the FSLM, they put their differences away in a common cause. And at the same time there was the liberal type party, what's called the 12, who were the 12 most respected men in Nicaragua, they were kind of liberals, they weren't Somoza's puppets, and they joined forces with the FSLM too and they became great heroes.

There was this newspaper, the only paper that criticised Somoza, called Black Parenza, and this guy called Jose Chemaro, he was the editor, and he actually went to school with Somoza and they'd always hated each other.

In 1978 he was assassinated by the National Guard and that provoked another storm of riots.

Finally, in 1979, leading up to July 19th, there was open warfare in every city, and the Sandinista guerrillas, they joined with the people.

Everybody was being slaughtered and persecuted and they had to go to the people to survive, and work with them.

On July 19th, 1979, the revolutionaries swept into power, but most of the fighting was done by people between the ages of 14 and 25, and I read a bit of paper from the Nicaraguan Solidarity campaign, and it said at one point the National Guard was pulling up or shooting anybody between those ages.

In other words it became a crime to be between the ages of 14 and 25. I felt it was really important.

Well I was told about it by a guy called Armstrong in California, because there was no information about all this in the press.

And I felt it was specially important, apart from the fact that they got rid of a dictatorship that had been there since 1919 and the people had done it themselves with teenage guerrillas, but the fact that Carter had a Human Rights policy.

Which meant that although they were trying all the things they could do in the world, behind the scenes, like they dropped Somoza at one point, but the fact is, that it was US Marines who had been in it all the way.

In fact the Foreign Department was quoted as saying, 'That Somoza guy is a hell of a son of a bitch. But he's our son of a bitch.'

And the fact that revolution and civil war had turned the country, and yet America has not sent in troops like Russia would or America would in any other way, like Vietnam, you could see what would happen if the Imperial powers weren't putting their fingers in.

But I only found about it from some crazy guy in California which is why we called the album, "Sandinista".

"LOSE THIS SKIN"

THIS features Tymon Dogg. This guy is one of those guys who has been chewed up by the music industry and left for dead a long time ago.

After he'd been chewed up by Apple and Threshold, the Moody Blues label, I met him some years later and I was just drifting around. So I became his bottle up down the tubes, we went to Europe and we had a lot of fun.

Anyway he was in New York and he went up to Mick Jones's hotel room, which was good in a way because it wasn't me pushing my mate on the rest of the band, it happened very naturally.

They started jamming around and he played "Lose This Skin", and he plays the violin like this, from the hip and that was the day Mickey Gallagher and Norman Watt Roy arrived.

But because he'd played that number on his own for all those years, he plays a five bar beat, it's not a regular thing and we couldn't get the hang of it.

So we went back to the hotel really depressed, but the next day, Norman's and Gluggo's jetlag had worn off and we hit it first time which is that take there.

"THE CALL UP"

THAT Clash single, "Call Up", you've got to give it to receive it, and if not then it's going to be like dog shit. So if you want immediate rock then you've got to get something else.

But it's still not a piece of shit like Paul Moreley called it in the NME.

That thing is like a circular mood and that's something you've got to feel good about before you put it on. So we are treading on thin ice because we're not going to get that kind of consideration.

But I want that kind of consideration, just that basic consideration that it might be good, or worth a listen without prejudice.

You see, the only place we're going to do anything is by starting here, (hand goes on heart) and those people who say they're going anyway, they're not helping at all.

They're doing . . . like you must not act the way you were brought up, and that's the way they're acting, the way they were brought up to act.

And I was a bit of a hippy when I left school, I felt that very strongly then, about conditioning and that's all that is.

We've got to stop moving with the flow, harming ourselves and work outwards.

I mean, why should the young people of this world slaughter each other again. How many times have we done it already?

We're the baby of the survivors and yet we're all too keen to go off again. And those boys on the single cover, they're all Russians, and I bet they're not too keen about it.

SPANISH STRUMMERS

Mike Nicholls | May 9, 1981 | *Record Mirror* (UK)

In the first quarter of 1981, the Clash amazed the world—and possibly themselves—by reappointing Bernard Rhodes as their manager. Apart from that, it was a quiet year.

There was no new material released under the Clash's name aside from "This Is Radio Clash"—a sparkling lyric with an unattractively angular backdrop—and some underwhelming B-sides to the singles mined from *Sandinista!* They also played on *Spirit of St. Louis*, an album produced by Jones for then-girlfriend Ellen Foley. The record was a failed but noble experiment in which Strummer and Jones ventured into intriguingly alien songwriting territory: ballads and European theatrical pop. Otherwise, the Clash concentrated on live work, building toward a ferocious touring schedule that would later lead Strummer to conclude of the band's career, "If I had to sum it up, I'd say we played every gig on the face of the earth."

This report from the road appeared in *Record Mirror*, the most pop-oriented of the British music weeklies. Despite the publication's lightheartedness, the report managed to touch on some weighty issues. One was a masterplan by Rhodes to spurn the UK market, something which would culminate in the Clash's UK fan base being hollowed out. The other was Topper Headon's heroin addiction, which would culminate in the drummer being sacked. Like Kris Needs's *Flexipop!* feature later in this text, it also captures the fact that, for all their earnestness in song, the Clash had a lot of fun on tour.

Notes: (Freddie) Laker was a pioneer in cheap transatlantic consumer flights.

The Clash adopted a band songwriting credit one album previous to the publication of this article, not two.

For "London's Calling" read "London Calling"

For "Bank Robber" read "Bankrobber"
For "Someone Got Murdered" read "Somebody Got Murdered"
For "Harlem Globe Trotters" read "Harlem Globetrotters"
For "Luis Buneul" read "Luis Buñuel" —Ed.

HASSLES SURROUND The Clash like oversexed iron fillings round an electromagnet. A band of extremes still obsessed with the romantic notion of the rock 'n' roll outlaw, their every action is garnished with a side-order of wind-ups.

Tour managers are driven to distraction, hotel managers to calling the police and their own managers are swopped almost annually. As for record companies, promoters and Press personnel—well, you chose your job, mate.

But occasionally the electromagnet is switched off and they become regular human beings. Joe Strummer, in particular, is more than human: he's one of the warmest, compassionate and genuinely concerned people I've ever met. To many the personification of The Clash, he sets increasingly high standards for himself and expects to see this attitude reflected in those around him.

It's this strong sense of moral purpose that caused him to complete the recent London Marathon without having gone into any prior training; to treat his own money with outright scorn; and to flog himself into the ground, relentlessly improving himself both mentally and physically. This may take the form of playing 'till he drops or immersing himself in the language, history and street culture of every country he visits.

Sure, he's no saint. Strummer womanises, gets wrecked and bad-mouths others like the best of us. But his huge capacity for living makes him a fascinating travelling partner. And as an extension of this, The Clash are probably the ultimate band to go on the road with.

Ironically, the interview was originally to take place in Ladbroke Grove on Saturday morning. But a unique combination of hassles and good timing conspire to find me muscling in on their debut tour of Spain. So exit the standard question and answer session . . . and into the front line.

I've known The Clash for some time now. My first dialogue with them was some time before I started writing for a music paper, at the French Mont De Marsan punk festival in 1977. After that I dropped in on them on every British tour and have had frequent conversations when running into each of them out and about London. Hitting Barcelona and Madrid with the band seems a just journalistic dessert for someone who has held the band in his highest musical affections these past four years.

A typical breakdown of communication between themselves and CBS means they aren't anticipating my arrival. This entails several hours of sleuth-work trying track them down at hotel, gig and first Press conference, their disdain for schedules meaning missing them on each occasion. Getting into the hall—the Pavillion Juventual Barcelona, no less—proves an even bigger problem.

Next to the local bouncers the average English gorilla is but a mere boy scout and since I didn't know the Spanish for "I'm part of the situation", it takes longer than usual to blag my way through.

Once inside, however, things start looking up. This is not entirely unconnected with the fact that quadruple tequillas are only half a quid a throw and there are some familiar fellow imbibers around. Like veteran roadie Jock who I've last seen passing out at Watford Gap Services after ordering "pizza—deep fried". He obligingly furnishes me with a backstage pass.

Then there's the famous PA supremo Roadent. Ever-ready to trade some juicy gossip for a beer he claims that it is his pallid self who is the subject of The Passions' falsely-titled 'I'm In Love With A German Film Star'.

But to the gig. The Clash haven't played for ten months and it shows. Apart from the fact that you can barely hear him, Mick Jones looks well slovenly and it's left to the rampant Stummer to single-handedly fly the flag.

The following night is a different story altogether. In the same way as a good Paddy Crerand performance used to make Man. United in the Best, Law and Charlton European Cup winning days, Mick needs to be on form if The Clash are to deliver. And in Madrid he enjoys his finest hour (and 40 minutes).

From the preliminary 'London's Calling' to the concluding 'London's Burning' he's at his most inspired, brilliant best, tossing out scintillating breaks and solos with effortless verve. His style embraces the best elements of HM as well as being particularly suited to the dub-orientated stuff of the past two LPs.

The beautiful 'Someone Got Murdered' can raise tears at the best of times but at the Real Madrid (basket ball section) stadium it caught another universe. The 7000 capacity crowd—almost double the number they generally play to in Britain and this is only their second-ever dago date—were also treated to red hot renditions of 'Bank Robber', 'Hammersmith Palais', Clampdown', 'Armagideon Time', Junco Partner', 'Jimmy Jazz', 'Janie Jones' and, of course, 'Spanish Bombs' and that's only the familiar stuff! Also up for grabs were about half a dozen newies but they kind of got mislayed in the brain-damaging circumstances of the next 48 hours (which they didn't play).

These begin almost immediately after the Barcelona show where start of tour high jinx co-incide with need to drown collective sorrows following the inauspicious opener. My unexpected appearance in the dressing room raises further mayhem. Whilst Joe introduces me to the non-plussed security guy and pumps me for news about cartoonist Ray Lowry's latest exploits, Mick and I chortle about unpaid rates bills.

Topper's greeting is rather more unorthodox. Having collapsed (with shall we say, fatigue?) at the end of the concert, his first action on coming round is to playfully toss half a brick in my direction.

Affecting a deft side-step, I manage to upset a trestle of (thankfully soft) drinks and from then on the lunacy never lets up. Frightened fans run for their lives as missiles strafe the air whilst back at the hotel room things are hardly a whole lot more civilised.

Bounteous supplies of duty free booze and other useful relaxants make for quite an unusual interview situation. This itself is punctuated by regular bathroom huddles comprising Mick, Joe and the ever-lurking Kosmo Vinyl, ostensibly the band's publicist but more essentially a major wind-up-artist. For example, the following morning my enquiry about which flight to book to Madrid is met with the astonishing non-sequitur: "You, know, I met the Harlem Globe Trotters in this airport."

Constant jokes are cracked about him being the Information Dept., other departments such as Complaints and Insults being occupied by Mick and bassist Paul Simonon respectively.

Head of the Ideas Department is Clash manager Bernie Rhodes whose re-appointment to his past position has been the most important development in the group's recent history. To recap a little, Rhodes took the group under his wing soon after his mate McLaren put together the Pistols and was responsible for The Clash's original urban guerilla stance.

Two years later he was ousted by his fully-grown fledglings but since his successors lacked the creativity of his fertile mind he has been recalled. His first major idea has been to abandon Blighty for the next nine months. He sees the whole music scene here as having returned to its pre-punk jaded self and reckons there's more inspiration crackling in the atmosphere of the newly-emerging rock 'n' roll territories.

Spain, with its healthily-growing post-Franco economy is a classic example, as are Portugal, Poland and Yugoslavia, all of which the band intend to play during their self-imposed exile. London, on the other hand, is bereft of any worthwhile rock clubs and TV shows but by the beginning of next year the situation may change.

Bernie tells me all this the morning after the night before at Barcelona Airport. The band are being unusually guarded. This might have something to do with my having crashed out on them a few hours earlier. Then again this personal first (falling asleep at gigs was last year's thing, maaan; Roky Eriksons in reverse are gonna be big in the summer of '81) did take place at 5am and the full effect of the previous evening's poor start to the tour is striking home.

The conversation with Rhodes, whose inter-Clash activities included "discovering" The Specials and Dexys Midnight Runners, continues during the flight to Madrid.

On asking him whether the band's political stance hasn't always been somewhat naive, his reply is "It had to come—like Laker. Politics is something which concerns every individual and the band are encouraging, rather than preaching, arousing interest in the likes of, say, the Sandinista rebels, so that people can investigate for themselves.

"An author of a history book doesn't necessarily agree with what he's writing about," he continues, "he's providing his interpretation of certain facts."

On the other hand, Joe Strummer disagrees that the band are merely passive observers. With the rain beating down on our coach roof as we leave Madrid Airport, he tells me that by the same token the band have no concrete political ideology other than "human rights."

"That explains 'Sandinista!'" he elucidates. "We felt sympathy with what they were doing (overthrowing the ruling family oligarchy in Nicaragua) and there was a total of media blanket at the time. So the title's useful. We're telling people about it. Yeah, I wouldn't say we preach but we are committed."

We? Although Strummer and Jones are generally acknowledged to be the band's songwriters, the last couple of albums have given all four members equal credit and 'Guns Of Brixton' was written by Paul.

Although in the light of recent events the song appears quite visionary, wasn't it somewhat provocative in 1979? "No," Simonon replies. "It was just about a situation where people could get pushed too far. And in the end they were—by the police."

Though rarely the most articulate member of The Crash, like Topper, he's certainly no fool, their "strong silent type" personalities admirably suiting them to their engine room role. Paul seems to come into his own at the stadium Press conference where a member of CBS Spain's International Department acts as interpreter.

When asked what he thinks of Mick Jagger's remark that the band "aren't even new for China" he jokes that the old Stone needs that kind of cheap publicity. Other ripostes show a similar degree of wit which is no less than the mainly banal questions deserve.

Although Joe's reply about the band touring Spain for "the sun the wine and the women" was not taken seriously by the assembled hacks, a later conversation with him reveals that it isn't far off the mark. Five years ago he hitch-hiked from Malaga to Madrid, having an enjoyable affair with a local senorita in the process.

It was his affection for the country that inspired the melody of 'Spanish Bombs', despite its stern political references. "It's a love song dedicated to myself and my father," he explains before going on to describe how one night, after a few drinks, his dad admitted to him that in the late thirties he'd had half a mind to fight for the Republican cause in the Spanish Civil War.

This return to politics and human rights leads me to ask where one draws the line in striving for freedom. Does he actually sympathise with the Red Brigade terrorists whose colours he's sported in the past?

"I don't want myself or anyone to go round killing people," he retorts bluntly, "I'd rather walk about in the sun with my hands in my pockets.

"That 'T'-shirt," he adds as an afterthought, was only a reaction anyhow—to that whole Rock Against Racism hypocrisy. Playing with phonies like Tom Robinson in that park and arguing about who'd head-line and use which dressing room. It was just a handy way of getting a big audience, with all the record company types getting in on the act."

Yet the band remain staunch propagandists, photographic images of assorted causes adorning their corrugated iron sheet stage backdrop, Projected slides show 'Right To Work' marchers in Detroit, devastation in Cambodia, dole queues in the UK and so on.

Equally varied is each of the band's taste in music. Few minutes of free time are spent not tuning into sounds blasting forth from portable tape machines they each carry everywhere. Whilst Joe and Topper listen to virtually everything, Mick specialises in reggae.

Paul is currently getting into rockabilly, compiling cassettes of all sorts of obscure stuff that few fans will be likely to identify if the odd riff finds its way on to the next Clash album!

We all catch a good earful of combos like the Shuffling Hungarians in Joe's room after the second gig but so, unfortunately, do our neigh-bours. Repeated rude demands from the hotel manager to shut up receive the requisite response: A five star hotel with 10 star-prices ought not to inconvenience its guests with no-star sound-proofing.

Following continual threats to call the police, the hapless manager finally keeps his promise and arrives at the door with two of the meanest suckers you ever saw. What *they* see is like something out of a surrealist movie. Lucky Luis Buneul is one of their countrymen.

Unconscious in one corner of the room is a fully-clothed Kosmo Vinyl who has at last succumbed to his most feared phenomenon—sleep. Sharing the ridiculous aluminium thermal bedspread we've draped over him like an Xmas turkey are a couple of, er, night birds (far more polite expression than groupie, eh Joe?) one of whom is staring blankly at the equally blank TV which no one bothered to turn off when reception ceases several hours earlier.

Not only all this but when Paul opens the door and the Carabinieri appear, Joe is so taken aback that he trips over the coffee (ha!) table and sends a whole pile of empty bottles tumbling to the floor. The domino effect somehow spreads to a neatly-arranged row of tapes which one by one kamikaze dive off the sideboard into the waste paper bin.

Miraculously the uniformed ones leave without making any arrests. The consequent adrenalin flow induced by the previous proceedings puts fresh life into him and he insists that we both "hit the streets".

"C'mon, man, let's go and find something to eat. I'm starving. Wow, the first pang of hunger!" he exclaims, holding his arms aloft.

In the half-light of that hotel room—dimmed by scarves draped over the soulless lamps—it was obvious that he considered this a triumph. A cossetted rock 'n' roll star with international fortune at his feet able to enjoy the easy temptation of Epicurean excess in favour of a fry up at some barrow boys' caff.

I hope Joe Strummer stays hungry and proud. I hope the rest of The Clash do likewise. Inevitably they all will.

HOW THE CLASH FED THE WONDERBREAD GENERATION, MADE THE MOUNTAIN COME TO MOHAMMED —AND OTHER MIRACLES

Mick Farren | June 20, 1981 | *New Musical Express* (UK)

Years after the Clash had split up, Mick Jones was asked by a journalist what he considered the highlight of the band's career. His answer would have caused brows to furrow in his home country but would have made perfect sense to American fans. He chose the media frenzy that surrounded the Clash in the States in June 1981 over their series of concerts at Bond International Casino, New York City. When the city's fire department objected to the venue's flouting of capacity limits, fans—facing the prospect of not being able to see the group—rioted. The band made the front cover of the *New York Post*, which screamed "'CLASH' IN TIMES SQUARE"—which fact, considering that the origin of the group's name lay in the preponderance of the word "clash" in newspaper reports, neatly completed a circle.

In Mick Farren's report from the heart of the proceedings, Mick Jones is rather sniffy about the United States and many of its denizens, but he and the rest of his colleagues soon became rather enamored of the burnishing of their legend the Bond affair engendered. (The Clash nobly agreed to perform seventeen consecutive dates at the venue until all ticket obligations had been met.) So important a place did it assume for the group in their own mythos that the title of a never-released Don Letts documentary about it—*Clash on*

Broadway—was, ten years later, given to their first box set. The latter was released around the same juncture that Jones braggingly recollected to the *NME*, "We ran this town. We took Broadway. De Niro was bringing his kids to see us, and the city stopped. The Clash were in town."

Ironically, such sentiments simply demonstrate how the Clash had lost touch with their home fans and their values: in Britain, the Bond affair had no resonance, a little-reported incident in a country that the Clash had always implied their fans should disdain. —Ed.

KOSMO VINYL shoots both fists heavenward, for all the world like a man who had just scored for West Ham at Wembley.

"I got the news on every channel! I got the news on every channel! I conned them all. I told them all that they were going to get an exclusive and then I stitched them all up!"

Bernie Rhodes may be back as The Clash's manager, but Kosmo is their conscience and one of their greatest psychic protectors. Right at this particular moment Kosmo is ecstatic over the fact that each of New York's seven major TV channels has run a substantial Clash item on their early evening news shows. The fact that, at the moment in question, The Clash may not be able to play in New York at all doesn't cause him a second's pause. There's nothing Kosmo likes better than the reckless danger of being a rock and roll Indian on the cowboys' own turf. Jerking the electronic media seems a fine prank.

In fact, The Clash are jerking around the whole of New York. They have arrived in the middle of a mini-British invasion. PiL, The Jam, U2, Teardrop Explodes and The Fall have all been through town in roughly the same timespace, but nobody has made anything like the same impact. The others are just rock and roll bands. The Clash, by a sweet combination of ignorance, arrogance, deviousness and plain blind luck, have become, if not a cause, at least a major talking point.

For a while, it seemed as though no British band was going to be able to top the PiL outrage of being bottled off the stage of the Ritz and then asked to play a return engagement. Then the Clash turned up in town, created two mini riots on Times Square, got themselves four solid days of saturation media coverage and, by the time the band has finished its New York stint, they will have played to some 32,000 punters.

The original idea was for The Clash to play an extended US tour. The usual gruelling round of 32 cities in 34 days or what have you. Unfortunately Epic, the band's massively corporate US label, refused, for their own reasons—reasons they don't want to reveal—to underwrite the tour financially.

The only other alternative was to play an extended season in a city like New York. Instead of taking the show to the fans, it was decided to bring the fans to the show. As Joe Strummer put it at the very first press conference before all the trouble started, "It's like the fans are going on tour instead of us, the mountain's coming to Mohammed."

The venue chosen for this Clash spectacular was a place called Bonds International Casino. Up until a few months ago Bonds had been a predominantly gay disco with lavish lighting effects, dancing fountains and a Flash Gordon staircase that bombards anyone walking up or down it with a frenzy of lights and tweeting sub-Eno electronics.

The main problem about Bonds is that the place is situated slap in the middle of Times Square, which is pretty much America's epicentre of vice, vulture shock, sleaze and dark doorway vampirism. Bonds' initial intention was to add a couple of thousand star spangled funksters to the midnight mess.

Unfortunately, it didn't quite work out that way. When disco failed, Bonds tried to stay in business by turning to live rock and roll. They ripped out the more lavish effects. The dancing fountains went and a stage was erected in their place. The first attempts were fairly modest, Burning Spear and The Dead Kennedys' New York debuts. Crowds increased when they presented The Ramones and later The Plasmatics with their exploding car. Booking The Clash for eight days straight looked, on the surface, like a move that would not only fit exactly with the band's needs but also put Bonds firmly on the map as one of the pre-eminent rock joints in the city.

What The Clash didn't know was that New York was in the midst of a rock club war. Over the past 18 months, far too many people had the bright idea that the way to make a million dollars was by opening a rock nightspot. Everyone except those involved knew the tide had to turn.

Since the start of the year, attrition has set in. The cavernous Heat, the chic and trendy Rock Lounge and the Anglophile and long-established

Hurrah have all closed. Others will undoubtedly follow. None of the other owners and promoters wanted to see Bonds pulling huge crowds right in the middle of town.

The real physical capacity of the ex-disco is around 4,000. That's the number that can be crammed in without their either being crushed, suffocated or driven axe-berserk crazy. The legal limit is 1,750. That's the number of people who can get out of the place in the event of fire.

Like most other New York clubs, Bonds sold tickets for The Clash up to and probably beyond the real physical capacity. Unlike other clubs, though, Bonds got caught. During the opening show the Fire Department received an anonymous tip. The firemen arrived just before the end of The Clash's set. The fire chief wanted to pull the plugs on the band but relented when Kosmo pointed out that if he did, the crowd were highly likely to rip the place to bits.

The Clash were allowed one encore, then the lights came on and the nightclub was cleared. The following day Bonds was informed that if they exceeded the legal limit on one more occasion they'd be closed. On the day after that the Building Commissioner also got in on the act and for 24 hours Bonds was actually shut down. Then, in the full glare of the local media, a compromise was reached. The shows could go on but not to more than 1,750 punters.

Unfortunately, something in the region of 4,000 tickets had been sold for each of The Clash's eight shows. The band, finding themselves caught in the middle of all this nonsense, decided that there was only one ethical course. They would add enough dates so everyone who has a ticket will get a chance to see a show. This means they will play a total of 16 days at Bonds.

It's a rugged stint, particularly for Joe Strummer's voice, following on a European tour. Doubling their expenses also means they take a financial loss. In order to reschedule the extra dates, Bonds are forced to blow out a date by The Stranglers and Gary Glitter's US opening.

IT SEEMS like everyone and their uncle now comes on stage to the strains of some stirring prerecorded tape. For The Clash in New York it's Hugo Montenegro's title theme from *For A Few Dollars More*. This spaghetti western opus is not only ironic, but for me it has the right touch of melodramatic, trashy bravado.

I figure if they had motorcycle gangs in the Soviet Union, The Clash are pretty much what they would look like. Jones is spiderlike in black, Strummer in a red, sawn-down Levi jacket, Simonon stone-faced in leather pants and a T-shirt, Topper stripped to the waist.

The particular show I'm talking about is the fourth into their NY stint. The opening night had been hot, crowded and, despite the fact that the audience had gone quite bananas, the band had been inclined to ernie about. At the end of normally taut, tight tunes they seemed unable to resist the temptation to fall into lengthy dub grooves, some of which were interesting, others just plain dull. Someone behind me whispered, "Jesus, they want to be The Grateful Dead when they grow up."

Four days in, though, The Clash are firmly on their feet. It's been a while since I've seen them, and the thing that's most noticeable is the stature they've gained. They've matured and they've acquired a definite authority. Where once they were enthusiastic but ragged and all over the place, they are now tight, tough and confident.

While Joe Strummer will never be a bel canto singer, he's learned to work extraordinarily well within his limitations and, when there's a danger of his faltering, he gets more than adequate vocal support from the other three.

Jones has become a passingly nifty guitar player with a pleasingly eclectic style that spans influences from JA to rockabilly as well as straight-ahead post-Chuck Berry knocking it out. In addition, he has gained a number of electronic toys including a pair of heavily gizmoed rototoms to keep us amused during the dub sequences. While Jones, with a mile-long guitar lead, leaps and bounces over the whole stage, Simonon, impassive as ever, sticks to his slot at stage right except when he fronts the band for the now topically prophetic (if slightly overstaged) 'Guns Of Brixton'.

The real surprise, though, is Topper Headon. Rock steady is a grossly overused cliche, but it fits so well. He lays down the foundation rhythm for The Clash with a dependability that can't be beat.

High points in the show include 'Ivan Meets GI Joe', the vintage 'Career Opportunities', the Vince Taylor classic 'Brand New Cadillac',

Strummer's traditional 'Junco Partner' and the newie 'This Is Radio Clash'. It's a long show, just short of two hours, and after all the grief of standing in line, switching dates and exchanging tickets, the audience isn't stinted.

There's more, however, than just the sum total of the songs. I used the word authority earlier and figure it's still about the most descriptive. There's an air about the band, an aura if you like. The only bands that have it are the ones who, barring accidents and lame-brain screw ups, are destined to be very, very big.

CERTAINLY THE Yanks seem to feel this is true. They want The Clash in the worst possible way. It's mid-afternoon on the sidewalk outside Bonds and a young woman is complaining into a TV camera. She has come down from Boston only to find that her ticket is now good for a show some eight days later.

"I mean, I can't come back next week. I already spent over two hundred dollars so far, what with the drugs and everything."

A woman with matted frizzy hair, the kind of skimpy outfit that Rolling Stones tour groupies wore in 1975, is offering to strip in order to raise the money for a ticket off a tout. She's clearly on the verge of hysteria. There was a time when loud, demented, star-fucker obsessives were simply a part of the rock and roll tapestry, but since Hinckley and Chapman they are treated with a little more care.

Nonetheless, the combination of boobs and high emotion attracts both the cops and the TV crews who have been camped on the block ever since Bonds' troubles started. It is, after all, New York's biggest punk rock fiasco since Sid stuck the knife into Nancy. The woman shrieks into a proffered microphone: "I should have backstage passes for every show!"

Even inside the club there are elements of the kind of hysteria that used to be the preserve of The Rolling Stones. In the space of one session of hanging out after the show, I encounter a woman handing around a nifty little nitrous oxide inhaler; Pearl Harbour, who's been hired by The Clash to DJ their shows, is spiked with acid and has to be taken to Bellevue Hospital; I also have my tape machine stolen.

Part of the problem is that America seems to need a big, bold, badass rock and roll band. For some reason they're unable to produce one for themselves.

Basically, The Rolling Stones' old slot is going begging after they lost it by being too old, too tired and too disco dreary. The contenders are not impressive. Jim Carroll doesn't have what it takes; The Dictators never made it and were ugly to boot; Johnny Thunders was too low-rent and The Dead Boys couldn't hold it together. Not even in America are Ted Nugent's carnivore capers seen as anything but strictly for laffs. The slot is definitely open and, if not the whole of America, at least New York seems anxious to shoehorn The Clash into it.

Mick Jones is not altogether happy with the situation.

"A couple of years ago it was never even on the cards for us to come here."

The Clash are clearly not convinced about this eager US audience. The American kids seem into icons where the band is into iconoclasm. The American kids are, apart from a few sore-thumb loonies, docile and pre-programmed. From where The Clash are standing it's not only the band who has to prove itself. The crowd has to do it too.

So far the crowd hasn't done too good a job. By far the largest majority have come to see a hard rock show but they don't give a tinker's cuss about The Clash's leftist principles or third world connections. They have come for their money's worth and nothing more.

When pro-El Salvador leaflets cascade from the roof, the audience grabs for them eagerly only to discard them when they find out that they're not free gifts. As Strummer puts it, "We play music that, hopefully, not only gets people dancing but makes them think while they're dancing."

Unfortunately, America is not thinking. Already there have been displays of the Bonds audience's thick-ear conservatism. They've been given the support acts, mainly chosen by The Clash themselves, as hard a hard time as any opener at a brute ignorant HM fest. First and worst victims were Grandmaster Flash And The Furious Five, one of the city's hottest rap acts. Their talkover funk interplay was clearly too much for three quarters of the crowd, white, Wonderbread-fed, post-Travolta kids from the suburbs. To them, rap is the anthem of the ghettos, the music of the kids with whom they fight in high school. The Furious Five flee the stage after a scant 15 minutes in a hail of garbage and Dixie cups. (Fortunately Bonds doesn't serve its over-priced beer in bottles.)

They have one final shot: "We've played a lot of places to a lot of faces, but we've never seen shit like this."

It was a similar incident to the one on the previous tour when toaster Mikey Dread was booed off the stage at the Palladium. Other support bands haven't fared much better. ESG, a multi-ethnic band from the South Bronx got the hook from the hooligans when they opened the Friday show, and even The Slits found themselves experiencing something of a negative response. Funkapolitan, on the other hand, despite doing rap material, were almost acclaimed. The final irony was that the most popular support with the mob turned out to be Siren, an all-female hard rock band not a million miles from heavy metal.

"It's disgusting, it's so fucking narrow-minded. I mean, it's an insult to us when you look at it. We picked the bands that opened for us, so, supposedly, we liked them and we wanted to turn the crowd onto something. They're too narrow-minded to open up to something new."

It seems that there is a hard core at the show who simply see The Clash as just another macho rock band and, if they are even aware of it, look on the band's political stance as just another gimmick—like the Stones' drug taking, Alice Cooper's monsters or Nugent's big game hunting. Mick Jones has a fix on this breed of Yank.

"They're like little kids with roller skates and Walkmans on their heads. I don't think our influence gets through to them at all. It's really cushioned here. It's the mass hypnotism."

He flips a hand toward the TV. A sickeningly cute child is telling us that he's going to be a top class basketball player by the time he's 18 because his mom feeds him on Wonderbread.

The cushioning of America is probably one of the most scary symptoms of the current malady. America (and that goes for a good deal of kids as well as the middle-aged) is still on its honeymoon with greed and Reagan. The cuts in welfare, aid to the old and education have yet to be felt. The serious unemployment has yet to come. Alexander Haig has not yet been allowed to start his escalating brush-fire war. The draft hasn't happened and neither has the polarisation of the racism that lurks just below the surface of the Clash audience. Overt fascism will only emerge from the swamp when America starts to hurt. Right now it hasn't even begun to care.

"On one level we're the same as them. We're just as irresponsible. On the other level, our stage performances, the records we make, the statements we make—we try and be responsible. Maybe not objective, but responsible and I don't see anything wrong with that, if you have information, to offer it as advice."

He looks for an example.

"Say you got to register for the draft, don't register and see what happens."

He suddenly grins.

"In fact, your high school turns you in. That's what happens."

The flip side of The Clash's coin is, of course, the situation in England. The US fan may want The Clash but not understand them, but if a mix of rumour and media are anything to be believed, there is at least one part of the English audience that seems to understand The Clash and not want them anymore. I put this to Mick Jones who seems concerned but not overly worried.

"We haven't played in England for a long time. I think when we do, everyone will see that there are plenty of people who still want to see us."

You don't think there are a lot of people with the attitude of fuck you, you abandoned your roots?

"I think there are some writers saying 'Fuck you, you abandoned your roots'."

You don't think that the very fact that you're making it tends to alienate some sections of the original fans?

"I don't worry about making it, I worry about not making it. If I don't make it then all the kids who are watching can say to themselves 'well shit, they didn't make it, they didn't get out, what hope is there for us to make it?' If *we* make it, then those kids know that *they* got a chance too."

I enquire if he could see The Clash taking over the old Rolling Stones slot of global bad boys into which the Americans seem so anxious to slide them.

"We don't really want it."

IT WOULD seem fairly certain that, barring accident, The Clash are on the verge of some sort of major breakthrough in the USA and, even in these depleted times, it is still the land of the big money and big exposure. They are a direct, almost traditionalist, four piece rock and roll band, and, in that, they are eminently acceptable in all areas of the country. It's their political attitude, their ethics and principles and their single-minded determination to use rock and roll as a mass medium, a means to hand out their very personal view of the conflicts in the real world, that sets them apart.

Not only are they on the verge of a breakthrough, they are, by very definition, on the verge of a whole set of problems. The role of a political band is about as relaxing as a brisk saunter through a minefield.

For The Clash it will be made doubly difficult because whatever breakthrough they make will coincide with the building of resistance to Reagan's right wing policies. They could even find themselves figureheads and anthem writers for a particularly bitter conflict.

They will find themselves not only a target for flak from the bad guys but also from some who are supposed to be allies. There is always the sniping of the ideologically pure and the inverted elitist who thinks that you can't have valid idea unless you're in penury and rags.

They will have to avoid the traps that eventually brought down The Doors and The MC5. They will find themselves at war with their record company (although this is nothing new for The Clash—all through the stretch at Bonds nobody from Epic seems to have shown their face) and at odds with a major section of the rock media who will never be satisfied with their efforts. They will also have the problem of simply maintaining their realworld perspective while being seduced and massaged by the trappings of stardom.

I doubt if I'd bother with The Clash except I still hold with the innocent belief that rock and roll music is a means of mass communication not yet totally in the hands of bankers and corporations, and that it still has the power to influence society as a whole—maybe not to the degree that I fondly imagined in the '60s, but that it can exert an influence.

I also believe that, of all contemporary rock and roll bands, The Clash have gone further in using this medium on a mass, politically-based level. As I'm writing this, the TV is telling me that Israeli strike planes have levelled an Iraqi nuclear plant which may or may not have been manufacturing atomic weapons.

I figure I'm going to need all the help I can get to survive this bloody decade.

CLASH CREDIBILITY RULE!

Paul Rambali | October 10, 1981 | *New Musical Express* (UK)

Joe Strummer had complained to Paolo Hewitt in December 1980 that journos didn't understand how "sensitive" musicians could be. Nobody could have been left in any doubt after reading this feature.

Strummer and Jones were promoting the Clash's first UK dates in nearly a year and a half but spent much of their interviews veritably spluttering with rage about the endless slights and put-downs of the Clash that appeared week in, week out, in the UK music press. (Such slights would occur not just in copy directly about the Clash but also as asides in reviews, features, and news items on other recording artists.) Strummer was especially vexed by what he considered the turncoat attitude of the *NME*, a paper that had once fawned over the band.

The two could have directed their anger at their manager and at fate as much as the British music press. The policy avowed by Rhodes to Mike Nicholls earlier in this book to forsake the UK had generated a backlash in the Clash's home country. Moreover, in the summer of '81, unemployment-related youth riots erupted across Britain, particularly in Brixton, London, whose racial tensions had been explored in the *London Calling* track "Guns of Brixton." At the time the Clash happened to be in—you guessed it—the USA. The unfortunate juxtaposition led to the inevitable cracks about how, when the white riots they'd claimed they wanted finally happened, the Clash weren't on the streets but across the pond sucking up to the Yanks.

Notes: William Whitelaw was UK Home Secretary.

> Right-winger Denis Healey and left-winger Tony Benn had recently been rivals for the post of deputy leader of the British Labour Party.

For "Bon's" read "Bond's" —Ed.

"I don't wanna know about what the rich are doing/I don't wanna go to where the rich are going . . ."
—'Garageland', 1977

TONIGHT, like most nights, the rich are going to Privilege, the chicest of chic Paris nightclubs. In the alleyway opposite, there are three tramps, and in the cafe next to the alleyway, there is Joe Strummer, nursing a cold beer, an aching throat, a sore conscience and a wounded pride.

"You saw those blokes lying out there in the gutter," he says hoarsely. "A lot of your readers ain't so far away from that young bloke in the middle . . .

"When I read the *NME* now, this is what I think, and this is really heavy . . . If they're teaching the readers to hate us, then I'd like to ask the *NME* who they're teaching the readers to trust? Which groups? Which ideas? I'm looking hard, and I can't see anybody."

Whoa! I don't believe it! I thought the *NME* was supposed to dote on The Clash . . .

"You must have a fucking long memory. *You* don't notice every little pin-prick—obviously not. I mean I don't care—my skin is thick enough by now, otherwise I wouldn't be able to get on stage, I'd be hiding in a cupboard somewhere. And I can deal with hard criticism. It's something I'd *like* to deal with, because if I'm no good I wanna know it . . .

"But how come the managing director of Warner Brothers isn't being whipped with the same stick? How come *TV Eye* sent him on a one-way trip to palookaville *(World in Action in fact—Ed.)* and not the fantastic combined intellectual power of the *NME*? Is it because of IPC?"

I tell him it isn't (though I may be wrong).

"Well that's even worse then, isn't it?"

THOUGH BOTH would probably like to deny it, The Clash and *NME* had a symbolic relationship over the years, mutually furthering each other's separate causes: *NME*'s sales, The Clash's exposure.

However there is, or there was, or there should be, a cause in common: the hippie activist ideal of rock as a protest, a provocative current carrying ideas and nourishment to the counter-culture. Of course there is no counter-culture any more, only subcultures. But this ideal is the reason why *NME* has done so much to shape, define, fuel and sustain something called the Clash Myth. In words, in pictures, and in cosy idolatrous cahoots!

"It's the positive things most of all," complains Strummer. "Quite often, I tell you more often than not, I've felt . . . *Leave it out!* I've felt almost sick! So I can't win. If it's good I feel sick because it doesn't do me any good to read that shit, and if it's a slagging off I feel sick because I feel I'm hard done by . . .

"They have a cupboard with a ruler in it which is called the Clash standard of honesty, truth and what the fuck is this world doing with . . . rich creates poor, and they take it out and they measure it with us and then they go off on a fucking 19-day whisky and cocaine binge! . . . Don't look so funny, because most of the music business is only interested in cocaine and alcohol in as much quantity as possible and at all times of the day and night and if you don't know that you must be living in Epping!"

Those pin-pricks must have found their mark. What that was, I don't know. Somebody said the Myth is dead. Somebody else said no it isn't. Somebody else asked where are The Clash now that the white riots have begun? I ask Strummer about the Clash book of Rebel Poses.

"You either attract people or you repel them," he replies, smiling. "And if you repel them, then you're wasting your time and theirs. That's what I say about the Clash book of Rebel Poses. Look, we could do it two ways. We could write the same songs, perform the same way on stage, but we could all wear C&A outfits.

"Either you go up there for people to look at you or you stay at fucking home! When I see people going on stage in any old shit, I think: you mugs! Do you think people *enjoy* standing down there? They want to see something. It's such a hideous thing anyway. You might as well make the effort."

Whatever happened to breaking down the barrier between the audience and the group, I ask, on behalf of our older readers.

"Tell ya, the audience can get through to any group if they give them encouragement. You don't know what it's like. It's ten times better than amphetamine. Same the other way around, mind you."

So you don't feel you've started something you can't live up to with the Clash book of Rebel Poses?

"No man. I'm *improving* on them! I don't see the shame, if you're hinting that there is . . ."

It depends on how sincere they are. (Can a pose be sincere?)

"*Sincere!*" he laughs. "Tell you this . . . Principle one of acting: a physical action denotes an emotion. It's the first rule, and it's true. Once you realise this, everything becomes clear."

Are you saying that wearing those poses brings out something in you?

"No, no, no. I mean *yeah*, obviously yeah, but . . . Drama is very powerful. Supposing we had the best script, and we were bad actors. Could we get it over? I don't think so. It'd be really hard."

Joe Strummer was born in Ankara, Turkey, 29 years ago to a father in the diplomatic service. He lived in Cyprus, Mexico City and Bonn before being sent at the age of nine to a boarding school called City of London Freeman's, "a kind of private comprehensive. If you got three 'O' levels you were top of the list. I got three. History, English and Art."

He went to the Central School of Art, which was as much of a failure in his eyes as he was in theirs. He says he became politicised through "experience, plus Bernie Rhodes".

"See those guys out there, down the alley? See the angle they see all this from?" He waves his hand to indicate Privilege across the street. "I saw it from that angle. I was 18, or 19, and I couldn't be fucked to . . . to play the game. I saw it from their angle, literally. In this city too. And that's what politicised me more than anything.

"Bernie Rhodes made me realise it could be sung about. Which is something I was kind of groping towards, singing about VD and squatting.

"Ever heard of Jack London?" he asks. "He was a writer from California who came to London for the Coronation in 1905—a bit like that wedding we just had. Instead of getting a seat in the stands in the Mall, he went down the East End.

"All these people were just sitting around on benches, really the *poorest* people. 'What do you think of the Coronation?' he said. And they said, 'It gives us a chance for once to be able to sit down all day without being moved on'. And that's all they said . . ."

I am honestly touched by the anger and compassion in Strummer's voice, just as I have been inspired in the past by these qualities in his music. It's easy to see why some people at *NME* lionise him as they do (despite his protests); easy to see how one French critic could romanticise thus: "They got Lennon and Baader. Are we going to let them get Strummer too?" Hard to imagine how anyone could live up to being Joe Strummer—heir apparent to rock's rebel crown.

THE CLASH are in Paris for seven shows before coming to England to play there for the first time in 17 months. Their repertoire now is virtually all highlights, with a handful of new songs. Their stage set looks like a border checkpoint, and they come on stage to the sound of wailing sirens. Their backdrop is painted by the New York subway artist Futura 2000, who works with his spray-cans and a ladder, while the group are on stage.

Seventeen months is not such a long time but rock has a short memory, as The Clash seem acutely aware. In 17 months they have hooked again with their former mentor, toured Europe and played New York, and seen the clashes they foretold come true on the streets of England.

"A prophet is never welcome in his own land," says Strummer, licking a wound that seems to be causing a disproportionate amount of pain. "Where were we during the riots? . . . Where was Karl Marx in 1917? We were playing a residency at Bon's in New York."

You and me and Joe Strummer and even William Whitelaw know that it wouldn't have made a brick through a window's worth of difference if The Clash were in Toxteth or Timbucktoo at the time. And *that's* why the wound hurts!

Whenever that kind of activity has happened in the past, rock music has been there to inspire it, catalyse it, crystallise it, or at least provide some kind of soundtrack for it. But not this time—or at least, not The Clash . . . And that's a bitter pill to swallow for anyone who still believes, as The Clash and Bernard Rhodes believe, that rock music can perform the same function for alienated white youth as reggae performs for alienated black youth.

"We were sitting there in New York saying, it's ridiculous us being here and this going on," says Bernard Rhodes. "But I don't know whether the riots were that major in terms of people being clear about what was going on. It was just a fracas.

"The Clash are interested in politics rather than revolution. Revolution sets a country back a hundred years. Revolution is very, very dangerous. I don't think we ever were revolutionary. I think we were always interested in the politics of the situation. And I think we still are. But I think that England's less interested.

"Politics could be, well, Healey got in just above Benn or Thatcher can't keep interest rates too low because America is doing the opposite and their system seems to be working . . . But that isn't it. It's about youth and where they get their information from, and how they deal with that information. And I think that's what we're about. Information comes to youth through the mass organisations like record companies and TV and that. In order to create an ethnic scene that these kids feel part of, they have to have their own sources of information.

"If The Clash are less relevant, or their profile in England lower . . . I think it's only because there's a right wing mood in England, and everything turns to suit the mood of the government in power. Usually you find that when it starts to turn the other way, the people responsible for turning it are the people who were considered the outgoing party at the time.

"Providing we can deliver to the best of our abilities, and providing we're critical enough internally, I think it'll be good. But it's still very difficult because of what the music scene is, with all its deficiencies, and you are prey to those just by being involved in it."

Bernard Rhodes seems unusually calm and optimistic, almost happy. Pennie Smith says the group have more arguments since his return, which I gather is one of the reasons why he's back. She says one of Rhodes' first moves was to rule no more hats!

Pennie also says The Clash are a very tactile group. "Most groups will stand the regulation English foot apart if you pose them against the wall, but The Clash touch each other all the time." She says their relationship is unusually close. "They quarrel a lot, but it's like lovers' quarrels, they're over as soon as they start. Most of the quarrels can be traced back to their laundry anyway!"

And what of The Clash's music? The Clash's music has lost a lot of its abrasive power over the years—the short, sharp, volatile statement has been replaced by the long, meandering and convoluted. The impact in a song like 'Washington Bullets', for instance, is diluted to a trickle by the music, which is too insipid to match the sentiment, and doesn't work too well as a piece of Brechtian discord either. I should have been shocked by 'Washington Bullets', shaken into the rage that I have to assume compelled them to write it, I want to be able to *feel* compelled them to write it.

The Clash shouldn't be afraid to do what they do best, orthodox as it may be. Their progress has been in terms of variety and experiment, straying across idioms in what seems at times like a vain search for another way of saying what can only be said as loudly and directly as possible! The Clash's progress as musicians has been at odds with their progress as politicians.

It's as politicians rather than musicians that they hold out the highest hope. But that's the Myth again. And the Myth is dead. Anybody know any better ones?

AN INTERVIEW WITH MICK JONES

WHY ARE you such a superstar?

People usually say rock star. But that still hurts. I feel it. I don't want to be just that. But, yes, there are some traditional elements to my work. A good guitar solo in the right place, a little bit o' tension added to the show. There's nothing wrong with having respect for the stage, because you're also out there entertaining.

There was a time when behaving like that was—

I couldn't give a shit! I do what I do and if you think I'm a big arrogant superstar then you're entitled to your opinion. I think I'm more than that. If I felt any moments of inflated ego, if I felt I was rushing to the stage just to please the audience . . .

You say I write soppy songs and I think I'm better than I am. Since the time you wrote that I am better than I was, I've been practising and playing. I ain't Liberace, man! I do me best. And I'm going to do better. If I'm rejected I'll work twice as hard! Slag me off, I want it! because I'll be *better* then.

Were you disappointed with the response to the Ellen Foley album you produced?

Yes. I was disappointed. (Angered) I thought it was a *great* record. I'd like to do the next one and make it even better and fix all our mistakes and *do it* this time. If she stands by her guns, I'll stand by her.

Will you get a chance?

I might. I might not . . . Not really. I'm not well liked in industry circles because I have way out ideas. You might think they're not. You might think they're really fucking straight! But I ain't a fucking straight. I ain't no sell-out either! You said Bernie's right, and we should have faced a trial for betraying our fans. So how come he's back with us if he thinks that?

Because he's got an awful lot of faith in you. But you obviously don't think you've betrayed your fans . . .

No. I don't. I think I done what's right.

Do you feel you owe them anything?

Yeah, and that's why we're going to play. We feel we have to play there. But it mustn't be like it's just gonna drag us down and we're going to split up! We want it to be great, not some *downer*.

Is that what it was getting like?

Sure it was getting like that! I felt *dragged* down, because you have to be on *their* level . . . I don't know, that's how it seemed. Now we seem to have our senses about us and we're ready.

A lot of people asked where you were this summer.

What am I supposed to say to that?

Implying that you had some sort of obligation to be there because of what was going on.

. . . I don't think I'd make such a great rioter . . . I don't even know if I agree with them. Destroying your own places. Especially if the government ain't going to give you another one—it seems really *double* dumb. I do my thing and it's a creative thing—that's how I feel I contribute to that. And if my absence is conspicuous on these occasions then I say don't look to me in the first place. I'm not the street fighting man. I still got a belief in the power of reason. That's how I feel.

You understand why people asked where are The Clash, don't you?

Yeah, I do. But I think I'd be really *stupid* to think I could go out and lead the people. I can help, maybe pass something on as I'm going along. Maybe if they were kicking my door down . . .

I don't think people expected you to be manning the barricades . . .

They *do* expect us to! But I don't feel that to participate I have to be in the riot. I think they should have a little more patience, these people.

I think they shouldn't look to you in the first place.

Yeah, *sure*. I think that too. Really, I honestly think that. Because it's a *lumber*. It's a big lumber! I can't do my thing so good if I'm distracted by nonsense! And I'm not saying the riots were nonsense . . . But a lot of it is just horseshit, right? *Horseshit!* What we have to put up with . . . especially at home. The *jeering* . . .

Do you like the Clash Myth—the image that has been built up around you, as much by others as by yourselves, although you've gone along with it . . . The Clash book of Rebel Poses and so forth.

Some of it's nonsense. But it has its aspects . . . It's the best way to travel, without a doubt. We have our arguments, because we wanna try and do it right. We're having a go . . . It's a very English thing, isn't it, having a go? But it's a drag because it's an oppressive thing. It's an oppressive thing that happens to me and that's what we're coming back to do, to try and make it a more positive situation, and we don't know, we'll see what dent we make. I mean it's just a sniff in the arse to the New Romantic, it's just another perfume, ain't it?

But I'm looking forward to it, I consider it a challenge. I don't consider it a comeback, because I don't consider that I've gone anywhere. We've got to get better at it. We've got to make ourselves *understood*.

THE CLASH and the critics—how much do you think they've defined The Clash?

They *have*. Too much. To their own ends.

A lot of them think The Clash are, or were, on some kind of pedestal—

It feels more like a coconut shy!

. . . holding the rock and roll grail. How does it feel to be a screen for all these fantasies to be projected on?

It can be uncomfortable at times. And it can be exhilarating other times . . . At least I don't have to wait until I'm dead to recognised. Like Edvard Munch. I like the odd slide, it's like a memento, you know, looking back . . . But it's usually projected onto an entity called The Clash, not us as individuals.

Why you? Why not, let's say, Generation X? Or The Police?

Because we always had our foot in the door. We were always going: Hey! What about us?

You reckon?

No . . . There's something about the four of us that makes it different, I suppose. I don't know. You're trying to say: do they project their fantasies on us?

Yeah, and they obviously do. Right from the start. That piece by Tony Parsons. The light shone down from your guitars. And it's gone on ever since, and of course you've failed to live up to these wild expectations, and you've had to live with it.

Yeah, and live with it, and live with it and live with it! And I know it's not me a lot of the time, but I still sort of . . . give that, because I think The Clash is probably more important, I mean the myth . . .

There is something to be said for that. That what people project on The Clash, the myth, is as important as what The Clash actually are.

What do you think about it? We've been called a Russian bike gang, or the Westway Wonders. What do you think, because you're going to do it, in some way?

I think you contain so many of the key images anyway, images from the rock tradition—Joe's Chuck Berry, your Keith Richards, the rebel stances, the quotes in your music—that people sought to complete or embellish the picture.

There's nothing wrong with people having imagination.

You were complaining just now about what it was putting you through.

Puts me through a lot, but there's nothing wrong with them doing it. I can't stop them. I *can't*. I wouldn't know how to. Sure these things are projected on us. I think it's cool.

So do I. But it leads to great disappointments.

Yeah, disillusionment. That's the trouble with imagination, ain't it? It never turns out how you think it's going to. Doing a painting or something; some of the songs . . . You imagine it and . . . like meeting famous people is a bit of a disappointment, generally. That's to do with myth again. You want to get to the bottom of the myth, but I can't help you.

Have you met any famous people that have lived up to your expectations?

I haven't met that many, but I'd have to say . . . Martin Scorsese, Robert De Niro and, um, Patti Smith.

It's often said that Bernard Rhodes is the group's mentor. Is that a fair description of his role?

He's part of the chemistry.

How did you meet him?

I met him at the Nashville one night (laughs). Deaf School were playing. They'd just won the *Melody Maker* competition. I thought he was a piano player. He seemed like a really bright geezer. We got on like a house on fire.

Does he give you a hard time?

Yeah.

Yeah. He gave me a hard time when I interviewed him once. But I liked him for it.

I imagine it's different on a daily basis. I see him more often than you do.

What did you think when he suggested you wear those clothes, the Seditionaries zips?

I don't remember him actually suggesting it. We probably thought the paint was pretty good at the time. I don't know if we were ready for the zips, but we were into them, no problem.

Were you already together as a group?

Some of us, not Joe. Me, Paul and Terry Chimes off and on. But we needed someone like Joe. I mean we had Bernie, and he was sort of putting it together. Eventually we decided it was gonna be Joe so we went about getting him. Good job too.

Did you go to art school?

Yeah. I went to Hammersmith, which became Chelsea halfway through my stay. I did a year of 'A' levels, then I worked during the second year and I went to night school, because I thought if I get a folder together I'll get four years of grants.

I got accepted for a foundation course, which wasn't really that hard. It's what happens afterwards. In my case, nothing much. One day they said you haven't done any paintings this term, and I said, Hey! Look at this (his shirt). Loads of people were really getting into it. Painting shirts. Before like Johnson's and that all caught on and started selling it.

We used to do it over everything. Over guitars, over the amps, all over the place. But they could never relate to that at school. They weren't the happening geezers. They always had chips on their shoulders. They wouldn't allow anyone to be happening. You had to be traditional. I spent a whole year just doing life drawing before I could do my own painting, which was all razor blades and Marilyn Monroe and limousines and so on.

Pop iconography! Yeah, I can imagine. It's what you do now with The Clash!

(Mick Jones laughs heartily at this and makes no attempt to deny it.) . . . Art school was just a fill in, though. I knew exactly what I was going to do. I had hoped to meet other musicians . . . I met some great people there though, and I wonder what happened to them now.

They're in advertising, if they're lucky. Otherwise they're in sanatoriums.

Yeah, the good ones, not the ones who could explain themselves well and bluff their way through exams, the ones who did good work, coming in and painting all day and working at home at nights . . . at the end of it, these people never got any jobs, nothing. The best ones never got any jobs, but the arseholes and the bullshitters did. I suppose it's the same in the music business . . .

Doesn't say much for you!

Well, there's always an exception.

And yet crass things seem to be the ones that succeed.

Oh yeah, sure. It's the lowest common denominator. But what we gotta do is find a place where the reality, and the art, and the entertainment can all meet. When we can bring that together, I think that's when we'll be really successful, because it won't be a crass thing.

That's what I hate about the music business. It *is* always the lowest common denominator. *Rubbish* always makes it. Everybody likes muck!

UP THE HILL BACKWARDS

Charles Shaar Murray | May 29, 1982 | *New Musical Express* (UK)

When a full-scale Clash biography, *Last Gang in Town*, belatedly appeared in 1995, it was appropriate that author Marcus Gray subtitled it *The Story and Myth of the Clash*.

Rarely has a group so mythologized itself. Many Clash interviews are peppered with lies and half-truths: exaggerations of poverty-stricken childhoods; fanciful excuses for the interview nonappearances of Terry Chimes; idealizing of song genesis (e.g., pretending that "I'm So Bored with You" wasn't once a fixture of their rehearsals and live set but was instantly changed to " . . . with the U.S.A." when Strummer misheard Jones's lyric); tweaking of biographical detail to make it more punk-friendly (e.g., claiming that the 101'ers were named after the torture room in Orwell's *1984* rather than Strummer's street address); insinuation of apocalyptical confrontations with record company bosses that were in fact perfectly cordial meetings; eulogizing of work with producers hired for their legendary status (Lee Perry, Guy Stevens) but who in reality hadn't worked out . . . Because of this propensity for mythmaking—an in extremis variant of the punk movement's Year Zero self-aggrandizement—lying to journalists became second nature to the Clash. Rarely, however, were they so dishonest as they were in this feature.

In the last week of April 1982, it was announced that Joe Strummer had been missing since the twenty-first of the month. Rhodes put out a statement in which caustic reference was made to the Clash's low fortunes in the UK: "I think he feels some resentment about the fact that he was about to go slogging his guts out just for people to slag him off." While the singer was away and the Clash camp supposedly frantically searching for him, the band's new album, *Combat Rock*, was released. A single disc, it was more focused than *Sandinista!* but rarely achieved the quality of the triple album's highlights. However, sentimentality engendered by Strummer's apparent torment caused reviewers to show more charity to the Clash than they had for years, while the combination of the publicity resulting from Strummer "doing a runner" and the vagaries of a dubious new system of compiling the UK charts sent the LP straight in at number two.

A few days after Strummer surfaced on May 18, it was announced that Headon was leaving the group due to "a difference of opinion over the political direction the band would be taking." Charles Shaar Murray met up with the remaining trio shortly after these tumultuous events in Clash-land. The *NME* scribe was apparently unaware that Strummer's disappearing act was a profile-raising ruse dreamed up by Rhodes after ticket sales for their UK appearances had proved abysmal (although Strummer did cause Rhodes genuine worry by not going to the location he had instructed). He also seemed unaware that Headon had in fact been fired for a heroin habit that was making a mockery of Strummer's antismack lyrics. Accordingly, Strummer, Jones, and Simonon led Murray a merry dance around the truth (Strummer: "I just wanted to prove to myself that I was alive"), although the reverential journalist admittedly seems happy to be spoon-fed.

All this worked out better than Rhodes could have imagined. So recently a laughing stock in their homeland, the Clash's brace of sold-out gigs at London's Brixton Fair Deal were doused in such goodwill that another date was quickly added there. Even external events seemed, for once, to be working in the band's favor. The beginning of April had seen the start of the Falklands War. The hypocrisy and unnecessary carnage said conflict represented for their constituency served to suddenly make the Clash's values seem relevant once more.

The salutary fact is that, had journalists and fans known at the time of how they had been deceived (the truth about Strummer's disappearance wouldn't be revealed until the band was no longer extant), the backlash might conceivably have finished the Clash.

Note: "Going Underground" and "Ghost Town" were singles by the Jam and the Specials respectively that had recently topped the UK singles chart despite hard-hitting political lyrics. —Ed.

HALF PAST ONE on Portobello Road. Past the chippy, opposite the bookshop, within earshot of a man with an amplified mouth-harp honking and scything through Little Walter's greatest hits. The sun comes down hard on the cast of the street parade, on the bikes and push-chairs and the stalls, a crowded pavement where money changes hands, time is passed and everybody seems to be waiting for something different to happen.

And it does: one by one, The Clash appear. First Paul Simonon, dressed in his usual black, then Mick Jones in khaki pants, bleached denim jacket and huge Rasta cap, then Joe Strummer, greasy, stubbled and buttoned into his trench-coat.

OKAY! HERE WE GO!

JOE'S BACK AND TOPPER'S GONE WHAT ELSE DO YOU WANT TO KNOW?

That's approximately what Kosmo Vinyl had said a couple of hours earlier on the phone, so we deal with that.

This is Saturday, while the F.A. Cup Final is going on, and the previous Thursday, The Clash reunited in Amsterdam to play the last ever gig with Topper Headon. Strummer had returned after weeks of rumours—working as a navvy in Marseilles, fished up out of the river in Glasgow, what did *you* hear? Did you believe it?—from a sojourn in Paris, during which time two career politicians in dead schtuck with their punters while their countries were falling to pieces embarked on a joint military adventure to distract attention from the home front and wave a few flags around, an entire British Clash tour was cancelled and rearranged, and 'Combat Rock' had reached number two in the album charts.

Obviously, there are a few things to discuss.

First Topper. Why'd he go?

"It was his decision," Strummer replies. We're squeezed into a booth in the corner caff. Strummer hunched in the corner, Simonon and Jones opposite, Kosmo Vinyl at an adjoining table and Bernard Rhodes leaning over Strummer's shoulder anxious to answer the questions first.

"I think he felt . . . it's not too easy to be in The Clash. It's not as simple as being in a comfortable, we're-just-entertainers group, and he just wanted to do that, just play music. He's a brilliant multi-instrumentalist—what used to be called that—and it's a bit weird to be in The Clash at the moment. Well, it *was*. He has to sort of strike out in another direction, because I don't think he wants to come along with us. There are things that we all want to do . . ."

"We all feel the same," Jones chips in, "and he don't, really."

"We're going to continue as a trio," resumes Strummer.

"I'm going to play the drums," announces Simonon brightly.

"We're gonna get some guest drummers in, and they're gonna play with us whenever we want to make a record or play some shows."

OKAY. Why'd you vanish?

"Me? *(Who'd you think, Lord Lucan? —Ed)*. It's a long story."

Gonna tell it?

Strummer sighs. "Well . . . it was something I wanted to prove to myself: that I was alive. It's very much like being a robot, being in a group. You keep coming along and keep delivering and keep being an entertainer and keep showing up and keep the whole thing going. Rather than go barmy and go mad, I think it's better to do what I did, even for a month.

"I just got *up* and I went to Paris . . . without even thinking about it. I might have gone a bit barmy, you know? But anyway, I went to Paris, and I knew that there'd be a lot of people . . . the fans were disappointed, the road crew had sold their motors to pay the rent fucking around with this lot. I knew a lot of people were going to be disappointed, but I had to go and I went and I'd recommend anybody else to do that if they have to.

"And once I got there . . . I only intended to stay for a few days, but the more days I stayed, the harder it was to come back because of the more aggro I was causing that I'd have to face there."

What about the agreements that you'd broken by going? Were you thinking of them?

"Yeah! We'd *never* blown out other gigs except for the time that Topper got stabbed in the hand with a pair of scissors. Even when the gear doesn't arrive and we're in a foreign city and the trucks are held up at the border, we'll still play the show by borrowing stuff off the support band or whoever we can get it from. We've got some *pride* in that direction—the show must go on blah blah—than to cut out *permanently,* you know?"

So what would have happened if you *hadn't* gone?

"I think I would have started drinking a lot on the tour, maybe. Started becoming petulant with the audience, which *isn't* the sort of thing that you should do . . . but it's very different now that Topper's left. It's back to the old trio now," he concludes with what can only be described as anticipatory glee.

So what did Simonon and Jones feel about the wandering Joe's pilgrimage?

"Well, I felt that anything he does is all right," replies Jones, staring out from under his cap. "Obviously we were disappointed that we weren't going off on tour and everything, and we were disappointed that some of our fans would be disappointed, but—I said this before while Joe was away—I felt sure that whatever he had was a good reason. And he's such an extraordinary person that it was fine: we could handle it. Hold the fort was what we did."

Were you in contact while Joey was away?

"No," volunteers Simonon. "We knew he was all right because he phoned his mum. He'd told her to keep schtum but I think Kosmo wore her down."

While you were away, did you consider not coming back at all, doing the full vanish?

"I don't think I had the . . . it's pretty hard to do that, to disappear for ever."

"Bernie was saying," says Jones, indicating the general direction of Rhodes' manic grin and impenetrable shades, "'Now this is like Brian Jones or Syd Barratt or something, now you're one of *these* group' so it *is* possible to vanish forever. Okay! We're The Pink Floyd now! And," he continues, warming to his theme, "Joe was Syd Barratt."

Yeah, but he didn't vanish *physically*.

Jones considers this. "Ah no, that was Vince Taylor, wasn't it."

Was Joe thinking while he was away about what was going to have to be different when he got back?

"No, not really, I was just pleased to have an . . . escape. It's great bunking off work, really great—as you well know—and it was a bit of that. I was just enjoying being alive. *I just wanted to prove to myself that I was alive* . . . that I existed, that it wasn't over. It was okay. We're doing this firstly for ourselves . . ."

"And it helps clear the air, anyway"—Simonon—"The fact that he went just cleared the air and made you realise more of where you stood individually as well as to two other people, three other people, or whatever. I knew he was coming back."

Strummer picks up the thread again. "I was saying that we're supposed to be doing this for ourselves, and when you lose sight of that, you're in trouble, because you start to think, 'Those people out there don't really *care*'—that's the people who come and see you and buy your records. It's been a bit of a desert for us lately, but we're Number Two this week with the album—which is a real shock, I can tell you . . ."

OBVIOUSLY! While the sheer fact of a record's presence in the charts is not necessarily a relevant signifier, 'Combat Rock' is the most extreme and direct Clash album since the first, and its ready acceptance and acknowledgement by the purchasing public indicates that there's far more support than is often supposed both for The Clash themselves and for the militancy that they once again represent.

See, The Clash had become first accepted then absorbed, then declared quaint, obsolete, null and void. As soon as it became 'safe' to like them and they started touring the States, it then became 'safer' not to. It was a short step from American pundits hailing them as the new greatest rock band the world—the new Stones! The new Who!—to British True Punks and post-rock hipsters alike to regard them as just another Anglo-American success story, like Costello before he withdrew, or The Pretenders. Not hard enough for the Oi Polloi, too rockist for the dancetariat.

And I mean they really show their roots: there's good old Greasy Joe with his rockabilly fetish, and Ranking Paul skanking with the system, and Mick's *such* a poser, always playing too loud . . .

Plus all this romantic rebel guerrilla chic, and the ethnic snippets . . . hopeless, boys. *Hopeless.*

The trouble is that—in the wake of 'Combat Rock'—none of that washes any more. X. Moore did the album all due honours a couple of weeks ago, so it only remains to state that it's a very *clear* album: the work of people who know exactly what they want to say and exactly how they want to sound. There is virtually no 'hard rock': none of the bulldozing rabble-rousing power-chord anthems left over from 'Give 'Em Enough Rope', none of the easy warmth of parts of 'London Calling', none of the musical tourism and lucky-dip oddments of 'Sandinista!'. They haven't united their sound and their vision more perfectly since their first LP, though both have broadened almost beyond recognition in the intervening period.

Listen to the way Strummer sings 'Straight To Hell' or 'Ghetto Defendant'. What you're hearing is not a presumptuous or impertinent attempt to associate with the alleged glamour of revolutionary war or urban oppression, but genuine compassion for the victims of organised human stupidity and greed, an expression of a desire to draw attention to intolerable circumstances and to mobilise public opinion towards eradicating them. I don't know about you, but I respect that compassion.

'Combat Rock' says that playtime is over. Strummer says that it's very hard being in The Clash, and if they are taking what they're doing as seriously as the album would suggest, then it sounds like he's right. It's also very hard being *around* them: not in the sense that they're unpleasant or antagonistic, but they carry an atmosphere of tension with them, just as they did when they were starting out. A very strong sense of *purpose*. 'Combat Rock' was—as is obvious to anyone with any knowledge of the logistics of record-making—written, recorded and designed and packaged long before the Falkland Islands represented anything to anybody who didn't have relatives there, but synchronicity is *not* a myth and this album isn't just selling because it's good product from a popular band. I think it's selling because a large and significant number of people want to hear what it says. There's an edge on the album and there's an edge on The Clash again.

Once again, they are a profoundly *unreasonable* band. There is a lot of excellent entertainment about, and it is by no means all reactionary, but it *is* reasonable. The Clash aren't.

"AND we're going to go over to New Jersey and start a four-and-a-half week American tour, and then we're going to come back here and do the British tour that we should have done before—that's if we can find a drummer. After that we don't have any plans."

Mick Jones: "After that, we *all* disappear."

So what do The Clash *want* to do?

"We want to consolidate something—like *us*," replies Jones. "Coming together and then exploding out. Out of captivity, the captivity of people's expectations of us . . . and of being contained by the music industry, that situation of not being able to get out."

So how do you get what you want out of them without them getting what they want out of you?

"Simple!" snorts Strummer. "Make sure that you're in a position to be able to *say* what you want, make sure that you're ahead. But as soon as you're not in a position to do that, if you're not independent enough to do that, if we couldn't keep this thing going to the right pitch, then we'd be . . . CBS were coming around to us saying, 'Right, we've got these suits here and we've got a nice little number written by Andrew Lloyd Webber . . .'"

"And a nice idea for a new haircut," interrupts Jones.

". . . and that would become what we were putting out. It wouldn't be anything to do with us. You have to be independent enough to remember what you were there to do in the first place, or you're fucked. They've all got their lawyers and their legal scene well worked out before we were even born. It's very hard to go in there and not go under. I mean, the whole game is to get you so that you owe them so much money so that you can't say, 'No, I don't wanna do that' without them saying, 'So how are you gonna pay this?'"

Bernard Rhodes at this point launches a high-velocity dissertation on the subject of Control In The Media and the fact that The Clash don't seem to reap the benefits of the airplay shop-window. (This is, after all, only right and proper. I, for one, don't want a load of depressing rubbish about knowing your rights and not heeding the call-up on *my* shiny yellow airwaves).

". . . in fact," Jones sums up. "We've written a song about it. It's called 'Complete Control' and we hope to have it out for the summer."

Well, you can by-pass the radio if people will buy your singles whether they get airplay or not.

"We can do that because we've always put singles out whether they got played or not. People have said that we should just do albums, but we like singles too! But since 'Capital Radio' we haven't been played on Capital Radio." Mick doesn't sound too surprised about that, as it happens.

"I never thought we'd be Number Two in Britain. I really didn't," Strummer muses. Rhodes quietly tips a slug of brandy into Joe's cup of black coffee. "There really seems to be something against us here . . . over the last few years, since we started going round the world."

"People don't *understand*," Simonon interposes fiercely, "what 'Bored With The USA' was about. They haven't got a fucking *clue*. If people say 'Oh, The Clash did 'Bored With The USA' and they're always going over there' . . . they don't understand the bloody song in the first place!"

"I think that Britain is really insular"—Strummer—"They don't realise that there is a world out there. People who spend any amount of time in London can't believe that anything outside *London* exists. I like to travel . . ."

This would appear to be the case.

Another new factor in the existence of The Clash is the removal of one of the all-time great millstones: their financial debt to CBS Records. This liberation is due to the much-abused and admittedly unwieldy 'Sandinista!', which has quietly and unsensationally contrived to be purchased by approximately 197,000 people in this country alone. They are now out of hock for the first time, a state of affairs which they find highly satisfactory. It is, after all, at least as valuable in terms of independence as cash.

Kosmo Vinyl recounts that nearly every American college the band had visited last time round had featured a bulletin-board offer to tape anybody's choice of an hour's worth of 'Sandinista!' for around $3. American release of 'Combat Rock' has been delayed so that the sleeve can be reprinted without the 'Home Taping Is Killing Music' health warning. "We don't care *how* many people tape our records," he declares proudly.

What The Clash are in the process of becoming is—in spite of CBS Records—a genuinely Underground band (I am choosing, thoroughly arbitrarily, to define an 'underground band' as one which is denied access to radio and TV exposure for reasons other than unpopularity). This means that their music actually has to be *sought out*. To see The Clash you have to go to their gigs (whenever they happen to be), and to hear The Clash you have to buy their record (or tape it off someone else who's bought it). Embarking on this course means an awful lot of hard work: it means that the band have to stay in touch with their audiences and keep their interest—and in the case of The Clash, that also means retaining their trust—in order to make sure that their work continues to be sought out. Especially in the current climate, one is unlikely to hear 'Know Your Rights' or any of the vital album tracks on daytime radio or down the pub.

Current pop wisdom sayeth as follows: in order to create a popular success, something shiny must be dangled in front of people's eyes via electronic media. The only other way is via discos and the club scene, and The Clash are no more welcome there (apart from isolated break-outs like 'Magnificent Seven' and *maybe* 'Overpowered By Funk' from 'Combat') than they'd be on a Capital playlist.

Doing it The Clash's way on a worldwide basis therefore demands an insane amount of gigging, and as a famous '60s smart-ass who got very little airplay himself once remarked "Touring can make you crazy". The danger of thereby developing intermittent strangeness of the mental process would seem to be substantially increased by this policy, which would also deliver them right back into the got-to-tour-to-sell-the-records/got-to-sell-the-records-to-finance-the-tour noose that they've just got themselves *out* of.

The Clash are almost messianic in their intensity when it comes to 'providing an alternative' on the US live circuit. "Maybe they'll just think we're Van Halen with short hair," Strummer will surmise grimly. "Maybe they'll just be grunging out on the bass and drums and guitar."

"Maybe we could put on false beards and stovepipe hats and stick pillows up our T-shirts," suggests Mick Jones helpfully, "and put out a nice country and western song to get on the radio there . . . then we could do some dance stuff for the hipper areas . . ."

Three the hard way. I mean, up the hill backwards isn't half of it. In terms of conventional careerism, The Clash are nuts. They are a gang of loonies. They are out of their fucking minds.

They have created an objective which—virtually by definition—debars them from utilising crucial means necessary to achieve it. If they doubt their ability to get successful without getting sucked in, then they'll set it up so that they won't succeed. In other words, not getting sucked in is more important than succeeding on any but the most stringently proscribed terms.

To reiterate: The Clash are totally unreasonable. They work on the principal that the distinction between method and objective is artificial and spurious, and that therefore compromise must be kept to a minimum (noises off: rising murmur of 'CBS! CBS! Train In Vain!' etc). The thing is that the amount of compromise necessary to get a single as hard as 'Ghost Town' or 'Going Underground' on the air does not appear to have been crippling.

However, I admire The Clash's intransigence, and the best of 'Combat Rock' is as powerful as anything anybody's done for a while. Long may they continue to piss everybody off.

JUST NOW there was almost a minute of uninterrupted gunfire on the radio, and the sound was almost too neatly set off by a police siren outside. Right now everybody's supposed to be jacked up to the back teeth with war fever, but just the same there's that dippy song about peace from the Eurovision Song Contest as Number One single last week and 'Combat Rock' mashing up the album chart.

There was a song I wanted to hear just then, but it wasn't on the radio It went:

> "*It could be anywhere*
> *Any frontier*
> *Any hemisphere*
> *No man's land*
> *There ain't no asylum here*
> *Go straight to hell, boys . . .*"

THE GOAT LIES DOWN
ON BROADWAY

Kris Needs | February 1983 | *Flexipop!* **(UK)**

This Mick Jones interview has a completely different tone to all the previous chapters in this book.

Partly this is because *Flexipop!* was a publication with a uniquely jocular approach. Partly it's because often the repartee between Jones and early Clash champion Kris Needs is just as silly as it can be when two old friends converse. Above and beyond that, however, is a factor never before present in Clash exchanges with the press: happiness.

When he wasn't "throwing a strop," Jones had always been the most gregarious of the Clash's personnel. Here, however, he positively gushes. So would most people if they'd had the kind of year—the interview took place just before Christmas 1982—he and his cohorts had.

Following Strummer's return and Headon's dismissal, the Clash had re-recruited Terry Chimes—whose conservatism now perhaps seemed more attractive after the sobering experience of the foibles of a junkie drummer—and set off to "tour" *Combat Rock*. The band worked America with a single-mindedness that tipped over for many into a sellout. When they played second banana to old-guard band the Who in American stadiums, UK fans couldn't help but pose the question of whether the Clash would have dared commit such a wholesale breach of punk taboo in Britain. Either way, the result was a top-ten US album and a bona fide American hit in the shape of "Rock the Casbah," and both were genuinely worthy achievements in the context of a then very staid American music industry.

As they had started the tour in the unusual position of not being in debt, this meant that, by the end of it, the Clash were on the brink of riches. Not only were considerable record royalties on the way, but the end of May would see the group pick up half a million dollars for playing the US Festival in San Bernardino. What with that, the wherewithal to finally make some of their long-cherished dreams a reality—Jones brings up a plan to open a club—and the fact of their great rivals/enemies/bookends the Jam having split, what now could possibly go wrong in the Clash's career?

Perhaps a clue lies in Jones's unkind crack about enjoying Strummer's disappearance. Perhaps another can be discerned in the fact that, partway through the interview, Paul Simonon decides not to enter the West London café in which it's taking place. At the time, Needs put it down to the bassist not seeing his colleague. In later years, he would wonder whether Simonon turned on his heel precisely because he *had* spotted Jones. —Ed.

"What we'll do is get the fried eggs and put them on here!" MICK JONES' hazel peepers light with glee at the prospect of mischief . . . but then he seemed well lit most of that afternoon.

What's prompted this zesty impersonation of a seasonal Selfridges? Mick, known to get down when the traps are open and the pressures mount, ended 1982 full of satisfaction at his group's achievements and positively brimming with ideas for the New One.

But first . . .

Let's stick our horns firmly into a fave Clash subject, little known but an almost daily figment of intergroup conversations. Beasts! Masses of them! Stoats, gnus, hamsters . . .

"Some people are crazy about pigs," muses Mick over his beans. "'78 was a very popular year of the wildebeest. I feel that this is the Year Of The Goat overall . . . or the Year Of The Amoeba! Ha ha!"

And did you hear those wildebeests howling on 'Should I Stay Or Should I Go' . . . ?

Flexipop! waited two years for this interview. This is The Clash. It's also 1983. As usual music is generally watered down, nostalgic, low-denominator whale-spew. This bears heavily on The Clasher this day.

"It's pathetic here!" Mick's beans machinegun the ceiling of Mike's Café. "It's REALLY pathetic. At least we've been interesting. We ain't been boring in a suit. I mean it's terrible. The state of music is this country is dreadful. It's also a see-though plastic bag and so much washing powder really."

Who can you mean, Mick? ABC?

"Well not them particularly. I just don't see it as a very creative contemporary scene. I saw ABC and thought they were good really – for a group that are boring in suits. I saw them in New York and they had quite a swish show. I was nearly fooled. I thought it was the New York Philharmonic but it was ten girls from Sheffield girlschool playing violins!"

The Clash – still going, battered but now triumphant out of the '76 Holocaust – have steamed on at an outstanding rate of creativity. Out on their own, they won't stand still and a bull's pecker to you if you're not there. Mind you, last year's tour proved there's still plenty who want them and now America has joined the boisterous herd. The Jam have gone. Why is the most volatile combination of them all still foraging?

The reply is an unrehearsed volley:

"We respect each other and because of that we've got our own self-respect. We still believe in what we're doing and we enjoy it. Give me any other reason.

"We try and be . . . at the same time taking good things from the past, we try not to be retro about things. Show me a contemporary scene here and I'll laugh it off. There really isn't anything in Britain that doesn't tend to look back totally. Look at Billy Fury or the Beatles f'rinstance. That's the scene, right? That will always be there in America. It's okay but it kind of takes away a lot of the contemporary listeners, puts them in a shade of melancholy or something. There's no sense in being sentimental about something that happened about twenty years ago."

Somehow their old friends The Press drift in – they would love to bury The Clash after all.

"They would love to . . ." sighs Mick. "Maybe it's because I've been away on tour so much I haven't read many music papers. Hip? Hip hop hippity hop! What would they put there instead? Perhaps they can give one of Paul Weller's old suits to Martin Fry and it'll be alright.

"All this stuff's really nice and it works well in a small environment, like London. People can be hip putting down other people. It don't work so well in a place like America. It's a bigger deal, a different league . . . not a different league really. This country's still the most creative country as far as I'm concerned. I mean, the most creative things have come out of this country – it has its good points as well. But creative people – that's not much to do with who some critic thinks is a hip-hop."

Talking of Mr Weller, he said The Clash should have knocked it on the head moons ago. Like he has, I s'pose.

"I don't remember him! He looks a bit '60s. It's 1983. They should have split up in '61. They're alright, The Jam, but they're just basically very straight, conservative in a sense, traditional. Those things that we are, they are too. But if the cap fits . . ."

Mohican

Something like Joe's runner . . . the Press LOVED it!

"Yeah, I loved it an' all. No, horrible. I guess I'm envious."

You wish you'd done it?

"Yeah, but once it's been done, it's been done. You can't do it. You have to do something else. Maybe I'll top meself."

Cut an arm off?

"Yeah, spike myself."

How does Joe's Paris-flit sit now with The Clash? Apart from envy, the quick break to grow face-fungus, guzzle booze and run marathons breeds . . . contempt? No, LAFFS!

"They made a big thing about it in America. Once we said in an interview when they asked 'what's happening with Joe?', and I said, 'he's gone off to have a sex change operation'. So then you see all these pictures of girls doing aerobatics and the caption is 'Joe Strummer – the operation worked out!

"Put him right in it there, but he didn't mind. You only have to get one gullible bloke to go, 'Oh really? I'll alert the Media immediately!'"

Funny if that really had happened!

"Mm. We'd be in Curved Air then!"

He had a Mohican instead.

"Yeah. One morning I woke up and we were Discharge. He's not anymore, he's got a skinhead. I'm in a group with two skinheads. The 2-Skins! Ha ha ha!"

Is Terry Chimes a full-time drummer now?

"No, I don't think so. He stays in Northampton. I don't know what he wants to do. And I don't know what's happening with Topper."

Momentary sidetrack: Topper's currently breaking in a new band with ex-Pretender Pete Farndon, which may be called Samurai and contains other known faces. A new-wave Asia! (Only joking.)

Back to over-egg musings . . .

"What've we been up to? Well, we toured all year, except for three weeks off when Joe went away. We'd just finished 'Combat Rock' on January 3. We've been touring all over the bloody shop. A tour of England and about ten tours of America."

Did the trick though, didn't it? The Clash currently slink up both album and singles charts, which is no mean feat.

"Yeah! It's really nice. It makes a change at the end of the year to be able to look back and not feel like you've wasted 365 days. Some of the things that have happened this year have balanced it out, you know what I mean? I think that losing Topper really had a great effect on us.

"I thought the best gig was the last Brixton one. I'm not that into the big ones, but when we went out and played with The Who it was really good for us. We (grin) sold lots of records, y'know? And probably picked up a lot of their fans. So we shouldn't complain. We went out there and did a job really. No big deal. We're matter of fact about it. We just went out and played, trying not to be phased by it all."

So you weren't pelted with Foreigner albums then? You won 'em over?

"Yeah. I think we did. People haven't got anything else to do as far as America goes. Let's say they really still believe in music more. It's their way of life, which is why you get thousands and thousands of them in row after row of megastadiums.

"It was The Who's audience. It wasn't our audience, but we did good there. The Who were gentlemen. They treated us very well, everything was just right.

"It's great. Townshend just goes 'ping!' on his guitar and they go woooaaahhh!!"

There were also massive solo-sorties through the States, including colleges in the Mid-West! Quaaludes! Beer! Burp! Hurl! Grope! Rockan Roll!

"You name it, we've played it, except for Kalamazoo. We haven't quite managed that. New Orleans was great.

"We went down to San Antone, pretending we were at The Alamo. We all played! Paul was Colonel Travis, Kosmo was Davey Crockett, Joe was Jim Bowie and I was the wall (chuckle). Bernie (Clash manager) was a cannonball. Joe Ely (manic country-rocker) was there too – a real authentic cowboy riding round on his cow!"

Donkey Kong

Despite these frolics, Mick hankered for life round Ladbroke Grove – Mike's, the Westway, sound systems, dogshit.

"I miss it. I love to live here. It's where I live, innit? I don't know who Yosser Hughes is. But I sure know a lot about Smurfs and Pacman! And Donkey Kong."

Donkey dong?

"Donkey Kong."

Do you absorb all these American crazes and grossities? How does it all rub off on Mick Jones from Royal Oak?

"Well I still kind of believe, personally for myself, that we're a lot more primitive than that. All that stuff is based on shit. There's certain things I like about it. I'm interested in the history going down at the moment.

"They just did this thing where they executed this guy in Texas about two weeks ago. They tied him down and injected this solution through a tube into his arm. Apparently you just yawn and go out. The guy died. He's a murderer.

"The paper had big headlines like, 'KILLER INJECTION BY THE NEEDLE OF DEATH!' Very strong, terrible images.

"Next day, a little thing in the paper: 'The executed man may have been the wrong bloke.' Probably was."

Sandwich

Do you feel BIG over here with all this achievement over there? How's it compare?

"No, I'm my normal size (Asked for that one). I know Joe feels funny he has to do things. He's got to get a flat now."

But hold! All this tour-talk has to take a back seat for the time being. They were due to be off again in the New Year but that's been shelved.

"We were going to go, but . . . after a while you just look at yourself in the mirror one day and steam's coming out of your ears. You know you've got to stop for a couple of days. The old cogs in the engine room . . ."

Is touring still the crack it was in the days of 'Sort It Out', 'On Parole' and 'White Riot' packages? My mind flicks back to a post-gig hotel in Leeds three years ago when an innocent cheese sandwich was ritually danced around by the entire Clash team chanting 'Sandwich! All hail the sandwich!' before being rent asunder by a cruel blade. Not [to] mention the goat impressions and a wide variety of jolly japes on Bernie.

"Sometimes it is, but it's got a lot more efficient. It's not quite so funny. But the real joke was on us, because all the things that were funny we had to shell out for and then were in debt. This year was the first time we haven't been in debt. Just being all-round good blokes probably stood us in good stead with the people, but they can't think very much of us if they take advantage of us like that."

At this moment, Paul Simonon appears at the café's window with his dad. He peers through the greasy glass. Mick waves but is non-spotted and Paul wanders off.

"He saw me and ran away!

"Once Paul said he wouldn't go on unless he had a rabbit costume. So we went to a costume hirers' place and got a whole rabbit costume with bunny ears and everything. He was walking around dressed in it, going 'ooooooooweeooocrooo!' (waves arms and legs) being a rabbit. He should have worn it for the encore, sort of hopped on."

Never mind, he can still mate with Captain Sensible and unleash a plague of bass-wielding bunnies.

Does he still throw salad at Bernie?

"Oh, last time round it was (polite voice) 'hello, how's it going?' And then Paul really does torture him. They lift him off the ground and play with him like he was a toy. But I think that's rotten!"

Quite right. Now what subversive influences are creeping into The Clash at present?

"Oh well, I think we're about to . . . we've done a year of consolidation, sticking ourselves really strongly together, so the next thing is to agree on something as soon as we can agree on something and then we'll do something, maybe a single. An anthem about cockroaches."

Sudden memory burst.

"Oh! We are going to record a record. We're going to record a record with Janie Jones."

For younger readers, Janie Jones is the legendary Vice Queen who was hit hard by law and scandal in the Swingin' 60s. The Clash immortalised her on their first album.

It won't be Janie's first vinyl outing – about twenty years ago she cackled her way through a thing called 'Witches' Brew'. The planned team-up is of more serious tone. It's a new Strummer song called 'The Judge'.

"It's on Vice Records!" says Mick. "I met her twice, once in '77 and once in '82. Joe wrote her a song when he was in hiding."

Mick's just produced and played on a twelve-inch rap single by Futura 2000, he of the onstage graffiti backdrop. Anything else like that?

"I don't know if I'm going to do very much. I have to really like it. There's some stuff in New York I really like. They've got a great scene there, it can be really good, as long as they don't get too bigheaded about it. But they ain't got that here."

Furry Legs

Mick does have plans for his own ambitious project though. He wants to write a musical.

"That's something I'm doing privately. That's me writing. I think it will be a musical! Ha ha! A Jewish 'Roots' with a bit of coalmining in it, and a touch of Russia."

Off the road but all systems go the offshoots, shrapnel-style.

"I think we're gonna do other things, like open a club."

This has been in the air for a long time.

"Yeah. We can be talking about it forever. We're going to do something about it now.

"It's gonna be a wedon'thavetoagreeonwhatsortofmusicwe'regonnaplay-type club. We're selfish, you know what I mean? Somewhere around this area (Notting Hill).

"One big room with a really big sound system, and one big room with a bar and no sound-system. So one room's for dancing and the other room's for talking. It'll be Uncle Bernie's Club!"

And there we must leave Mick to prance gazelle-like into the distance to enjoy his Christmas shopping. Antlers raised to the heavens, a mighty tail whisks. The Clash are now a mountain on the globe. With furry legs!

THE CLASH ACCORDING TO "TORY CRIMES"

Sean Egan | 2002 and 2014 | Previously unpublished in this form

Terry Chimes admits he was always the "odd man out" in the Clash—hence his punning, mocking billing on the sleeve of the first Clash album. Nonetheless, his drumming bookended the career of what most people would term the "real" Clash.

Although he had a second stint with them, he never got to make a second studio album with the Clash. By the end of 1982, with current live commitments fulfilled and the future of the group in doubt, he drifted away.

This is a composite of two Terry Chimes interviews, one conducted in 2002, the other 2014. The material—most of which has never previously been published—explores two contrasting stages in Clash history. In the first, the band were novices living in poverty. In the second they had graduated to the status of global stars yet, Chimes found, still had their problems. —Ed.

You seem to have had a very happy childhood.

My parents definitely wanted children. When they got them, they put the children at the center of their lives, which is the best upbringing any child can have. It's unconditional love, which sets you up for the rest of your life.

What did your dad do?

He used to make photographic plates for the *Sunday Times Magazine*. In those days, pre-computer, you had to physically make a metal plate to print pictures. A highly skilled [job] in the day. He got out just before the big Wapping riots, when they tried to kick the unions out. He took his golden handshake retirement weeks before that happened, so he was very lucky.

He was obsessed with music. We always had music in the house: clarinets, guitars, pianos. He regarded musicians as the highest form of life. I think it rubbed off on the rest of us, 'cause all three of us—his three sons—became professional musicians.

Did he not try to be a professional musician himself?

No. He had kids. That meant he had to earn a steady living. He did earn money, though, playing. He went out every weekend and played in bands.

When did you first become seriously interested in playing music?

About fourteen, fifteen. I listened to Alice Cooper and Led Zeppelin albums and copied all the things they did on the drums. I was completely self-taught. I didn't have any lessons, which is probably not the best way, but it's just the way it was.

Did you have favorite drummers?

John Bonham was always my favorite. No one had quite the power he had. He just used to command the whole stage and I always thought that's much more impressive than a hundred-thousand beats per minute. Any song is so much better if you've got a really powerful drum beat behind it.

But you're not that that kind of drummer yourself.

When punk came along, it was like, "Okay, we've got to move at a hundred miles an hour—and have the power with it." It was a hybrid. I always used to like Ian Paice of Deep Purple. He was different, he was really fast. I think I got somewhere between the two of them.

Were the Clash your first serious band?

Yeah. I was quite young. I was nineteen when I first come across them.

How did you join?

I answered an ad. Bernard met me first and talked to me. I thought he was a raving lunatic, because he wanted to talk to me to see if I was the right kind of person before I auditioned, but I thought, "Let's go on and see what happens here." The band turned out to be Brian James and Mick Jones and Tony James. That was the London SS. (That wasn't mentioned to me at the time but, looking back, it was one of the names they had). I played with them for a few hours. I hung around and chatted with them a bit. I thought it was an intriguing setup. I think they had the spark of something interesting there. We said we'd talk about it, and then no one called me and I didn't call them.

I saw another ad a little while later. I called that one as well. It was Bernard again. He said, "Oh, I think I know you." I said, "Yeah, I think I know you!" So we chatted about what we'd been doing and then he said, "Well, this is a different band." I think his words were, "One of the guys you met the first time has now graduated from that stage and got some other guys around." So I came down and this time it was Paul on bass, Mick on guitar, Keith Levene, and Billy Watts was singing. Again, we bashed out songs and that felt pretty good as well. I had very long hair at the time. I was dressed completely out of touch with all the other guys. I remember walking from the room to the caff and, as we were walking along, these guys were all dressed differently and they've all got lots of people looking at them: "What are these weirdoes?" Like a little gang. I remember thinking it would be kind of nice to be in a gang. Again, we had this, "Oh we'll chat and we'll see." And then I get the call again to say, "Come back, we've had more changes."

This time it was in Camden Town, Rehearsal Rehearsals. I arrived and said hello to Paul and had a chat with Mick and [he] said, "By the way, we've got a new singer," and Joe arrived. They said, "Joe, this is Terry. He's a drummer." He went "Hello" and then looked away again. Quite cold, really. Joe just seemed really strange to me. Just my first impression: strange-looking guy and he sounds really strange. I knew nothing about the 101'ers. I'd enjoyed working that day with Billy Watts and I thought he was pretty good. I saw Joe and compared him with Billy Watts, which is a mistake of course. His singing was really weird. I didn't appreciate what he was at the time. I don't know how long he'd been there when I met him, but perhaps he wasn't sure about a few things so he was being a bit cautious or a bit cagey.

How pivotal was Bernard Rhodes?

He was essential. You wouldn't have had a Clash without Bernie. He created it. He hired the rehearsal studio, he put the ads in, he interviewed everyone, he put them all together, he had a lot of say in what we did.

How many songs had Mick and Joe written at the time you joined?

Not too many. When I rehearsed with them before Joe came along, there were very few original songs then. Then when Joe arrived there was a few, and then in the coming months they came out of nowhere, loads of them.

Were they always intent on writing political songs?

Oh yeah. Partly it was the way they were, partly Bernie had said you've got to have this social comment going on: you've got to mean something, you can't just write a song for the sake of a song. In fact, Joe took me aside trying to explain what they were trying to do and said he saw the Pretty Things when they played somewhere and said, "All their songs are just nonsense 'cause they didn't mean anything to anyone. The song has got to say something to someone about something."

Did you consider the Clash part of a musical scene or movement?

Absolutely. Right from the start. The first gigs we did was supporting the Sex Pistols. That scene was already there, so we just jumped in on it. Before we knew where we were, we were being carried along with it, so it was really fortunate timing.

Punk hadn't hit the mainstream yet?

Oh no, it hadn't hit at all. I can remember being around the Clash for quite a long time and then suddenly you had people in the *Sun* newspaper with safety pins and things saying, "This is punk," and it seemed really weird that something I was involved with in the real world, in the physical world, appearing in the media like that.

At the time, it was a five-man lineup. How did three guitars work?

I think Bernard was trying to create a certain kind of setup. He was trying to create a climate to work in where a certain kind of attitude was formed. Keith was very strong in that way. Keith's attitude was very powerful—he was a strong character, full of energy, very challenging. He was good in that way. He was what we needed. He provided that side of things so Bernard liked having him around. But it was too many guitars—and probably too many egos.

And Keith was never quite settled. He never seemed very happy. He was always challenging and arguing and questioning everything. Keith would attack immediately, whereas Joe would say, "Well, what is it then? Tell me what it is," and then decided whether to criticize. Joe was much more open to ideas.

Keith seems to have been the most musically proficient band member.

Well, that was the idea: he was supposed to be the guitar soloist. Mick was supposed to be the one that wrote the songs. Joe would sing and strum away. It was a sort of weirdness; there was always something not quite right about it.

Bruce Springsteen always seemed to feel obliged to give Clarence Clemons a sax solo. Was that what the five-man Clash was like?

I do remember Keith going, "Oh I must come up with a solo for that song and for that song." There was a little bit of that. When in fact, looking at the first album, there wasn't a whole lot of soloing going on really, was there?

Was Mick leading from the back, like Keith Richards does with the Stones?

He was writing large amounts of material, which obviously gave him certain power, but he wasn't so much interested in throwing his weight around. I think he fancied himself as a star, but he wasn't really interested in power in the band. He was happy to let the thing unfold in front of him rather than trying to control it or make it happen the way he wanted.

Did the band seem to have a coherent vision of what they wanted to sound like?

I don't think it was all that preconceived. It was an evolving thing and there was quite a creative attitude generally. We came up with some really strange ideas sometimes. I remember coming in one day and Joe saying, "Mick's written two mini-operas." The mini-operas were songs over two and a half minutes long. I think "Remote Control" was one of them. They were both slightly longer songs with lots of different parts in.

I'd grown up listening to John Bonham so I wanted to be the hardest-hitting rock drummer in the world. I wanted to really splat that beat down hard and that kind of fitted the Clash's material. I think Joe just felt that we needed to work harder than everyone else and have more energy than everyone else. Joe and I really wanted to have more energy than everyone else and the other two felt more in terms of music.

Were the Sex Pistols considered the biggest competition?

I remember talking to Joe much later, I think during the first album, and saying, "We're judged compared with them and we need to try and better what they do somehow." And Joe said, "Yeah, I agree," but Mick said, "I don't see it that way at all. They're just another band and it's good we're all doing this stuff."

I felt they were the ones to beat, but I always felt a sense of camaraderie and they always seemed to be very happy to have us play on the same bill. They really helped us a lot, actually.

Where did the Ramones fit in?

Keith loved the Ramones. I think the rest of us thought they were a great band and it's great that they're there and it's really fun what they do, but it was like a different thing altogether and we didn't want to be like them.

Was there a discernible reggae influence?

They liked what reggae bands were about. The reggae bands were doing it for the music. They weren't rolling around like Pink Floyd were in their own jet and all that. They wanted to be a kind of rock equivalent of that. Not to play the reggae, but to be like them in their attitude.

Your partner in the rhythm section, Paul, was the only one of you who wasn't a fluent musician. Did that cause problems for you?

From one gig to another to another, he rapidly improved . . . I think because he looked the way he looked and he had the right attitude and he was willing to work and he fitted in and he got on with everyone and he had this artistic streak—he could paint and stuff—that I don't think anyone ever questioned that he could do it. We knew that if he kept playing he would get there and become fluent. A lot of people laughed at the fact that he couldn't play at first, but he always held his end up. He's an easy bass player to play with, actually. Having played with dozens over the years, he's a very solid bass player.

The songs were about English working-class life, especially London life. Were you worried there might not be a market for such parochial material?

I just wanted to play music. I wanted to get on a stage and have a load of people jump up and down screaming. With the Clash I was able to do that, so that was great, and if they wanted to sing songs about the Westway or whatever, that's fine, let them do it . . .

I sussed early on that the songs were good and I enjoyed playing them. I always figure if I enjoy playing something then someone else is going to enjoy listening to it. I didn't worry about the market, although I never really knew how big or small it would be.

What I did worry about—and this was the thing that led me to leaving the band really—was these attitudes of politics and so on . . . We used to argue politics. It's not really left- and right-wing, it's more I always think governments should interfere less and they were like, "Governments should do this, should do that." So we used to argue and they would hit back with, "Oh, he's a Tory—Tory Crimes . . ."

They would say things like, "We don't wanna have any money," and I would say, "Well you've just said you want to be the biggest band in the world. How the hell you going to have a road crew and all the things you need to get on the road and do things?" I think that irritated everyone because that would be like spoiling the fun. I would put a fly in the ointment by saying, "That's not practical . . ."

Joe never found a way round the fact he wanted to be really famous on a massive stage but didn't want to be considered to be a pop star. In fact, right at the end—I saw a documentary—he said, "We became what we started out to destroy." But that was always going to happen.

But I always maintained that just because you're famous and playing to a live audience doesn't mean to say you're Pink Floyd—all that lounging around in studios doing concept albums and ghastly music. There's no reason for the Clash to become that. But Joe just had this fear of being accused of that. He had the problem of worrying about what people think of him. You can never worry about what people think of you, really. You don't go in that business to become anything other than a famous rock musician . . .

In fact, Bernie said that I was a foil. In other words, when they come up with these things, I would always say to them the things that journalists would say later on and give them a bit of practice. But I felt really that it was me versus everyone else in these discussions. It got on my nerves. We got on okay. We just had disagreements all the time. Also, we worked very hard. We worked seven days a week, and a lot of hours, and that grinds you down a bit sometimes.

In your book, *The Strange Case of Dr Terry and Mr Chimes*, you seem to say that the Clash's political outlook or demeanor was the result of their troubled childhoods. That's quite a statement to make.

Yeah, but every single one of them came from a broken home. And the crew, and the management. All of 'em. I don't know anything about Bernie's upbringing, but I'm sure he must have come from a broken home as well.

Does that mean that they weren't genuine?

No, but when you come from a broken home you easily get angry about things, and you get told the world's a horrible place and you sort of tend to agree.

I was always the odd man out and I realized writing my book what it was. I didn't know it at the time. I had this pretty happy upbringing and was always smiling and happy and they were all railing at the world and all the injustice and angry with everyone. Bernie very consciously tried to bring that out in everyone and amplify it and in that process I was feeling more and more like "I'm in the wrong place here, because I don't feel like that at all." It's only when you write a book that you start thinking hard about this stuff. When you're nineteen, you don't understand it.

Would it be fair to say that you were from a more middle-class background than Mick, Keith, and Paul?

[*Laughs uproariously.*] No. I was from the East End and they were from Maida Vale, so it was the other way round, if anything.

You were said to be quieter than them . . .

I suppose because I'd gone through an educational process—I got A-levels and things.

How much rehearsing were you doing before the first gig?

Tons of rehearsing.

Were any of you in day jobs?

I think I was just in the middle of leaving one then. The other guys never had any money. I remember being the only one who ever had any money in his pocket, but Bernard would come and bail us out now and again.

What do you remember about an early Clash song called "For the Flies"?

I did some weird drum beats on that. Really strange thing. I asked Joe about where that song had gone. He said, "Well, after you went, we didn't bother with it 'cause it had that funny little drum thing in it and we didn't know what it was."

What do you recall about the genesis of "Janie Jones"?

I remember that day that Mick came in and announced it. He was all excited. He explained the drum beat he wanted, so we worked that out. He had quite a clear idea of the whole thing in his mind, so we did it and it worked perfectly immediately.

You made your debut supporting the Sex Pistols at the Black Swan in Sheffield on July 4, 1976. You'd only been rehearsing a month at that point. Do you think it was a bit too early to make your debut?

Was it a month? In my head, it felt like six months. Maybe [it's because] I was young at the time. I think we were ready for that gig because we were rehearsing seven days a week and we felt like we wanted to go and do it somewhere. We didn't want to spend our time in Rehearsals. We wanted to get out and do it.

We got up at the crack of dawn. I think we met each other at five in the morning at Rehearsals. We got this big truck and went up there and it turned out the gig wasn't until that evening. But it was the enthusiasm of the first gig. We had hours and hours to spend.

There was one or two hairy moments, but we survived it okay. We felt good afterwards, although looking back we would probably say it was a load of rubbish . . .

I remember some people coming up afterwards and saying, "The rest of the people in Sheffield don't get this but we love it." They were all dressed in full punk stuff. The rest of the audience were just looking. They weren't hostile, they weren't going wild, they were rabbit-in-the-headlamps: "What the hell's all this about?" Which was the case all round the country: a few mad punks at the front and a lot of other people that have got one toe in the water.

Was everyone nervous beforehand?

Mick was always the one who was nervous. He was always nervous before the gig and always happy afterwards. That was right through all the time I knew him . . . Joe was always fine beforehand and depressed afterwards.

How many songs did you play?

It was a short set, maybe twenty-five minutes.

It's been said that "48 Hours" was written for the second gig?

I remember it being a rush job.

You played your next gig in August at Rehearsal Rehearsals. Can you describe the place?

It's just a big room. We kind of tarted it up. We put some curtains on the ceiling and made it look a bit posher. It looked like a warehouse before that.

How did this second gig compare to the first?

We were rapidly developing. We were getting more fluid and confident and better.

How big was the audience?

Not a vast number. Twenty-five people, maybe. Caroline Coon was there. I remember her saying very nice things to us.

It wasn't long after that that Joe and Paul got caught up in the Notting Hill riot, which led to the composition of "White Riot." Do you remember them telling you about what had happened?

All I remember about it was I just felt that when you have a carnival you sometimes have a bit of aggro and it's no big deal. They were talking about it like it's some major event in world history. In fact, it was just a few punch-ups at a festival, which happens all the time. I remember thinking, "What's the big deal about it?"

Did you think it was a good idea for a song?

When we played it, it felt good because it was really fast and furious and we all enjoyed playing fast, furious stuff.

All of the early gigs, we used to get on that stage and try and overwhelm the audience with energy. That was the unspoken intention. Joe was a front man—you always knew he was going to go mad and give as much energy as he could.

I think "1977" was written slightly before "White Riot." What did you think of that, and the message "No Elvis, Beatles, or the Rolling Stones in 1977"?

It was fun hearing the lyrics when Joe came up with them. It was like, "We're new and the old ones should move on." That seemed like a reasonable thing to say, really.

What did you think of "Remote Control"?

We learned it and it seemed like a load of disjointed different bits stuck together, but once we'd played it a few times round, you just got used to it. It does sound more dated than the other stuff maybe.

What about "Hate & War"?

That was the other mini-opera.

What do you remember about Keith leaving?

Joe, Paul, Mick, and myself were sitting there and Joe was moaning that Keith is the phantom guitar player: he comes in and he disappears again and he didn't really see him as part of the thing. I remember thinking, "Well what do you want him to do, then? He comes in and plays his solos." And then Mick said to him, "So do you think he should leave then?" and Joe said "Yes" and turned to Paul and he sort of nodded in agreement. I thought, "What the hell's going on? One minute he's in the band, then suddenly . . ." I found that really odd.

When Keith arrived, they all put this opinion and he obviously wasn't very happy about it, having done a lot of work in the band. I argued that this isn't the way to decide the future, just on a whim. I realize, looking back, they were right and I was wrong. The feeling had been growing in all of them and they just expressed it and found they all agreed and that was that. When Keith accepted the fact, picked up his guitar, and walked out in a huff, Mick looked round and said, "I better learn to play guitar."

How did Bernie feel about what had happened?

He was a little bit miffed, but he accepted it fairly quickly.

Did that cause a big change in the way you operated as a group?

Because we had two guitars there and we didn't really need a solo in every song, after Keith left we sat down and played all the stuff without him and thought, "Well, actually we can do this and it's less complicated with less people."

When did the new four-man lineup begin to gel as a group?

I think right away.

But then you yourself started coming and going . . .

I got to a point where I said, "I'm not happy. I'm going to leave the band." There was a bit of argument about it. They felt let down, I suppose. It was always me versus the rest of the band and the manager and everything else. Just got fed up with all that. We set a date, which was just before the Anarchy in the UK tour [December 1976]. They had a various number of stand-ins . . . I carried on doing loads of gigs because they couldn't find anyone. When they finally found Topper, they were happy to move on with him, but up to that point I kept jumping back in to do things.

How many gigs did you play with the Clash in the seventies?

About twenty, I would guess.

You did some recording with them, firstly demos for Polydor records. The Polydor sessions were produced by Guy Stevens. What did you think of him?

I really liked Guy Stevens. I still think he was really the natural producer for the band. He was known to be a drinker and on the sessions I remember Joe saying to me that the guys from Polydor and the engineer "got him numbered." Meaning, "They're watching him to see if he drinks and they want him out." The way I saw it, he felt the band were with him but the company and so on weren't and he cracked under the pressure and started boozing before the end of it and blew it. Which is a shame, 'cause he knew how to get the best out of the band.

The Polydor playbacks must have been the first time the Clash had properly heard themselves?

I really love it, because you could hear that power come off the tape. Because we were such a tight band, we could go in there, play the stuff, and it would sound just right, so the backing tracks sounded really solid.

The first album and the Beaconsfield demos and the Polydor demos, all of it is really just us going into the studio and doing what we did live.

After the Anarchy tour you came back temporarily when Julien Temple recorded you—music and film—at Beaconsfield film school.

My impression was we got the place free to practice recording while they practiced their technique of filming. We were all playing with acoustic screens, headphones, and all that.

The proper recording came when the Clash were signed by CBS. Was the £100,000 deal with CBS on the table when you left?

Before I left. Chris Parry [of Polydor] was looking and then Bernie suddenly switched and went with CBS. They'd outbid Polydor, basically. And of course Bernie at the time thought, "Oh this is good, I can talk Terry into coming back on board now because we've got money." He could never figure me out at all, bless 'im. I felt sorry for him, really . . .

I remember at that time Joe making one more attempt to persuade me to come back on board 'cause there was money coming in. I knew it was the right decision. I was pleased to do the album because, having left the band, it was like making a permanent record of what I'd done so far. I remember Bernie coming to me and telling me that they'd found Topper. He said, "You must be really upset now that you haven't got a chance to come back." I said, "Well, if I'd wanted to come back I could have done all those months before . . ."

People have asked me this so many times. They can't understand how you can walk away from a £100,000 record deal, which was a lot of money back in those days. But if you're not happy, there's no point. Money's not really a big motivating factor for me. It's always there whether you go for it or not, it's just always around. I'm a hard worker, of course. Money doesn't really make a big difference, 'cause whatever I do I'm gonna earn money anyway.

The Clash wrote quite a few songs about themselves. There's one on *London Calling* called "Four Horsemen" and it contains the line, "They picked up a hiker who didn't want a lift from the horsemen." Did you realize that's almost certainly you?

No, but I'm not surprised, because Joe never forgave me for leaving the band. Even years later, after coming back and doing another tour and then years and years later—we weren't working together—I bumped into him a few times, he would still go on, "You shouldn't have left the band, you did that." Unbelievable. He would never let it go.

Why was he so upset?

Joe worked very, very hard to get the Clash off the ground—we all worked really hard—only [for me] to walk away from it. He couldn't understand how you could put so much into something and then walk away. I tried my best to explain it but he could never get it.

He was a funny bloke really. He was a lovely man in many, many ways and very impressive in many ways. He had his flaws like everyone. We got on very well, but we were always arguing about something. Just the way he was. He liked to argue because I think he found an argument was a way of figuring out where he stood on things.

The "White Riot" single is slower compared to the Beaconsfield/album version.

I can't remember consciously slowing it down.

Some people think it's also tamer?

I don't think so. When that record came out, you were hearing stuff like Smokie on the radio. Even slowed down, whatever you compared it with—like the Eagles—it was going to sound pretty wild.

What did you think of CBS Studio 3, where you recorded the single and the album?

Someone mentioned that the place cost zillions of pounds per hour to hire and there was an awareness going in there that we can't faff around for ages.

A row started between Mick and Paul because Paul wanted this really thick reggae-style bass sound and Mick wanted a harder-edged sound. I think Joe and I didn't really have that strong opinion either way. They really dug their heels in very deep and it went on for hours. I'm sitting there thinking, "We're wasting all this money on studio time"—although it shouldn't have bothered me 'cause I wasn't in the band then. Simon [Humphrey] come up with this whizzo idea of saying, "Record both sounds on separate tracks and we can argue about it later." After hours and hours of standoff, here's a compromise and nothing else was said.

Was there ever any discussion about Mick playing the bass lines?

No, because Paul had played 'em all live [and] it sounded great, so there was no need.

Simon Humphrey was the engineer assigned to you by CBS. What did you think of him?

He was like lots of engineers: very easy to get along with, very affable . . . Simon was a good engineer. He intervened when necessary and he sat back and let us do our own thing.

Did you have an idea of how you personally wanted to sound?

I insisted right at the start I wanted it to be a live drum sound. I don't think the rest of the band had thought about the drum sound. I remember saying if we had that "deadened" sound it would sound like the Eagles. "Okay, we'll have a live drum sound." We probably went a bit over the top with it.

The whole thing was very live anyway. Lots of ring in the drums. If you put a lot of tape on a drum, make it "dead," you can control it more but it's not as aggressive. On the top of that, they put this gated kind of sound, gated reverb on the snare. It's very, very treated, the snare. In "Deny," there's a lot of it on there.

Mickey Foote, the Clash's live sound man, is credited as producer on the early singles and the album. How seriously can we take that?

He was there throughout, trying to run things. I think he left the engineering to the engineer and he left the arranging to Mick and he just did the other bits, which weren't much. With the exception of "Police & Thieves," it was just a case of bashing out the live set.

Were you set up in a circle in the studio?

[Yes.] I could always see Joe. Joe was like an anchor man. Sometimes he'd sit there and nod and do things even if he wasn't recording. He kind of took the responsibility of counting and nodding at everyone.

How many takes of each song were you doing?

Averagely three or four. It was very fast. The backing tracks went down very, very fast. Joe was quite good actually at doing that: playing on the backing track so we knew where we were in the song, and looking over and nodding at the right time and all that. Mick tended to be in the control room, listening to how it sounded.

Did you watch the vocals being recorded?

Once I'd done my bit I tended to get out the way.

Joe has credited Mick with the architecture of the tracks, the arranging.

I think we only realized when we got in the studio that Mick had that talent for arranging things and putting little finishing touches on the song. Mick's backing harmonies live were always kind of shouting. He didn't do the subtle stuff. If you listen to "Police & Thieves," there's a lot of subtle stuff on there. He didn't do *that* live.

Mick fairly quickly realized the potential of the studio. The rest of us would just do what we did live and he was doing other things to make it better. He was definitely the arranger of it. [Joe] was more concerned with the mechanics of laying the track down, making sure there's no mess-ups and that's it. Mick was more concerned with the layers going over what there were.

Your tattoo on "Janie Jones" is the first sound we hear on the album. "Janie Jones" seems a strange album opener, as opposed to something explosive like "White Riot."

I thought that was well-cool, that being first on the album. If you listen to "Janie Jones," it starts with drums, then it's got layers coming in one by one. It's a classic buildup to begin the song. "White Riot" gives it all away straightaway—bang, and that's it.

There's some absolutely wonderful drumming on "Cheat," as if the intention was to make the track as frenetic as humanly possible.

As you can tell, I talk very fast. When I hear myself on speech recordings, I think "I can't be that fast, can I?" It's the same with the drums: I play very fast, but it didn't seem fast while you're doing it.

It's been said "Cheat" was never played live. Is that true?

Yeah.

How did you get the idea to do the phasing on "Cheat"?

Simon come up with that. I think someone said something about phasing. He said, "Well let's put some on and see what it sounds like," and he put it on and looked round. I said, "That's fantastic!" I think everyone thought it was fantastic.

Why record "Police & Thieves"?

That was a song we used to play sometimes to warm up in Rehearsals to get going. Playing the set over and over just felt like work, so we'd play something else. We would do "Roadrunner" by Jonathan Richman and the Modern Lovers and we'd play "Police & Thieves" for the same reason. I don't remember what point it was decided it was going to be on the album, but we warmed up in the studio on "Police & Thieves" and everyone was enjoying it and it was the same thing again: if we enjoyed playing it, maybe someone'll enjoy listening to it.

We consciously thought, "Let's just put a rock beat to this and see how it sounds," and, although it sounds a bit odd, it kind of works. It felt good. So we just said, "Well keep it like that, then."

Sometimes, we just used to play the backing track without the singing. When we went in the studio to put it down, it was only when Mick's harmonies came on—which we'd never heard before, because we never did those in rehearsals or live—I thought, "Wow, that sounds really good." When he put all these little touches on it, it sounded much better.

What's your favorite song on the record?

At the time my favorite track was "Garageland."

It's a sad song.

The lyrics might be, but it really is quite up-tempo, quite lively. It made me roar with laughter—still does—when in the fade-out, Joe says, "One guitar . . ." I've never spoke to him about this, but I just assumed it was a sarcastic comment on *Tubular Bells*. *Tubular Bells* goes, "One guitar, four synthesizers, fifteen harpsichords," all that. I just thought he was taking the mickey out of *Tubular Bells*. Joe's got a hilarious sense of humour.

I think they might have just started doing it [live] before the album. I like it 'cause it gave me an opportunity to do some weird stuff on the drums: doing a ride on the snare and then that tom-tom at the end.

The album has got this murky sound to it.

I was a little bit disappointed with the quality of the sound, but I felt it was a faithful reproduction of what we did live. The quality sounds awful. It sounds a bit muddy somehow. But I don't know if there's any way you can get round that, because you don't want [an] overproduced, dead kind of sound. It captured that raw energy we had live and that was good enough really.

On the album sleeve you're credited not by your actual name but as "Tory Crimes."

I think I'm disappointed at that. But then when you leave something, you can't really leave it and also say I want to have control or have a say in what's going on . . . I don't know who decided to put it on the album, but none of us ever dreamt we'd be discussing this forty years later, because we're young and you do things on the spur of the moment. It didn't bother me that much because everybody knows who I am anyway.

Were you surprised that the album went to number twelve?

Not at that stage, because the punk movement had gathered that much momentum. You were seeing stuff in the daily papers about it all the time.

How do you feel about the way the first album is now perceived as an all-time classic?

It's just a piece of music and if enough people like a particular piece of music it becomes a classic. I think back at the time I couldn't have had someone compare what we did with the Beatles or Hendrix or anything like that because they were huge names to me, but with hindsight every generation produces something. That album is held up as one of the better ones of its generation.

Did you ever have regrets about leaving the Clash the first time round?

I've played with Billy Idol, Black Sabbath, Johnny Thunders, Hanoi Rocks ... The funny thing is with my career, there are some people who say they know all about Black Sabbath but have never heard of the Clash, other people who know Billy Idol but have never heard of Johnny Thunders. I wouldn't compare the people I've played with because they're just different. I've no regrets because, when I was eighteen, I wanted to be in a famous band just to see what it would be like and I had more than my fair share of that in my life.

You went into computer programming for a while. Is that not a bit like manual labor after having been in a rock 'n' roll band?

Little phase I had. I had this grass-is-greener thing: "People that do normal jobs have a much nicer life." Of course, when I did it, I realized quickly that yes, there are those advantages, but on balance you're better off in the rock business, so I went back to that. I just needed to try being a normal person.

This is when computers were quite new. I learnt how to program computers. I enjoyed the challenge. I did a computer program, made it work. I thought, "Great, that's really good." They said, "Now do another one like this." I thought, "Hang on a minute—suddenly this is becoming work rather than fun."

Would that have been your life forever if it hadn't been for the call to come back to the Clash?

Oh no, I'd have gone back to bands one way or another. But that was a convenient jumping-off point.

How did you end up rejoining the Clash?

I rejoined in 1982 because, when Topper went, they asked me to come back in a big rush . . . It was a snap decision. I met with Bernie and Kosmo, we discussed it. They needed an answer there and then, so I said, "Okay, I'll do it . . ."

I remember Mick saying to me, "I bet you've heard none of the albums," and I laughed and said, "No I haven't actually." I hadn't followed them very closely at all. It didn't matter. I soon learned the songs and carried on . . .

It was a steep learning curve because the trouble with Joe, he can't make it easy. He would have a completely different set list every night taken from a large pool of songs, so instead of having to learn fifteen songs like you normally would, I had to learn about forty songs from which fifteen would be chosen each night.

Were you surprised at how they'd developed?

I was surprised at the diversity of it. Stuff like "Magnificent Seven" and the *Combat Rock* album, some of the funk stuff on there, "Overpowered by Funk." They'd moved in more different directions than I expected. I always knew they had a bit of reggae in them, but the other stuff was a surprise.

Did you find it difficult to reproduce the tricksy rhythm track of "Straight to Hell"?

No. It was like the old days when I was learning to play. I listened to it, decided I've only got one pair of hands—I can't do double-tracking—so I worked out a way of using the snare drum without the snare and the hi-hat and toms. That was probably my favorite song to play live 'cause I liked the way Joe used to sing that one.

How had the Clash setup changed?

It had changed a lot. There was more people in the audience, more money flying around, more staff around to do things . . . We used to argue about ideology frantically all the time at the beginning and that all stopped because obviously they were no longer saying in '82, "We don't want to have any money" and all this sort of thing. They'd grown up, and so had I.

The main problem was Joe and Mick weren't getting on. Probably the sensible thing would have been to say, "Let's all just disappear and have a break for six months and then see what happens," but bands don't seem to do that and really the management should suggest that sort of thing. I suppose Bernard was losing his grip on the band.

Had Joe and Mick been best mates before?

I don't know if you'd say that, but they were definitely hostile to each other whereas they'd been getting on fine before. There was a resentment and a kind of grudge building up. There was nothing I could do to change that. Mick was enjoying the fame and being a bigger band and having more things and Joe was, I guess, embarrassed by it. That's where it all stemmed from. [Bernard] was on Joe's side always.

It does seem that they'd all decided that they'd had enough of poverty and were embarking on a concerted attempt to make money?

Oh yeah. I remember one of the road crew moaning to Joe that this road manager, he won't do this, he won't do that. And Joe's answer was, "Look, I'm sick of going on a tour all round the world, working really hard and at the end of it we sit down with the manager and they say, 'We've just lost a hundred grand on that tour and therefore we've got to go out again and try and get that back.'" He was sick of that struggling. It will always wear you down. Of course, I was thinking that right from the beginning: when you start saying you're gonna give all your money away, what's the point of that? You can't sustain that.

Did some of it strike you as a bit mercenary: gimmicks like stickers, stencils, Clash clothes?

I dunno. It's the business we're in. Everyone does it and because the Clash started out by saying, "We're not going to make any money or do anything commercial" they set themselves up in an impossible way. They were always going to turn round and sell some things and that was always going to be greeted with, "Ah, see—they've sold out," so you can't win.

Paul had started out parroting bass lines taught to him by Mick. How did you find Paul as a musician, five years on?

[He'd] got better, because he could sing and play at the same time and do his moves.

Some people think that, in some ways, supporting the Who at the iconic Shea Stadium was the highlight for the Clash.

Seventy thousand [people] and we did two nights. I think for the Americans, they see that as the high point of fame. Musically, you could argue about it. I think we were pretty much at the peak at that point.

The *Live at Shea Stadium* Clash album was finally released in 2008. Most live albums are doctored—was that one?

I played the album when it came out and it sounds to me like what we did. I'm sure someone's fiddled with something, but it was basically what we did.

You left for the second time around the end of '82. Why was that?

They didn't want to make me a full member, like a partner in the thing. I felt, "Well why not do that, because I did all that work at the beginning, I came back . . ." But they felt that they had done seven years' work and why should I come back in and just take equal share when I'd been doing other things. That was one that I don't think we could get over. They weren't going to offer that and I wasn't going to accept anything less.

Were you shocked when, after you left, Mick was sacked?

No, 'cause they'd talked about it. I knew it was on the cards. Whenever I would argue with them about the future of the band, Joe and Paul would say, "Well, there's no point arguing about that until we decide what we're gonna do about the issue with Mick," so it was in their minds sometime during '82. We did loads of touring. We toured all over the States, then we toured England, then we went and did that Who tour . . . We did that Jamaica thing . . . We did loads of stuff. After doing that for six months, I was saying, "Okay, this obviously is working, shall we make this a permanent arrangement?" and they were like, "Well, we don't know what we're doing yet anyway with regards to Mick."

Did Mick take the attitude that because he was so talented, "They're nothing without me"?

It was something along those lines. I couldn't say he ever said that, but it felt a little bit like that. Which, of course, wound up Joe and Paul. I thought, "So he's big-headed. That's just him and he'll grow out of it." I never saw it as a big deal really, but they said, "We've had seven years of this—you've only just come back and had a little bit of it."

Was the idea of sorting out the "issue with Mick" always discussed in terms of sacking him?

Not at first, but by the end that was the idea that Bernie and Kosmo were working on. I always thought, "That's nuts." At first, I thought they were joking. I thought, "No, that won't work," however annoying he could be at times. (He's not now, he's completely changed.) You just can't have a Clash without Mick. But of course, when you're in a heated argument in the middle of things, they get these ideas in their head, they think that's gonna work.

Do you remember the moment you decided to leave again?

It didn't really happen that way. We finished touring. We did that little gig in Jamaica at Christmas, which was a sort of Christmas holiday as much as anything, and at that point we all went home. Because of what had been said prior to that, I thought, "This is it now, they're not going to get this all back together again," so it just kind of fizzled out.

Was there a possibility that you might play with them at the US Festival in May 1983?

I'd gone before it was even suggested. But I knew that that gig was only going to be one gig. There was no way they were going to go back on tour for three months across America. It was just never going to happen again. After that, they got rid of Mick and got these two guitar players to replace him, which is kind of odd. That was a different thing.

They made an album called *Cut the Crap*.

I just never got round to listening to it. When I heard Bernie had produced it, I felt, "Oh my god, that is just so wrong." I didn't want to listen to it 'cause I knew I'd be disappointed.

Topper once said, "I think the band would have died with punk if I hadn't joined. With Terry Chimes on the drums they wouldn't have been able to evolve into anything more musical." Meaning he didn't think you would have been able to play the sort of signatures and styles to be heard on *London Calling* and *Sandinista!* What do you think of that?

Well, we're different, obviously, different styles of drumming. I don't think we'd have died. I think we'd have gone in different directions. It's like *Back to the Future*: you never know if you change one thing what the future holds.

Would you have been happy to try jazz and reggae, etc.?

I'd have been willing to try different things, experiment a bit, but my nature is a hard-hitting, hardcore rock drummer. I'm not turned on by fiddly drummers, jazzy types. So that's what I would have been leaning towards always, and if you've got a drummer like that it will take the band a bit down that direction.

You decided to give up music in 1987.

Yeah. I thought, "I've had enough of this. I'm gonna do something different now."

Has healing always been something you're interested in?

Oh yeah, massive. Healing's a passion because if someone's suffering and their life's a misery and you can turn it around, it's hugely satisfying.

You could have gone into any strand of medicine. Why chiropractic?

Because it's drug-free. They've gone completely down the wrong path of modern medicine. Way too many drugs, way too much surgery. The body is an incredibly finely tuned mechanism, it's very sophisticated, and to try and adjust it so that it works well is the way to go. Modern medicine with drugs and surgery is like taking a clock that's not working and hitting it with a hammer to see if it might improve.

How many patients have recognized you as an ex-musician down the years?

Thousands of them. I've done a quarter of a million treatments so far.

You've become spiritual in recent years. Was it a Damascene moment?

Yeah, it was really. It was more important than anything else that's ever happened to me. It was a turning point completely. Once that's happened to you, nothing can ever be the same.

People who have spiritual awakenings often seem to be at a vulnerable point?

Inspiration or desperation, that's when things like that happen. My father had died a year previously, which hit me pretty hard, so it might have been a delayed reaction to that in the sense that it really shook me to think, "Actually, we're not here forever." That might have been a factor.

You returned to playing drums after a gap of twenty years. Was it hard to pick up again?

It's very easy. Just went straight back like it never stopped, except your arms ache afterwards until you get back into it.

Can a fifty-something drummer be as good as a twenty-something drummer? There is a physicality involved that there's not with guitar playing.

Oh, I think so. You probably need to make a point of keeping fit. I talked to Topper. I said, "Are you doing any drumming?" He said, "No, I can't these days. I haven't got the stamina." Which I found a little bit odd because, if you get down the gym, anyone can get stamina.

THEY WANT TO SPOIL THE PARTY— SO THEY'LL STAY

Bill Holdship | October 1984 | *Creem* (US)

Replacing the drummer of the Clash was perhaps no big deal. The appointment of Pete Howard to the vacant stool in time to play a string of American Clash dates culminating in the US Festival on May 28, 1983, seemed a smooth process that augured a near-future follow-up to the breakthrough *Combat Rock* album.

On September 1, 1983, however, the Clash released a press statement that was as momentous as would be a communiqué from the Rolling Stones that announced that Keith Richards had been sacked. It stated, "Joe Strummer and Paul Simonon have decided that Mick Jones should leave the group. It is felt that Jones had drifted away from the original idea of The Clash. In future, it will allow Joe and Paul to get on with the job The Clash set out to do from the beginning."

Strummer announced a new Clash lineup early the following year. Curiously, said lineup comprised a quintet. Augmenting Strummer, Simonon, and Howard were guitarists Nick Sheppard and Vince White, a three-pronged attack that it had been concluded was too unwieldy back in the Keith Levene days. It was almost as though Strummer was on some level acknowledging the disproportionate importance Jones had possessed for the Clash.

The straightforwardly guitar-based music the new Clash proceeded to purvey was a deliberate repudiation of the exotic musical directions explored by the band in recent years. This reassertion of the back-to-basics values of punk featured in Strummer and Simonon's justifications in the press for the drastic decision to fire Jones—they complained his recent song demos were dominated by beatboxes, synths, and samples—but most of the talk was of Jones's unreasonableness. "We were begging him to come out of his hotel room. That kind of atmosphere," Strummer told the *NME* in February 1984. This will have struck a chord with those who'd seen or heard of Jones's prima donna airs, but in some quotes Strummer seemed even to be resentful of Jones's evident happiness of late.

While Jones lay low, Strummer and co. took to the road. This feature was written during the first foray to America of the new Clash. It saw Strummer explaining to the country that had only just taken the band to its bosom why they now looked and sounded very different.

Contrary to the described machinations of Kosmo Vinyl, by the way, the Clash were not accorded the cover of the magazine.

Notes: The discussion of the controversy the Clash caused at the US Festival is a reference to the fact that—angry at ticket prices being higher than they'd been informed—the Clash refused to take the stage until festival sponsor Steve Wozniak agreed to donate $32,000 to a summer camp for disadvantaged youth.

"SDS" was sixties protest group Students for a Democratic Society.

For "Bony Maronie" read "Bony Moronie" —Ed.

CREEM contributor Mark Norton and I were talking several days before the Clash "invaded" Detroit, and we began discussing the concept of "armchair activism" and how the Clash probably fit into that category. Mark pointed out that there's currently a voguish literary movement of poets and writers speaking out against the turmoil in Central America, and (using Joan Didion's recent book on Salvador—which he says is "terrible"—as an example) he added that, for the most part, it's a pretty limp-wristed political mechanism. "War is bad," they say, "but evil dictatorships should be stopped." To which the only sane reply might be: "How perceptive!" (Or an alternative reply, courtesy of Lenny Bruce, might be: "What 'should be' is a lie.")

It seems if these artists were *really* serious, they'd follow the lead of Ernest Hemingway and other writers during the Spanish Civil War, and put some action where their words are. These earlier writers not only spoke out in favor of the anti-Fascist Spanish loyalists, but they raised money and actually went to the center of the conflict to help out. Artists literally became soldiers, donning military fatigues for more than fashion's sake; and while they lost their cause, no one could ever accuse them of being limp-wristed.

On the other hand, as I grow older, I'm beginning to believe that there simply are no political solutions. It's just a fact of life. Sure, "war is bad," but we've always had it, always will. No one can possibly agree on everything (or sometimes it seems like *anything*), and the '60s "do your own thing" message proved to be bullshit because I'm sure Charlie Manson would argue that's exactly what he was doing. For socialism to come to America, nearly everyone would have to suffer first—and almost no one is willing to do that. (Former SDS president on why the activism ended: "Paranoia—and we liked air-conditioning too much.") America should have learned a lesson from Nixon, but it still elected Reagan, who actually makes (the) Dick look better in retrospect. Or going back to the Spanish Civil War for another example, Hemingway warned both America and Europe if they failed to support the fight against Franco's Fascists, Hitler and Mussolini would overrun Europe, creating the second world war. No one listened to him. Things rarely change. Everything remains the same. Fatalistic? Perhaps. Realistic? Definitely.

Which is why something like the Who's "Won't Get Fooled Again" or Elvis Costello's brilliant "Peace In Our Time" makes more "political" sense to me than most of the Clash's combined output. Don't get me wrong. I thought the band's debut LP was great, while Give 'Em Enough Rope had some great moments, particularly "Safe European Home." But even back then, it was the energy and humanistic attitude that impressed me as opposed to what often sounded like empty political rhetoric. On top of that, I was still an idealistic college kid who believed that rock 'n' roll could "save" the world, and that everyone who listened to (and grew up with) a certain kind of music had to share a similar world view. (What a chump, eh?)

London Calling was the Clash's masterpiece—but what made it great was (once again) the attitude and the traditional "roots rock" position, right down to its Elvis Presley cover art. (Who could resist Joe's growl right before Mick's solo on "Brand New Cadillac," one of the great vocal moments in rock, right up there with Otis's whistle on "Dock Of The Bay" and Elvis's "Yeah!" on "I Need Your Love Tonight"?) But the bubble burst with *Sandinista!* (or *Give 'Em Enough Vinyl),* an overblown, pretentious affair, while *Combat Rock* was the absolute pits. What were the

Clash trying to say? Nothing, unless you wanna count doubletalk, and it seemed that the band was finally being consumed by its empty political stance. And, of course, there was the million-dollar question: what does an orange Mohawk have to do with changing the political structure in the 1980s?

It was about this time that the Clash's offstage actions started to reveal a bit of hypocrisy and inconsistency as well. Topper Headon's heroin addiction and Mick Jones's "rock star" posturings seemed to represent the very image the band had once denounced. Joe Strummer's rhetoric made him an almost comical character (an image CREEM has manipulated to the hilt). There were the hit singles, MTV videos ("rebel" rock or big business?), and, especially, the US Festival fiasco, where at least a few Clash fans sat in the dirt and heat while the band decided whether they'd take the stage or not. Even recently, Dave Marsh's *Rock & Roll Confidential* accused the "new" Clash of crossing a picket line of striking house technicians at a concert in Long Beach, CA.

For me, the final blow came when I heard Lisa Robinson interview Mick Jones on her radio show shortly after the release of *Combat Rock*. She said "Should I Stay Or Should I Go?" reminded her of classic Yardbirds and Who (?!?—as Rick Johnson pointed out, the song sounded better when Mitch Ryder recorded it as "Little Latin Lupe Lu"), and she asked if the Clash compared itself to these great '60s bands. Jones's reply? "We feel there has never been another band in the history of rock as great as the Clash!" To which my reply (as Lennon, Holly, Moon and assorted others probably rolled in their graves) was "You pompous ass!"

So this probably would have been an even more negative story if the Clash had refused to talk to us again, as they had the last three years in a row. The band was reportedly unhappy with the negative review R. Meltzer gave *Combat Rock* in CREEM, as well as the fact that we wouldn't guarantee them a cover story, which sounded like a "rock star" attitude to me. One of our correspondents at the World Music Festival in Jamaica two years ago reported that the Clash absolutely refused to talk to anyone from CREEM. I finally confronted Kosmo Vinyl, the band's press liaison ("whose speaking voice," John Mendelssohn wrote in another publication, "makes Joe Strummer's singing voice sound like Tony Bennett's") on this issue.

"I didn't want to talk to you because you wouldn't put us on the cover. I'll admit it. I don't mind. And if people say that's wrong, I'll say I don't go on about publisher's meetings and all the things that get spoked. I know about publisher's meetings! I understand the game, and I play it quite openly. I know for a fact that certain magazines don't get interviews with certain people unless they guarantee a cover. Your magazine chose not to put us on the cover. I chose not to do an interview. It's only mutual."

But isn't that a pop star attitude, the same thing Mick Jones got canned from the Clash for?

"No, that wasn't a pop star attitude. That's a hustler's attitude! I know that even *Time* Magazine guarantees covers to the right people."

Weren't you angry about the negative review of *Combat Rock* in CREEM? "Nah! Not too much. I thought it was quite interesting. The worst review you gave us turned out to be our biggest selling record!"

Fair enough, I suppose.

I finally get to talk to Joe Strummer two days after the Clash's Detroit gig with new guitarists Vince White and Nick Sheppard. Admittedly, the "new" band sounds tighter and better than the old line-up (Joe attributes it to better amplification—"Before, we had a very loud stage sound, and Mick had the attitude of 'Stuff it, I'm having my guitar as loud as I want it.' So we lost control of the P.A. sound, and it was a mess"), although the new songs, possibly excepting "Are You Ready For War?," leave a lot to be desired.

Joe seems to have mellowed with age, although part of his new calm may have something to do with his recent repudiation of drugs.

"We're not born again or anything like that. All we want to do is think clearly, and you can't think clearly on any drug. And I've found that my life is much better. Too much marijuana is a bad thing. You can deal and cope with life. I don't think people on marijuana realize how much it affects them. It's like taking their legs away or something. It's such an insidious drug because it claims to be harmless, doesn't it? But it's a bad drug."

Whatever the case, he doesn't spout off in his previous "violent" manner. When he wants to make a crucial point, he relies on eye contact, and he'll touch your arm for emphasis. He seems much friendlier than he was in previous days (cf. Dave DiMartino's Clash story in CREEM, Dec. '79). He compliments me on my "Elvis/Sun Studios, Memphis" T-shirt (I mean, how can I dislike this guy?). He worries there's too much noise in the bar for my recorder to tape our conversation. (In seven years of interviews, I've never had a subject in the least concerned about that.) And wonder of wonders, when some spittle escapes Joe's mouth and lands on my recorder, he graciously wipes it off.

He talks about everything from Jesse Jackson being the best candidate ("the only *real* opposite to Reagan") to the Russians ("They can't even build a color TV that doesn't break down. How are they going to conquer the Western World?"). Granted, the leader of the "anti-violent" Clash still often contradicts himself ("I've seen people come to blows over the Clash, and that made me feel great. What else can we really argue about that would inflame our passions to the point of physical violence? And more power to it!"), while a lot of what he says still sounds banal. Cases in point:

ON WHY THE "NEW" CLASH ARE TOURING WITHOUT A RECORD: "In my mind, I liken us to a new platoon, and we're going to go out and crawl right in front of the enemy lines, get fired upon, and then look at each other to see how we're bearing up. Can I rely on this guy when my gun jams? We're under fire, and we're sharing that experience. And that's what is going to make our record great." Huh?

ON WHY THE "ANTI-WAR" CLASH WEAR MILITARY FATIGUES ONSTAGE: "What is the opposite of a highly trained Green Beret? I'd say it was a shambling, wino-junkie hippie. So that's not good enough. We wear those clothes in a spirit of self-defense. The more organized they are, the more organized we will be. And that's the way it'll be in the future." Hmmmm.

ON THE CLASH'S 1984 "POLITICAL PLATFORM": "Get up off your chair, turn off the TV, go outside and deal with real life. What I'm talking about in 1984 is the 'on' and 'off' switch on all appliances, and I would urge all Americans to put it in the 'off' position for a change. I turn off everything when I come here—TV, air-conditioning. Dammit. I don't want that Top 40 radio, MTV in my mind. Turn off everything. Exercise your right upon the switch. That's our message in '84." Which does make sense, but if everyone turns everything off, how will they hear the Clash's messages?

But fair's fair, and I gotta admit that I kind of liked Joe Strummer. The man is definitely concerned and sincere, if a bit politically naive. I asked him what I considered some tough questions, and he answered them, without anger, the best he could. What follows are some excerpts from that conversation.

The Clash have always had a lot of political rhetoric, but I'm beginning to believe that there are no political solutions. Don't you ever feel it's a lost cause?

Yeah, but I don't think we can know what will happen. The reason the political thing isn't going to be a solution is that we don't know what the truth is. Just suppose the right people, who aren't puppets, started running for office and were elected. The climate would change. And within that climate, you might even get truth in the papers, on TV and on radio. And when the new generation is subjected to a bit of truth, who knows what might happen? Compare the Black Panthers to Martin Luther King—who achieved more? It was really King's message in the long run. And a thing like that should be studied.

Sure, King achieved more, and he got shot. Most of the Panthers later embraced the establishment. The '60s taught a lot of lessons, and we still have Ronald Reagan as President.

Yeah, but Ronald Reagan is a product of the drug culture. The two are synonymous in my mind. Reagan is there because we didn't care. We kept goofing up, we copped out, and we let Reagan in. The same with Thatcher in England. Maybe we have to be burned to learn. Hopefully, people are going to be less apathetic about it now or nothing will be left.

I mentioned the poet-soldiers in the Spanish Civil War. Don't you think real activists should go to Nicaragua and help the people out?

Yeah, I think it would do some good, really. But even so, I don't think anything can stop the U.S. Army from killing every man, woman and child in Nicaragua. And that's what they have to do because that's the only way the U.S. is going to stop them. America is following the wrong policy because Nicaragua would be friends with the U.S. It's the same as Southeast Asia. When realize that Ho Chi Minh was in touch with U.S. in 1949, you begin to see things differently. They drove Cuba into the arms of the Kremlin. It's all paranoia. I'm sure that Americans could get on well with Nicaragua and Cuba—even if they are socialist, Marxist states. So what? They want to trade. Why is it the Western policy to uphold the worst dictators—anything but letting socialism come into it? It's madness.

But don't you think that activism goes beyond your song lyrics?

Well, yeah, but it's first things first. We're musicians. I started by playing "Bony Maronie," and that was enough for me when I was learning it. We're musicians, but we know there is going to be a struggle between one economic order and another—the have and have-nots will come to a conflict, and the music is going to play a part in creating an atmosphere for that struggle. But first you have to have that cultural input. First, you have to have the spirit raised before any activism can begin. I mean, the Vietnam War was a target that everyone concentrated on, and I really believe the antiwar movement stopped the war. But that was because there was one clear issue to think upon. Without that clear issue, the left is in complete disarray. But again, I think the issues will eventually become clearer, and I believe that our music will play a part in that struggle. When you're talking about activism, I'm not pretending to be an activist. That's going to be another thing completely.

I heard Mick's out of the band because he developed a "pop star" attitude.

I don't think he could help it. He was a bedroom kid—one of those kids in the bedroom dreaming that someday he'd be as big as the guys on the posters, learning his chops in the bedroom. That's something I never went through at all, but he did, and he just doesn't realize that the '80s are different. He still thinks the world's the same as it was when he was in his bedroom. He still believes in the hierarchy of rock 'n' roll. What it came down to was, in the end, we were going "Look, these heavy metal bands are turning people into oafs and idiots. We've got to get out there, and stick in another oar. We've got to work." And he'd say, "I think we should take six months off." And I couldn't convince Mick that it wasn't the '60s out there anymore.

And then there's the fact that I don't believe anyone is that great that they don't write crap sometimes. Mick wouldn't have that. In his mind, he was a great artist, and great artists don't write crap. It was dangerous. I think Mick's got a tendency to bring "yes" men close to him, and shut out people who will tell him the damn truth. Remember, I'm supposedly his buddy and partner, and I said to him, "Mick, I don't think you can produce." What I meant was that you just can't sit in the chair, move some faders, and claim to be a producer. And it was "You bastard! I thought you were my friend." I worry about him because I don't think he has anyone around him telling him the truth.

There was a piece in Rolling Stone *where Mick's lawyer said in time Clash fans will discover that they haven't been told the truth.*

Ah, fuck that. Rubbish. He ought to get something going. I mean, it's been six months. What's he doing? All I've heard is that he's fallen out with Topper. He's auditioning drummers, and they're calling it T.R.A.C.—Top Risk Action Company.

Since the Clash promote harmony to a degree, isn't it a paradox when the band itself can't get along?

Yeah, it does seem like a paradox. I just feel that's real life. The only way it went wrong was because we couldn't tell each other the truth. When any relationship gets to that point, you might as well forget it. We argue constantly here, but nobody takes it personally. Everyone realizes that we're trying to get the best out of it. That's why I think this is going to work.

I liked everything up to London Calling, *but thought* Sandinista! *and* Combat Rock *were terrible. What happened?*

What's wrong with *Sandinista!* was that there was too much to give every track a good mix. It was brave to try, but unsatisfying in the end. To understand *Combat Rock,* you have to realize it was a salvage operation. It was a home movie mix—which led me to tell Mick he couldn't produce—and I finally had to take it to Glyn Johns, an outsider, to save it. Mick's attitude was that I ruined his music. Fifty percent of *Combat* Rock was great rock, but the other fifty was what Phil Spector would call "wiggy."

From what I see, hasn't punk—especially hardcore—evolved into just another cliche? It's like heavy metal with a different uniform.

Well, I think we're too successful for a lot of those kids. They don't follow us anymore because they've forgotten that punk is an attitude—and not a uniform or even a form or style of music. Punk was never those things. They were by-products. But the hardcore scene ain't exactly a hotbed of creativity—the things I always check for.

I'm only reading it from a distance, but I think they've forgotten that it ain't studs, it's the thoughts.

You were criticized after the US Festival. On one hand, it was admirable that money be donated to charity. On the other, a lot of people were there to see the Clash, and you made them wait hours in the heat.

Yeah. That was a screw-up. We knew that we had a two-fold purpose there. We're not a band that protects our ideals at home. We have to deal with the music industry, and that weekend, the whole industry was looking at the festival as *the* state of rock 'n' roll. So we had to go in there and show them that we wouldn't be pushed under the carpet. Our second purpose was to spoil the bloody party, because I'm not going to have some millionaire restaging Woodstock for his ego-gratification and tax loss in his backyard and get away with it. If Wozniak had said "I'm having a beer fair, a T-shirt fair and a computer merchandizing fair, and we're going to have some music on the side to draw crowds," that would've been honest. Instead, he said "Unison, Unity—US." Our first reaction was to go right in there and ask, "Does anyone know what we're unifying around? Does anyone know what the definition of US is?" Dead silence. People forgot to check that out, and rushed to get walkie-talkies. As we rode out of there, Kosmo was singing to the tune of "T For Texas": "It's Vietnam mixed up with Woodstock." Don't tell me that you can recreate Woodstock in the Me Generation of cocaine California in 1983. We had to go in there and spoil the party because nobody else was. Everyone else was sitting around going "Hey, man. It's cool, man." And on the Van Halen day, someone got clubbed to death over a drug deal. Anybody could've seen that was going to happen.

But there were fans there specifically to see the Clash . . .

Yeah, but you see we got caught. We were juggling with too many balls. We were having it out with the press before we went on, and I don't think we should have done that.

The press did criticize your attitude.

Yeah. Well, I'm glad. Let's stand up and be counted. But what I thought as we left was how none of the other bands on the "new music" day stepped forward and said, "Hey, I think this is a lot of jive, and I want to say something, too." In fact, the only guy with any guts the entire weekend was Eddie Van Halen. Because with all that stuff going down, he walked alone, unasked, right into the middle of our trailer, and stood there grinning, with his hands spread wide. And I thought—well, I drank to him over that.

I take it you won't do another US Festival?

Well, I don't think an invitation will be offered. But, you know, I like a good argument, especially with Californians.

You were criticized in Dave Marsh's Rock & Roll Confidential *for crossing a picket line of striking house technicians in Long Beach.*

Well, if there was a picket line, it must have been manned by ants or something. (Reads *RRC*) Yeah! This is what we want. More of this kind of stuff . . . I didn't see any picket line. I mean, I've usually got an eye for those picket billboards.

Would you have crossed it if you'd have seen it?

No, I wouldn't have. Definitely not. But usually when we go into a town, I can spot a picket line 200 yards up the road. Even when it's only manned by two or three people, I can spot it. I think I'm going to investigate this a bit. We drove around the building several times. There wasn't a soul. Hell, it's not above their ability to come and talk to us, is it? Still, I guess if it's true, we have to take it on the chin.

You once sang "No Elvis, Beatles or Rolling Stones in 1977." The Clash have existed as a successful band almost eight years now, and by this time, in chronological terms, the Beatles had split. Elvis was in the army and the Stones were in decline. Aren't you afraid in 1984 the Clash may be peddling their own form of punk nostalgia and "phony Beatlemania"?

Not really, because those scenes were founded on the aura of mystique. "See the star, worship the star, don't touch the star." One of the facts that we've tried to bring out is anybody can do it. We've always tried to talk to anybody after a show who wants to talk to us because we're intent on showing them that we're just another bunch of idiots like anybody else. And the fact is we play three or four chords. On a good day, we might hit five. But dammit to hell, I challenge anyone not to be able to learn five chords in three weeks. God, I could get a penguin to do that. Or Flipper. Flipper on the fretboard. Twenty years ago, people swallowed the "star" thing, and you'd think we'd have progressed. But, oh, no. 1984. Duran Duran. Boy George. Still swallowing it. Phony Beatlemania definitely ain't bitten the dust, but I'll be damned if I'll support it. You know, I like to tell people to hate us. Get out from under our shadow, be your own person. I'm proud to inspire people, and from then on, they should take it from there.

Why call this band the Clash? It's weird. The Pretenders are continuing with brand new people. Johnny Lydon has a bunch of faceless sidemen doing "Anarchy In The U.K.," and they call themselves PiL. Wouldn't it be more honest to call this Joe Strummer's new band?

No. We are the Clash. I say in all my arrogance that we need the Clash, and we're it. Even if Vince and Nick weren't in the Clash before, they were buying the records and standing in the front row. The fact that they learned to play is great because we can use them now. But we are the Clash because it certainly ain't U2, and it certainly ain't the Alarm, and it certainly ain't the make-up brigade, and if certainly ain't the heavy metal thing, and it certainly ain't Mick Jones. *We are the Clash* and I'd hope that if I started to act funny that I would be fired, and the Clash would continue to roll on without me.

So there you have it—Joe Strummer in 1984. Still as arrogant as ever (he told me Mick Jones was right in calling the Clash the greatest band ever "because you got to believe that, whether its true or not"), he remains steadfast in his beliefs, and you have to at least respect him for that. On one hand, the Clash haven't produced a really good record in nearly five years, and I'm afraid their time may have passed them by. On the other hand, I'd rather hear Joe Strummer telling a crowd of Detroit teenagers that "Sex Mad War" is dedicated to "a time when a woman can walk alone in the park at midnight without being afraid—which is her divine right" anytime over Motley Crue's "We love fucking the girls in Detroit because their pussies taste so good!" (Can someone get these morons to crawl back under their rock? Please?)

After I left the interview and was digesting some of the things Strummer had said, I drove past the American Legion hall in Royal Oak. I swear that two Army sergeants were out front leading a group of pre-teen kids in army uniforms through complete military drills. I couldn't help thinking of Hitler Youth (Reagan Youth?), and wondering if maybe Joe Strummer was right. Maybe we do need the Clash. After all, a little optimism ain't a bad thing.

But then, I guess that I just don't know.

HE WHO LAUGHS LAST

Lenny Kaye | March 1986 | *Spin* (US)

The new-look Clash certainly wasn't the prolific proposition of the previous incarnation. In their first thirty-nine months as a recording outfit, the Clash released four albums (one a double, one a triple), two EPs, and several stand-alone singles and B-sides. The gap between their fifth album, *Combat Rock*, and its follow-up was forty-two months.

With bizarre synchronicity, that follow-up appeared within days of *This Is Big Audio Dynamite*, the long-playing debut of Mick Jones's new group, whose name was designed to be readily reducible to the acronym B.A.D. True to Strummer's previous claims, it showed that Jones had embraced modern musical styles without equivocation, including nonmusician personnel, drum machines, elastic song structures, slogans as lyrics, shrill blasts of synthesizer, and the new art form that would become known as sampling (although appropriating film dialogue rather than snatches of records). Contrary to what B.A.D. member Don Letts claims herein, it was anything but rock 'n' roll. Whatever the genre in which they operated, however, B.A.D. at this point were a rather trendy proposition. That perception may not have lasted much beyond the second of their nine albums, but there was no doubting who had come out better in the head-to-head.

Although the new Clash debuted powerfully with "This Is England"—a heart-wrenching dissection of economic decay—that single's parent album was widely derided, whether it be for the purposeless Americanism of its title, *Cut the Crap*, or its music's bellicose, unintentional parody of punk music. As Strummer couldn't bring himself to promote it, it spent a mere three weeks in the UK album chart, peaking at number sixteen. In the United States it made number eighty-eight, a figure all the more pitiful for the fact that its predecessor was a certified US million-seller. When Jones then spurned Strummer's overture to rejoin the band, the Clash were no more.

Not only was the title of this *Spin* feature appropriate, but Lenny Kaye was a logical figure to question Jones about the second act to his career: he was the compiler of *Nuggets*, the garage-rock compilation so influential on punk. He is, however, a little negligent when it comes to challenging Jones over his explanation for leaving the Clash: the guitarist makes it sound like a resignation, rather than a dismissal. In later years, Jones would freely admit that his self-absorption made him the architect of his own misfortune. —Ed.

It's a long way from World's End to the end of the World. Down on New York's Avenue C, along the cutting edge of the next urban frontier, Mick Jones has brought his traveling medicine show to town.

B.A.D. Big Audio Dynamite. Light the con-fuse.

Did he fall or was he pushed? The question seems useless in retrospect. Once in the air, the force of gravity takes over. You splatter unless you learn to fly.

Mick Jones was more than a member of the Clash throughout the glory years of what has come to be known as the Nouveau Wave. The musical oversoul of the band's ruling triumvirate, he translated their tangled social philosophies into stylistic action, aligned them conceptually with both white and black rockers, and combined reggae and garage punk with rockabilly and metalesque anthems. Joe Strummer would rant, rave, and rabble-rouse; Paul Simonon would smolder; Mick would keep extending their sonic textures: "I'm So Bored With the U.S.A." "Tommy Gun," "London Calling," "Know Your Rights."

By the time the Clash finished, *Combat Rock* had gone several shades of platinum. As unofficial heirs apparent, they opened for the Who at their farewell New York City performance at Shea Stadium, where all good rockers go to be enshrined in immortality. Like most bands who take a contra-stance, the Clash proved they thrived on adversity. Given mainstream success, they had no choice but to turn their M-16s on themselves.

Bye bye, hey hey, maybe we will come back someday. But don't bet on it.

Mick Jones wants a riot of his own. He's worked too long and hard on Big Audio Dynamite to turn tail now. Two years in the making, his latest project is subtle in execution and impact, a surprise for those expecting either one-sided sloganeering or partying. The music has become a swirling, cinematic montage of jump cuts and fleeting images, densely layered like so many cels of animated cartoon or bits of a newsreel.

Don(ovan) Letts, a film and video director, picked up his camera in 1976 just as other punks-to-be reached for electric guitars. At the time, Letts was running a vintage clothing shop in the basement of one of London's Kings Road antique markets and working as a reggae DJ at night. His super-8 documentary of the early British punk scene, *The Punk Rock Movie*, is a classic piece of you-are-there home movie-making. Don's dub instincts served him well on film and through his current collaboration with Mick (he co-wrote seven of the eight songs on the debut album), he's now come full circle.

Big Audio Dynamite's aural collage is a shuffled deck of fast-forward images that—like life—often seems incongruous, only making sense when seen as a whole. "We juxtapose a lot of stuff," says Mick, "stick it all on top of each other. I like that mixture of the samurai sword and the Sony Walkman, the Dickensian London and the Wild West London of 1985–86.

"I think we've got a chemistry that couldn't exist anywhere else, apart from London," adds Don. "There's a kind of cosmopolitan mix that we still have. It isn't like segregated minorities; there's still a mingling between the subcultures. The people are still into each other's ideas of music."

"Yeah," Mick says. "Like if it was in New York, it would be two groups, and one would be in Brooklyn with a couple of these guys, and another in Manhattan with me and the rest. In London, they're still mixing on the street."

This Is Big Audio Dynamite blends its varied styles without being buried by them. It's not an easy album and rewards repeated listenings. The beat-box rhythms, the sing-along choruses, the special effects and voice-overs, the impressionistic lyrics whose scattered imagery creates its effect through cumulative force rather than narrative—we are far removed from the Clash's explicit political statements. Jones has not forsaken his moral stance; he's merely filtered it through personal revelation. The resulting ambiguity removes him from the cross upon which the Clash were granted their crown of thorns—the purgatory of a "White Man in Hammersmith Palais." You think it's funny, turning rebellion into money?

I remember the first time Mick Jones played me an unmixed tape of that song in his apartment, and how it seemed to sum up the cross-cultural contradictions of the late '70s. The Clash believed, therefore they transcended.

Later, we watched the end of a movie he'd taped off television called *Zulu*. Its climactic scene was a showdown between African tribesmen and their 19th century British colonial adversaries: the English are besieged in their fortress, surrounded by Zulu troops. In an unmistakable cadence, the Africans begin to sing their battle song.

The British commander exhorts his troops to sing back in kind. These competing voices fill the air, a harmonic blend that at first "clashes" and then seems as one song. The melodic lines intersect, dancing off each other, stopping, starting, a mixage honoring all combatants. Seeing it in 20th century London only made it the more real.

"Zu-zu-lu—come out to play," sing B.A.D. from the World stage. And so they have.

> When you reach the bottom line
> The only thing to do is climb
> Pick yourself up off the floor
> Anything you want is yours

"It was always going to be a group," says Mick. "It wasn't like I'm going solo now and get myself some backing people. I could've easily cashed in on my previous success, gone out and done 'Train in Vain' or 'Should I Stay or Should I Go' for big audiences. But that's not what I wanted to do. I didn't want to be doing it *then*, so I couldn't see why I should want to be doing it on my own."

If one of the lyrical themes of Big Audio Dynamite is a phoenix-like rise from the ashes, you can't blame Mick for keeping his spirits up during what must have been a period of painful reevaluation. That he's so chipper today, reclining on a hotel bed in a white raincoat that makes him look like a gleefully mad scientist, is an indication of how far he's traveled since the Clash split up. The black leather Jones of *Rude Boy* seems a lifetime away. Talking quietly, confidently, without malice, he makes a marked contrast with the more volatile Letts; dreadlocks and moonlight.

They go out at night. Don wears his shades. At the Milk Bar they look like shadows pressed against the white walls. There is an air of incognito around them, despite the fuss that Mick's presence causes among the more knowledgeable scenesters. Don plays Ilya Kuriakan to Mick's Napoleon Solo.

"What's on?" asks Mick at one after-hours soiree. "What's the entertainment?"

"You are," comes the answer, and in perfect juxtaposition "B.A.D." booms over the sound system.

"I wanted to make a dance record," Mick says. "I was very influenced by standing in a lot of New York clubs and thinking, wow, this is what we need at home. I was impressed with the scene. The beat box just took me on. I wanted to stick rock 'n' roll guitar on this dance rhythm, and I wanted to do my quirky vocals on it, and I wanted to get a couple of unknown musicians, and that would be enough. I wanted to get non-musicians as well and stick it all together, because when you get fresh heads you get fresh ideas.

"Where Don's coming from or where Dan's coming from—they're not used to the studio. If you go, well, what about if we did this? and then you're told you can't do that, we do it this way, most musicians would go along. When Don or Dan suggest something, I'll say, let's try it out, and that's how we get these mad explosions in the music and stuff, because it starts from completely non-musical ideas.

"But you know what that is, this mix of unknowns and non-musicians? That's punk rock."

The magic words. Both Jones and Letts are old (young?) enough to remember when punk meant more than a rigidly defined chainsaw musical style and a fashion statement. In many ways, Big Audio Dynamite is their attempt, along with bassist Leo "E-Zee Kill" Williams on bass, drummer Greg Roberts, and "conductor" Dan Donovan (who plays

Jerome to Mick's Bo Diddley), to revive punk's sense of attitudinal possibility and personal discovery.

"What I like about this," says Don, "is that it's a springboard for creativity. People feel like they can get involved. That was the thing about punk rock that I genuinely miss. It wasn't just the Sex Pistols onstage. There were all these people who also felt like they wanted to do something, and pretty soon there was a new magazine, or a shop opening up, or a new band.

"We don't want just fans. When we go out, we like to get turned on by the fans. We're looking at what they're wearing as much as they're looking at us. Or seeing what they're thinking, or what they regard as cool or uncool. I like that two-way thing.

"I wised up when I saw the Pistols," recalls Letts. "I realized I could dig what they were into but do my thing as well. And maybe they could respect me as much as I respected them. That's what happened. Before punk rock, I was a shop manager, and after punk rock I was Don Letts reinvented. If I hadn't seen those guys, who knows where I'd be today?"

Don often considered the transition from making videos to starring in them, but hadn't planned on working with Mick "'cause there were bands out there, doing a job really well, and through what they were doing, I could relay it and also express myself. But, as it turned out, that hasn't been the case the last few years. I cannot relate to this soft, safe music, ugly guys, and people ain't sayin' nothin'. So I found myself with a bit of spare time, funnily enough, at the same moment Mick was at a loose end. Instead of waiting for other people to inspire me, I thought, fuck it, I'm going out there and try to do it myself. I might add that if other people were doing it the way I like to see it done, I might not be in Big Audio Dynamite. I was tired of waiting, and I'd suggest everyone else shouldn't wait either, but go and make it happen."

Jones suffered similar frustrations in his final months with the Clash. There were indications of his B.A.D. self in previous work—"Rock The Casbah," "This Is Radio Clash," "Magnificent Dance"—but his efforts at broadening the Clash sound were often met with skepticism. "I mean, they used to call me Wack-Attack," he laughs, "and say that 'you've got your usual New York environment around you.' But they really didn't have anything else to put in its place. It was kind of a negative approach to things, and I never used to like that, really, because I was always into going forward, moving ahead.

"And then when it started coming around to revival time . . . if I didn't love the guys dearly, I would've been gone. But I happened to wait around. I thought we could work it out together. I was a bit wrong in that. That's all a shame, really, because if we'd have talked to each other, it probably wouldn't have happened, but we weren't even on grunting terms. I was the biggest voice of dissent, and when it started going backwards, that was the time I had to be moving on."

Mick hasn't given up the political idealism from which the Clash drew much of their inner fire. "I still think it's important. The political thing is difficult, but these things have to be said. I think the problem was the way we said them. Now we're taking a different approach. We don't want to be bludgeoning people with our stern, preaching message. We've taken our soapbox and kind of tidied it up and made it look like a pink Cadillac. We try to make it a bit more glamorous, have a bit more to do with life.

"We wanted a celebration. When we went in and made the record, we were really enjoying ourselves. And when we get onstage, we enjoy ourselves. That's what I drum into the lads all the time. You've got to be enjoying yourself, because if you're not there's no point to it whatsoever. What we're serious about is our sense of humor. Any other way, you've immediately got tactical problems. How are you going to say it and have people wanting to listen? Not even that we want to get them listening immediately. If we get them dancing . . . and then maybe the message comes later and the message is a simple one: how are we going to live? That's the message of all music."

The two shows at the World deliver the Big Audio Dynamite philosophy in action, although the group returns to the dressing room after Thursday's debut in a temperamental mood. The previous night in Boston, the mostly collegiate crowd had been theirs from the start. Here, the seen-it-all multitude remained watchful and not a little wary throughout. After a few initial attempts to rouse the audience, the band backed away from confrontation.

"We turkeyed," Mick moans in the dressing room afterward. He folds his body into a corner and grimaces. Josh the photographer tells him to "get with it. You know what New York is like; if they fuck with you, you gotta fuck them back." Even as Joey Ramone makes his way backstage, Mick sits preoccupied, his mind on the next night's performance.

Friday makes all the difference. Despite a guitar string broken at a crucial moment, and the drum machine, which decides to drump its programming, the band never loses its groove. "You're still a bit cool," jokes Mick, getting the crowd to yell "party!" before tearing the roof off the sucker with a monster encore version of Prince's "1999." No oldies-but-goodies for this lot. Post-gig, the dressing room mirrors steam with flushed excitement and the slapping hands of camaraderie.

Among the well-wishers is Rick "Def Jam" Rubin, who remixed "The Bottom Line." How did Mick like it? "I like it very much," he nods vigorously. "Because he's taken the essence . . . in fact, I want to collaborate with Rick some more on the next record, whatever it is, because I don't feel we'll have to record so much stuff. He kind of simplifies it. I like that simplicity. Plugging in and getting the right channel straightaway."

The album itself, produced by Mick, grew over a year of playing little-announced spot dates, where the unnamed B.A.D. opened for such groups as the Alarm and U2. "We wanted to be able to play the music live," says Don. Audiences went away impressed, and the low profile allowed the band to fully develop its complex array of sounds and technologies. Make no mistake: from Mick's synth guitar to Letts's sampler, this is a high-tech combo. Don: "The thing is we're not afraid to deal with technology, as long as we're pulling the reins, and it ain't pulling us. If a fuse blows, I think we can still rock the house."

Mick agrees. "We did all the stuff beforehand. We did about a year of pre-production, getting it right before we even went near a studio. We demo-ed it all out, everything, so we could go in there, hook the shit up, and I could read the *FT* [*Financial Times*]. Six weeks later the LP comes out the other side. Occasionally I'd have to whip the band into shape."

Don: "I'd be in the corner working on my pelvic thrust in the mirror."

Mick: "You shouldn't be too precious with it, really. We wanted to get it out in '85. Then we want to do another LP after the new year so we can have something fresh out for the summer. We're looking for a much simpler approach on the next one. It's going to have just as much meaning, just as much going on, but we're going to look for even more space. It's not going to be packed with information the way this one is. Space is as important as the music." Work is scheduled to begin on the new album in London this month.

A song like "Medicine Show" makes it seem like Big Audio Dynamite has seen one too many panaceas proffered. They allow that they may be a part of music's ongoing spaghetti western, "but it's also about people's gullibility. I think they swallow a lot of stuff that's pretty unpalatable. In 'Sudden Impact' we start talking about heavy metal music, and how it encourages people to think that devil worship and abusing women is cool, so on and so forth. To live a non-spiritual existence. To be fucked up. And that's supposed to be cool.

"Well, I don't think it's cool and I don't know anybody else who does, but a lot of young kids are influenced by that and educated to that kind of attitude, which leads to a lot of fucked-up people out there. We're aware of the effect musical formulas have on their specific audiences. We don't seem to have a specific audience. We seem to be picking up people from all over the place. Sometimes it's not who you'd expect."

This has not exactly endeared them to highly formatted American radio stations, to whom B.A.D. is a polygon of indeterminate angles trying to fit into a square hole. "When we started on the radio here," Mick grins, "they had us in the Unfit for Human Ears category. We're trying to change their minds, not ours."

Don similarly shrugs. "They seem to have a problem with this classification thing. I don't know about anybody else, but I think it's rock 'n' roll. It's '86 rock 'n' roll, dealing with the fact that you can use the media as an instrument, scratching and cutting it up. I thought we'd get a fringe of people who are dissatisfied they can't latch on to anything else. Like me. I can't identify with what's going on out there."

"I kind of get the best response from people on the street, really," Mick continues. "Not that I'm pretending or patronizing or anything. I'm not in touch with the kids. We're pretty sophisticated guys now; we're not street urchins or anything. But you can tell if you're happening or not. When you're walking around, and they come up to you and say 'shit, the gig was great,' or 'when are you playing next?' or 'I've heard about you or heard your record,' you know there's a buzz."

All is grist for the Big Audio Dynamite "sausage machine," as Mick puts it. Using the sampling capabilities of modern synthesizers, which can reproduce the waveforms of everything from symphony orchestras to barking dogs, bits of movie sound tracks, sound effects, and other found arcana are grafted onto the storage discs Don carries around with him in a canvas bag. Used as exotic spicings for the basic B.A.D. recipe. "By the time we're finished with them, we've made them ours," says Mick of such recycling. The effect is arguably more screenplay than hit single.

"We don't place our values on record sales, though we're not doing bad here. More people are getting wind of us through word of mouth or whatever. But we're not on any big world domination trip. We're not gonna do tours; we'd rather showcase events in each individual place. Take each town as it comes. And go back home and kind of chill and consider what the next thing there is to do. To do each one as best as possible, but not jump back on the treadmill, or conveyor belt, and lose your soul for rock 'n' roll."

Perhaps he's learning a lesson from the problems the current Clash are having. *Cut the Crap*? Cut the Clash is more likely, as two weeks after the José Unidos (a pseudonym for the production team of Joe Strummer and manager Bernard Rhodes) collaboration hit the stands, drawing ironic comparisons with B.A.D.'s debut, a terse communiqué advised that Joe and Paul were preparing to start from scratch.

"We have parted as friends," read Joe's statement, regretfully announcing "the departure of Nick Sheppard, Vince White, and Pete Howard. The decision is mutual . . . me and Paul would like to thank them for the dedication and enthusiasm." Also severed was their relationship with Rhodes and longtime publicist Kosmo Vinyl. In an interview on the *Old Grey Whistle Test* TV show in England shortly before leaving for New York, Mick alluded to Bernie as the catalyst behind his leaving the band.

Strummer immediately took off for Spain, where "me and Paul are going into the studio to record our next tune, called 'Shouting Street.'" The poor reception which greeted *Cut The Crap*—with the shining exception of the moving "This Is England" single—must have hurt Joe, and maybe he'd foreseen that his bold effort to recreate the battlements where "Two Sevens Clash" and "wise MEN and street kids together make a GREAT TEAM" was a futile attempt to turn back the clock. For further information, Joe advised, consult the latest releases by the Clash and B.A.D., and Topper Headon's *Leave It To Luck*. Hmmm . . .

Jones has been through that and is determined not to be trapped this time around. Like he sings on "Sony": "We put the past on to Fuji / Then we erase it totally—yeh!"

"I know how power ultimately corrupts," he admits. "For me, now, leaving the Clash was a really great thing. It set me free, because as far as the music was concerned, it was becoming a cage."

Mick pauses, considering the struggles of the last two years. "The most important thing to yourself is your frame of mind. You can't dwell on the past. If you get that straight, you can do it. That's what punk taught me originally. You can do anything you want to do. I would add now that you need the right frame of mind to do it."

JOE STRUMMER: AFTER

Sean Egan | 2000 | Previously unpublished in this form

This is the second part of the transcript of the Joe Strummer interview from 2000, which focused on his non-Clash musical activities.

Strummer had recently emerged from a ten-year recording hiatus after disputes with his record label. As such, he displayed the euphoria of a released prisoner as he discussed his new solo album, *Rock Art and the X-Ray Style*. When conversation turned to the Clash, however, melancholy set in, especially over *Cut the Crap*, an album he discusses here at unusual length.

Note: "Cantona" is French soccer player turned actor Eric Cantona. —Ed.

Could it be said that *Cut the Crap* was your first solo album insofar as you'd by this point taken over the Clash?

Yeah. That's probably a Joe Strummer/Bernie Rhodes album, because we'd agreed that he wanted to produce it. So obviously he wanted a hand in picking the tunes or he'd say to me, like, "Put half of that tune with the other half of that other tune you've got there." So that was Bernie's go at the production chair.

Mick had been your great musical foil over the years. Was it strange having to write on your own or with Bernie?

Yeah, it was strange. Bernie had manipulated me into a situation where he'd [used] me to sack Mick Jones in order so that he could get into the driving seat. So I think that was a bit shitty, but then again I blame myself for falling for it. You've always got to blame yourself, especially when you're licking your wounds in the middle of the night. If you're blaming other people, you ain't going to get to the truth.

The album has "Strummer/Rhodes" songwriting credits.

Yeah, that surprised me.

So you would disagree with those?

Fifty-fifty would probably be well in his favor, let's say.

There's actually some good tunes on that album.

There's a few. I really like "This Is England." "North and South" has a vibe.

"Are You Ready for War" ["Are You Red..Y"]—I've always liked that.

Yeah, that's another one.

How would the album have sounded without Bernie producing it?

It's difficult to say because, having flung out Mick, straightaway on that studio floor you've lost a great player and arranger and a writer. If we'd have kept the team as it was before that happened, say Bernie managing, me and Mick writing, and the guys playing . . . But then again we'd have wanted Topper Headon to make it proper and he'd been sacked about eighteen months before all this shit went off, so the whole team had disintegrated, unraveled from the first stitch. But supposing all those things were in place—we still had Topper, still had Mick, and Bernie was managing—yeah, it would have been a big album, definitely. But then again, everything would have been better.

Is there somewhere in the vaults what you might call a director's cut of *Cut the Crap*? In other words, a tape before Bernie started doing these weird overdubs?

No, because we worked together.

We were doing it in Munich and he went back to England for a week. Do you remember that Boney M stuff, the famous disco records? Well the guy playing the funky guitar on the Boney M massive hits—I can't remember his name, to my shame—but I got him in. I remember we put some really cool—using a slide-guitar type thing—air-raid sirens over "This Is England." But played on an open-tuned. I remember thinking all that was mega. One day maybe I might phone that guy Ulli [Rudolf, studio engineer] in Munich and see if he kept a monitor tape of that one. When Bernie got back he nixed that 'cause it was put on when he wasn't there. "Let me get control of my project again" type vibe. But apart from that, I can't really think there's anything there, no.

It does sound like Nick Sheppard and Vince White weren't allowed to make much of a contribution. Did it feel like a proper band?

No, not really. Imagine we were them coming in on the tail-end of something been running for about five years, it was fairly massive. It must have been really weird to suddenly be thrust in the midst, with Bernie raving, me out of my mind, Paul standing around grumpily. It must have been a nightmare. So I think somewhere between the rhetoric and the bullshit they were forced to shut up.

I did hear that Pete Howard is hardly on the album at all?

I think it's all drum machines.

So what happened there?

I think it was a great security blanket to show up at a studio, put down all the drum tracks in three hours using a drum box, and then sketch in the rhythm chords, block in the chords, so at the end of a day and a half you had the whole album that you could listen to. I think he felt that was a great security blanket for him 'cause he'd never engaged in this kind of thing before. That's why I think Pete Howard didn't get a crack.

Was Pete just hanging around the studio waiting for his chance to play?

Well I think Bernie decided to work in Munich 'cause it was away from the studio grapevine. Again, we can see signs of nerves showing here . . . Also, he's always loved a cheap deal. I think he got a cheap deal in the studio in Munich. So he just flew people over there. He probably flew Pete over for a week hanging about. So really it was more like Bernie marshalling his pieces and using them against each other or one by one in order not to have his authority challenged.

When it came out, it does seem that you almost disowned the whole album?

Well, I did. This is all my fault by letting this thing happen. Firstly letting Bernie manipulate myself into getting rid of Mick. Which Mick helped by being the grumpiest sod you've ever seen in your life permanently, but I should have known he was only joking in a way. Then the actual recording process became more and more horrible as I realized what I'd done. And frankly I was tired out of my mind 'cause we'd done sixteen sides of vinyl in five years and played a thousand million gigs. Finally, all this went off in my face. CBS had paid in advance for it, so they had to put it out. I just went, "Well, fuck this," so I just fucked off to the mountains of Spain to sit sobbing under a palm tree while Bernie had to deliver a record.

In the *Clash on Broadway* box set booklet there's no mention of *Cut the Crap* even existing. Do you think it would be better to just acknowledge it as a sad finale to a great band, rather than just not mention it at all?

Oh, I think definitely you mention it, yeah. That's why I'm quite pleased to chat with you about it. Even though you might not use any, at least it'll be somewhere on tape, 'cause these things have to be examined. Also, Jon Savage did a nice thing in that book he wrote called *England's Dreaming*. That was the only good review that album ever got, where he called it maybe a slightly overambitious sound collage—which I think would have pleased Bernie. Also, it's got "This Is England" on there, so it's not a complete dud. I think it has to be mentioned, but obviously *Clash on Broadway* was put together with Mick Jones. I think it was a pathetic attempt not to offend Mick Jones.

When you went off to the mountains, as you put it, I do remember there was a press statement saying that the other three guys weren't going to be in the band anymore, but you and Paul were going to make a single called "Shouting Street." The impression given was that the Clash would continue in some way.

I can only think that Bernie might have put out that press release. That sounds like a bit of a Bernie Rhodes–Kosmo Vinyl jib to me, 'cause I think I was well beyond any thoughts of continuing.

So would it be fair to say that even before *Cut the Crap* hit the shops that you'd washed your hands of the whole thing?

Yeah. Mea culpa. Definitely, yeah.

I did hear that Bernie was thinking of auditioning people to replace you?

Yeah, he did in fact hold perhaps two or three auditions. Him and Paul and Kosmo.

Paul was in on it?

Yeah. He was. [Laughs.] That definitely happened.

Would this have been Paul and the other three guys?

No, I think that it was just Paul. Not being there, it's hard for me to say which of the other three guys were included, but it would be a plan that Bernie and Kosmo had hatched up.

You'd become disillusioned with Bernie. I'd have assumed that Paul would have too.

Apparently not.

There was this period, just after *Cut the Crap* came out, when you cut a very forlorn figure 'cause you were following Mick around.

I was trying to undo my mistake. We always hit each other off-time. Like when he was dead into "Let's re-form the group," I wouldn't be, and when I was into it, he wouldn't be. Big Audio was taking off, so he just laughed at me.

When was he into re-forming the Clash?

Some years had gone by and it must have been after a few Big Audio Dynamite albums, perhaps when the first Big Audio Dynamite left Mick. I think what had happened, he'd supported U2 when they were massive on a stadium tour around the world and he got fed up of being the used brush in the third support band, down the hall with three sandwiches and a crate of pale ale, seeing U2 flitting in and out on helicopters. It must have got his ambition going or his rock 'n' roll star thing going. So that must have put the petrol in that engine. Eighty-something.

What was your reaction at the time?

Well I was quite keen, but I'm terribly loyal in a stupid way and I knew that the best combination was Strummer/Headon/Simonon/Jones on the floor and Bernie Rhodes managing it. 'Cause I'd got Bernie back in when we were faltering somewhere in the middle period. I'd thrown a power play and got Bernie back to manage us for the final two years of glory or whatever, or the big times. So I knew that that thing worked. Mick was trying to promote his then-manager to manage the band. That's when I realized that we were in a real bad position 'cause its almost like a juicy piece of meat—if you can imagine the commercial ramifications of putting the Clash back, especially back then. I realized that all these piranhas would start swarming in and I didn't really want Mick's manager to manage the Clash.

You weren't thinking of Bernie managing though, were you?

Yeah, I was. Yeah.

Really? After all that had happened?

Yeah, definitely. I'm terribly loyal, and still loyal to this minute.

So was Mick saying, "Well if you're not going to have my manager . . ."

" . . . it's not on."

I can understand Mick thinking, "Well, I'm not going to have Bernie managing," after what Bernie had done to him.

True, but you have to look at the track record. Things began to smoke, as they say, with Bernie in charge and us doing the business.

To a lot of people your peak period was the _London Calling_ period, when Bernie wasn't managing.

True, but that sold about three hundred thousand copies, _London Calling_, in America.

I'm thinking artistically.

True, but "Straight to Hell" is a fantastic track and there are tracks in the next few years after that that are fantastic. Also, we were making the cultural explosion, like seven nights on Broadway, and seven nights in Sydney, and seven nights in Tokyo, and seven nights here, really blasting it out.

So this period, just after _Cut the Crap_, when you followed Mick to where he'd gone on holiday and you told journalists that you hoped to get the band back together, would you say that was your lowest ebb in life?

Yeah.

And how long did it take you to come to terms with the fact that the Clash was over?

It took me about eleven years. [Laughs.] From then 'til now.

Obviously Mick said, "I've got Big Audio Dynamite together; I can't pull this band apart now that I've set it up." What was your game plan then?

I was too exhausted to have one, I think, 'cause it had been an exhausting five years. A real rocket ride to Venus.

So were you not thinking about the future at all?

No. I'm not very practical really. I'm kind of an instinctive person. Perhaps what I should have done was held some auditions, got some great players, and made a group that would still be going now, but I didn't have the capacity to think like that.

Your kids were very young then, weren't they?

Yeah and all that: your parents die, your girl has a kid. Suddenly everything had changed, in a personal situation.

When you were commissioned to do those songs for the *Sid and Nancy* film [1986], was that the first creative thing you did after *Cut the Crap*?

Yeah.

How did that come about?

Well, after Alex [Cox, director] had shot *Sid and Nancy* and it was all in the can, I got invited to the wrap party. He asked if I'd write him a song called "Love Kills," so I went and did that for him. Then I got involved in his universe of making movies. If I had a game plan, that would have been it: to sort of get out of people's faces in the rock 'n' roll world and try and maybe do some movie composing or do a bit of acting.

Mick came in to do overdubs on "Love Kills"?

Yeah, he came in and played guitar on it, 'cause we were kind of helping each other. I worked quite hard on his *No. 10, Upping St.* album, the second B.A.D. album.

With regards to the *Sid and Nancy* film, I've always been surprised at the way Sid Vicious is indulged by people who knew him. Wasn't he just a psychopath?

No, not at all. He was sort of part aggro monster and part really sweet guy. I mean, I always tell this story [about] that first night when I saw the Pistols. At the Nashville, you had to walk through the dressing room to get onto the stage. The Pistols showed up to do their sound check. We were already there sitting in the dressing room, so they had to kind of walk through us in Indian file, and at the end of the line was this guy in a gold Elvis Presley jacket, one of those Las Vegas jackets. I thought—'cause we were sort of staring at these people— "Right, I'm going to mess with one of them to see what they're made of." So the last guy reached me. I said, "Oi mate . . ." And he went, "What?" I said, "That's a nice jacket, where d'you get that?" And in this sort of cool-out atmosphere, it's quite tense. You'd think that Sid Vicious would have gone, "Oh fuck off," but he said, "Oh, do you like it? I think it's brilliant as well. I tell you where I got it, mate. Do you know that stall on blah, blah, blah, up the stairs, to the left . . ." Sid was a very cool, nice person, until I suppose he decided he had to thump someone.

This was when he was just a—

A camp follower. And then I used to hang out with him quite a lot and he was planning this group called the Flowers of Romance, with him and Viv [Albertine] from the Slits. We should have given them some encouragement 'cause I remember one night in some flat he was going, "And this is how I'm gonna sing," and he made this great shape holding this kind of coat stand as a microphone stand. I think he would have made it on his own. He was dead flash.

I only knew the nice side of Sid. Maybe it's been overplayed, the psychopathic side, but he did have a tendency to go off.

Do you think the *Sid and Nancy* film was a fairly accurate portrayal of him?

I wouldn't like to comment on that, because when it got into Nancy Spungen and they got into heroin and then went to New York, or they were dossing around London, I wasn't really part of that scene. In fact, from the minute he joined the Pistols, and they went off to America on that tour, that was about the last time I saw him.

Being as you were always a little bit suspicious of this newfangled electronic music, did you subtly try to nudge the *No. 10, Upping St.* album in a Clash-y direction?

No, I did the opposite, in fact. I bumped into him in Soho and he grabbed me by the arm and he said, "Look, you've got to help me out because I've got to deliver this album and we haven't got any lyrics." I heard they were in Trident down in St. Anne's Court and so we did a bit of recording there and I said, "Well, look mate, if what you're saying with this stuff is that we've got the freshest beat, yo, it's the dopest thing ever, shouldn't we go to New York and record it there?" 'Cause I had great memories of doing *Sandinista!* there and stuff, so I kind of pushed the project over to New York in order to up that factor.

You got the gig doing the soundtrack to *Walker* [1987]. As you've always acknowledged that your chief talent is lyrics rather than melody, were you not a little bit apprehensive about doing an instrumental soundtrack?

I'm slightly idiotic and I just jump into things. I don't remember feeling apprehensive. The great thing I had on my side was that I'd spent ten weeks working as an extra on the film down in Nicaragua, so I'd spent ten weeks walking around in that weird heat, and we were in a really southern town, Granada in southern Nicaragua, way away from anything. Spend ten weeks in a spot like that and you can soak stuff out of the soil or the buildings, so I found myself walking through the long afternoons when everyone was asleep in the town and the tunes started to come to me.

You had all these session musicians working for you. Did you find it a bit intimidating saying, "You play this part, you play that part"?

Yeah, that was intimidating, especially for someone like me, but I had a great stroke of luck. A lot of these great players that are on *Walker* were playing on Taco Bell adverts. Their main meal ticket was playing on these kind of cruddy adverts, so when I showed up in the studios and I'd just say to them, "Come on, this is music, play the bad notes," meaning, "Play the notes you're not allowed to play when you're doing a Taco Bell advert," I encouraged them to open up and they loved it so much that they gave their best.

There were some very good reviews of that album when it came out. Were you surprised?

Yeah. I do remember having a bit of a chuckle. Because the press had sort of written me off, as one would expect after the *Cut the Crap* debacle and all this, the reviews were incredibly reluctantly good. It was sort of, "Well this shouldn't be any good but for some reason it seems to be not half bad." They were kind of gritted teeth.

Trouble is—

No one's ever heard it, but never mind.

Well the other thing I was going to say is—like to a lesser extent *Sid and Nancy*—it's a good soundtrack to a not particularly good film.

Yeah, the film was a bit crap.

Do you feel in a way that the music was wasted?

Well not really, 'cause on the other hand Alex Cox had the vision to point at me and say, "Right, you do all the music to the whole movie," which was a great thing. And it's great to just work with a director, 'cause I have worked on other films with a committee of people. They're really big on committees now in Hollywood. It's really hard trying to make music to please, say, ten different people round a table. Alex just said go ahead and do it.

You did the *Permanent Record* soundtrack [1988] and those were actual songs. Would you have written those songs anyway if you hadn't been commissioned?

No, I don't think so. The best thing we hear on that one was "Trash City." I was looking for something to make it interesting, i.e., the basic rock 'n' roll format, and got into the timbales and congas and the Latino. That got me running on that for a few years.

You actually recorded more songs than they actually used in the film, is that right?
Yeah, but I think they're all pretty substandard.

Was that just done quickly then?
Yeah, it was a sort of quick knock-off job. Perhaps I wasn't feeling that inspired, but I did meet musicians on those sessions that played with me over the next few years on *Earthquake Weather* and went round the world in the Latino Rockabilly War.

With regards to the acting, I did hear a rumor that you were offered the role of the hit man in *The Hit* (1984), the Tim Roth/John Hurt film. Is that correct?
Yeah. I accepted the role and then Bernie and Kosmo came to me and persuaded me not to do it. I think they were frightened of losing control. When I think back on it, perhaps they thought, "Well shit, if he's in this film and it goes over big then he might want to become a movie star and then we've lost control of the whole bandwagon." It was me who suggested to them that they get Tim Roth.

Do you regret that now?
No, definitely not, 'cause Tim Roth is a brilliant actor and that was probably his first break into a movie, although he'd done that *Made in England* skinhead thing on the TV, which was why I suggested it to the *Hit* people. When you come down to it, acting's for the actors.

Apparently you did enjoy acting in *Straight to Hell* [1987] and *Mystery Train* [1989].
Yeah, but only 'cause it was a bit of a laugh or something different. I never felt I did anything worthwhile in that world.

What's the story about this single that you recorded for *I Hired a Contract Killer* [1990] which ended up not being released?

[Laughs] I wish I had a copy. It's so funny. Aki Kaurismäki, a Finnish film director, and I recorded "Road Train Driver" and "Afro Cuban Bebop." Aki, he does everything at the bottomest level in order to keep people from telling him what to put in his movies. I think it's a really remarkable thing that he's got going, 'cause he can make movies without begging the suits for a bunch of money and the suits then try and influence the content. But he does it by keeping it very low-dollar and he found the cheapest pressing plant in the world which was in Eastern Europe and he had fifty promotional discs printed up with one song on one side, one on the other. But the hole wasn't quite in the middle, so there are fifty records out there with an off-center hole with this tune on it.

Was that intended to be a commercial single as well, eventually?

No. None of this was run along the lines of any kind of intelligence. Things just happened. Like Aki said, "I want you to write me a song for this movie." And I said to him, "Okay, what do you want it to be about, Aki?" And he thought for a minute and he looked at me and he went, "About life!" Then we just kind of blundered on from there.

You went on tour with the Pogues in 1987–88. What was it like trying to step into the shoes of Shane McGowan?

I've got to reiterate, I did this as a favor to the group because they couldn't afford to cancel the world tour, 'cause you get cancellation fees on every gig and there was eight of them in the band and six more in the crew. I knew them personally. I think I had about a week's warning when they decided that Shane just had to be put in a rest situation. So I kind of jumped in there, which is something perhaps I shouldn't have done. I don't regret it, but it was weird. Once we got out to Austria, the skinheads in the audience, they didn't understand the situation, so they thought I was there trying to knock Shane out of his job. That kind of thing could get hairy—or did get hairy.

In 1988, you did the Rock Against the Rich tour with Class War, the pressure group. You got a bit of stick for that at the time. The perception was that you'd made a fair bit of money with the Clash, you certainly weren't living in a squat anymore, and here you were aligning yourself with not just anarchists but people who it's rumored have been involved in violent action. Do you feel it was a mistake?

I think so, but what it stemmed from was a concert at the Hackney Empire, where they badgered a lot of people to do it and I agreed to do the show. This was drunken pub talk. Then when the word came through that the council wouldn't have it or it was cancelled, the drunken pub-talk escalated until it was, "Well fuck them, we'll go on a tour." Suddenly we were on the bus. Having said that, it was a brilliant tour as far as being with people and having a laugh and getting around.

When you started out in the Clash you had literally nothing, living in a squat or living in Rehearsal Rehearsals, so it was easy in those days to align yourself with an organization like Class War, or whatever the equivalent was, whereas today you've got kids to support and you've earned money. Do you feel that the Joe Strummer of 1976 is a very different person to who you are today?

Yeah, I think so, because you realize certain things. For example, Stalinist organizations, you realize with the onset of maturity that—if you did give these people power—the first thing they'd do is put you up against a wall and shoot you for being a degenerate or a spliff smoker or a loose cannon. Then you begin to think, "Well, what the hell am I doing?"

You mentioned the Latino Rockabilly War. That band never seemed to get going properly. Would that be fair to say?

Yeah.

What happened with them?

We did *Earthquake Weather* [1989], which is a good record, although I buried the vocals from a feeling of insecurity probably. We did quite a vicious tour, all around America, all around Britain, all around Europe, and at the end of the tour I was completely exhausted and the accounts were twenty-four thousand in the red. I remember looking at this sheet and I felt completely mentally and physically exhausted, and I thought, "Well, why didn't I just sit here and tear up £24,000, and be really fit and happy?" Also, the record sales were absolutely dismal. So it was me who knocked that on the head. I said, "Well, look, if we're going to lose twenty-four grand, I'm going to have to start driving a cab. This isn't on." If you just remember that the Clash sold *Sandinista!* and we didn't get any royalties for that in order to make it three for the price of one [*sic*]. We were too far ahead to ever recoup the great riches that have been recouped today by punk groups selling ten million albums. You have to remember that people don't send you fivers every time your name's mentioned.

Were you happy with the *Earthquake Weather* album?

Except for the fact that I buried the vocals. There's some great tunes on it, like "Shouting Street," "Dizzy's Goatee," "Jewellers & Bums," "Leopardskin Limousines," "Sleepwalk." Those are five tunes that are as good as any tunes on any album by anybody.

We finally got to hear "Shouting Street." Did you record a version with the Clash?

No, I think I wrote it after *Cut the Crap*. Or perhaps it was considered for *Cut the Crap*.

Is that the only song on that album that was left over from the Clash days?

Yeah.

Is it true that Epic/Columbia refused to promote the album?

Well put it this way . . . Imagine you're Sony, who have by now bought Columbia, and you've got Mick under contract with his Big Audio, and then you've got Joe Strummer under contract with whatever he's doing.

Now if you kind of under-promote these efforts, sooner or later you're going to force them together and then you can get back to making huge amounts of money. That was part of the reason why I shut down shop after *Earthquake Weather*—'cause I realized I was contracted to these people on a never-ending contract, i.e., one-off, but their option.

Does Mick feel the same way as well?

Well I don't know. Funnily enough, we've never got round to discussing it yet. But I would think that would be a fairly logical game plan when they saw that neither of the things was going to catch fire and sweep the world like the Rolling Stones. They must have thought, "Well, let them put out a few records and get fed up, and then when they're skint we'll put the band back together."

When you went on strike, did you officially say to the label, "I'm not going to make you any more records"?

No. I just took to the hills.

Did your contract not have a thing where it said your next album must be delivered by X date?

I can't remember exactly how that worked, but I remember that it was one-off with their option. Because I had a descendent of the Clash contract, if I went into a studio, that was the contractual signal of them having to cough up the advance, and they realized after *Earthquake Weather* that the advance was way too big for the returns. So they were not keen for me to go in a studio at all, 'cause it would kick in a new phase of the contract. So I was stuck between a rock and a hard place there. So for the next eight years I figured how to get out of the contract.

But couldn't they have said to you precisely that: that they would rather you not record anymore?

True, but because they'd taken up the option on the second solo offering, I should have realized that I could have sued them for loss of earnings or something. Also, being in a giant corporation, it's very difficult to get any kind of progress on any paperwork, 'cause quite frankly nobody cares and it's so big that there's a lot of other things going on. Michael Jackson is big in town—never mind these insects. And so I realized I was going to have to try and get out of that situation. I knew that I couldn't afford to get a lawyer 'cause I watched that George Michael thing. I had the same contract. Five million quid it cost him *and* they found against him. So I realized I was kind of fucked and I decided to bore them out.

Weren't you bored as well, because you'd been so prolific with the Clash?

True, but it dovetailed really, because its almost like saying you've been yakking at the party for three hours—you've got to sit down and shut up now. It dovetailed with the way I was feeling because I wanted to sit down and shut up as well and let someone else have a go. Also with kids, you don't really want to be away.

Also I was learning to record. I bought an old eight-track. I made a soundtrack to a film called *When Pigs Fly*. The film never was released, but I did the whole soundtrack to it and I just got a fax from Rykodisc the other day surprisingly saying, "Even though the film didn't get general [release], we feel this music is too good to sit in a vault and how about making a release date for this soundtrack to the film that never was?" So that might see the light of day. That would have taken about a year to write and record, and then we went down to Rockfield to do the final sessions on it. I had always things going like that.

When did you get official confirmation that the label where happy to let you go?

Oh, it was terrific. I got them to let me go on the grounds that if the Clash ever got back together then we're contracted to Epic, but on solo stuff I could be free. It was about four years back that I got the nod, but it took a further year to get the actual paperwork onto the lawyer's desk and to actually get him to sign it. You get kind of embarrassed or tired of ringing up. This is the god's honest truth: eventually I rang up and I said, "Look, I've tried to be patient, but a year has gone by. If we don't get that contract out of you within a week I'm going to come up to the lobby of your new headquarters and I'm going to stand outside and I'm going to prevent anyone entering or leaving the building until you bloody get that contract out of the bottom drawer and sign and release." In order to get released I had to frighten them. I seriously frightened them, 'cause they thought do they need some idiot coming up in a bad mood.

How long did it take for you to assemble your new band, the Mescaleros?

We started on Valentine's Day last year, me and Antony Genn and we started to record and we began to assemble them from that minute. I knew Pablo Cook from trying to start a group for Richard Norris and also Bez—me and Pablo and Bez tried to start a group.

What happened to those groups, by the way?

Well three of the tracks are on *Rock Art and the X-Ray Style*. "Yalla Yalla," "Sandpaper Blues," and "Diggin' the New" were vestiges of the attempt of me and Norro to . . . We had a group called Machine that we were trying to get going. He was coming from acid house and I was coming from punk. We both fought our corners very hard and eventually we fell out, although we're mates now. I think it was just too much of a bold maneuver. He saw the singing—because he was used to acid house—as being one of the tracks on the board. I was coming from punk rock where the singing was part of the song and the song was made before the recording, therefore the recording was about the song and the singing was about the song.

Then after that, me and Bez and Pablo, we did some music for a short Cantona film, *A Question of Honour* it was called. It's ten minutes, Cantona sort of trying his go at acting. We did the music for that and then thought we could maybe get a group going, but again we couldn't get it going. So I was sort of sitting on my heels until I went to a Fat Les session to play rhythm guitar on the giant flop "Naughty Christmas," and that's when I bumped into Antony again.

Does Antony write the tunes and you the words?

Yeah, I'd say we could put it like that.

How does writing with him compare to writing with Mick?

Well it's different. We can start with a beat and a groove and a feel, and then we move into the actual writing, whereas back in the day you'd probably do that with just an acoustic just to get it going. I still do all my writing on an acoustic, just to make sure that it works in its simplest form, but we work somewhere between the two.

Was "The Road to Rock 'n' Roll" really written with Johnny Cash in mind?

Yeah. And rejected. Rick Rubin put out the word that they're going in to do a Johnny Cash comeback record. So I leapt at it, and I knocked off "Road to Rock 'n' Roll" and sent it over to Rick. When I met Johnny after a gig a year or so later, Rick said, "Oh, this is Joe. He's the guy that sent us that 'Road to Rock 'n' Roll' song," and Johnny turned round to me and bent over—'cause he's like ten feet tall—and he went, "You really confused me with that song, boy." That's what he said to me, word for word. And I went, "Urm, er . . ." It was backstage and he was swept away in a crowd of well-wishers, there wasn't a chance really to take it further than that, but that's when I thought, "Well, fuck it."

Is that the first tune you've ever done bespoke, as it were?

Yeah, I think so. I tried to imagine him singing it and I wrote it that way.

Did you sing with a deep voice on the demo?

I tried to. To help it get in there.

You sound very excited about the Mescaleros. Are you going to try to crank up the productivity, try to get an album out a year or something like that?

Well it's best not to make any insane thoughts like that, 'cause if I've learnt one thing it's take it as it comes, and then you can see what you're doing. I like just tipping along and thinking, "Well, we've got a good group, if we hold this, we can go and record some good tunes and maybe make another great record and just go along from there." And not try and think ahead too much.

You wrote some songs with Brian Setzer for his *Guitar Slinger* album [1996]. How many songs did you write with him altogether?

We wrote "Sammy Davis City," "Ghost Radio." I wrote several others with him, but I can't remember offhand. I think those two made it onto Brian Setzer albums, but there are a few more that we're cooking up. I quite like writing with him. It's sort of different 'cause he's such a wizard on the guitar.

He used to have this love of roots rock 'n' roll the same as you have, but he's doing something slightly tangential to that now with the Brian Setzer Orchestra. Can you see the logic to that?

Well, we actually came to blows over this. I know it sounds ridiculous, but you can imagine me and Brian rolling around the floor in a wrestling match. Before it really kicked off, I'd say to him, "What the fuck are you doing with all this, Brian?" I'd go out and see him and I'd take a Cornershop record or something and I'd play it really loud and say, "Check this out," and so we kind of came to blows over musical content.

You and Mick and Paul and Topper have all done your best work together. Have you ever thought of just working with each other, without having this burden of the Clash name?

Yes, but the world's a much crueler place than we can imagine and they've put into contract that if I'm in the same studio with Paul, for example, then that thing is called the Clash and is owned by Epic, and if I'm in a studio with Mick it's a similar thing. So I don't think there's any way we could get around that. And anyway, what's done is done.

In the Clash documentary *Westway to the World* you seemed just about to cry when you were talking about the Clash splitting up.

Well it was a bit heavy, all that. It was kind of like being on the shrink's couch all of a sudden. But I'd say let it be, to quote the Beatles. What was, was. Also you have to remember that people live their lives to this soundtrack. I'm continually meeting all the people that were at all the concerts and I'm very aware that it's part of people's lives. At least if you saw the Clash live at the Manchester Apollo in '77, that's something that is always yours and it can't be given to someone today. 'Cause people live their lives for it, and with it, and to it, and by it, and it's a serious thing. I'm really conscious to keep that from being besmirched or cheapened.

AN INTERVIEW WITH PAUL SIMONON

Ben Myers | November 2004 | 3ammagazine.com (UK)

Paul Simonon has said he was the dark horse in the Clash, a reference to the fact that he could be posited as a painter who was just biding his time as a rock musician. Since the split of the Clash, Simonon has dabbled with musical projects like Havana 3am, Gorillaz, and the Good, the Bad and the Queen, but he has otherwise concentrated on the life at the easel from which his time in the Clash diverted him.

This interview coincided with the twenty-fifth anniversary deluxe edition of *London Calling* but covered numerous other things, including Simonon's childhood, his painting, and his perception of the Clash as almost ancient history.

Ben Myers is not the only one impressed by Simonon's "aesthetic perfection." During the Clash's lifespan, assiduous attention to his body saw Simonon blossom from a waif with fine cheekbones into a cross between James Dean and Charles Atlas. It wasn't a huge surprise when, in 1982, readers of *Playgirl* voted him one of the ten sexiest men in the world.

Note: "The TV thing" seems to be a reference to John Lydon's recent appearance on reality show *I'm a Celebrity . . . Get Me Out of Here!* –Ed.

It's all about poise. If you don't have poise – definition: "balance; a dignified and self-assured manner" – in rock 'n' roll, you're nothing. Paul Simonon had it in abundance. And still does. Look at any footage of The Clash and you're struck by the aesthetic perfection of their bassist; the way in which he just hung there, cool but coiled, aloof but ready. Joe Strummer had the politico credentials and Mick Jones had the Keith Richards flash and swagger and natural musical ability, but Simonon had poise.

Born in 1955 he grew up on the streets of Brixton and Ladbroke Grove, often one of the few white faces in black neighbourhoods. His father Gustav was a Communist Party member and art lover, whose appreciation of paintings was passed onto his son at a young age. In the late Sixties – around about the time that Desmond Dekker was introducing ska sounds and styles to British mods who, in turn, would soon develop the burgeoning skinhead culture – Simonon spent a year in Rome and Siena when his mother's new partner had won a scholarship to study Italian baroque music. Skipping school, it was here that he saw the great works of the Renaissance masters close-up and his lifelong interest in fine art began.

Returning to England in 1969 he became a sharp-suited skin and immersed himself deeply in dub and reggae, as well as the film and soundtracks of the then-popular Spaghetti westerns. Simonon was too smart and multicultural to be attracted by the racist undertones of the skins; he was into the sharp lines, the street-tough look and the outlaw stance that would soon become integral to the presentation of The Clash.

Despite having no inherent musical ability, his looks, intelligence and attitude were more than enough for Mick Jones and manager Bernie Rhodes to invite him to play bass in the band they put together in 1976. Joe Strummer was poached from London's premier pub rock band The 101ers and The Clash was born. For Simonon it was a task he threw himself into with gusto when he moved straight into Rhodes' Rehearsal Rehearsals at Camden Lock, marking the band's territory with a vast Ballardian mural depiction of the Westway, that looming landmark at the centre of The Clash's psycho-geographic London. With the aid of his dub favourites Simonon mastered the rudimentaries of the bass and within nine months they were a signed band heading the punk vanguard.

By the time of 1979's *London Calling* he had developed into a skilled player, penning such songs as perennial favourite and much-sampled 'Guns Of Brixton', and a thrusting enigmatic presence in the band's increasingly thunderous live shows. Simonon provided the film star glamour to an otherwise motley bunch of homemade haircuts and bad dental work: it was he who developed the band's early paint-splattered

Pollock-inspired look and whose fascination with guns and outlaw culture led to their mid-period black military look – all straps, angular zips and reinforced gussets. Riot gear. Street-fighting togs. And, later, with *London Calling* and beyond again it was Simonon who looked effortlessly natural in their Golden Age Hollywood suits, hats and overcoats. In the words of Mick Jones, "He was just *there*, looking fantastic . . . the bastard."

When The Clash split in the mid-80's – Simonon remained until the bitter end – he travelled America, recorded the Latin-influenced Havana 3AM album, and dedicated more and more time to his paintings. He now regularly exhibits and is a respected figure in the art world. Equally as importantly, he is producing technically-accomplished paintings that are traditional – classic, even – in form, yet stunning enough to find favour amongst a scene cluttered with charlatans and conceptualists.

Today he's relaxed, affable, interesting and interested – everything you'd have hoped for. Once again he finds himself talking about his time with a once-in-a-generation band, a career that ended when Simonon, the youngest band member, was still in his twenties.

"The label said they wanted to do a 25 anniversary release of *London Calling* and, coincidentally around the same time Mick Jones was moving house and came across a box full of tapes," he explains of the recent reissue and the official reason we're talking today. "He said he recognised them immediately as copies of demo tapes of the album, the originals of which were lost somewhere on the Circle Line in 1979. We thought it would be a good idea to put them on as well, and Kosmo Vinyl, who worked for The Clash in our heyday had been sitting on these video tapes with footage of us making the album in the studio. He thought they'd badly deteriorated and wouldn't be of much use, but we had them sent over anyway and had them checked through. It was on a format that doesn't exist anymore but there was some character somewhere who had a machine that could transfer them. There was a lot of footage of Guy Stevens at work, physically and mentally producing The Clash. So now we've become – would you believe – a Sony 'legacy' act. Or is it 'heritage act'? Whatever you want to call it . . ."

3AM: How does it feel today, looking back on footage that only previously existed as memories?

PS: You do feel displaced in so far as thinking 'Who are those handsome young men?' (laughing). But, yeah, it's strange looking at yesterday and seeing yourself documented in that way. It's shocking but it's hilarious because back then it all seemed normal. At that age you're like an open book because you're less experienced, so when the producer comes in and starts smashing chairs and throwing ladders around you think, 'Oh well, this is what happens . . .' To a point, anyway.

3AM: You've said on many occasions that the making of this album was one of the happiest times for you in the studio – when you came into your own as musician.

PS: Really it was Guy's injection of a live energy and enthusiasm that was contagious. We tended to stand up when we were playing a number, and occasionally sit down, but once Guy was in the room there was no time for sitting down because either a chair or ladder might crack you on the head. The thing about *London Calling* is that it has the quality of a band playing live then and there, which comes down to Guy Stevens, as opposed to the different role of Sandy Pearlman on the previous album [1978's *Give 'Em Enough Rope*]. Sandy Pearlman was able to extract the live Clash performance and produce it in a very technically spot-on way, whereas Guy's approach was to go in all directions, leave the tape running, charge ahead and everything would be great. Record one song, move onto the next one. *Give 'Em Enough Rope* is a solid rock record but it was quite different to our debut too. Sandy Pearlman wanted to put the lab coat on and create this supersonic sound, which I think he achieved, but on *London Calling* Guy was able to translate what we were trying to do in a more human form.

3AM: As with so many people before me, listening to The Clash document and mythologize London was a major factor in me moving down from the North to the city. I now live in the Camberwell-Peckham area.

PS: Well, I know Camberwell very well: I used to go to Camberwell New Baths a lot and the cinema, which used to be the Odeon. My old school is around there too, though you've got to understand that I went to a lot of schools.

3AM: You made London sound like an adventure playground. 'Guns Of Brixton' was a pretty bleak and violent little commentary, but I thought: 'I want to go there'.

PS: Well, you've got your fair share of things going on up North in . . . where is it? . . . it sounds like a Durham accent (laughing). You just need someone to sing about it. I suppose you've got Roger Whittaker. Perhaps he could update 'Old Durham Town' into something more contemporary. That was always a big thing with The Clash: writing about what's on your doorstep. But after a while we had become grown men, certainly by *London Calling* and, having travelled, we had become more worldly and our thoughts more international, as opposed to being eighteen, nineteen, and getting the group to sing about 'Career Opportunities' or 'Garageland'.

3AM: When did you first become politicised?

PS: To be honest, I didn't have much choice. When I was pretty young my dad decided we didn't have to go to Catholic church anymore, and went on to join the Communist Party. But what I couldn't get was how comes I was the one out delivering the leaflets and he was the one at home watching the telly! So I was aware of the political system and also, obviously, because I grew up listening to a lot of reggae – music that had more edge than a lot of contemporary music as far as political content – it seemed normal. For Joe it was folk music, people like Woody Guthrie or Bob Dylan. For all of us there was the knowledge that a song can be about things other than love, kissing and . . . having a nice dance.

3AM: Was there a lot of discussion in the early days about the band's presentation as a political force, or was it more natural process?

PS: Very much. You have to understand that Bernie Rhodes was integral to the birth of The Clash. After rehearsals we'd sit down and ask each other what we wanted out of it and there's that famous line about Terry Chimes replying 'I want a Lamborghini', which was fine for him. But, yeah, we cross-referenced with each other, and asked 'Where are were going? What makes this band different?', rather than 'Let's all get drunk, pull birds and play guitars and that's it'. We wanted more depth, a more human approach.

3AM: Would the band have been as powerful or effective without the aesthetic edge? A lot of which came from you: the Jackson Pollock clothes, the military look . . .

PS: That was why we had so much trouble with our record company, because they were used to groups who didn't have a clue about where they were going, how they wanted to dress or whatever. But because of Bernie everything needed to be in-house: all ideas came from the group itself, which was why we were such a tight unit in that respect. This was especially true during *London Calling* because we'd parted with Bernie and left our rehearsal studio in Camden because it belonged to him, the Pistols had split up, Sid had died and we felt quite alone in some ways. We found the place in Pimlico and became even tighter. In this type of environment you get tighter, to the point where you didn't even need to talk when you were playing, because there was a natural communication there.

3AM: In Johnny Green's book it really becomes apparent how skint the band were at that stage, something perhaps which the punk police and critics failed to recognise as you began to progress from being a punk band to an international rock 'n' roll band.

PS: That's it. You could say that our backs were against the wall and we had to get on with the job at hand, which is why the album came out the way that it did. The second album hadn't been very well received and people were throwing accusations around that we'd sold out.

3AM: You were criticized – as many political bands are – for being idealistic, but I've never seen idealism as being a negative thing. It's often from idealism that great ideas flourish.

PS: That was up to us – we could be as idealistic as we liked. If someone knocked us down for that then that was up to them, but it was our group and we did things our way. It might be the wrong way, but at least we were trying: why don't you go and try your way if you think it's better? Better to be idealistic than the opposite . . .

3AM: You were the member of The Clash who was actually most friendly with the Sex Pistols and John Lydon's circle of friends. What are your memories?

PS: The first time I saw John was at the Nashville. I sort of knew Steve, Paul Cook and Glen Matlock, and I knew of John because Bernie Rhodes talked about him, but had never met him. John seemed like he had a pretty strong attitude towards the audience – or anybody – insofar as it wasn't 'Pleased to meet you, this is my little group' and more a case of 'I don't give a toss about you, I'm on the stage and I'll do what I like'. If you think about that period most of the world was still in flares and had long hair, and here's this character with a ripped-up jumper and cropped hair. The first time we had a conversation was outside the Screen On The Green and he was with a bunch of his mates. I went over and asked him if he knew where I could buy some cigarettes and he said (sarcastically) 'Yeah, there's a shop about two miles in that direction'. We giggled at each other, he showed me the shop and it went from there. I haven't seen John in ages, but we seemed to have a respect for each other from the start. We both came from non-musician situations, which might have something to do with it.

3AM: Were you fans of his later work with PiL?

PS: Yeah, I thought it was brave to jump in at the deep end after the Pistols, but that's John, he doesn't do things by half measures. He's always been very clear on where he's going. A lot of people slagged him off for doing the TV thing but I thought it was good to do because people have the wrong idea of him – like some sort of fat, bean-slurping idiot like in that Alex Cox film [*Sid & Nancy*]. That pissed me off, making him look like an idiot. Whereas when he did the TV show the rest of the world saw a very sharp, intelligent human being and that surprised a lot of people. They expected him to be a mindless idiot, but John has a fantastic wit, a wicked sense of humour.

3AM: The Clash were confrontational, but by 1979 punk had dissipated to a degree into a subculture interpreted by many as an excuse for violence. Did you find yourself in any particularly hairy situations?

PS: Well, we didn't feel particularly comfortable walking the streets of Northern Ireland and having our photos taken dressed in what could have been seen as some new military wing of the British army: black leather jackets, SWAT-style Clash trousers. But the reason we did that session was to really promote the idea of other bands coming over to Belfast to play, because no one would. There was more trouble in the early days too when people didn't quite understand what the group was about. There'd be times you'd come offstage and there'd be darts imbedded in the backdrop (laughing). That's probably why we moved around so much . . .

3AM: You set out to change people's ways of thinking and you succeeded in some ways, if only by galvanizing new groups, writers, designers. Do you look back on such achievements with pride?

PS: To inspire people, even just for one second, is worth something. To be honest, we were blokes with guitars, and it's unlikely we could change the world, but at eighteen you at least think it's possible – and it is, but maybe not in the way you first think. The amount of people who come up and say we changed their lives and gave them a whole different concept of how to look at things, is fantastic. I'm not saying we were holier than thou, we were pretty regular blokes.

3AM: And that's why people got the band: they saw something real they could relate to.

PS: What made a big difference was the open door policy we had. Anyone who wanted to come backstage could, and it was never a problem. I don't know whether other bands did that. It was good for us to meet people who had come to see the group and converse with them, ask them 'What's it like in your town? What, there are no clubs here? So what do you do?' It was about sharing information and it was good to know what was going on out there, and how people were dealing with their lives. And that spread right across the world.

3AM: What are your opinions on The Clash film, *Rude Boy*?

PS: It was a confusing period for us. It's great for the live performances, but I remember on many occasions asking the director what the film was about. Mick and Joe certainly asked the same, and no one seemed to have much of a clue. The directors were busking it. As a documentation of the time it's fine, with the rise of the National Front and so on, but it's nothing more than that. The story was a bit weak and the whole situation with the black guys in Brixton . . . I don't know what they were trying to set up but it was a bit unclear and careless. I didn't even know that stuff was being filmed. The film-makers generally just followed us around and put the camera on from time to time. There were a few scenes that were staged or based on a loose sketch of a script, but that was about it.

3AM: You must get asked the same questions relating to the band day in and day out. Are you happy to talk about The Clash so long after the event?

PS: Actually, I don't talk about it all the time and don't really sit around thinking about it, to be honest. But then situations like re-releases or seeing new footage of Guy Stevens is like poking the pond and all the information is floating to the top again. It is a bit odd sometimes talking about it all again. It's like me doing an interview and asking you about your school, you know? It seems so far away.

3AM: What are you working on at the moment?

PS: Right now, I'm working towards another exhibition. It's not going to be London scapes this time. It'll be something very different. I'm busy, I'm productive, and that's what I fancy doing at the moment. Maybe in two years time I might fancy making an album.

3AM: Really?

PS: Maybe, maybe not. I might fancy writing a poem. Who knows!

3AM: The London scapes were very impressive. I thought the one with Battersea Power Station in the background and the light bursting through the cloud was the strongest one of that series.

PS: Thanks. That one was actually my favourite, and it was also the last one to sell, which is strange. But it's on to the next show now. I'm hoping to put it on next year. I'm working away at the moment because I like to get a large collection together so I can pick and choose about which paintings make the grade. I spend a long time pondering which works should be shown, I'm very brutal in my selection. It has to be top notch.

3AM: Do you have regular working routine when you're painting?

PS: Yes, I do. When I was doing the Thames painting I didn't have a studio at the time, so I tended to work outside. Now, though, I'm very fortunate to have a place about five minutes away from where I live and it's under the bloody Westway of all places! I can't get away from that bloody bulk. I remember seeing it being built as a kid and it's still there now. I'll probably be buried underneath it as well.

3AM: You must have seen a lot of changes in and around Notting Hill/Ladbroke Grove?

PS: You're telling me. I'm probably one of the few local yokels still living here – a lot of people have been priced out. But then again there's a good ecosystem around here, because there's still a lot of the same housing estates, and also a lot of new businesses and fancy shops that have opened up. A couple of blocks away from me it's like Bond Street or something. The rich come in and buy their goods and maybe meet a few of the local trouble makers who might relieve them of a bit of cash, and everybody goes home relatively happy one way or another.

3AM: That's what makes London so fascinating – the fact that millionaires can rub against some of the roughest estates in the country.

PS: It's mad. But Ladbroke Grove and Portobello has always been like that. If you look in the history books you can see that on one side there was Holland Park with its fancy houses, and on the other side, pig farmers, gypsies and brickies. It's odd.

3AM: Who are you listening to at the moment?

PS: The most recent thing I bought was Dexy's *Greatest Hits*, but like everyone else I've been listening to The Libertines. I still listen to music, and I still play at home, but not professionally in a club or whatever any more.

3AM: What type of stuff would you be playing if you [were] 20 today? Do you think it would be like The Libertines or would it be vastly different? Would you even pick up a guitar?

PS: Er . . . I don't really know. When I did Havana 3am we were veering towards a lot of Latin stuff. It's hard to say because every few years your headset changes. I've had various ideas, but I've put them aside because I'm really just thinking about the painting at the moment. I'm too distracted by art to seriously think about music at the moment.

3AM: Well, thanks for the time Paul.

PS: That's all right, it was nice talking to you. And good luck in Peckham!

TOPPER HEADON: "JOE WOULD BE TURNING IN HIS GRAVE"

Sean Egan | 2008 | Previously unpublished in this form

When in "(White Man) in Hammersmith Palais" the Clash mocked "new groups"—particularly the Jam—for "turning rebellion into money," they were leaving a giant hostage to fortune. Over the following years, the line would on many an occasion be thrown back in their faces.

It was bad enough that, toward the end of the Clash's life span, their modus operandi began to exhibit the type of tackiness and avarice they had once scorned: gimmicky record giveaways, diva-esque demands on the media, a plan to market the stylized military fatigues they by now sported on stage, playing as support act to the Who in soulless stadiums . . . In the aftermath of their active career, however, this developed into what often seemed to be full-blown mercenariness.

The CD version of their 1988 best-of, *The Story of the Clash Volume 1*, retailed at an eye-popping £22.99. *Clash on Broadway*, their 1991 box set, executed the traditional exploitative trick of offering a handful of substandard outtakes to entice fans who already owned the bulk of the contents. Highlights from their limited catalog were regularly excerpted for compilations that seemed both similar and pointless. They appeared intent on deferring to the USA with which they'd once been so bored: *Clash on Broadway* had an American-centric title, liner notes by US writers who knew little about the social conditions that gave rise to the band, and for two and a half years was only available to UK residents as an expensive import. They showed none of their own record-collector hinterland: they never did release a compilation that properly mopped up all the singles, B-sides, and rarities unavailable on album. Even *Sound System* (2013) failed in this respect, despite twelve discs and a price tag of £100 or more. Some argued that all this hardly mattered now that the group no longer existed and the fires of punk had long died, but as Clash biographer Marcus Gray so acutely put it, "There is no statute of limitations on integrity."

This 2008 interview with Topper Headon—most of it previously unpublished—originally coincided with a new slew of Clash product: concert album *Live at Shea Stadium*, DVD *The Clash Live: Revolution Rock*, and a coffee-table autobiography, *The Clash by The Clash*. Although happy to reminisce about his time in the band—and although in later interviews he would be very enthusiastic about *Sound System*—the drummer is here scathing about the way that the Clash's values now seem to stand for nothing. He is also fascinatingly off-message about Simonon's bass-playing, Terry Chimes's drumming, the irreconcilability of the Clash's ideals and ambitions, and his own reasons for joining the group.

It's noteworthy that Headon seems to date Strummer's conviction that the Clash had sold out to his own time in the band. If true, one can only imagine how the singer must have felt in the period after the drummer's dismissal, which is when the big bucks really started to roll in. —Ed.

What do you remember about succeeding Terry Chimes?

When I went for the audition, I was really blown away by the energy of the group and the power and the look of the band, but I wasn't that impressed with the musicianship. Don't get me wrong: I did like the first album, but musically I didn't think it was that great. I thought I'd hang about for a year and make my name and then maybe move on to play some—what I call—proper music. But it changed. Even with *Give 'em Enough Rope* we were doing stuff like "Tommy Gun" and "Julie's Been Working for the Drug Squad." It became more musical, as far as I was concerned.

Did you let them know that your intentions were to leave after a year?

No. I wanted to be a successful musician and I thought this band was a good stepping stone, but when I joined the band it was a catalyst for the band to start playing good music. By the time we were recording *London Calling*, I was loving the music. We'd become more of a rock band as opposed to a punk band. We kept the punk ideals, but we were playing jazz and soul and funk.

Even when I had to go round playing the first album, that was enjoyable 'cause it was just sheer energy. Then when we came to record the next studio album, the music evolved. I think the band would have died with punk if I hadn't joined.

Really? Even with Mick being steeped in the lore of rock 'n' roll?

He might have been able to take it forwards, but that first album was a very basic punk album. With Terry Chimes on the drums they wouldn't have been able to evolve into anything more musical.

Before the Clash, was your mind set on joining a band permanently?

Yeah. When I found the right band. I hadn't made any plans. I just wanted to be a gigging, living, successful musician playing music I loved, and that happened with the Clash.

Both your parents were teachers, is that correct?

Yeah.

Would it be fair to say you come from a fairly middle-class background?

Yeah, definitely.

With you, was it the syndrome of taking up the drums to rebel against that?

No, not at all. [I took] up the drums 'cause I love music.

You're a multi-instrumentalist. What do you play other than drums?

Well, that's kind of been exaggerated. I play the drums well and I mess around on the bass and the piano and guitars. I only qualified, for want of a better word, to play the drums.

Who were your favorite drummers as a kid?

Keith Moon. Terry Williams was my all-time favorite. He used to play with a band called the Manband [Man], a Welsh band. But I also love Billy Cobham. Buddy Rich I saw many times. I just love great drummers.

Do you favor the virtuosos?

Well they're the ones that obviously catch your eye, or catch your ear, but also Charlie Watts I used to love because of his rock-steady timing.

How did you find the Clash as people?

When I first met the band, they were all kind of intimidating because they had that punk stance, but very, very quickly we became great friends. I think we was at our closest when we did *London Calling*. When we were rehearsing and writing the music for *London Calling* and playing football together, we were like best friends.

But within a couple of years we just got sick of the sight of each other. We didn't take any breaks and we were either in the same van or the same coach or the same aeroplane. We were constantly together twenty-four/seven and, as with any relationships, in the end what attracted you to someone in the first place started to piss you off.

What role did each member play?

It was pretty much a collective thing, but everyone brought something different to the table. Joe I suppose was the elder statesman . . . I became a heroin addict. Paul was in charge of the group's looks. Mick wrote the music. Joe was the spokesman . . . It's really hard to define what the chemistry was between the four of us, but there was a definite chemistry that just worked.

Some people find Mick a nice, sensitive bloke. Others thought he was a diva. How did you find him?

He was a fucking nightmare. He was a total rock diva. I'm still good friends with Mick today. He'd be the first to admit that he was impossible to get on with on the road . . . Mick became more and more—what did Joe say about Mick?—"Like Elizabeth Taylor on her period."

Paul Simonon was your partner in the rhythm section. Do you think he's an underrated bass player?

Not underrated. I think what he did was underrated. Mick taught him how to play the bass and that's all he did. He didn't improvise. He wasn't what I would call very musical. But once he'd been taught a bass line, he just stuck to it, which meant onstage it was phenomenal for myself. If I'd been playing with an—inverted commas—proper bass player then it would have been a whole different feel. Onstage, he was fantastic to play with because you always knew where he was gonna be. I could embellish in stuff and go wherever I wanted, across the beat and do all those jazz-type fills, and know that Paul was just holding it together.

There have been rumors that Mick played some of Paul's bass lines on Clash records.

Yeah, he did.

On every record?

On a hell of a lot, yeah.

Did Paul mind?

No. Paul's role in the band was mainly onstage and in charge of the artwork and the look of the band.

Your first Clash record was "Complete Control," on which the band were slagging off your own record company.

We never got on with the record company through the whole time that I was with the band. They didn't want a double album, full stop, let alone for the price of one. They didn't want a triple album, full stop. They didn't like the way we wouldn't do *Top of the Pops*. Really, there's no way we should have made it. We wanted to be the best band in the world and the biggest band in the world, but we wouldn't do *Top of the Pops* and we wouldn't charge more than this for a ticket and we wouldn't play seated venues. The first time we played New York, it was sold out at the New York Palladium. We didn't do any of that slogging.

After a honeymoon period, the British music press were constantly attacking the Clash. Did you find that upsetting?

Yeah, of course. No one likes to be slated and I think a lot of it was resentment. The punk thing in England was very local. It was the Pistols and the Damned and the Jam, and none of those bands made it in the States. When we changed our music from punk into a different type of music and when we changed the look and then when we started to break into the States, there was a lot of bitter sniping in the press from those punk journalists.

But "I'm So Bored with the U.S.A." was a hostage to fortune.

If only people would understand what "I'm So Bored with the U.S.A." was about. It was about how you put on the television those days all it was was *Kojak, Ironside, Starsky & Hutch* . . . Everything we watched in England at the time seemed to be American.

The Clash have always been a bit dismissive of *Give 'em Enough Rope,* but is it that bad an album?

It's not a bad album really. Speaking personally, it was my first album that I'd ever played on and to have a band like the Clash to play with, with the lyrics that Joe and the songs that Mick wrote and then a great producer like Sandy Pearlman . . . It was a great drum sound on that album.

I think it was a transitional album from the out-and-out punk album that the first one was to what *London Calling* became. "Julie's Been Working for the Drug Squad" was a New Orleans–type number. "Safe European Home" was an out-and-out rock song. I think it's much maligned, but it was probably our worst album. I think *London Calling's* where we peaked with the chemistry between the four of us.

The Clash have always given Guy Stevens a lot of credit for _London Calling_, but does that do a disservice to Bill Price?

Bill Price was a fantastic engineer.

We had this attitude we wanted to record all these different types of music. By then I was playing all the percussion and I was loving it. I was just enjoying being in the band. We wanted to record a double album for the price of one, so we had our kind of agenda. Guy Stevens kept the whole thing live. I remember when we recorded "Brand New Cadillac." Bill Price had got all the sounds together and we started recording it and Guy Stevens just pressed the intercom, he said, "Take—that's perfect." I said, "Fuck off, Guy—it speeds up." And he went, "All great rock 'n' roll speeds up." And we just kept it. And that kind of set the template for the rest of the album. He didn't let us overcomplicate it. He didn't let us disappear up our own arses, which is what began to happen with _Sandinista!_

Speaking of speeding up, how do you deal with click tracks?

I've never tried. But I did record a track recently with Zero 7. Henry Binns and I were in the studio and Henry was saying about how the Clash records sounded great and I was explaining to him that we recorded in big churches, huge great rooms, and it was kind of live and there was spillage between the four of us playing. We put this track down and then he started using a computer and dissecting it and bringing this bit back . . . With the technology today, you've lost a lot of what you used to have when you were playing live.

I remember when we recorded "Rock the Casbah." I'd only played it twice round. I'd done an intro, a couple of verses, and a chorus. When the rest of the band walked in I said, "This is an idea I've got." They said, "Well that's perfect, we'll just do the vocals over the top of that." I said, "Well it's only half the length it should be," so we just spliced the tape.

And that's you playing piano on the track?

Yeah, and bass and percussion. It's only Joe over the top of that, in fact.

Did Joe say, "I've got a lyric that can go over this"?

No, he went off into the toilet and wrote it.

It was accused by some of racism at the time, exploiting anti-Iranian feeling in America.

[Laughs]. Was it? I don't think that happened at the time. That's probably stuff that people have invented since then. It wasn't anti-anything.

When you were making *London Calling*, did you realize how slick and polished it would sound?

No. We were recording it in Wessex and we never took any time off and we had such a deadline. We had an American tour to start. So we finished the recording and we didn't have time to mix it. We left it in the capable hands of Bill Price and Guy to do all the mixing. We were on the tour bus in the States and we got the first tape sent out, and it was like, "Wow, this is fucking great."

It just happened. We rehearsed down in Pimlico and all those songs came together and we wanted to get a producer. Guy Stevens had worked with the band previous to me joining and Bill Price had produced the *Cost of Living* EP. When you put Bill and Guy and the four of us together, there was just that chemistry.

***London Calling*'s considered a classic album now, but the perception of some when it was released was that it was a sellout, the Clash going American or commercial. Barney Hoskyns of the *NME* said that "Brand New Cadillac" was the only good song on the album.**

Unfortunately in life there's always people who don't like something. That is just an insane thing to say really. I feel kind of sorry for him today. Not only has he got a horrible name, but he must feel like a bit of a lemon today. But he's perfectly entitled to his opinion.

Did you think you were going to go mega during the *London Calling* **period?**

We always hoped for that. Right from when I joined. I thought, *This band is gonna be big, I'm gonna hang about here.* We always wanted to be the biggest band in the world, but at the same [time], we had a certain naivete that said, "Okay, we want to be the biggest band in the word but we're not doing *Top of the Pops*, we're not playing seated venues, we're not supporting anyone"—we never did support tours—"and when we go to the States we're not going to just do an ordinary tour, we're going to have Bo Diddley supporting us."

When you look at the Jam's endless run of hit singles, do you think it was a mistake to refuse to play *Top of the Pops*?

No, definitely not. Basically, we were the only band of the punk thing to conquer the world. And we're the only band to have done that ever since. Oasis have never made it in the States and Japan, and nor has Robbie Williams . . . I've just got back from the South of France and I never realized how huge the Clash were in France . . .

There's a thing in this country where we look at big bands and think, "Oh they're huge," but in the world they're not. I do remember when, after we split up, people thought we must be rich, but because we had released albums for the price of one and had all these self-imposed limitations on what we actually did, we hadn't made a fortune actually. It's only in recent years or whatever since that it's continued selling. We sell more records than we ever have done.

Even with the illegal-download situation?

Yep. We still sell more records than we ever have done. I've started going back into schools to talk about the dangers of drugs. I spent twenty-odd years in hostels for the homeless and busking on the underground, squats, prison, bankrupt . . . I just went back to the boys' grammar school today where I was a pupil and all the kids there have heard of the Clash.

When did the heroin addiction start?

When I joined the band I didn't use heroin or cocaine, and gradually over that five-year period I just started using and then became addicted. It was just the way the band evolved.

You got your first song on *Sandinista!*, "Ivan Meets GI Joe." What inspired that?

It was just something I was working out on the piano. I'd had that song for a while and, while I was laying down the piano and the backing track, Joe went to an amusement arcade with one of those little ghetto blasters and went round recording all those sound effects. That was an amusement arcade in Shaftesbury Avenue or Charing Cross Road or somewhere. When he came back we merged the two together. Joe wrote the lyrics and I sung them. Under protest I might add, because I hate the sound of my own voice. It's in tune but [that's] why I played the drums and wasn't a singer.

Why was *Sandinista!* a triple album?

It was Mick's idea. This is where Mick took it to the extremes and wanted a triple album for the price of one [*sic*]. I think it would be an amazing single album, a very good double album, but there's no way there's three albums worth of material on it.

Members of the band were spending a lot of time in America. Were you conscious of the fact that you were moving away from the lifestyles of your audience?

Yeah, course we were. That's why Joe became more and more unhappy with the band 'cause we did become what we'd set out not to become. The stuff on the first album was singing about their experiences, and as the band got bigger and bigger it was harder to keep to that punk thing, especially in this country, because we were writing about stuff that happened all over the world and we were staying in lovely hotels and we were flying everywhere.

Was it only Joe who was agonizing about that?

I think so, yeah. In fact, I know so.

Combat Rock is a weird album. Half the songs are great and half are not too good at all. Do you think Joe and Mick were suffering a lack of inspiration?

It's weird. There's two songs on that. There's "Should I Stay or Should I Go" and "Rock the Casbah" and they both became huge hits worldwide, but the rest of the stuff . . . "Overpowered by Funk" wasn't particularly brilliant. Actually, I like "Sean Flynn." Mind you, "Should I Stay or Should I Go" was never a number one 'til we'd been apart for years. I'd been thrown out by the time it was released.

When Joe returned to the band after disappearing, you left almost immediately. Was this a "He goes or I go" scenario?

Yeah, that's it. That was the power play within the group. I don't really enjoy talking about all this sort of stuff. It's all been documented since. Bernie had been brought back at Joe's insistence and then Bernie and Joe wanted me out of the group. Joe sided with Bernie and did that disappearing trip to Paris and basically said, "The band can't survive without me. I want Topper out."

And that's one of the best things of all. I think every band has a shelf life. We never grew old on the stage. We had five years, we released all that material, toured incessantly, and then imploded right at the top. Within six or seven months, Mick was out . . . It was just the best five years of my life and I'm really proud today that the records are still a global phenomenon.

What do you think of the new book _The Clash by The Clash_?

I was against the book coming out because it's a transcript of [2000 Clash documentary] _Westway to the World_ with photos. It's nicely packaged, but I think it's time to draw a line under the Clash. When [editor] Mal Peachey came down to do the book, I said, "Listen Mal, I don't think there's any need for another Clash product on the market." I did get a copy of the book and it is attractive, it is a nice coffee [table] book and there's a lot of photos that I haven't seen before. But that's all it is: it's a transcription of *Westway to the World*.

But the fact that there's an audience for this material suggests the fans do want the stuff.

It's new fans, I think. I think Joe would be turning in his grave if he'd seen what the band have become today. When the book was first mooted, I said, "It's just regurgitated stuff from thirty-odd years ago."

There was talk of an official Clash biography ten years ago or so. I remember speaking to a publisher back then who was going to publish it and in the end he threw his hands up in the air and walked away from it. I got the feeling from that conversation that he found the Clash to be a corporate entity.

It has kind of become that, I'm afraid. Joe said, "After Topper left they never did another good gig." Unfortunately, that was the case. All of a sudden they've got the fucking Shea Stadium thing coming out and it's not really the Clash. It is the Clash, don't get me wrong . . . No objection, but the Clash was a chemistry between the four of us. If Paul had gone or Mick had gone, any one of us had gone, that chemistry would have been destroyed and it wouldn't have been the Clash. They tried to limp on without me and it only lasted another year afterwards.

But Terry had been there at the beginning.

Fair enough to Terry, he's a very nice bloke, but he could only play the first album. Have you heard that *From Here to Eternity* [1999 live Clash album with tracks spanning 1978–1982]? You can tell when it's me or Terry.

I'm sure the album will do well, I'm sure the book will do well, but I do think we have become a bit of a . . . People making money out of the Clash. And, at fifty-three years old, can I be bothered to object to it anyway? How old are you? You know what the Clash originally stood for, and we don't stand for that anymore. Nowadays, there's money to be made and all the singles are repackaged every year. Last year, the singles were all released in their original art sleeves in a box. The Clash are dead, Joe is dead literally, the Clash were thirty years ago, none of us are really that bothered anymore, and so people are moving in and making money out of it. The Clash book and *Live at Shea Stadium* are classic examples. And if it's all right with you, I'd like to leave it there.

ABOUT THE CONTRIBUTORS

Lester Bangs was a "gonzo" rock journalist, placing himself prominently in the reports he filed, often to prick what he saw as the pomposity of established musicians. He started his writing career aged twenty at *Rolling Stone*, going on to contribute to *Creem* (which he also edited), the *Village Voice, Penthouse, Playboy*, and the *New Musical Express*. He authored books on Blondie and Rod Stewart that bizarrely juxtaposed glossy photographs of their subjects with scathing critiques. He died of a drug overdose in 1982, aged thirty-three.

After writing in the seventies and eighties for *Melody Maker* and the *NME*, **Chris Bohn** became editor in chief of the *Wire*, a magazine devoted to alternative, underground, and nonmainstream music. He has also written under the name Biba Kopf.

Caroline Coon is an artist, political activist, journalist, and author. In 1967, she cofounded Release, a civil rights organization for people arrested for drug possession. She was one of the journalists who championed and named punk rock.

Sean Egan is a writer and editor specializing in arts and entertainment. His two dozen books include works on the Rolling Stones, the Beatles, *Coronation Street*, Tarzan, James Bond, William Goldman, and Manchester United.

Mick Farren wrote for legendary hippie bible the *International Times*, and went on to edit it. His 1976 *NME* article "The Titanic Sails at Dawn" is considered to have articulated the malaise caused in music by the rock aristocracy, as well as its punky solution ("it may be a question of taking rock back to street level and starting all over again"). He was a prolific author of both fiction and nonfiction. He was also a musician, recording with the Deviants and as a solo artist. He died in 2013.

Mikal Gilmore has contributed to *Rolling Stone* since 1976. In 1984 he received an ASCAP Deems Taylor Award for his music writing at the *Los Angeles Herald Examiner*. His 1994 family chronicle, *Shot in the Heart*, won him the National Book Critics Circle Award for biography/ autobiography.

Paolo Hewitt started his journalism career at *Melody Maker*. He has been chiefly associated during that career with mod, the Small Faces, the Jam/Paul Weller, and Oasis. Among his many books is *The Looked After Kid*, his critically acclaimed memoir of being brought up in foster and local-authority care.

Bill Holdship has been editor of *Creem*, *BAM*, *Daily Variety*, and *New Times Los Angeles*. He has contributed to almost every publication that has covered music during the last four decades, including *Mojo*, *New Musical Express*, *Los Angeles Times*, *L.A. Weekly*, *Rolling Stone*, *Classic Rock*, *US Weekly*, *Spin*, the *Village Voice*, and numerous alternative weeklies.

Lenny Kaye is a musician, writer, and record producer. He has been a guitarist for Patti Smith for more than forty years and has worked in the studio with such artists as Suzanne Vega, Jim Carroll, and Allen Ginsberg. He has written the life story of Waylon Jennings (*Waylon*) and an impressionistic study of the romantic singers of the 1930s, *You Call It Madness*. *Nuggets*, the anthology he compiled of sixties garage rock, has long been regarded as defining a genre.

Nick Kent was once told by the Beach Boys' Brian Wilson, "You look more like a rock star than me." Kent's writing for the *NME* in the seventies may have gone hand in hand with him living a dissolute rock 'n' roll lifestyle, but his journalism is among the most well regarded of the era. Some of it sought to rehabilitate the reputations of the likes of

Wilson and Syd Barrett in an age when nostalgia was frowned on. Also a musician, he briefly played with both the Sex Pistols and the London SS.

Charles Shaar Murray's journalistic career got off to an explosive start: the 1970 "Schoolkids Issue" of underground paper *Oz* in which he made his print debut led to an obscenity trial for its editors. He joined the *NME* in 1972 and went on to become a founding contributor of *Q* and *Mojo* magazines. His writing has also appeared in the *Evening Standard*, *Guitarist*, the *Guardian*, the *Independent*, the *Independent on Sunday*, the *Observer*, *MacUser*, *New Statesman*, *Prospect*, *Vogue*, and the *Word*. He is the author of the award-winning *Crosstown Traffic: Jimi Hendrix and Post-War Pop.*

Ben Myers is a journalist and award-winning novelist. He has written for *Mojo*, *New Statesman*, the *Guardian*, *Melody Maker*, *Caught by the River*, and the *NME*. His novels include *Turning Blue*, *Beastings*, *Pig Iron*, and *Richard.*

Kris Needs was London correspondent for *New York Rocker* when he saw the Clash play in Leighton Buzzard in October 1976 in what was their sixth gig. He has been both contributor to and editor of *Zigzag*. He currently writes for most leading music publications, including *Mojo*, *Record Collector*, *Classic Rock*, *Prog*, *Vive Le Rock*, *Electronic Sound*, and *Shindig!* His books include *Joe Strummer and the Legend of the Clash.*

Mike Nicholls was a journalist at *Record Mirror*, for whom he interviewed many of the top music stars of the late seventies and eighties.

In the late seventies, **Tony Parsons** became synonymous with Julie Burchill when they became staffers at the *New Musical Express* after both answered an advertisement seeking "hip, young gunslingers." They both championed punk and the Clash, before turning on both in their scabrous book *The Boy Looked at Johnny*. Having had his first novel published when he was twenty-three, Parsons developed this talent further, with *Man and Boy* being particularly applauded. He also became a television personality and newspaper columnist.

Mark Perry was born in Deptford, South East London. He was editor of premier UK punk fanzine *Sniffin' Glue*, which he started after hearing the first Ramones album in July 1976. In 1977, fed up with just writing about the music, he went on to start a record label, Step Forward, and form his own band, Alternative TV, which continues to the present day.

Paul Rambali has written for the *NME*, *The Face*, and *Arena*. His books include *Barefoot Runner*, a biography of marathon man Abebe Bikila.

Since starting with the *NME*, **Chris Salewicz** has written for quality newspapers and magazines across the globe. He is the author of many books, among them *Redemption Song: The Definitive Biography of Joe Strummer*.

Steve Walsh was a prominent face on the early UK punk scene. As well as writing for the *NME*, *Zigzag*, and *Sniffin' Glue*, he played guitar in Sid Vicious's pre–Sex Pistols band Flowers of Romance. He later went on to play in Manicured Noise, one of the most original bands in the 1979–80 post-punk scene.

A Philadelphia native, **Susan Whitall** grew up in metro Detroit and was a writer and editor for *Creem* magazine from 1975 to 1983. A music and feature writer for the *Detroit News* from 1983 to the present, she is the author of *Women of Motown* and *Fever: Little Willie John's Fast Life, Mysterious Death and the Birth of Soul*.

CREDITS

"Clash: What, Them Again? Fraid So. No Apologies . . . on the Road Fax" by Nick Kent. First published in *New Musical Express*, December 2, 1978. ©Time Inc. (UK) Ltd. Reprinted by permission of the publisher.

"Clash: Anger on the Left" by Mikal Gilmore. First published in *Rolling Stone*, March 8, 1979. © 1979 Mikal Gilmore. Reprinted by permission of the author.

"Yes, It's Strummer in the City (Boilin' Red Hot)" by Charles Shaar Murray. First published in *New Musical Express*, June 30, 1979.
"Up the Hill Backwards" by Charles Shaar Murray. First published in *New Musical Express*, May 29, 1982.
©Time Inc. (UK) Ltd. Reprinted by permission of the publisher.

"Clash: One Step Beyond" by Chris Bohn. First published in *Melody Maker*, December 29, 1979. ©Time Inc. (UK) Ltd. Reprinted by permission of the publisher.

"The Clash Clamp Down on Detroit—Or: Give 'em Enough Wisniowka" by Susan Whitall. First published in *Creem*, June 1980. © 1980 Susan Whitall. Reprinted by permission of the author.

"Joe Strummer Answers the Call-Up" by Paolo Hewitt. First published in *Melody Maker*, December 13, 1980. ©Time Inc. (UK) Ltd. Reprinted by permission of the publisher.

"Spanish Strummers" by Mike Nicholls. First published in *Record Mirror*, May 9, 1981. © 1981 NewBay Media. Reprinted by permission of the publisher.

"How the Clash Fed the Wonderbread Generation, Made the Mountain Come to Mohammed—and Other Miracles" by Mick Farren. First published in *New Musical Express*, June 20, 1981. ©Time Inc. (UK) Ltd. Reprinted by permission of the publisher.

"Clash Credibility Rule!" by Paul Rambali. First published in *New Musical Express*, October 10, 1981. ©Time Inc. (UK) Ltd. Reprinted by permission of the publisher.

"They Want to Spoil the Party—So They'll Stay" by Bill Holdship. First published in *Creem*, October 1984. © 1984 Bill Holdship. Reprinted by permission of the author.

"He Who Laughs Last" by Lenny Kaye. First published in *Spin*, March 1986. © 1986 Lenny Kaye. Reprinted by permission of the author.

"An Interview with Paul Simonon" by Ben Myers. First published on 3ammagazine.com, November 2004. © 2004 Ben Myers. Reprinted by permission of the author.

INDEX